# MEAT!

**ANIMA** Critical Race Studies Otherwise

A series edited by Mel Y. Chen and Jasbir K. Puar

# MEAT!

a transnational
analysis

edited by
Sushmita Chatterjee & Banu Subramaniam

DUKE UNIVERSITY PRESS
DURHAM & LONDON   2021

Designed by Aimee C. Harrison
Typeset in ITC Franklin Gothic and Warnock Pro by Westchester
Publishing Services

Library of Congress Cataloging-in-Publication Data
Names: Chatterjee, Sushmita, [date] editor. |
Subramaniam, Banu, [date] editor.
Title: Meat! : a transnational analysis /
edited by Sushmita Chatterjee and Banu Subramaniam.
Other titles: ANIMA (Duke University Press)
Description: Durham : Duke University Press, 2021. |
Series: Anima | Includes bibliographical references and index.
Identifiers: LCCN 2020024604 (print) | LCCN 2020024605 (ebook)
ISBN 9781478009955 (hardcover)
ISBN 9781478010951 (paperback)
ISBN ISBN 9781478012481 (ebook)
Subjects: LCSH: Meat—Social aspects. |
Meat—Moral and ethical aspects. | Meat—Political aspects.
Classification: LCC TX556.M4 M438 2021 (print) |
LCC TX556.M4 (ebook) | DDC 641.3/6—dc23
LC recordavailableathttps:// lccn.loc.gov/2020024604
LC ebook recordavailableathttps:// lccn.loc.gov/2020024605

Cover art: Detail of Mithu Sen, I CHEW, I BITE, 2011. Dental
polymer and artificial teeth, paint, glue. Shown at Mediations
Biennale, Poland. Courtesy of the artist.

# CONTENTS

## ACKNOWLEDGMENTS

MANY THANKS TO the University of Michigan–Ann Arbor's Institute for Research on Women and Gender (IRWG), particularly Heidi Bennett and her team, for enabling us to come together as a group and converse about everything meat-related. This opportunity provided much synergy and excitement. The coeditors are also deeply grateful for the enthusiasm, collaboration, and inspiration that each of our contributors has provided. This has been a truly incredible experience with much to learn, relearn, share, and enthuse about.

Duke University Press has been the perfect venue for this volume with its *Anima* series, and much thanks to Mel Y. Chen and Jasbir K. Puar for inspiration and support. Courtney Berger, our editor at DUP, has provided invaluable help throughout the process. Much gratitude to Sandra Korn at DUP for handling details and keeping us on track. We would also like to thank our anonymous reviewers for this volume. They provided generous, constructive, and generative feedback and suggestions. This volume was much strengthened because of them.

Introduction | SUSHMITA CHATTERJEE
AND BANU SUBRAMANIAM

# How to Think with Meat

MEAT noun \ mēt \
1 FOOD; the edible part of something as distinguished from its covering (such as a husk or shell)
2 FLESH; animal tissue considered especially as food
3 the core of something
—*Merriam-Webster Dictionary*

BY TRAVERSING THROUGH THE HEART OF EMPIRE, and along its meandering transnational routes, this collection of essays thinks with "meat." Meat, we contend, is a critical site, mobile and porous, where multiple political debates cohere. The twelve essays in this volume serve as a catalyst to open up conversations about ethics, consumption, science, race, gender, sexuality, colonialism, and postcolonialism, through a focus on meat. At first glance, meat seems like a self-evident category. Yet, as will emerge through this collection, meat proves to be much more tension-ridden: we explore how, what, and when objects become meat, the criteria by which diverse objects such as sexualized bodies and edible products may all be rendered into meat, and the invention of fake, substitute meats and meat-like products. Meat has become the center of a diverse set of politics—food politics, environmental politics, sexual politics, gender politics, body politics, maternal politics, disability politics, class politics, religious politics, international agronomy, political economy, international law and trade through patents and trademarks—and it is important to a diverse set of issues such as social justice, vegetarianism, sustainability, climate change, pornography, and capitalism. Meat, as we discovered, mutates constantly as an object and thus needs to be studied through divergent scales of place, time, and their many entanglements. In this volume, we unravel how meat is consumable flesh, animal, food, a currency for empire; it is mother, oftentimes exotic, a sexual and racial signifier, a fetish; it can also be fish, vegetable, plant, technology, and a fierce conduit for biopolitics.

The topic of meat has a curious history and has been implicated in diverse framing mechanisms when thinking about animals, gender, sexuality, race, transnational orbits, bodies, and materiality. As a frame for consumable flesh, meat is often assumed to be dead, without agency or a voice to scream out its name. Thus, heterogeneity is collapsed under the universal equivocation of meat; sexuality and gender positioning are subsumed under its politics, and so are the violent histories of racism, slavery, misogyny, colonialism, and imperialism. We usually invoke meat to talk about a hunk of steak, women as meat, and objects, lives, conditions, divorced from social agency. But curiously, the ambit for meat keeps increasing the further we choose to see. Authors in this volume trace the transit of frozen meat, manifold technologies of making meat, becoming meat, eating meat, and bodies rendered meat through governance, sociality, and economics as the essays on beef bans, yoga, chicken, pig, and fish demonstrate. As we move through frontiers, oceans, and bodies, human and nonhuman, we encounter a rolling horizon that constitutes meat. However, it is important to underline that we do not say that everything is meat. Rather, we delve into the politics of becoming meat. As successive chapters in this book demonstrate, we are concerned with what and who becomes meat; the rendering of meat highlights configurations of political economy, identity, and technologies of power. The book aims to work toward fathoming some of these technologies, traveling with it, and showcasing its workings.

We approach "meat" as politics, a site for transnational flows, colonial circuits, and varied mediated significations of gender, race, and class. Drawing from colonial and postcolonial studies, transnational analysis, feminist science studies, queer theory, critical race theory, animal studies, and disability studies, this volume aims to push conversations in animal studies, food studies, and eco-analyses toward the volatile and power-saturated meaning of meat, an understanding of meat as a signifier of power. These transdisciplinary mediations help draw out the potential interconnections and sites of political solidarity.

Contemporary politics is rife with activism around meat. For example, at the last Climate Change Summit in Paris, activists made a plea for less meat consumption. Paul McCartney tweeted "Less Meat = Less Heat."[1] New dietary guidelines announced in January 2016 in the United States recommended less meat for boys and men.[2] The growing sexual politics around anti-meat, grounded in ecological and ethical considerations, has been construed as "feminized" and unleashed its own backlash in movements such as MEAT (Meat Eaters Alliance Transnational), "Mankind for the Ethical Treatment of Humans," and dedicated to "the preservation and inhalation of meat and meat related products."[3] Missing from these conversations are questions of what constitutes meat. How do we respond to a global phenomenon such as climate change when keeping to local and straitjacket framings of meat? By widening the conversations about what constitutes meat, we highlight how the push and pull in conversations around meat move with a curious arrogance that seems to know the meat it talks about, notwithstanding the transmediations in every body and configuration: political, geographical, economic, and material. By highlighting the politics of what constitutes meat, we seek to draw out its varied constructions based on social exigencies, disciplinary framings, and economic rationalities.

Through the push and pull in conversations around meat and its many complexities born through capitalist, racialized, and patriarchal structures, we would like to frame the environmental consequences of a meat-eating culture, the ecological catastrophes that revolve around it. The rise of meat-eating and production among emerging economies has been accompanied by a racist backlash and global anxiety about its accompanying ecological damage. Anti-meat activists highlight the unprecedented greenhouse emissions and unsustainable levels of pollutants in air, water, and land; the spread of new kinds of viruses and bacteria; and myriad other environmental consequences that meat production entails. Not all meat has the same environmental consequences, and oftentimes eating beef is named as a major problem. But, as we shall see, these anxieties and accusations are embroiled in problematic global politics. While the environmental damages are indeed real, the renewed focus on the Third World as the site of ecological degradation is striking, especially since many of these regions are on the front lines of the devastation of climate change. As the essays in this volume show, growing ecological consideration should contextualize our understandings of anti-meat politics, as we theorize its complex entanglements with global capitalism, including the rise of the technological innovations such as genetically modified organisms, and the emergence of fake meat. This volume contributes to environmental conversations around meat and its consequences, by signaling the importance of taking account of race, gender, empire, and power politics in rendering meat a consumable object. We beckon toward a larger picture, one that takes into account flows and forms, transits and consumption, beef bans and body politics, hog waste and xenotransplantation, to be able to build the conversation around consequences with deepened responsibility and an understanding about how different bodies are involved as meat. As conversations around environmental racism and the increase of toxicity have emphasized, we cannot presume homogeneous effects when framing these conversations, and thus we endeavor to draw attention toward power configurations on a transnational scale in order to inspire forms of action that are attentive to histories of colonialisms, racisms, ableism, and sexisms that frame "meat."

Meat is a quintessentially global object. We contend that in contemporary global politics, meat has emerged as a useful site where multiple ideologies, politics, and actions cohere. Meat changes in meaning as we travel through the world across territorial, political, cultural, and academic disciplines. An illustrative case of meat's changing meaning-play are the potent politics of the recent bans on beef-eating in certain regions of India. As several of the essays in this volume allude to, these bans cannot really be counted as a democratic insurgency toward vegetarianism, pacifism, or an anticapitalist ethos, targeted as it is toward religious antagonisms, revitalizing ideas of Hindu supremacy, and class-based politics. With the rise of religious intolerance, we see stark examples of how the politics of meat is tied to the politics of religious communalism, class interests, regionalism, ethnic and racial politics, and political party agenda-setting. Colonial expansion across the globe had its own politics of meat through widespread transportation of frozen meat, or in the introduction of new meats to territories around the world.[4] Much of colonialism transpired through the affective, the disgust in what the "other" chose to eat. As Parama Roy writes, "the stomach served as a kind of somatic political unconscious in which the phantasmagoria of colonialism came to be embodied."[5] Roy looks at the "alimentary habitus" as central to the colonial encounter.[6]

Meat also allows us to trace the postcolonial condition through its "alimentary habitus," through the stomach, arteries, flesh, senses, in communion with different spaces, through mobile transnational trajectories and border crossings. Aptly, Donna Haraway reminds us, "Follow the chicken and find the world."[7] Understanding the routes of animal trade, dietary habits, food economics, avian flu and bioterrorism, labor, ecological politics, and bodies requires an understanding of meat. Indeed, meat is mediated through complex power relations of nation, gender, sexuality, race, class, disability, and empire, all of which need to be understood in their temporal framings. Our volume will engage with its transnational politics or the ways through which place and time territorialize and deterritorialize conceptions of what constitutes "meat."

Through different essays, this volume presents the astonishing range of issues, ideologies, and politics that cohere around meat globally. Rather than claiming "global" representation in the choice of subjects and issues surrounding meat, our volume looks at different spaces critically—the geopolitical framings of meat. The attention to geopolitics highlights connections and the interweaving of issues as they travel the world. To some, it will seem that our essays are curiously centered on South Asia, and specifically India. While our own intellectual and affective histories likely play a part, we believe that it is important to trace meat through its colonial histories, and the focus on South Asia enables us to showcase how deeply implicated meat is with colonial, anticolonial, regional, religious, and cultural politics of the subcontinent.

The various essays in the volume highlight the deeply resonant and fraught place of meat and its framing through local and global confluences. Thus, by signaling the power politics and varied stratifications premised on meat, we present glimpses into the shifting terrains of transnationalism, that is, how different communities of belonging are created and re-created through the emphasis on meat. We are attentive to the politics of framing a region as singular or monolithic as, for example, in South Asia. Thus, we complicate the construction of a region by pointing out the confluence of myriad forces, international and national, that frame an issue, and we work with a transnational methodology to pry open the politics surrounding the creation of nations and communities. Our attention to the recent beef bans in India reflects this methodology. We think together about how meat works as a conduit in transnational politics to showcase the creation of borders and the figuration of cohesive communities that refuse to be contaminated by meat-eating. By coalescing around a particular region, and critically engaging with it, we work toward illuminating the politics traversing transnational geographies and the mapping of bodies and spaces.

Meat is not easily categorized. It is not merely a singular object, sign, symbol, or one that embodies a unitary, local, or singular politics. Rather,

5

we understand it as a "meta" object of sorts that reveals the various nodes that connect meat; it brings together and reveals the multiplicities, complexities, and contradictions of contemporary politics. A quick perusal of the topics our authors will engage with include: How do we define "meat"? For example, is fish meat? How does fake, "bloody" vegan meat challenge our conception of meat? How do we queer veganism? Does a petri dish hamburger constitute meat? How do we make meaning of some of the varied transnational and cultural meanings of meat across the globe? How do the legacies of colonialism and empire endure in the contemporary politics of meat? How does meat figure in ethnic identity politics? Why are so many disgusted at consuming human milk, while they consume the milk of other animals unproblematically? When does cow's milk become a trope for nationalist politics or ecofeminist politics? How does meat-eating change in the context of postnuclear violence? What do North American indigenous relations tell us about eating meat and interspecies relationships? How is chicken connected to the politics of respectability for African American men? Different from the flesh of animals as meat, what are conditions under which the sacrifice of human flesh stands for hospitality and gift-giving? How do we respond to technologized, painless meat? How does the politics of beef-eating connect to yoga? What does following the pig tell us about race, gender, biotechnology, and empire? What is the relation between ash and meat? This is a large list, we admit—a veritable smorgasbord of issues, topics, methods, methodologies, histories, genealogies, and circuits! But that they all cohere around meat highlights the significance of meat as an object of inquiry. All these conversations remain productively haunted by the selective malleability and rigidity of what constitutes meat as it travels the world and its varied ethical imports.

Understanding meat as an assemblage of race, gender, sexuality, nationality, and disability means noticing the curious companionship of antagonistic ideologies. Despite the assertive declaration that "meat is bad" made by individuals and parties on different sides of the ideological spectrum such as vegan studies scholars, the Hindu right, ecological activists on climate justice, and others, we see a surprising lacuna in these conversations about what constitutes meat. Carol Adams's critique of meat as a homogeneous term based on an "absent referent" remains important in signaling unthinking consumption, lack of knowledge as to the origin of the flesh, and its sexual politics.[8] Maybe understanding meat has to grapple with this unknowability, its expanding constitutions and arterial flows. Meat as matter and political signifier has fascinating histories through space and

6

time, whether seen in the significance of dead animals as trophies, mutinies over eating pig or cow, how curry travels the world, McDonald's happy global family, or the increasing popularity of sushi as healthy food.[9] This volume looks at the entangled nature of conversations on meat and their mediated boundaries. We study meat through different spaces and time periods to reflect on what Elspeth Probyn terms "alimentary assemblages." As Probyn writes, "Now, beyond a model of inside and out, we are alimentary assemblages, bodies that eat with vigorous class, ethnic and gendered appetites, mouth machines that ingest and regurgitate, articulating what we are, what we eat and what eats us."[10]

Meat as alimentary assemblage is at the heart of contemporary debates in multiple fields. It can open up conversations in food studies and animal studies toward new and interesting directions. The growing popularity of animal studies on questions of binaries between human and animal, the nature of humanism, the status of nonhuman animals, animals in art and culture, anthropomorphism, and other questions has received a dizzying level of attention.[11] Some would even like to think of animal studies as divided into subgroups such as "critical animal studies, human–animal studies, and posthumanism."[12] The rich literature in animal studies has opened up different disciplines to their exclusions and investments in the "human," inspiring multiple transdisciplinary conversations on animality and animals. In addition, it has grown through critiques of its own exclusions with regard to topics of concern, areas of study, and critical deciphering of who is the "animal" and the "human" in animal studies—positions laced with power. For instance, Julie Livingston and Jasbir Puar succinctly point out that "much of posthumanist thought as well as animal studies suffers from an often unmarked Euro-American focus and through that, ironically, a philosophical resuscitation of the status of 'the human' as a transparent category."[13]

The volume also highlights the relationship of meat to food studies. The various essays highlight how "taste" is critically modulated through cultural, environmental, ethical, and technological landscapes. Moreover, the connections between animal studies and food studies are obvious, but they are oftentimes separated as different and distinct forums, journals, programs, and scholarly endeavors. Food studies, like animal studies, has evolving frames and pursuits on questions of food access, food sovereignty, the cultural politics of food, histories of food, and many other concerns. In critical engagement with food studies, Kyla Wazana Tompkins urges us to consider "critical eating studies" rather than food studies with its investment

7

on an object as "By reading orificially, critical eating studies theorizes a flexible and circular relation between the self and the social world."[14] Moreover, Henry Buller and Emma Roe draw our attention to the dissociations between "food" and "animals," and urge an integrative analysis.[15] They point out that "contemporary food and animal studies share a certain preoccupation with alterity and with it, a febrile engagement with ethics."[16] Engaging in these conversations on eating, food, animal, human, and differences, meat seeks to inspire conversations between animal studies, food studies, critical eating studies, feminist and queer theory, and environmental analyses to study the alimentary assemblages of flesh, climate change, technology, taste, desire, environmental justice, and many other pressing concerns of our times. Meat is food. It is animal. It is also human. Meat is eaten. Sometimes it is sacrificed without being eaten. It is tied to technology. It could also be vegetable. By drawing attention to interstitial connections, meat's maverick politics gnaws at the borders of programmable methods of inquiry.

Overall, this volume will constitute a unique intervention in thinking about animals, food, eating, and environmental issues, for many reasons. First, meat could be either dead or alive, and thinking about meat has to reckon with "animacies." As Mel Y. Chen writes, "Considering differential animacies becomes a particularly critical matter when 'life' versus 'death' binary oppositions fail to capture the affectively embodied ways that racializations of specific groups are differentially rendered."[17] Chen's critical intervention in animal studies makes us reconsider binaries between animate and inanimate, dead and alive. Meat continues this conversation through transnational trails, land and ocean bodies, toxic meat, hospitality and flesh, fake meat, xenotransplantation, meat technologies, and other issues. Second, it is important to emphasize the transnational focus of our volume. A transnational understanding of meat is indispensable in enabling analysis that moves beyond one-dimensional framings that, even in their critique of meat-eating, remain embroiled in making others meat through an ignorance of how bodies move in the world. For instance, how would vegan studies respond to the beef ban in different parts of India where outlawing meat, contrary to its meaning in some other parts of the world, stands for communalism, caste, and class violence? Invoking Jacques Derrida, it is important to understand that "One never eats entirely on one's own: this constitutes the rule underlying the statement, 'One must eat well.'"[18] Working with transnationalism necessitates an understanding of complicity and contamination between varied bodies and nations; thereby

8

we also situate analysis of transnationalism within nations, not simply international, as attention to indigenous relations necessitate. Third, studying meat necessitates a transdisciplinary orientation that would simultaneously de-discipline itself in order to move beyond prescribed borders. An understanding of meat in its diffused, malleable, changing connotations would add greatly to conversations in the fields that often remain stuck on static ideas of animal, vegetable, space, and time despite many attempts to maneuver otherwise. We hope that *Meat!* will act as a useful catalyst through these spaces.

## Organization of the Anthology

The volume is organized into twelve essays. We start with Elspeth Probyn's essay, "When Fish Is Meat: Transnational Entanglements," which explores the framing of fish as meat, as white meat, or even as "chicken of the sea." Showcasing the insidious entanglements of fish with the politics of race, the north plundering the seas of the south, fascination for white-fleshed fish, eating fish more than a hundred years old, and many other insights, the essay draws analyses of "relatedness" further, through webs of colonialisms, sexual and racial imaginations of the north and south, and how fish swim through and get embroiled within these regimes of power. The north very much controls the market in terms of taste and naming, or even being practitioners of what counts as sustainable fishing practices. Inspiring our imaginations through deep waters, the essay helps us fathom the rolling borders of sea, fish, animal, and meat through the framing of the transnational politics of fish as meat.

Irina Aristarkhova's essay, titled "Eating the Mother," pries open questions about cannibalism by analyzing the "mother as food." Aristarkhova looks at Jess Dobkin's exhibit *The Lactation Station Breast Milk Bar* to analyze what constitutes food as liquid, solid, mother, self, and milk. She asks: "Is the mother food? And if the mother is food, then what kind of food: meat, drink, solid, liquid?" By provocatively positioning how we are all cannibals from birth, the essay moves the analysis of cannibalism toward the mother's body and drinking milk. In fact, as the author argues, life is actualized by eating the mother. The mother is meat and drink offering food to the life that she sustains. Questions of incorporation, digestion, gestation, reproduction, and other bodily co-becomings frame the analysis in this essay toward an understanding of meat that is often rendered invisible, like the mother.

9

Jennifer A. Hamilton, in her essay "Reindeer and Woolly Mammoths: The Imperial Transit of Frozen Meat from the North American Arctic," studies meat's entanglement within the politics of indigeneity and imperialism. By studying frozen meat in transit alongside the circulation of images and its racialized politics, the essay discusses how understanding "transits" is indispensable toward fathoming the global food supply line amid colonial and imperial processes. Brief interludes allow the author to draw out the connections between the figure of the Eskimo, meat, and its relation to "civilization" through consumption of whale blubber and specific animal products, and other images that centralize the framing of indigeneity alongside technologies of freezing and the consumption of meat. As the author points out, "I have traced how seemingly disparate phenomena—woolly mammoths and reindeer, canned meat and breakfast cereal, racial science and its nonhuman familiars—operate as nodes in the imperial transit of frozen meat."

Sushmita Chatterjee, in "Beefing Yoga: Meat, Corporeality, and Politics," invokes the transnational spread of yoga and the national beef bans spreading through many states of India. Urging us to discern stratagems of politics, the essay looks to extend conversations about "trans-corporeality" as coined by Stacy Alaimo, to understand the craft of politics and thereby situate "meat at the heart of government politics." The author asks: "What do beef and yoga as 'meat' tell us about a transnational body politic?" Comparing, contrasting, and showcasing the entangled nature of the beef bans and the emphasis on yoga, the essay uses the image of body politics to frame meat as politics. The essay emphasizes the opposing and incalculable pulls that frame body politics in transnational times, and its unforeseeable effects. Through an emphasis on "mischievous trans-corporeality," the essay unravels statecraft that works through meat.

Anita Mannur's essay, "Eating after Chernobyl: Slow Violence and Reindeer Consumption in the Postnuclear Age," examines "exotic" meat in the context of postnuclear violence. Specifically engaging with reindeer meat, the essay studies the entanglements of the right to food, environmental justice, indigeneities, and what constitutes local and exotic food. By drawing our attention to various locales, from Jungle Jim's in Cincinnati to London's Borough Market, New Nordic cuisine and its spreading through Finland, Iceland, Greenland, and Sami herders in Scandinavia, the essay interrogates questions connected to culinary framings and its politics. Mannur showcases the many erasures in framings of local meat as safe and without contamination, and frames how in our attention to fetishizing the local we forget the transnational effects of nuclear catastrophes, which makes thinking of pure local food or meat a naïve proposition inattentive to the many forms of violence.

In "Romancing the Pig: A Queer Crip Tale from Barbecue to Xenotransplantation," Kim Q. Hall writes about entanglements between barbecue, xenotransplantation, queerness, and disability, which formulate an intimate politics of empire. As Hall writes, "My focus on romancing the pig aims to get to the heart of the matter about the materialization of the pig as a biopolitical site of a transnational politics that circulates beneath the skin and distinguishes between self and other in discourses of health, disability, and belonging." By critically engaging with frontiers, borders, and territorial movements between and through bodies, skins, and waste, the essay frames how pigs "become meat." Contesting notions of purity in meat and in politics, the essay contextualizes the racism and ableism sweeping through much of what becomes meat. Contesting romanticized notions of meat, and romancing the pig by deconstructing its usages, politics, and ethics, the essay foregrounds the "messy hybridities that make up bodies and worlds."

Parama Roy's essay, titled "On Being Meat: Three Parables on Sacrifice and Violence," uses three parables from early modern England, ancient Indic, and contemporary India to decipher varied frames of carnivory in relation to human self-sacrifice. These examples of human edibility and interspecies sacrifice instantiated for the flourishing of nonhuman life signal toward an "ethics not wholly governed by anthropocentrism." Taking up varied instances of "killability" in human bodies as different from animal life, which has dominated discussions, the essay points toward instances where flesh and life are separated as such, and the differences between consumption of flesh and sacrifice of flesh. For instance, Roy narrates instances of gift-giving that involve giving one's ears, eyes, hands, and other parts of the body, as seen in Buddhist literature. The gifts, as Roy illustrates, are "composed simultaneously of flesh and spirit," and constitute a "sacrifice of the bloody animal sacrifice demanded by Brahmanical ritual." It thus constitutes the "sacrifice of sacrifice." And, in this moment of self-sacrifice and becoming meat, the body is transformed into a higher being and qualifies to become Buddha.

In "'I Hide in Plain Sight': Food and Black Masculinity in Vince Gilligan's *Breaking Bad*," Psyche Williams-Forson examines representations of black masculinity through meat, especially chicken. Through a close reading of the character of Gus, Williams-Forson demonstrates the close association between black men and chicken used to affirm and play against stereotypical framings. As the author points out, "chicken is used to shield as much as it is used to highlight Gus's blackness, his masculinity, and his performances of respectability." Gus works at keeping his illegal activities hidden by using chicken, and it is this mechanism that enables him to be a respectable actor. The author demonstrates the intricate workings of the politics of meat in identity work, among black men in this case, to showcase the myriad ways through which it works. While chickens are used to stereotypically portray black men and women and with racist tones, chickens are also used by black men and women to affirm themselves and to subvert the status quo of one-dimensional associations.

Neel Ahuja, in "On Phooka: Beef, Milk, and the Framing of Animal Cruelty in Late Colonial Bengal," writes about dairy practices in the context of cow blowing. Ahuja writes about the reverence bestowed on the cow as mother by Hindu nationalism, and the colonial state with its animal welfare policing. The construction of "the bovine question," Ahuja argues, helps us understand the continuation of cow protection vigilance and its rhetoric. As the author writes, "In its uneven representation of human–bovine intimacies, the colonial archive—especially legislative debates and administrative memoranda concerning animal welfare and dairying practices—offers a path for rethinking the disjunction of beef and dairy that guides most historiography of cow protection." By drawing our attention to the practice of phooka and intense debates surrounding it in colonial Bengal, this essay helps frame animal welfare policing around practices of witnessing that help validate claims of certain forms of cruelty, while obscuring others.

Angela Willey's essay, titled "Fake Meat: A Queer Commentary," uses the means of autobiography to queer vegan food and fake meat. Framing the "sexual politics of meat" in terms of queer vegan politics, this essay draws us through storytelling practices, the practices and pleasures of place and identity working in what constitutes meat, and the author's own narrative in making meaning of the confluence of events, relations, and people that cross her life and thinking about meat. Framing the issue of fake meat around sexual ethics, and with sparkling humor, Willey writes, "we might yet queer veganism by cultivating a far richer lexicon for practices of undermining cultures of killability."

In "The Ethical Impurative: Elemental Frontiers of Technologized Meat," Banu Subramaniam explores the purity politics in religious frames around the beef bans in India, and the technological imperatives of making safe meat separate from the ethical, political, and ecological concerns around eating "real" meat. Questioning the ethics and the purity politics around categories of meat, vegetable, plant, technology, and religious politics, Subramaniam writes, "I worry that ethics is not the best frame through which to examine the politics of food." Confronting categories believed to be pristine and pure, the essay challenges the meaning of meat and its effects. By inviting readers into her own personal history, the author bridges conversations on meat between the personal, political, technological, and ethical. Dispelling myths of a vegetarian India, the essay traces the horrific violence surrounding beef bans in India. Concomitantly, we also notice the ironic proliferation of new technologies, "technologies of harm reduction," which muddy the borders between categories of meat and plants and "de-animalize the animal." By drawing attention to and prying open questions of "purity" surrounding meat, the author presents analyses in food and animal studies with a provocative impetus.

In an afterword, Mel Y. Chen in "Fire and Ash" reckons with the politics of meat by noting that "meat is a truly weird thing" that connotes substance and "nonintegrity" through widely varied meaning-plays. By noting how meat and air work environmentally, in tandem, and coagulate with fire and ash, Chen urges us to think through the "interconnectedness" of bodies, meat, air, and ash, noting all the while that "they are not the same ash." Indeed, thinking with meat, "How to enflesh this air-meat's nonintegrity?"

## Conclusion

Overall, in considering meat as a transnational object, our attention to transnationalism works with varied mappings. Meat, here, does not simply displace the universal Western human critiqued as the bias of animal studies and food studies. Instead, we study mappings, transits, and movements to understand the slippery oscillations between nationalism and transnationalism; we track nationalism's ability to rear its head stubbornly over and over again; and we trace the multiple, intersecting transnationalisms even within nationalisms. We traverse with our analyses from global oceans to cellular levels when studying fish as meat or xenotransplantation. Attention to mappings has to reckon with their constructed nature, with technologies of intervention, and the constant oscillations of time. With attention to mappings, the essays in this volume study contemporary uses and forms of meat, alongside examples from the past, cognizant of the fugitive mobility of time in keeping intact and changing formulations of meat. We look anew at constructions of "local" and "global," through examinations of transits of

13

frozen meat and the transportation of exotic meat. Technologies of meat in terms of real or fake meat enable us to study its configuration from laboratories to farms, queer sexual politics, and body politics. Continuing the conversations on "entanglements," "intimacies," and "viscous porosity," this compilation of essays studies framings of meat through empire and imperialism with a serious attention to mappings and their undoing in space and time.[19]

In addition, the question of ethics—the "right" and/or "wrong"—remains a vexing problem for most of the essays. Rather than a quick denunciation, which loses the many nuances in the questions under review, we work with ethics as a mode of understanding entanglements and curious similarities and differences that prevent an easy solution. When becoming meat is also tantamount to becoming Buddha, how do we stake a morally higher ground on all forms of meat? When fake meat could signal a queering of veganism, is there a straight response? When yoga and the beef bans are connected, and yoga also helps millions around the world, should we practice selective appropriation? What is pure meat, and how do we reckon with its contaminations and retain a pure ethics? Is there an ethics beyond anthropocentrism? Multiple questions jostle for attention through this volume, its collage demanding thinking with complexity about the multihued politics of meat. As we hope to demonstrate in this volume, it is important to "Think with Meat," and how we do it has to be attentive to power relations: geopolitics, gender, sexuality, race, and empire, among others.

## Notes

1 "Paris Climate Change Summit, and the Taboo of Meat-Eating," *Euronews*, September 12, 2015, http://www.euronews.com/2015/12/09/paris-climate-change -summit-and-the-taboo-of-meat-eating/.

2 Anahad O'Connor, "New Diet Guidelines Urge Less Sugar for All and Less Meat for Boys and Men," *New York Times*, January 7, 2016, http://well.blogs .nytimes.com/2016/01/07/new-diet-guidelines-urge-less-sugar-for-all-and-less -meat-for-boys-and-men/.

3 Meat Eaters Alliance, Facebook group, https://www.facebook.com/Meat-Eaters -Alliance-Transnational-MEAT-128168027255496/info/?tab=page_info.

4 See Lizzie Collingham, *Curry: A Tale of Cooks and Conquerors* (New York: Oxford University Press, 2007); Joanna Radin and Emma Kowal, eds., *Cryopolitics: Frozen Life in a Melting World* (Cambridge, MA: MIT Press, 2017).

5 Parama Roy, *Alimentary Tracts: Appetites, Aversions, and the Postcolonial* (Durham, NC: Duke University Press, 2010), 7.

6 Roy, *Alimentary Tracts*, 7.

7 Donna J. Haraway, *When Species Meet* (Minneapolis: University of Minnesota Press, 2008), 274.

8 Carol J. Adams, *Neither Man nor Beast: Feminism and the Defense of Animals* (New York: Continuum, 1995), 16.

9 See Harriet Ritvo, *The Animal Estate: The English and Other Creatures in the Victorian Age* (Cambridge, MA: Harvard University Press, 1989); Anita Mannur, *Culinary Fictions: Food in South Asian Diasporic Culture* (Philadelphia: Temple University Press, 2010); Elspeth Probyn, *Carnal Appetites: FoodSexIdentities* (London: Routledge, 2000); Uma Narayan, *Dislocating Cultures: Identities, Traditions, and Third World Feminism* (New York: Routledge, 1997).

10 Probyn, *Carnal Appetites*, 32.

11 Matthew Calarco traces the multidisciplinary origin of animal studies and lays out two incessant questions that define much of the field: "One question concerns the being of animals, or 'animality,' and the other concerns the human–animal distinction." Matthew Calarco, *Zoographies: The Question of the Animal from Heidegger to Derrida* (New York: Columbia University Press, 2008), 2.

12 Laura Wright, *The Vegan Studies Project: Food, Animals, and Gender in the Age of Terror* (Athens: University of Georgia Press, 2015), 11.

13 Julie Livingston and Jasbir K. Puar, "Interspecies," *Social Text 106* 29, no. 1 (2011): 5.

14 Kyla Wazana Tompkins, *Racial Indigestion: Eating Bodies in the 19th Century* (New York: New York University Press, 2012), 3.

15 Henry Buller and Emma Roe, *Food and Animal Welfare* (London: Bloomsbury Academic, 2018), 11.

16 Buller and Roe, *Food and Animal Welfare*, 13.

17 Mel Y. Chen, *Animacies: Biopolitics, Racial Mattering, and Queer Affect* (Durham, NC: Duke University Press, 2012), 10.

18 Jacques Derrida, "'Eating Well,' or the Calculation of the Subject: An Interview with Jacques Derrida," in *Who Comes after the Subject?*, edited by Eduardo Cadava, Peter Connor, and Jean-Luc Nancy (New York: Routledge, 1991), 115.

19 See Karen Barad, *Meeting the Universe Halfway: Quantum Physics and the Entanglement of Matter and Meaning* (Durham, NC: Duke University Press, 2007); Nancy Tuana, "Viscous Porosity: Witnessing Katrina," in *Material Feminisms*, edited by Stacy Alaimo and Susan Heckman (Bloomington: Indiana University Press, 2008); Kath Weston, *Animate Planet* (Durham, NC: Duke University Press, 2017).

# When Fish
# Is Meat

## TRANSNATIONAL
## ENTANGLEMENTS

### White Fish

For those who grew up in middle America in the last century, Chicken of the Sea might evoke white tuna fish on white bread sandwiches, maybe with a glass of milk: a nice white lunch. For some, the mention of chicken brings back racist stereotypes of African Americans through food choices. As Psyche Williams-Forson writes: "a black-faced man with large, extended red lips, was typically symbolic of how whites would stereotype black people with food to endorse various products like fried chicken."[1] Here the transformation is: "a celebrated food of the South . . . turns into an object of ridicule and defacement."[2]

For others, chicken of the sea is just downright confusing. An infamous moment on *The Newlyweds* in 2003 had Jessica Simpson wondering what she is eating: "I know it's tuna, but it says chicken by the sea. Is that stupid?"[3] While Simpson had to play the role of the blond bimbo, her question for non-Americans is maybe even more hilarious than it was for those who knew the reference, bringing to mind the image of chickens strolling along "by the sea" eating tuna.

The actual name came about in 1914 when Van Camp Seafood Company used the name that fishermen gave to the albacore tuna that used to be plentiful along the Southern California coast.[4] In the history of fishing in California, canned sardines were pushed aside by albacore tuna because it was white and had few bones—unlike sardines. A former sardine canner, Albert P. Halfhil, realized that when tuna is steamed it turns "an appealing white color and has a pleasantly mild flavour."[5] As food blogger Erin Nudi writes, "Perhaps even back then Americans generally preferred fish that's not too 'fishy.'"[6] Roberto Ferdman writes that "It was precisely canned tuna's blandness that the industry latched on to. Early advertisements touted that canned tuna tasted like chicken long before international tuna canner Chicken of the Sea decided to turn the likeness into its name."[7]

Despite now being owned by the multinational company Thai Union, "chicken of the sea" is a particularly American invention. It uses albacore, which is the only tuna that can be labeled "white" under federal regulations.[8] The American love of this white-meat tuna resulted in albacore being fished out in California. While Italians and Spanish love preserved tuna, their taste for it is more adventuresome, and their canned or bottled tuna includes yellowfin, skipjack, and even bluefin species.

The idea of white fish that tastes like chicken combined with a disdain for brown, bony, and fishy fish is emblematic of a particular white American middle-class habitus, one that grew up on the white purity of milk[9] and white bread.[10] As Rachel Slocum argues, these white foods "were promoted to strengthen the white American body."[11]

In her review of race in the study of food, Slocum makes the argument for including race within a political economy of food. This then "might connect hunger and race, climate change and biopolitics, neoliberal disasters and anti-racism."[12] She points to how "the industrialized agriculture landscape of the US is made through racial ideologies active in the labor market and the institutionalized racism that removed African Americans, Mexican and indigenous people from the land."[13] While on the surface white fish seemingly begs an analysis in the terms of critical whiteness theory, here I focus on how the desire for white, non-fishy fish is deeply shot through with racial and ethnic inequalities between the Global North and South. I map this through fish and fishing in the southern oceans. As many have explored, the continuing effects of colonialism have an ongoing impact on how natural resources in the south are developed and traded. Daniel Pauly and his team describe how "'south to north' trading patterns, would largely eliminate fish from the markets of countries still 'developing' in 2050."[14] I use a framework I developed elsewhere[15] to draw out the complex entanglements of more-than-human fish. The intimate and intricate connec-

18

tions between and among fish and human foreground questions of class, gender, and ethnicity in the divisions of the Global North and South. This is about the survival of some forms of fish, certain human populations, and the environments in which we live. As an object of research, this demands relational thinking. The objective is to get at the thickness, the complex and deeply unequal distribution of matter in which we are always differentially related. There is the exigency of figuring how matter is always "enmeshed in a variety of relations."[16] Some of the entities to which or in which more-than-human fish are related are the marine environments, colonial legacies, climate change, laws and regulations, technologies, and—most pressingly—global and regional interrelated markets.

Toothfish is the new whiter-than-white fish on the market, which is the subject of this chapter. The tale of *Dissostichus eleginoides* and *Dissostichus mawsoni* encapsulates the global and the transnational, Global North and South, and the battles over scarce fish played out in the very deep seas of the southern oceans. The analysis of this epic tale may tell us something about the weird entanglements of taste, the unequal relations between Global North and South, and the precarious future of more-than-human fish, all in the rush to catch a fish that doesn't taste like fish.

It was on a field trip in Nelson investigating New Zealand deep-sea fisheries that I first encountered the entangled nature of toothfish. I asked Graham, the resource manager at Sealord, why toothfish is so popular, and so astonishingly expensive. The nearly blue-white deep-sea fish is caught in Australian and New Zealand seas around Antarctica, and it sells for AU$95 per kilo. That's about as much as good-quality wagyu beef, and a little less than lobster. Graham reflected briefly, and replied: "Well, it's about those American chefs. You see, toothfish doesn't look like a fish, doesn't smell like a fish, doesn't taste like a fish—so it's perfect for American appetites."

Austral Fisheries in Australia markets toothfish as Glacier 51 (further taking the fish out of fish), and describes it as having a "snow-white flesh and broad scalloping flakes [that] display a clean and sweet flavour. The elegant balance of flavour and texture . . . provides a culinary versatility rare in fish fillets."[17] Austral plays up the epic nature of their fishery: "Isolated deep in the sub-Antarctic, a staggering 4,109 km from mainland Australia lies one of the most inhospitable islands in the world—Heard Island." They brag about their epic fishing trips, and the Marine Stewardship Council certification of the fishery. "Gale force winds, horizontal snow, ten metre swell and as little as four hours of light per day display the raw power of mother nature surrounding this incredible Marine Stewardship Council (MSC) certified sustainable fishery."[18] As of 2016, Austral took another move and showed "it cared enough to act," and became a carbon-neutral fishery company. As Austral's director of marketing Dylan Skinns puts it, this is another way to show that "our industry has many more sexy stories to tell than the happy chickens and the grain-fed cows in the animal protein sector."[19]

People go out of their way to describe toothfish in unfishy ways. Rick Moonen of New York's Oceana restaurant loves its high fat content, as do other chefs. He says, "It's like a perfect date" (with high fat content?). He further describes the fish: "Think of eating a perfectly ripened mango—that's exactly what it's like to eat this fish." He expands on why chefs in particular fell in love: "It's bullet-proof. . . . You can cook it hours before you need it and re-warm it without harming its flavour or texture. Everyone had to have it: it became a gold rush."[20] Moonen's assumption about his customers, his "culinary sophisticates," is that "they had never been comfortable with non-white fleshed fish."[21]

That encounter at a large fish company in New Zealand started me thinking about toothfish, orange roughy, and other very deep-sea fish. News of inhabitants of the very deep is a tabloid favorite. The very term the deep conjures mock/shock horror: "It can be easy to forget that an alien world lives right beneath us—the mysterious ecosystem of the deep ocean, where the creatures of your nightmares lurk far below the surface."[22] Another account focuses on a scene where "a monstrous pale creature writhing around aboard a small fishing vessel as confused fishermen poke it with a stick. Boasting a nasty-looking set of fangs, the white-ish pink eel-like creature looks like something straight out of a sci-fi movie."[23] In yet another account, a longnose chimaera is described as "a winged fish with evil eyes." This admittedly somewhat strange and beautiful fish usually lives thousands of meters deep in tropical seas. Recently, however, a Nova Scotian fisherman found a chimaera when trawling in the frigid Atlantic. He was shocked, and the fish was dead. "Like much of the fish pulled in as by-product while dragging nets for cod and redfish, the chimaera died due to the pressure change. . . . It was eventually loaded onto a conveyer belt and dumped back in the ocean."[24]

The appearance of some of these deep-sea denizens may be due to ocean warming. The southeast coast of Australia (where I live) is now registering one of the highest global increases in ocean warming, and this of course deeply affects fish. The habitation zones have kept shifting south over the past several years. This has brought tropical fish to Sydney, where they winter over because of the warmer waters. This means snorkelers can now flirt with clownfish in Sydney Harbor, but it also means that fishers are going further south to find their usual prey. Marine biologist Alistair Hobday writes: "Just as Nemo was carried south to Sydney by the East Australian Current, large open ocean fish like tuna and billfish are moving south with these warming waters."[25]

The world is coming south on a major scale. As the waters of the Northern Hemisphere are increasingly fished out, large-scale trawlers and processors are going deep into the deep south. "[T]he unthinkable is finally happening: we are running out of fish. The global catch of fish reached its peak in 1989. Every year that passes, another decline is recorded, and vessels have to ply the seas ever longer and cast their lines ever deeper. They have to go into new territories and catch unfamiliar species just to keep tonnages up."[26] The privileging of the north is deeply embedded in the science that is supposed to be the basis upon which environmental conservation programs make claims. As Boris Worm and Trevor Branch found in their review of global catch data, even in "the most comprehensive database on fish biomass there is an inherent spatial bias, in that 90% of those assessments currently come from North America, Europe, and Oceania, and only account for 20–25% of global catch."[27] They state that a "common factor among these [fisheries-conservation] hotspots is the prevalence of highly mobile foreign fleets, which may in part be driving increasing catches and exploitation rates."[28] In other words, the north is pillaging the seas of the south. A *Washington Post* journalist comments: "As they went farther and deeper, fishermen have brought back fish that people didn't have recipes—or even words—for."[29] In short, we have no idea what we are eating, or what we are doing to these unknown fish and their ecosystems.

"Farther and deeper": finding fish and naming them are not innocent endeavors. Individual toothfish, *Dissostichus eleginoides*, first appeared as bycatch from trawlers in Chile's deep waters. As Bruce Knecht describes it, what fishers found was a revelation: "elephant fish, congrios, grenadiers, sea squirts, shoe mussels, and picorous. The creatures were even odder than their names. . . . The grenadiers had what appeared to be thorns on its skin, eyes so big they covered half its head, and a tail not much thicker than a strand of spaghetti. 'Some people call them rat fish.'"[30] Out of this odd assortment, the "only halfway-normal-looking creature was a Patagonian toothfish."[31] Lee Lantz, an American fish salesman, quickly renamed toothfish as Chilean sea bass, although it is neither a bass nor only particular to Chile. They inhabit waters around sub-Antarctic islands and the submarine plateaus of the Southern Ocean.

21

1.1 Patagonian toothfish. Source: Royal Geographical Society.

The story of Lantz's renaming is now infamous. In 1977, he was in Valparaiso looking for new, cheap fish to sell in the United States. Lantz did indeed spot something new: "an exceptionally large, fearsome-looking grey-black fish. . . . Close to 1.5 meters long, it looked as if it weighed nearly 50 kilograms. With its dark skin and bulging eyes, a protruding lower jaw that was studded with teeth so pointy they looked as if they had been honed by a pencil sharpener, even this lifeless specimen looked menacing."[32] The title of Bruce Knecht's book encapsulates part of the story: *Hooked: A True Story of Pirates, Poaching, and the Perfect Fish.* The fish tasted bland, but "the blandness could even be a plus."[33] "It had a texture similar to Atlantic cod's, the richness of tuna, the innocuous mild flavor of a flounder, and a fat content that made it feel almost buttery in the mouth. Lantz believed a white-fleshed fish that almost melted in your mouth—and a fish that did not taste 'fishy'—would go a long way with his customers at home." Lantz probably quite rightly thought that Americans wouldn't know much about Chile—even though Salvador Allende had been ousted by a CIA-backed military junta in 1973—but he liked the exotic touch of "Chilean." A year before Lantz "discovered" the toothfish, on the other side of the Southern Hemisphere, another species was dragged from the deep. *Hoplostethus atlanticus* is commonly called slimehead because of the mucus canals in its comparatively large head. It is actually quite beautiful with its orangy-red coloring, which led to its common renaming, orange roughy.

In 1978, after a little research, orange roughy was targeted as a commercial fishery in New Zealand. Its flesh is white and it is a mild-flavored fish that is easily deboned, so again good for people who don't like fish. It was an instant hit with chefs like Gordon Ramsey, who praised it as a good substitute for more popular and overfished Northern Hemisphere fish such as wild salmon.[34]

While the fish was a wild success in the kitchens of upmarket restaurants, the problem was that the science lagged far behind the ability of the

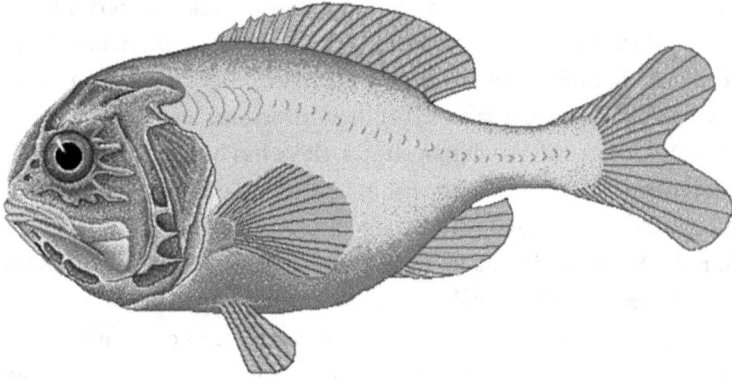

1.2 Orange roughy. Source: Robbie Cada.

roughy fisheries to scoop up the fish by the ton. It is a deep-sea fish, though not as deep as the toothfish, and it likes to hang out with other rough-ies on deep seamounts, especially when it is young. This makes it an ideal candidate for trawlers, who went crazy in what was termed the "gold rush." The New Zealand, and to a lesser extent Australian, fishing frenzy lasted for three years until the orange roughy was near extinction. When the sci-ence finally caught up with the trawlers, it was discovered that the roughy is exceptionally long-lived—some have been dated as 150 years old. And it doesn't come into sexual maturity until it is in its mid-thirties.[35] This means that stocks taken now would take thirty years to replenish.

There is something viscerally upsetting about the idea of eating a 150-year-old fish. It says a lot about the disconnect between fish eaters and fish that many of us would have no idea what age our dinner is. In 1996, research conducted by Gwen Fenton[36] demonstrated the true age of roughy and other deep-sea, slow-maturing species. Following this, New Zealand im-posed strict limits before it was completely decimated. The government then commenced accreditation through the Marine Stewardship Council. By 2016, three fisheries, accounting for 60 percent of New Zealand's orange roughy catch, achieved MSC certification.[37]

For many customers, seeing the blue logo is the end of the story—MSC says it is sustainable, so it must be. This trust curtails asking important questions that the MSC isn't interested in—including socioeconomic and cultural ones about labor practices and fishing communities. The MSC doesn't even do the science; some would say it merely crunches the num-bers that the FAO (the UN Food and Agriculture Organization) gathers from member states about fish catches. However, many fisheries buy into the often-lengthy MSC process in hopes they will gain a premium. As more and more big multinationals like Walmart commit to stocking certified sustainable fish, the race is on to get that prized blue logo on your product, although, as Peter Marko demonstrates, there has been a great deal of species substitution even when the fish is labeled as MSC-certified.[38]

It is widely recognized that the MSC was a game-changer in focusing on fish rather than marine mammals. As Stefano Ponte states, "In little over a decade, the MSC has single-handedly created a market for 'sustainable fish' and has brought it into the mainstream."[39] It is quite amazing how fast the MSC conquered the market with its eco-logo, and it encouraged a market for fish labeled sustainable. However, there is increasing criticism of the MSC. Scientists are worried that the third-party certification can be overly generous in the application of the guidelines. Rainer Froese and Alexander Proelss[40] found that 31 percent of MSC-certified fisheries were in fact overexploited. Claire Christian and colleagues[41] followed up on their study and examined the process of objecting to MSC certification. Objections are lodged (often by other NGOs such as Greenpeace) when there is doubt about whether the certification took into account certain factors. For instance, in the case of New Zealand hoki—a "sustainable fish" very widely used in restaurants—it was objected that the bottom trawling on the seafloor created environmental damage. It costs $8,000 to object, and objections rarely get upheld. Jennifer Jacquet and Daniel Pauly share a scientific skepticism about the workings of the MSC despite the fact that Pauly was one of the gang of superstar marine scientists brought in at the inception of the MSC. Jacquet notes that there is "not only growing concern among scientists about the effectiveness of seafood eco-labelling in general and the MSC label specifically, but an increasing willingness for scientists to take on rigorous research in response to that skepticism—research that the MSC should probably be doing itself."[42]

More germane to my argument, it is increasingly apparent that the organization is massively geared to the Northern Hemisphere and the Global North. Ponte writes: "while the market for fish in general has indeed become more global in the past three decades . . . the market for certified fish remains a Northern affair."[43] As part of the process of decontextualizing knowledge that such organizations trade in—in part to vaunt their scientific credentials—the focus tends to be on species rather than milieu. For instance, tilapia is lauded by organizations such as Monterey Bay Aquarium's Seafood Watch because it is easily farmed and, as a noncarnivorous

24

fish, doesn't require fishmeal. Its abundance as a farmed fish has led some to call it "the aquatic chicken."[44] It is part of the cichlid family, and was and remains important in Africa—although its main market is now in the north. In Australia, however, tilapia is often called the rabbit of Queensland's waterways, and not because it is cute. It is classified as an invasive noxious fish.[45] Of course, as Karen Cardoza and Banu Subramaniam remind us, evoking "invasion" is never innocent.[46]

## Southern Fish

I have used the terms *north* and *south* somewhat loosely. They are obviously loose and messy appellations straddling both cartographic and political and economic understandings. In Jean Comaroff and John Comaroff's argument, "'the South' . . . describes a polythetic category, its members sharing one or more—but not all, or even most—of a diverse set of features. The closest thing to a common denominator among them is that many were once colonies or protectorates."[47] There is an "inchoateness of the line between the hemispheres."[48] In an interview, John Comaroff expands on this: "The Global South has multiple referents, multiple meanings . . . its primary denotation is geographical: it signifies, hemispherically, the lower half of the planet, its underside. But this is a grotesque simplification, a realist—and often racist—conceit."[49]

Margaret Jolly raises "the respective positions of rich and developed nations of Europe and North America and the poor and underdeveloped countries of Africa, Asia, South America and the Pacific."[50] Jolly asks, "What is the effect of making such a link, and our embodied association of 'up' and 'down'?" This representation of the south as "down under," as on the bottom, replays gendered and sexualized binaries of passive/active, top/bottom, further complicated by colonial and postcolonial contexts. This is also the south of Raewyn Connell's critique in *Southern Theory* whereby ideas and social theory don't emerge from the south.[51] "'South' is a source of data but not ideas."[52] Connell's project is to reverse this ordering and to examine and circulate the ideas of southern thinkers from India, South America, and Africa who "refuse to be captive to the false claims of universality and the totalizing metanarratives of the North, as they address the diverse specificities of . . . life and the regional potential for progressive politics."[53]

If the Comaroffs and others are revitalizing what the south means politically and conceptually, there aren't really equivalent champions of southern fish. Indeed, the Southern Hemisphere is represented as a no-man's pot to be plundered.[54] This is clearly conveyed in this quotation, which comes from the BBC's highly respected production department, Earth: "There's enough fish there to make up 1.3 tonnes per human on the planet. If you take and harvest 50% of that, turn it into fishmeal and then feed it to chickens through agriculture or pigs, you're creating 4.3 kilos of animal protein per human per day. So, you've got people starving on the planet right now through food shortages, and here's a huge larder which we haven't even touched."[55] As we've seen, this representation of the southern oceans and fish is becoming naturalized: "We've run out of fish, so let's go down there." As we have equally seen, the ignorance about fish in the south is colossal, and replicates Connell's framing of the south as provider of material and raw resources, not ideas.

This paradigm was evident in the near-eradication of Patagonian toothfish once it became Chilean sea bass, and equally so in the case of the renamed slimehead. The collusion between those with good intentions (to practice fish substitution to relieve the pressures on overfished northern species) and the sheer ignorance and greed about the realities of fish stocks and communities that rely upon them is all too familiar.[56]

To further explore this, I return now to the cousin of the Patagonian toothfish, the Antarctic toothfish. As I've said, they are different: *Dissostichus eleginoides* and *Dissostichus mawsoni*. The latter is named for Sir Douglas Mawson, described by Wikipedia as "a key expedition leader during the Heroic Age of Antarctic Exploration."[57] The anatomy of Antarctic toothfish differs from the Patagonian one. It possesses antifreeze glycoproteins, which allow it to survive in the subzero waters of the Southern Ocean below sixty degrees latitude.

The governance of Antarctica is a very complicated web of global and international agreements. It remains deeply marked by colonial and imperial conflicts. As in the title of Klaus Dodds's book, some of Antarctica is pink ice[58]—named for the ways in which the British Empire colored maps of their colonial territories in pink. Numerous flags have been raised on Antarctica over the decades and centuries, including the Stars and Stripes and the Tricolor. Nearly half of the continent is under the Australian colonial-looking flag—with its Southern Cross and a small Union Jack—because in 1931 Britain "gifted" it to its former colony. Nicoletta Brazzelli argues that "Antarctica is not properly a postcolonial country: it has no native population, no specific language or culture; its history seems to coincide with the history of European explorations."[59] Sanjay Chaturvedi makes this point more forcefully: "The penetration of both polar regions (the Arctic and the

26

Antarctic) by the imperial and colonial forces need to be seen as an extension of similar but much larger process emanating, at least to begin with, from Europe and unfolding differently in various parts of the world."[60] One can readily see this in some of the names—for instance, the South Shetland Islands, which are nearly 9,000 miles away from the Scottish Shetlands. As Victoria Rosner puts it, all these nations "that have staked claims in Antarctica are engaged in a struggle to define belonging in a place that nobody has ever called home."[61]

As several feminist accounts demonstrate, the colonial history of Antarctica is deeply gendered.[62] In the past, the wrangling between and among nations was motivated by what Christy Collis calls an "imperial spatiality" produced through the sheer desire to conquer, "leaving behind flags and cairns of possession." This was then followed by "colonialism [and] the subsequent practice of spatial possession by occupation."[63] The imperial claims are all hotly contested. As was evident in the Falklands/Malvinas war between Argentina and Britain, a lot of lives have been lost in attempting to stake out bits of icy land. While Margaret Thatcher wanted to demonstrate her iron fist, she was more than likely aware of the lucrative claims that would have flowed from having the Malvinas in a British pocket. In laying claim to land, Argentina and Chile went as far as "flying down pregnant women so they could give birth to Antarctic children in the late 1970s."[64] Dodds writes that there is now "a new era of continental exploration and international rivalry, the Antarctic is now as much a symbol of global anxiety, as it is a site of ongoing scientific collaboration and knowledge exchange— snow, ice, and the cold are new geopolitical and scientific front lines."[65]

The claims to the land in Antarctica became more vexed in 1982 with the UN Convention on the Law of the Sea (UNCLOS) ruling that a nation, including any far-flung territory, had the exclusive economic right over the two hundred nautical miles that stretch from its coastline. Exclusive Economic Zones (EEZs) lie very uneasily with the overarching frame of governance— the Antarctic Treaty. The 1961 treaty rules the governance of Antarctica. It includes the guarantee of freedom of scientific investigation and the exchange of scientific findings, and the nonmilitarization of Antarctica and the Southern Ocean.[66] Australia was one of the twelve original signatories to the Antarctic Treaty, signed in 1959. Six other countries—Argentina, Chile, France, New Zealand, Norway, and the United Kingdom—have territorial claims.[67] Australia's (highly contested) claim on the continent, which amounts to 42 percent, translates into an EEZ of 2 million square kilometers of the Southern Ocean.

It is often pointed out that while the treaty serves to protect terrestrial Antarctica, it does little for its seas and the Southern Ocean. This omission led to the creation of the Commission for the Conservation of Antarctic Marine Living Resources (CCAMLR) in 1982. CCAMLR was established to manage living marine resources contained within the "CCAMLR Convention Area," which is roughly defined as all waters bounding the continent of Antarctica, north to the Antarctic Convergence. It is, however, widely described by NGOs as weak, especially, it seems, when it comes to protecting the toothfish.

CCAMLR has no powers to prevent IUU—illegal, unreported, and un-regulated—fishing. As the price rose for toothfish, so too did the spread of piracy. In 2001, 90 percent of Chilean sea bass (aka toothfish) sold in the United States came from illegal fishing.[68] The boats were not the ram-shackle affairs of the Somali pirates,[69] but modern, highly technological industrial ships mainly owned by Spanish concerns. Ships like the *Viarsa* could carry three hundred metric tons of toothfish, worth $3 million. The owners of the pirate fishing boats can disappear behind a complex network of international regulations and techniques. They routinely use flags of noncompliance (FNC), which effectively means they operate as "unregu-lated vessels." They have multiple shell companies and offshore bank ac-counts to hide the profits. The result is that "fitted with onboard factories and vast freezer holds . . . they could pull fish from the sea in quantities that domestic fishermen could not have imagined."[70]

Thanks in large part to a protracted Sea Shepherd campaign, the last of a pirate fleet, called the *Bandit 6*, was shut down in 2016.[71] In March 2016 the Spanish Ministry of Agriculture fined Vidal Armadores €17,840,000 and disqualified them from fishing. They found that "the target of the interna-tional business structure was to manage and operate four fishing vessels: KUNLUN, SONGHUA, YONGDING and TIANTAI, all of them involved in IUU in the region managed by the Commission for the Conservation of Antarctic Marine Living Resources (CCAMLR)."[72] This again demonstrates the difficulty that CCAMLR faces in preventing the degradation of the seas that surround the treaty-bound land of Antarctica. It also points to the strange logics that MSC deploys. It certified several toothfish fisheries after the piracy had stopped, including the Glacier 51. This was despite the long-standing gaps in fisheries science about the lifecycle of the fish, and the damage fishing wreaks on the environments of the deep south. Fish stocks are monitored by tagging juveniles. Knowledge of the prevalence is largely dependent on accepting the fishermen's word. In a weird twist of the more-than-human, killer whales have now learned how to eat toothfish off the long-liners. They can't dive to the depths of the fish's natural habitat, but they pluck them off as the lines surface. The marine biologists who first noted this are, of course, fascinated: "here we have a human activity and the whales have switched their behavior to take advantage of it."[73] This has profound implications for measuring sustainability because no one knows how many fish the whales take as their natural right.

The Ross Sea, which New Zealand claims as its dependency, is another casualty of the treaty. Little did I know when I talked to the manager in Nelson that the company he works for is one of the major companies fishing in the Ross Sea—widely considered one of the last pristine and intact marine ecosystems. Few others do either. As the New Zealand journalist Mike White writes in a piece entitled "Hypocrisy on the High Seas," "while New Zealand regularly sermonises about the evils of Japan's Antarctic whaling, few realize that our own boats are involved in controversial fishing nearby."[74] I have to admit that, like many others, I didn't know much about the Ross Sea: "It's at the bottom of the ocean at the bottom of the world. It's a place where few see what's going on and no one knows exactly what's happening."[75]

Sealord, which is the second largest owner of toothfish quota, is 50 percent owned by Nissui (a mega Japanese company) and 50 percent by Maoris under the Maori Fisheries Settlement. In 1996, it conducted exploratory fishing for Antarctic toothfish in the Ross Sea. In 1997, Sealord commenced a commercial fishery, joined by a multinational fleet of fishing boats from members of CCAMLR. Adult fish are located nearly a nautical mile deep into the ocean, and grow to six and a half feet in length and up to two hundred pounds in weight. Juvenile toothfish, however, hang out together on seamounts and banks, in nearshore areas, and in shallow areas around islands. This behavior makes the juveniles an easy target. It's what Pauly calls "strip mining the ocean."[76] Huge industrial fishing boats are needed to get to the fishing grounds. The mid-water trawlers scoop up the juveniles, and the long-liners go for the adults deeper down. One long-line can have up to 8,000 hooks. *The Last Ocean*, a documentary directed and filmed by Peter Young, is an affecting account of what is happening at the bottom of the world.[77] The scenery is truly breathtaking, and the film captures the huge variety of wildlife—from Adelie and emperor penguins, to Weddell seals, to a variety of killer whales that only exists in the Ross Sea. The arrival of fishing trawlers into this icy blue-white seascape is quite shocking. As one marine scientist says, "this is the industrial world invading this pristine place."

Another estimates that 90 percent of the adult population has already been taken. And, as had already happened in so many parts of the world, it is the destruction of the ecosystem that is most worrisome. As the narrator says, it's about "things that eat toothfish and what toothfish eat." The removal of these big fish puts the ecosystem of the Ross Sea out of kilter.

## Conclusion

When is fish meat? For some it is obvious. As a long-term pescatarian, I knew that fish wasn't meat even though the category of fish-eating vegetarian is confusing for many. Catholics certainly know that fish isn't meat. Since 2011, English and Welsh Catholics have been obliged to abstain from meat every Friday. The Code of Canon Law Abstinence considers that meat comes only from animals such as chickens, cows, sheep, or pigs—all of which live on land. American Catholics in the south were glad to have it clarified that alligator is a fish, and I presume Australian crocodiles are too.[78]

In this chapter, I have sought to connect the white middle-class American predilection for fish that doesn't taste like fish. As we have seen, this is anchored in the early 1900s when it was discovered that if you cooked albacore tuna and then canned it, it could be passed off as chicken of the sea. This taste for white is enshrined in US federal legislation that only albacore can be referred to as white-meat fish. Those long-ago appetites endure and have found ever newer fish and developed highly lucrative markets. The chase for toothfish and the gold rush frenzy for orange roughy quickly depleted stocks of fish that can live longer than most humans. The high price on their unusual heads has galvanized industrial fishing that blithely ignores the territorial waters of southern nations, and violates one of the few places that is supposed to be set aside by treaty for peaceful investigations for all of humankind. With the seas of the north increasingly fished out, the "pristine" Antarctic is now up for grabs by illegal trawlers owned by European concerns.

Eating fish well necessitates being cognizant of a very complex system— it means getting into the heart of the more-than-human entanglement. It's messy. There are no clear-cut answers. Well-meaning, often middle-class, people in the north routinely deplore farmed fish practices in the south. And it is now clear that some employ horrendous human labor practices— the full extent of slavery or indentured labor is hard to fathom and to trace. And some fishing practices are decidedly not sustainable—for the fish, the environment, or for the fishing communities. But there are well-run farms

30

that provide much-needed employment. It is often easier to take a political stance against farmed shrimp from the south than to come face to face with the damage trawlers from the north routinely do in developing nations in the south. Beyond the piracy—which as we've seen in many cases is conducted by European boats—the aboveboard and sanctioned fishing trade by European Union and United States is stripping African nations of their main source of protein. They may get hard currency for giving up their EEZ rights to foreign vessels, but coastal communities are left with no fish. One can imagine what substituting potatoes for fish protein does for the bodies of the poor—especially for women and girls.

Ecosystems are entanglements. In many cases, such as Somalia, the stock is plundered by high-tech boats conducting voluminous illegal fishing. And we wonder why some Somalis took to the seas to exact revenge. When you take out the big fish, everything falters. When the sea becomes simplified, ecosystems have little resistance and simply close down. In this chapter, I have tried to trace out the relatedness of fish. As Stefan Helmreich writes, "things—refugees, nomads, weapons, drugs, fish—challenge borders because they are imagined to 'flow' across them."[79] It's hard to draw maps on the sea and even harder to ensure that regulations are followed.

I've argued here that the "crisis" of fishing and oceans is one of complex flows of colonial power and its legacies that mean that the Global South is seen as the "bottom" of the world that can be fished ruthlessly, with little concern for fish stocks or the communities that depend on them. Fishing has always been an intricate interplay of available technology, knowledge, and fish. As the north has developed ever more precise technologies—sonars, GIS, and planes that report on where the fish congregate—and bigger and faster boats that can go longer and deeper, developing nations are left behind on the shore. Their inshore fish stocks are gone, and their artisanal and more sustainable techniques do not allow them to compete. This unequal state is further destabilized through seemingly "good" initiatives such as the MSC that disqualify southern nations from joining in the burgeoning sustainable fish markets because of cost, or worse, because they no longer have the fish stocks to certify. The final straw is how the market for fish hinges on the tastes of consumers in the north for bland white fish. Drawn by outrageous prices, industrial multinational fishing fleets hoover up the denizens of the deep, now renamed to make them palatable.

It's enough to make you give up eating fish; it's certainly enough to stay away from white fish that tastes like meat.

31

# Notes

1 Psyche Williams-Forson, "More Than Just the 'Big Piece of Chicken': The Power of Race, Class, and Food in American Consciousness," in *Food and Culture: A Reader*, edited by Carol Counihan and Penny Van Esterik (New York: Routledge, 1997), 347.

2 Williams-Forson, "More Than Just the 'Big Piece of Chicken,'" 347.

3 Tina Smithers Peckham, "Jessica Simpson Recalls Her Infamous 'Chicken of the Sea' Debate," *ETonline*, November 29, 2016, http://www.etonline.com/news /203780_jessica_simpson_recalls_her_infamous_chicken_of_the_sea_debate.

4 It is now owned by Thai Union, which was at the center of the labor scandal in 2016, when it was found that they were effectively enslaving fishermen.

5 Erin Nudi, "Food History: Canned Tuna," February 12, 2015, https://www .erinnudi.com/2015/02/12/food-history-canned-tuna/.

6 Nudi, "Food History."

7 Robert A. Ferdhan, "How America Fell Out of Love with Canned Tuna," *Washington Post*, August 18, 2014, https://www.washingtonpost.com/news/wonk /wp/2014/08/18/how-america-fell-out-of-love-with-canned-tuna/?utm_term= .7d67a4f1281c.

8 Suzanne Hamlin, "Canned Tuna: In Search of Flavor and Texture," *New York Times*, August 6, 1997, http://www.nytimes.com/1997/08/06/garden/ canned -tuna-in-search-of-flavor-and-texture.html.

9 Melanie E. Dupuis, *Nature's Perfect Food: How Milk Became America's Drink* (New York: New York University Press, 2002).

10 Aaron Brobow-Strain, "White Bread Biopolitics: Purity, Health, and the Triumph of Industrial Baking," in *Geographies of Race and Food: Fields, Bodies, Markets*, edited by Rachel Slocom and Arun Saldanha (London: Ashgate, 2013).

11 Brobow-Strain, "White Bread Biopolitics," 31.

12 Brobow-Strain, "White Bread Biopolitics," 34.

13 Brobow-Strain, "White Bread Biopolitics," 36.

14 Daniel Pauly et al., "The Future for Fisheries," *Science* 302, no. 5649 (2003): 1361.

15 Elspeth Probyn, *Eating the Ocean* (Durham, NC: Duke University Press, 2016).

16 Sebastian Abrahamsson et al., "Living within Omega-3: New Materialism and Enduring Concerns," *Environment and Planning D* 33, no. 1 (2015): 10.

17 "The Fish," *Glacier 51*, n.d., http://glacier51toothfish.com/the-fish/.

18 "The Fish."

19 Interview conducted by author, January 5, 2017.

20 Bruce G. Knecht, *Hooked: A True Story of Pirates, Poaching, and the Perfect Fish* (Sydney: Allen and Unwin, 2006), 73–74.

21 Knecht, *Hooked*, 71.

22 Cheyenne MacDonald, "The Terrifying 'Alien Creatures' of the Deep: Russian Fisherman Becomes Online Hit after Revealing His Bizarre Catches on Twitter," *Daily Mail*, December 20, 2016, https://www.dailymail.co.uk/sciencetech

/article-4053490/The-terrifying-creatures-deep-Russian-deep-sea-fisherman
-online-hit-revealing-bizarre-catches.html.

23 George Mills, "What the F*** Is That: Viewers Horrified by Nightmarish
Alien Fish Dragged from the Sea," *Daily Star*, September 29, 2016, http://www
.dailystar.co.uk/news/latest-news/549326/fisherman-malaysia-captures-alien
-sea-creature-eel-goby-video.

24 Elizabeth McMillan, "Creepy Deepwater Fish Surprises Nova Scotia Fisherman," *CBC News*, March 7, 2016, http://www.cbc.ca/news/canada/nova-scotia
/lunenburg-fisherman-photographs-creepy-deepwater-fish-1.3479154.

25 Alistair Hobday, "Ocean Winners and Losers Revealed in Marine Report
Card," *The Conversation*, August 17, 2012, https://theconversation.com/ocean
-winners-and-losers-revealed-in-marine-report-card-8891.

26 Wilson da Silva, "All the Fish in the Sea," *Australian Financial Review Magazine*, 1999, http://www.wilsondasilva.com/all-the-fish-in-the-sea.

27 Boris Worm and Trevor Branch, "The Future of Fish," *Trends in Ecology and
Evolution* 27, no. 11 (2010): 594.

28 Worm and Branch, "The Future of Fish," 596.

29 David A. Farenthold, "Unpopular, Unfamiliar Fish Species Suffer from Become
Seafood," *Washington Post*, July 31, 2009, http://www.washingtonpost.com/wp
-dyn/content/article/2009/07/30/AR2009073002478.html.

30 Knecht, *Hooked*, 70–71.

31 Knecht, *Hooked*.

32 Knecht, *Hooked*.

33 Knecht, *Hooked*.

34 Theo Mertz, "Delia and Nigella Panned over Endangered Fish," *The Telegraph*,
October 30, 2013, http://www.telegraph.co.uk/news/earth/environment
/ecology/10413849/Delia-and-Nigella-panned-over-endangered-fish.html.

35 "Methuselah of the Deep," *Ecos* 68 (1991): 13–17, http://www.ecosmagazine.com
/?act=view_file&file_id=EC68p13.pdf.

36 In 2016 Fenton became the first female chief scientist of the Australian Antarctic Territory, a fact that will later become salient in my discussion of gender and
Antarctic research. http://www.antarctica.gov.au/science/meet-our-scientists
/dr-gwen-fenton.

37 The MSC was founded in 1997 as a joint project between the World Wildlife
Fund and Unilever, which was one of the world's largest seafood processors
(Unilever, cited in C. Christian et al., "A Review of Formal Objections to the
Marine Stewardship Council Fisheries," *Biological Conservation* 161 [2013]:
10–17). The MSC involves third-party examination of a fishery, a process that
may take a couple of years and can cost $100,000 or more. The public doesn't
seem to realize that the fishery—or in the case of the roughy, the government of
New Zealand—bears the cost. The MSC describes their three-pronged process:
recognize and reward fisheries that fish sustainably, work with fisheries and
commercial partners to build a market for sustainable seafood, and provide an

33

easy way for everyone to find seafood from a sustainable fishery: the blue MSC ecolabel. https://www.msc.org/about-us/standards.

38 Peter Marko et al., "Seafood Substitutions Obscure Patterns of Mercury Contamination in Patagonian Toothfish (*Dissostichus eleginoides*) or 'Chilean Sea Bass,'" *PloS One* 9, no. 8 (2014): e104140.

39 Stefano Ponte, "The Marine Stewardship Council (MSC) and the Making of a Market for 'Sustainable Fish,'" *Journal of Agrarian Change* 12, nos. 2/3 (2012): 304.

40 Rainer Froese and Alexander Proelss, "Evaluation and Legal Assessment of Certified Seafood," *Marine Policy* 36, no. 6 (2012): 1284–89.

41 Claire Christian et al., "A Review of Formal Objections to the Marine Stewardship Council Fisheries," *Biological Conservation* 161 (2013): 10–17.

42 Daniel Cressey, "Seafood Labelling under Fire," *Nature*, May 11, 2012, http://www.nature.com/news/seafood-labelling-under-fire-1.10626.

43 Ponte, "The Marine Stewardship Council (MSC)," 312.

44 G. W. Barlow, *The Cichlid Fishes* (Cambridge, MA: Perseus, 2000).

45 Garry Fitzgerald, "Tilapia in Australia," *Sweetwater Fishing*, n.d., http://www.sweetwaterfishing.com.au/tilapia.htm.

46 Karen Cardoza and Banu Subramanian, "Assembling Asian/American Naturecultures: Orientalism and Invited Invasions," *Journal of Asian American Studies* 16, no. 1 (2013): 8.

47 Jean Comaroff and John L. Comaroff, "Theory from the South: Or, How Euro-America Is Evolving toward Africa," *Anthropological Forum V* 22, no. 2 (2012): 126.

48 Comaroff and Comaroff, "Theory from the South," 127.

49 Lisandro Claudio, "Thoughts on Theorising from the South: An Interview with John Comaroff," *Johannesburg Salon* 10 (2016), http://jwtc.org.za/volume_10/lisandro_claudio.htm.

50 Margaret Jolly, "The South in *Southern Theory*: Antipodean Reflections on the Pacific," *Australian Humanities Review* (2008): 44, http://australianhumanitiesreview.org/2008/03/01/the-south-in-southern-theory-antipodean-reflections-on-the-pacific/.

51 Raewyn W. Connell, *Southern Theory* (Sydney: Allen and Unwin, 2012).

52 Jolly, "The South in *Southern Theory*," 44.

53 Jolly, "The South in *Southern Theory*," 2.

54 This sounds like Garrett Hardin's infamous "tragedy of the commons" (1968). However, where he blamed a universal tendency of man to destroy communally held entities, this is more precisely about the greed of some and the historical conditions of colonialism that enable it. Garrett Hardin, "The Tragedy of the Commons," *Science* 162, no. 3859 (1968): 1243–48.

55 David Cox, "The Race to Fish the Larder Living in the 'Twilight Zone,'" BBC.com, January 16, 2017, http://www.bbc.com/earth/story/20170113-the-race-to-fish-the-larder-living-in-the-twilight-zone.

56  By this I mean in terms of other fisheries, but also about how "good intentions" have wreaked havoc on indigenous human and more-than-human populations. Probyn, *Eating the Ocean*, chapter 5.

57  "Douglas Mawson," *Wikipedia*, n.d., https://en.wikipedia.org/wiki/Douglas_Mawson.

58  Klaus Dodds, *Pink Ice: Britain and the South Atlantic Empire* (London: I. B. Tauris, 2002).

59  Nicoletta Brazzelli, "Postcolonial Antarctica and the Memory of the Empire of Ice," *Le Simplegadi* 12 (2014): 127–41, http://all.uniud.it/simplegadi.

60  Sanjay Chaturvedi, "Antarctica," in *International Encyclopedia of Human Geography*, edited by Rob Kitchin and Nigel Thrift (Amsterdam: Elsevier, 2009), 133–39.

61  Victoria Rosner, "Gender and Polar Studies: Mapping the Terrain," *Signs* 34, no. 3 (2009): 490.

62  Lisa Bloom, *Gender on Ice: American Ideologies of Polar Expeditions* (Minneapolis: University of Minnesota Press, 1993); Victoria Rosner, "Gender and Polar Studies: Mapping the Terrain," *Signs* 34, no. 3 (2009): 490.

63  Christy Collis, "The Australian Antarctic Territory: A Man's World?," *Signs* 34, no. 3 (2009): 515.

64  Klaus Dodds, "Settling and Unsettling Antarctica," *Signs* 34, no. 3 (2009): 508.

65  Klaus Dodds, "*Scott of the Antarctic* (1948): Geopolitics, Film and Britain's Polar Empire," *Acme* 65, no. 3 (2012): 59–70.

66  "Antarctic Treaty System," Australia Department of Agriculture, Water and the Environment, http://www.antarctica.gov.au/law-and-treaty.

67  "Antarctic Treaty System."

68  Knecht, *Hooked*, 89.

69  The Somali pirates came to the world's attention in 2009 when a NATO alliance force led by the UK took on the pirates. "The Somalis would seize an entire commercial vessel and crew and demand a ransom." Dan De Luce, "Why Is It So Hard to Stop West Africa's Vicious Pirates," *Foreign Policy*, September 23, 2016, http://foreignpolicy.com/2016/09/23/the-world-beat-somali-pirates-why-cant-it-stop-west-african-piracy/. It is a fascinating tale, which unfortunately I haven't got the space to do justice to. The views about the pirates differ. Obviously, the business concerns in the West as well as the insurance companies condemned them. But as Johann Hari points out, "More than $300m-worth of tuna, shrimp, and lobster are being stolen every year by illegal trawlers. The local fishermen are now starving." During the height of the piracy the local fishermen found that their catch returned by more than 50 percent because the foreign trawlers were scared off. Hari details how nuclear waste was also routinely dumped in the waters off Somalia. Johann Hari, "You Are Being Lied to about Pirates," *Independent*, January 5, 2009, http://www.independent.co.uk/voices/commentators/johann-hari/johann-hari-you-are-being-lied-to-about-pirates-1225817.html.

70  Knecht, *Hooked*, 41.

35

71 Siddharth Chakravarty, "The End of the 'Bandit 6,'" Sea Shepherd, March 6, 2017, https://www.seashepherd.org.uk/news-and-commentary/commentary/the-end-of-the-bandit-6.html.

72 "Vidal Armadores Fined over €17.8 million by Spanish Authorities for Offences Relating to Illegal Fishing Activities," Sea Shepherd, March 19, 2016, https://www.seashepherd.org.uk/news-and-commentary/news/vidal-armadores-fined-over-17-8-million-by-spanish-authorities-for-offences-relating-to-illegal-fishing-activities.html.

73 Bridie Smith, "Whales Losing Killer Instinct: Marine Giants Have Discovered Take-Away Meals," *Sydney Morning Herald*, December 30, 2016, http://www.smh.com.au/technology/sci-tech/whales-losing-killer-instinct-scientists-find-marine-giants-have-discovered-takeaway-meals-20161228-gtj5os.html.

74 Mike White, "Fish out of Water: Hypocrisy on the High Seas," *North and South* (2010): 292.

75 White, "Fish out of Water," 292.

76 Daniel Pauly. "Ocean Leaders 'Shake Up' How We View the Seas." 2015. http://www.seaaroundus.org/magazines/2012/National GeorgraphicNew Watch_Ocean LeadersShapeUpHowWeViewTheSeas.pdf.

77 John B. Weller, director, *The Last Ocean* (Auckland: Fisheye Films, 2012).

78 Carl Bunderson, "Alligator OK to Eat on Lenten Fridays, Archbishop Clarifies," Catholic News Agency, February 15, 2013, https://www.catholicnewsagency.com/news/alligator-ok-to-eat-on-lenten-fridays-archbishop-clarifies.

79 Stefan Helmreich, "Nature/Culture/Seawater," *American Anthropologist* 133, no. 1 (2011): 137.

## Bibliography

Abrahamsson, Sebastian, Filippo Bertoni, Annemarie Mol, and Rebeca Ibáñez Martín. "Living within Omega-3: New Materialism and Enduring Concerns." *Environment and Planning D* 33, no. 1 (2015): 4–19.

Barlow, G. W. *The Cichlid Fishes.* Cambridge, MA: Perseus, 2000.

Bestor, Theodore. *Tsukiji: The Fish Market at the Center of the World.* Berkeley: University of California Press, 2004.

Brazzelli, Nicoletta. "Postcolonial Antarctica and the Memory of the Empire of Ice." *Le Simplegadi* 12 (2014): 127–41. http://all.uniud.it/simplegadi.

Brobow-Strain, Aaron. "White Bread Biopolitics: Purity, Health, and the Triumph of Industrial Baking." In *Geographies of Race and Food: Fields, Bodies, Markets*, edited by Rachel Slucom and Arun Saldanha. London: Ashgate, 2013.

Cardozo, Karen, and Banu Subramaniam. "Assembling Asian/American Naturecultures: Orientalism and Invited Invasions." *Journal of Asian American Studies* 16, no. 1 (2013): 1–23.

Chaturvedi, Sanjay. "Antarctica." In *International Encyclopedia of Human Geography*, edited by Rob Kitchin and Nigel Thrift, 133–39. Amsterdam: Elsevier, 2009.

Christian, C., D. Ainley, M. Bailey, P. Dayton, J. Hocevar, M. LeVine, J. Nikoloyuk, C. Nouvian, E. Velarde, R. Werner, and J. Jacquet. "A Review of Formal Objections to the Marine Stewardship Council Fisheries." *Biological Conservation* 161 (2013): 10–17.

Claudio, Lisandro. "Thoughts on Theorising from the South: An Interview with John Comaroff." *Johannesburg Salon* 10 (2016). https://jwtc.org.za/resources /docs/salon-volume-10/6Vol10SDinteractive.pdf.

Collis, Christy. "The Australian Antarctic Territory: A Man's World?" *Signs* 34, no. 3 (2009): 514–19.

Comaroff, Jean, and John L. Comaroff. "Theory from the South: Or, How Euro-America Is Evolving toward Africa." *Anthropological Forum V* 22, no. 2 (2012): 133–31.

Connell, Raewyn W. *Southern Theory*. Sydney: Allen and Unwin, 2012.

Dodds, Klaus. *Pink Ice: Britain and the South Atlantic Empire*. London: I. B. Tauris, 2002.

Dodds, Klaus. "Scott of the Antarctic (1948): Geopolitics, Film and Britain's Polar Empire." *Acme* 65, no. 3 (2012): 59–70.

Dodds, Klaus. "Settling and Unsettling Antarctica." *Signs* 34, no. 3 (2009): 505–9.

Dupuis, Melanie E. *Nature's Perfect Food: How Milk Became America's Drink*. New York: New York University Press, 2002.

Erdrich, Louise. *The Round House*. New York: HarperCollins, 2012.

Ferdhan, Robert A. "How America Fell Out of Love with Canned Tuna." *Washington Post*, August 18, 2014. https://www.washingtonpost.com/news/wonk/wp /2014/08/18/how-america-fell-out-of-love-with-canned-tuna/?utm_term= .7d67a4f1281c.

Forson-Williams, Psyche. "More Than Just the 'Big Piece of Chicken': The Power of Race, Class, and Food in American Consciousness." In *Food and Culture: A Reader*, edited by Carol Counihan and Penny Van Esterik. New York: Routledge, 1997.

Hamlin, Suzanne. "Canned Tuna: In Search of Flavor and Texture." *New York Times*, August 6, 1997. http://www.nytimes.com/1997/08/06/garden/canned-tuna-in-search-of-flavor- and-texture.html.

Hardin, Garrett. "The Tragedy of the Commons." *Science* 162, no. 3859 (1968): 1243–48.

Helmreich, Stefan. "Nature/Culture/Seawater." *American Anthropologist* 133, no. 1 (2011): 132–44.

Hobday, Alistair. "Ocean Winners and Losers Revealed in Marine Report Card." *The Conversation*, August 17, 2012. https://theconversation.com/ocean-winners -and-losers revealed-in-marine-report-card-8891.

Jacquet, Jennifer, and Daniel Pauly. "Seafood Stewardship in Crisis." *Nature* 476 (2010): 28–29.

Jolly, Margaret. "The South in *Southern Theory*: Antipodean Reflections on the Pacific." *Australian Humanities Review* (2008): 44. http://australianhumanities review.org/archive/Issue-March-2008/jolly.html.

Knecht, G. Bruce. *Hooked: A True Story of Pirates, Poaching, and the Perfect Fish*. Sydney: Allen and Unwin, 2006.

Marko, Peter B., Holly A. Nance, and Peter van den Hurk. "Seafood Substitutions Obscure Patterns of Mercury Contamination in Patagonian Toothfish (*Dissostichus eleginoides*) or 'Chilean Sea Bass.'" *PloS One* 9, no. 8 (2014): e104140.

Pauly, Daniel. "Ocean Leaders 'Shake Up' How We View the Seas." 2015. http://www.seaaroundus.org/magazines/2012/.

Pauly, D., J. Alder, E. Bennett, V. Christensen, P. Tyedmers, and R. Watson. "The Future for Fisheries." *Science* 302, no. 5649 (2003): 1359–61.

Pauly, D., V. Christensen, J. Dalsgaard, R. Froese, and F. Torres. "Fishing Down Marine Food Webs." *Science* 279, no. 5352 (1998): 860–63.

Pauly, Daniel, Reg Watson, and Jackie Alder. "Global Trends in World Fisheries: Impacts on Marine Ecosystems and Food Security." *Philosophical Transactions of the Royal Society B* (2005). https://doi.org/10.1098/rstb.2004.1574.

Ponte, Stefano. "The Marine Stewardship Council (MSC) and the Making of a Market for 'Sustainable Fish.'" *Journal of Agrarian Change* 12, nos. 2/3 (2012): 300–315.

Probyn, Elspeth. "Queer Fish: Eating Ethnic Affect." In *Visuality, Emotions and Minority Culture*, edited by John N. Erni. Amsterdam: Springer, 2017.

Probyn, Elspeth. *Eating the Ocean*. Durham, NC: Duke University Press, 2016.

Rosner, Victoria. "Gender and Polar Studies: Mapping the Terrain." *Signs* 34, no. 3 (2009): 489–94.

Russell, Denise. "Aboriginal-Makassan Interactions in the Eighteenth and Nineteenth Centuries in Northern Australia and Contemporary Sea Claims." *Australian Aboriginal Studies* 1 (2004): 3–17.

Simoons, Frederick J. "Rejection of Fish as Human Food in Africa: A Problem in History and Ecology." *Ecology of Food and Nutrition* 3, no. 2 (1974): 89–105. doi:10.1080/03670244.1974.9990367.

Tacon, Paul S. C., and Sally K. May. "Rock Art Evidence for Macassan-Aboriginal Contact in Northwestern Arnhem Land." In *Macassan History and Heritage: Journeys, Encounters and Influences*, edited by Marshall Clark and Sally K. May. Canberra: ANU Press, 2013.

Tixier, Paul, Nicolas Gasco, Guy Duhamel, and Christophe Guinet. "Depredation of Patagonian Toothfish (*Dissostichus eleginoides*) by Two Sympatrically Occurring Killer Whale (*Orcinus orca*) Ecotypes: Insights on the Behavior of the Rarely Observed Type D Killer Whales." *Marine Mammal Science*, February 1, 2016.

Weller, John B., director. *The Last Ocean*. Auckland: Fisheye Films, 2012.

White, Mike. "Fish out of Water: Hypocrisy on the High Seas." *North and South* (2010): 292.

Worm, Boris, and Trevor A. Branch. "The Future of Fish." *Trends in Ecology and Evolution* 27, no. 11 (2010): 594–99.

# Eating
# the Mother

JESS DOBKIN'S *The Lactation Station Breast Milk Bar* (2006–16) is an amazing work that could be described in a seemingly simple and transparent line: an artist offers donated breast milk to her audience members in a wine tasting setting. Hence, the title appears self-explanatory. In this text I engage with this work to expand on a specific topic raised recently but not yet engaged with extensively, in relation to new creative works of similar nature: of anthropophagy/cannibalism. In several such works made by self-identified mothers, the maternal body and its products are offered to be consumed in various ways (cooked, raw, mixed with other ingredients). Dobkin's work is unique in raising new questions about cannibalism and its as yet unexplored connection between autophagy and anthropophagy as a fundamental human condition: how we are all born cannibals. The new body of work, like the one by Dobkin, enables us to ponder what eating the mother is about. There are at least two reasons why the topic of the mother as food has not been explored more systematically to date. First, it is due to an omission from and acknowledgment of mothers in various productions (cultural, philosophical, and biomedical), as I discuss elsewhere in my work on hospitality and the maternal. Second, it is due to the challenges that the topic of eating the mother presents within feminist discourse. Jess Dobkin's work charts a new territory toward questions of postcolonial and queer frameworks of theorizing the maternal.

*The Lactation Station Breast Milk Bar* raises many important questions. I will focus on two:

1. Is the mother food? And if the mother is food, then what kind of food: meat, drink, solid, liquid?
2. Does the self and non-self relation of the maternal body imply cannibalism and anthropophagy, autophagy, or something else?

# 1

Is the mother food? And if the mother is food, then what kind of food: meat, drink, solid, liquid?

Jess Dobkin's project *The Lactation Station Breast Milk Bar* was first performed in 2006 in Toronto. It was later performed again in Montreal, and most recently at the FAB Gallery of the University of Alberta, in May 2016, as part of the exhibition New Maternalisms: Redux, curated by Natalie Loveless.[1] This was the time when I witnessed it and will be referring (unless specified otherwise) to the 2016 iteration. During the performance Dobkin and her assistant served, as hostesses, the breast milk in the setting of a wine tasting: several participants sat on bar stools around an oval table and were given a menu; various milk tastes were discussed, opinions exchanged, tastings happened, and a conversation ensued. The milk was donated by Edmonton-based nursing mothers contacted in advance of the performance. It was stored in a fridge and pasteurized before being served.

The artist and the critics who have written about the work emphasized that breastfeeding has been surrounded with disgust, which *Lactation Station* reveals: "Perhaps the most successful aspect of the show was its ability to bring to light the intense revulsion that surrounds breast milk, a substance that is inextricably linked to the feminine body."[2] Revulsion has been overdetermined, however, as a framework to approach the work: would it not be more repulsive to taste milk coming from udders/breasts of nonhuman animals, to do a cross-species tasting? But it does not play out like this in most cultures. Thus, if this revulsion and another term—disgust—have become tropes to understand the work, the questions of the maternal body as food and cannibalism are not addressed in depth or accepted without further critical consideration. I have written elsewhere that I can imagine another work, post–*Lactation Station*, where packaged breast milk is

40

advertised and sold in supermarkets as superior, healthier, and more "natural" than any other animal milk, because it is human, of the same species.[3]

I am not asking these questions for the sake of being outrageous, but rather to move the discussion of "disgust" into the recent scholarly literature on what it means to "eat well." Jacques Derrida argues that we cannot ever eat well—fully ethically, without violence, without harm to other, nonhuman beings—because this would mean cannibalism, eating just ourselves, and not consuming "others." Eating well, it is often argued in this vein, is a compromise, and at best, we want to lessen the suffering of those whom we eat. Therefore, scholars in animal studies often focus on "how" rather than "if": with less violence, with less pain, with more sense of ecological codependence and sustainability. But fundamentally, it is argued, eating is appropriation and consumption. In his dismissive discussion of vegetarianism, Derrida (rather quickly, too quickly) himself moves to this point: that appropriating plants is also appropriating life. That logic then comes full circle: because appropriating plants is also violent, there is no difference between eating animals and plants. Does it then mean, as Dostoevsky would ask, that "anything is allowed" just because we do not, at least in theory, spend a bit more time on the question of self-eating? Noneating and cannibalism remain unexplored, though they are as much part of our lives, as I show here, and should be given further consideration, because as much as we try to move away from cannibalism due to its taboo status, we are all starting as cannibals, as people who eat our mothers.

This fact—that we are cannibals—was recognized, almost inevitably, without much elaboration, by most who have written about Dobkin's work. This is its elegant power: in offering us, in the simple gesture of tasting, another person's bodily product, without making many statements about what "eating well" might mean, *The Lactation Station Breast Milk Bar* was about such primordial "eating well" as "eating the mother." Why look elsewhere? We have practiced this all along. Charles Reeves, writing about the first iteration of the performance in Toronto, provides one such reading prompted by Dobkin. Though still primarily focusing on the concept of disgust, he provides a substantive discussion of human breast milk versus human blood as food:

> The interest in the event bore out Dobkin's hunch that our curiosity about breast milk runs deep and that, because breast milk is both nutrient and bodily substance, a certain amount of attraction mitigates the disgust that it provokes. This mitigation explains why Dobkin's project

attracted a more mixed response than other attempts to turn people—or parts of them—into food. When, in 1992, the Australian restaurateur and food writer Gay Bilson publicly proposed to collect about three liters (more than six pints) of her blood, have it screened for possible contamination, then substitute it for pig's blood in a conventional recipe for blood sausage, outcry made her drop the idea, even though there was no question of harm to self or others. This contrast between the responses to *Lactation Station* and Bilson's proposal suggests that whereas we're unclear whether human milk is food, we're certain that human blood is not. Surely this difference springs from cultural expectations, since, when it comes to other mammals, we tend to consider most, if not all, of the animal—including its blood and milk—as potential food, eliminating bits from our diet in response to social norms or ethical considerations. Regarding humans, we reverse this perspective: nothing is food. Breast milk straddles this difference because we're familiar with the idea of breast milk as food, but that familiarity extends only to a mother nursing her child. Beyond that, we're not sure what we think. Dobkin's gambit was to isolate breast milk from the mother–child relationship by replacing children with adults, a simple switch that highlights our uncertainty about the liquid. Why is it food for an infant but not for someone older?[4]

The reference to cannibalism in relation to *Lactation Station* is also made by Jennie Klein in her review of the exhibition:

*Lactation Station Breast Milk Bar*, which Dobkin has performed in the past, brought the audience directly into contact with material—breast milk—that is and is not "alive." For adults—and the adults that night included Minister McLean's partner who held his own baby while sampling other women's breast milk—drinking breast milk feels cannibalistic, and thus taboo and unclean. While it is not on the level of the cannibalism that was implied by Zhu Yu's *Eating Babies* (2000), a performance for which most of the world has only photo documentation, *Lactation Station Breast Milk Bar* actually provided real breast milk. There was no question of whether or not it was consumed. What is more, the breast milk, which tasted so different, made the audience acutely aware of the degree to which the material world—food, diet, environment—could impact caregiving and nurturance.[5]

42

The authenticity of the claims to it being "real" has been pointed to or implied as an important quality of this work, and notably has not been questioned (though Klein in the same paragraph questions how authentic the work of Zhu Yu is). Tasting assured its realness (later in this chapter, Elspeth Probyn brings us back to this topic of really real in food studies). Milk's authenticity is also assured by the proximity in Dobkin's work to the materiality of the maternal body. I do not suggest that the importance is primarily in whether we are "cheated" (what is cheating in the realm of contemporary art?) by artists or anyone else who is involved in making these works. Their own claims to authenticity lead to the original question: If what we are presented with here as food to taste is not what it is supposed to be, then the work changes its meaning profoundly. Or does it? There is another undercurrent to the question, which interests me too: the multiple substitutions and transformations the authenticity question provokes. Historically, our human ability to substitute breast milk by anything other than the breast milk from another human mother has been mostly unsuccessful, and even to date often leads to unsatisfactory results (think of baby formula debates).

Moreover, the successful (resolved) substitution of breast milk with other types of food as the infant grows is seen as a major step in coming of age, of an ability to be independent, to survive in this world. In psychoanalysis, this important process results in the weaning off, in the separation from the mother, and subsequent forms of separation anxiety. For mothers, the process of separation, as is shown in contemporary art of the maternal, varies and could signify the end of a major dependence or bliss, or of their own independence from sustaining an ecology of being with an infant.

Any food, all future food that we eat after our birth, is a substitute for the mother. It is a substitute for her body, and the breast and its milk, because they could be seen as inseparable from the rest of the mother, from her flesh, her meat, her body that together make this milk, this food. Because that original meal is supposed to be the best one, the most comforting one, after which one is blissfully asleep, calm, and content, the relationship is psychosomatic in many ways—and hence its attractiveness, as Reeves and Klein noted above when writing about *The Lactation Station*. What is comfort food, after all? Isn't it about being at home with oneself through ingestion, digestion, and incorporation of the familiar? Long after nursing is over, the feeding and eating continue on substitutes, desires, and longing. Maybe it is a good thing we do not remember that feeling of bliss. What could, really, substitute for it? The need for the separation to resolve itself on different levels is what *The Lactation Station* reveals also.[6]

43

Eating the mother keeps us alive. Whether one wants it or not, whether one's own mother could be eaten, if you read this text, there is a mother whom one has eaten. Dobkin's work brings back all these substitutions, lays them bare in front of us in a kind of a circle: she desperately wanted to feed her own daughter, imagined it, but could not. That anticipation and the subsequent substitution led her to substitute her own breast milk not only for her daughter, but for all of us: we had a substitute mother and her milk for tasting as food for that day. This situation—of breastfeeding adults to support a cause (relieve hunger, make artwork, feed a sexual fantasy)—is not normal (at least, not yet). Dobkin's work also points to substitutions of animals and plants as food for humans, including the breast milk substitutes for human infants (soy, cow milk, etc.). Dobkin's work also reveals maternal actions, thoughts, and choices as the artist, the nursing mothers, and the audience members breastfeed, donate, contemplate, and discuss the process of feeding the other with their bodies as the only way to be that we know to date. Who else knows so well their role in generation, in life, than breastfeeding, nursing bodies? Who else is privy to our cannibalism if not those whom we cannibalized to grow inside of, to be born, to become, and to grow outside?

In fact, it does not matter if the milk Dobkin served was "real" in being human breast milk, as declared in the performance. The mother has been food beyond reasonable doubt.

Alternatives have been scarce, and many humans did not survive if they could not digest or did not have access to a human breast and its milk. Biomedically speaking, there are two major ways in which human reproduction ensures we consider the mother as food: first, the process of viviparous gestation through the placenta within the maternal body; and second, dependency on a very specific type of nourishment still tied to someone else's body (most often a maternal body), caregivers, and food providers. This is especially distinct in humans and few other mammals. For the first year of life, a newborn has limited or no mobility to procure food. And even when they grow and start walking, they are dependent on their community for survival much longer as compared to other mammals. The most recent "maternal turn" in contemporary art highlights these two directions, especially focusing on the question of dependency and its meaning for the mother, following the groundbreaking work of such artists as Mary Kelly.[7]

44    Apart from the breast milk, the placenta represents and demonstrates, as an organ, as matter of the mother, her meat, another type of food that the mother is. The whole placental tissue, with its attached umbilical cord

and the cord blood, is becoming today a more visible site of consumption, preservation, and exchange among "enlightened" global consumers, a part of a "paleo-friendly" diet. (This coincides with placental and cord blood research, especially of specific cells and tissues, in biomedical industries.) Today more mothers are reclaiming this part of their bodies as food and a cultural product, an artifact. Cookbooks with placenta as the main ingredient are sold online.[8] Though they elicit various emotional and cultural responses (evidenced by Amazon.com reviews), the general turn in making the maternal body more visible in its function as food for other humans, including the mother herself, is part of the larger cultural drive to articulate and change how the mother is eaten and incorporated.

New humans grow inside other humans. This means that the human inside of whom we grew was our food for growth. This sounds rather self-evident, but it has been surprisingly little written about or explored, and more often actively forgotten. But something does not grow out of nothing. We fed on someone else's air, blood, flesh; we literally consumed the other in the complex process of this growth. Biological sciences, especially the life sciences, have been studying these complex processes in their quest to solve the question of life. Their understanding of human generation shifted from seeing the maternal body as the "immunological paradox," a rather difficult "site" for the implantation of the early embryo into the walls of the hostile uterus, with its subsequent fight for survival through building a protective wall, the placenta, to today's model of a more cooperative mechanism of exchange and mutual nourishment between the growing "other" human within the maternal "self." New fields of evolutionary developmental biology (evo-devo) and epigenetics contribute to postmodern and new materialist feminist theorizing around the support of symbiotic theories of the human condition: on the cellular and genetic levels of human embodiment and its materialities, there is no life without various forms and processes of cooperation and enmeshment. Existence is a fragile equilibrium of coexistence. Various feminist theorists have proposed a similar vision and hence see new biomedical research as supporting their ideas, especially within symbiotic and positively theorized frameworks of the maternal–fetal relations. Concepts of intersubjectivity, co-becoming, being-with, and being-from, are offered to think through this new materialist vision that presents us with new ontologies of self and non-self.[9]

Therefore, can we conclude that the mother is food? From this point of view, yes: she provides, through her own body, nourishment that sustains life, and this is one definition of what food is. Without herself as food, there will be no being, or death. *Human life is a possibility realized only by eating the mother.* The mother eats too, certainly, but the pregnant body digests, and food becomes some other thing before it becomes food for the fetus. Food becomes part of her body, which then provides for the growing life. This particular process of transformation of one kind of food, which the mother eats, to become another kind of food suitable for the fetus is a challenge for biomedical sciences. They often (mis)represent a possibility of bypassing the maternal body to feed the fetus ectogenetically. Rather than bypassing, what biomedicine can achieve is partaking from another (human or nonhuman) body, then putting this through a process of mimicry of the maternal tissue (making it a substitute), and then hoping that enough will be absorbed by the preterm infant so as to accept what is transferred and to transform it into "food" and metabolize it.

Another matter of definition and associated production of meaning is the separation between the liquid food and the drink. When liquefied nutrients are given orally or through some other pathway into the body, they are usually called "liquid food." In this sense, because the newborn, an infant, cannot yet ingest and digest solid foods, the breast milk and its substitutes can be called food. As liquid food they are food, and not a drink. Though in Dobkin's installation the breast milk has been presented within a wine tasting setting, its ambivalent status as "liquid food" rather than a drink (wine, water) remained, as also noted by Reeves and Klein above.

But is the mother also a kind of meat? One of archaic definitions of meat is that it is "food of any kind." If the mother is food, therefore, she is meat: it is a simple logical outcome. As solid food (tissue, placenta), she is even "more" meat. However, breast milk, as a liquid type of food, is then a kind of meat (compared to blood, which needs to be cooked into a sausage—for example, a blood sausage, as quoted above—to become "meat"; otherwise it is a "drink of blood"). Here the method of ingestion (and not only the quality of the thing itself) is important: how it feels inside the mouth, whether teeth are engaged or not, and if it is to be drunk, swallowed with or without chewing. Infants, after all, do not have the option of chewing. Their meat needs to be liquid. The mother is also meat because she is a mammal (as opposed to fish or fowl); she is a "red meat" animal, giving her breast milk to the offspring like a cow.

*The mother, thus, is all kinds of food, liquid and solid; she is meat and drink at the same time.* She is air that the fetus breathes. She is water in which they bathe. She provides energy to be and to grow in its multiple forms.

In Parama Roy's *Alimentary Tracts: Appetites, Aversions, and the Post-colonial* (2010), the question of what and how we eat gets more scrutiny around the "we," formed by "what" and "how." Eating is entangled with the history of empires and colonizations, and we, of various sorts, come together to partake in memories and dreams.[10] The mother is a central figure in this beautiful meditative book, helping me to imagine this riskier, ethically challenging reading of Dobkin's *Lactation Station*. Thus, in her fascinating reading of Sara Suleri's memoir *Meatless Days*, Roy concludes: "We all begin, Suleri says, as cannibals, feeding upon our mothers' bodies inside and outside the womb."[11] Suleri partook of her mother's body in and through her dream, offered to us in a written scene of her mother's funeral:

> A blue van drove up: I noticed it was a refrigerated car and my father was inside it. He came to tell me that we must put my mother in her coffin, and he opened the blue hatch of the van to reach inside, where it was very cold. What I found were hunks of meat wrapped in cellophane, and each of them felt like Mamma, in some odd way. It was my task to carry those flanks across the street and to fit them into the coffin at the other side of the road, like pieces in a jigsaw puzzle. Although my dream will not let me recall how many trips I made, I know my hands felt cold. Then, when my father's back was turned, I found myself engaged in rapid theft—for the sake of Ifat and Shahid and Tillat and all of us, I stole away a portion of the body. It was a piece of her foot I found, a small bone like a knuckle, which I quickly hid inside my mouth, under my tongue. Then I and the dream dissolved, into an extremity of tenderness.[12]

She imagined it, but does it matter? (Unlike in Dobkin's *Lactation Station Breast Milk Bar*, where the reference to the "real" mothers giving the "real" breast milk for tasting by the "real" audience members seems omnipotent.) I follow Roy here, who engages with Suleri's text, to expand on her point that "the eating of maternal remains is the best form of memorialization, making the child once again flesh of her mother's flesh." Dobkin's work is generous in enabling this memorialization to be shared. In Suleri and Roy, the maternal body and food are connected to questions of belonging and being in place, in sociality where food is inscribed in a colonial relation (postcolonial, settler colonial, with various connotations of colonization as related to what, how, and when to eat as interconnected in the family and its larger community). In the case of *The Lactation Station*, and what interests me here the most, is how Dobkin's performance, installation, and the whole project engages with her audience to expand her personal story of single queer milk-less motherhood into such shared "memorialization" of our cannibalism. But is it cannibalism?

## 2

Does the self and non-self relation of the maternal body imply cannibalism and anthropophagy, autophagy, or something else?

Could it be that we—researchers, scholars, artists, writers, and critics—are too quick to assume cannibalism? In this formulation of the maternal body, cannibalism seems to be an implied outcome as far as Dobkin's, Suleri's, and other similar kinds of works are concerned.[13] However, the relation between the mother and cannibalism is not self-evident, for at least two reasons: (1) the person who eats another human's flesh did not choose to eat their mother in their fetal condition and infancy—unlike the audience at Dobkin's performance; and (2) In Suleri's written dream, the feeling of hunger was not presented as an impetus to eating. In both cases, the consumption was not based on hunger, to get nutrition, as in extreme cases of survival, imagined or real. If it is cannibalism at all, it is more of a cultural, religious, ritualistic kind, which has been questioned by many scholars and anthropologists.[14] Now there is a renewed interest in such new cannibalism, as in Derrida's quote above, by combining the cultural and ethical reasons with the questions of "having to eat to survive" and still "eating well."

Almost always for newborns the situation is reversed: they do not have a choice and they are hungry. Certainly, they could "refuse the breast," or not be able to digest human breast milk, be allergic to it, but in order to survive they have to eat, whether it is the breast milk of another human given to them or its substitutes. Hence, the question arises: Is it cannibalism at all if one is unconscious of one's surroundings and just eats to survive? If it is a forced, unconscious, infant cannibalism, is it then cannibalism at all?

The process of growth inside another's body is even more complex in relation to the concept and practice of anthropophagy (human eating). If we assume that the mother and her growing embryo are one and the same person, as they are, then it should be termed autophagy: eating the self. It is the maternal tissue that grows, because it is her body, not separated by anything or anyone (in fact, it is only in the early twentieth century when the embryo was "found" inside a dead mother by researchers, leading to what is now known as Carnegie stages of development).[15] But this ability to "see" and "separate" the embryonic body/tissue from the maternal body/tissue is relative to how one perceives the tissue of this person to start with: this is still one and the same body, it is her, one human being, as this specific body, no less than two or more bodies, beings, and selves. Whether one decides for whatever reason the beginning of another being starts on the first day of conception or later, it does not change the ontological fact that it does not exist without her; it is her, fundamentally. In that sense, what we have is self-eating, when the maternal body eats itself in the process of growing itself to become separated later into at least two. The other is eating the mother as it grows. This is what gestation is: eating your mother's flesh and blood in order to be born. Gestation takes place as digestion and ingestion of the self by the self. What makes, biologically speaking, an embryo an "other" is that part which came from the other human, and not herself; but once the embryo became part of her body proper (usually considered after implantation, though this process still takes place inside one and the same person, the same body), it is the self that digests oneself as a process of gestation.[16]

Therefore, in Dobkin's installation one could be considered a cannibal when the following three conditions are met: (1) one trusts that what one tastes is human breast milk; (2) one partakes of this "liquid food" for nourishment or out of curiosity, or fetishism, or another non-hunger reason; and (3) one chooses to ingest, digest, and metabolize another human. An infant, however, is a cannibal by circumstance of its existence. One does not choose to eat one's own (before birth, during breastfeeding) or someone else's (through donated breast milk) mother. What Suleri did in her dream, and what the audience members did at Dobkin's installation, is different from that initial act of cannibalism. In this first anthropophagic act the self and the other are distinguished symbolically more than biologically and ontologically (this difference is a later product of adult knowledge, human social contact, and imagination).

Metabolically, of course, the gestative processes are more akin to digestion, and therefore, self-eating and eating the other here are one and the same: cells are born, live, die, and get metabolized again, for the whole period of gestation. If it is about scale of comprehension and study, the mother provides it: one could zoom further inside or outside of her. The growth of the fetus is enabled by two pathways: from outside the mother (through the mother and her mouth, her environment), and from the maternal tissue itself, which also gets metabolized, especially if there is limited nourishment coming from the outside. On the cellular level, in terms of materiality, by-products get either reabsorbed or expelled from the maternal body, depending on the process in question.

What about the mother, one might ask? What relation does she her-self have to cannibalism? She cannibalizes herself because it is her self that grows, when another inside of her becomes this other, grows into the other through eating around itself, absorbing and metabolizing her own body, which is the other too. How different are gestation and digestion? Are there examples where they are almost the same? If a worm gets into her diges-tive system, starts absorbing the nutrients she eats, and grows inside of her, then there is a similarity (the same for a parasitic twin, for example). The gut bacteria and other living organisms inside of us get gestated in the process of our human digestion. Human gestation, evolutionarily speaking, is not a very efficient system of survival and reproduction (compared to oviparity, for example, or replication). The mother self-cannibalizes. The autophagist (the self-cannibal) is the mother. But is this, then, cannibalism? Or is it just life?[17]

After delivery, her cord blood, her placenta, and her breast milk can all be digested by herself and others, and sometimes do get consumed. If she eats her own flesh and drinks her own milk, it is, once again, autophagy. The distant sense of this as autophagy, with its connection to cannibalism as taboo, might explain why so many mothers mentioned to Dobkin during the tasting performance that they never tasted their own milk. Most of us, however, end up tasting our own blood, but the idea of tasting or drinking the blood of another human might be less acceptable. From the maternal point of view, however, the autophagy stops if she does not eat any of the by-products of her delivery. The autophagy results in the birth of another human being who has eaten her for months before that—by being her. That human being will continue to eat her or another person, thus happen-ing to be a cannibal, if and when partaking of human breast milk. Other than that, self-eating ends. She still forces, invites, makes, enables another to eat her liquid body as breast milk. Once that relation ends also, the question of cannibalism or self-cannibalism is forgotten, unless Dobkin, Suleri, Roy, and other artists, writers, and scholars bring it back.

While an audience member does have a choice to taste or not to taste an artifact, in Dobkin's offering of a product, food, from another human's body, the question of not tasting, of not eating comes in. I will explore this as a matter of restraint, as it also connects us to cannibalism and what it means to "eat well." Parama Roy, among others, also emphasizes food as a site of vulnerability and irony, implicating the subject's everyday decisions in the larger communal and familial framework of history and its discontents. "Eating and non-eating . . . are powerfully implicated in the politics of empire

50

and decolonization. But they are not, or not only, the by-products of these processes of historical and epistemic overhaul; they are also fundamentally constitutive of it, at the level of ideas, practices, figures, and debates/conflicts."[18] Roy, in her powerful *Alimentary Tracts*, engages with the most recent tropes about gendered and racialized embodiment and the colonial genealogies through eating and food studies, siding with those who do not see how violence can escape us as far as eating is concerned. She mentions not eating in relation to the vulnerability of eating. For her, as for Derrida, Haraway, and many other recent theorists of eating and ethics, being alive is about incorporation, consumption of the other, fundamentally violent because such consumption rests upon and reproduces inequalities (between humans, between humans and nonhumans, etc.). She concludes, upon thinking with Suleri and others, about "the ineluctable violence entailed in all eating and perhaps in all kinship."[19]

There is no better relation, it seems, to support Derrida's and Roy's argument than this self–other cannibalism one cannot escape when one is born of and lives off others in order to live. I agree with this point in a generalized sense of the ontological being who is already born and who is writing, thinking, and living. But that also presupposes that life and living are inevitable, with all the violence entailed. If not eating means not being, then what most recent feminist creative work demonstrates is that at the heart of the celebration of life-giving subjects—the mothers—there is a question of forced cannibalism, of forced eating, which needs to be posed as a question of forced life. In that sense, I start where others end: thinking further, beyond the recognition of the inevitability of the violence of living. I believe that Suleri's and Dobkin's works reveal the temporal inequality of the one who gestated and generated and the one who is living and thinking now about what it means to be born as a cannibal. Does being forced to cannibalize make cannibalism permissible because the one who was cannibalized upon, the mother, made the choice to be eaten (provided the pregnancy was consented to and chosen)? In the "gift of life," the receiving one cannot refuse taking. Roy's words about "vulnerability, uncertainty and dependence"—implied in all eating—are especially powerful in relation to eating the mother, the one who starts it all.[20]

In our rush to think through the ethics of eating others, especially nonhuman beings, the fact of having eaten the mother remains overlooked. The most recent creative and scholarly work, such as by Roy, Suleri, and Dobkin, among others, has started this difficult conversation. Creative mothers and nonmothers are taking the lead in approaching these questions, but

51

the most difficult questions are still to be explored, as *The Lactation Station Breast Milk Bar* demonstrates. How to acknowledge the labor of life-giving without disarming or disabling the question of autophagy? The sacrifice was not requested but needs to be responded to nevertheless. The only time the question is asked is when life itself is seen as a condemnation (philosophically, religiously, personally, economically, ecologically, and so forth). When the question is not addressed to the life-giving speaking, writing, and creating subject, the answers become part of epistemic violence rather than a dialogue—or worse, when some scholars and policy makers decide for (m)others who is more worthy and who is less of being born.

The question of autophagy and "forced life" does not lead automatically to anthropophobia, misandry, and misogyny. Various ethics that privilege nonbeing, because of the violence of life, are explored in Buddhism and Jainism, for example, but their interests in noneating have not gotten much traction in contemporary theoretical debates about "eating well" in contemporary scholarship. I started exploring this question elsewhere in relation to another relevant ethics—feminist ethics of care, which also omits the topic of autophagy.[21]

Certainly, the above paragraphs do not mean that we should stop planning to minimize and lessen the suffering of those we eat, incorporate, and digest. Another author on cannibalism in recent contemporary theorizing presented readers with an alternative concept, which I would like to end with: "restraint."

In her book *Carnal Appetites*, Elspeth Probyn traces how "the figure of the cannibal emphasizes the most human of attributes, as well as designating the limit beyond which humanity is thought to cease." Probyn focuses on racialized difference in definitions and approaches to cannibalism, providing us with another lens through which cannibalism could be reframed. If cannibalism is driven by hunger (rather than ritual, for example), it shows "hunger as the great life driving force."[22] Probyn's main concept in the text comes from an analysis of colonial white men theorized as more "savages" than so-called native cannibals (coming from the Spanish word for "savage," coined by imperial subjects who thus described indigenous populations of the "newly discovered" lands). Following Montaigne's point that "barbarism lies in the killing, not in the eating," as the murder in conquest, consumption of imperialism is a bigger savagery, Probyn shows. The indigenous "cannibal," after all, "is an omnivore with a sense of occasion" who shows restraint by not simply following one's hunger. Risking the Eurocentric notion of the "noble savage," Probyn makes the argument that there is more in the cannibal

52

trope for a contemporary cultural critical scholar than meets the eye: "If the cannibal is barbarous, it is because we have made him so."

In order to carefully avoid the trope of the "noble native," Probyn engages bell hooks's famous text "Eating the Other," which critiques the superficial consumption of racial difference to "spice up" the bland palate of the white Western subject. Writing in 1992 about popular culture and her white male students from privileged backgrounds, hooks noticed the behavior of the white male consumer-cannibal who was fixated on ingesting a static, dead, sexualized Other, devoid of life or resistance. This is what I believe Jess Dobkin managed to avoid and what distinguishes her, for example, from Rick Gibson's earlier cannibalistic performances:[23] *The Lactation Station Breast Milk Bar* took a lot of time to develop strategies to make sure that donors are present, speaking, participating subjects.

A video work showing interviews with donors and their experiences with breastfeeding was a central part of the installation and disrupted the commodification of breast milk by focusing on mothers themselves as speaking, asserting, and present. In promotional materials for the first installation in Toronto, Dobkin did appear to present herself and the milk as a curiosity item (the postcard of her squeezing the milk as it pours into wine glasses is currently displayed on her Wikipedia page).[24] Dobkin knew very well that in many previous works that dealt with breast milk, it often became an "exotic" and abject substance of the maternal body usually hidden from view, and now "procured" through some special process only for the consumer. Another element was the presence of donors themselves on the day of the performance, with the potential for a consented dialogue between them and those who tasted their milk. Dobkin's gratitude to donors was clear, and their decision to donate their milk to an art project, as an art product, was acknowledged as a complicated choice. Being aware of all those other ways in which the mother could be eaten symbolically, without any recognition—which is demonstrated in the title of the work and in the promotional materials—Dobkin builds her aesthetic strategies of non-consumption around engagement with the donors in an experience that makes their breast milk into a cultural product, an artifact of their own collective making.

Probyn, instead of rejecting cannibalism as cultural taboo or a compromised concept, pushes our conception of it further, to engage with its standing as "the threshold beyond which we cease to be human."[25] In order to achieve that, Probyn analyzes cannibalism tropes in Joseph Conrad's *Heart of Darkness* and its subsequent adaptation in Francis Coppola's *Apocalypse*

53

*Now*. In a reading that assembles a wide range of references, from Giorgio Agamben (through Michel Foucault) and Marx, to contemporary middle-class obsession with hip restaurants and references to "Aboriginal savagery" and "cannibalism" by right-wing politicians in Australia, Probyn argues that cannibalism serves as this liminal, border-making, edgy term often evoked today to find new definitions for what it means to be human, by linking it to another taboo—incest—and sexual appetites that "operate as our society's physic ground zero."[26]

Preoccupation with cannibalism faded with the emergence of modernity, but when the latter is in question, the former enjoys a comeback. Probyn wants the cannibal today "to operate as a limit term in revitalizing thinking about ethics and appetites" due to the fact that "as a historical spectre of Western appetite, the cannibal presents us with a visceral sense of restraint performed in the face of hunger."[27] After all, "the native cannibals" did not eat the white male protagonist in *Heart of Darkness*, though they easily could have. Moreover, they restrained themselves when they were especially hungry. Though for Probyn it did not seem to matter that the cannibals in question were products of Conrad's own imagination, it is important, I believe, to consider Probyn's notion of restraint together with my analysis of the mother as food. Perhaps what one needs to discuss is maternal restraint, and here the reading of Probyn and Roy together is productive: the weaning of the entire culture from its rapacious appetite, from its all-consuming cannibalistic hunger. The real hunger, as has been shown by many (e.g., Vandana Shiva), is rarely caused by anything but the all-consuming cannibalistic greed of global capitalism. Hunger is a problem of distribution.[28]

If Dobkin was conscious of slipping into fetishization of breast milk, there is a danger of fetishizing the materiality and reality of food in scholarship too. How does one analyze this obsession with food without refetishizing? With restraint, perhaps? For Probyn, "the present alimentary and economic conjuncture is bewildering. Food is now simultaneously a deeply fetishized commodity—the last difference?—and, as I have argued, the only thing that is held to be really real."[29] I believe that such a path, that questions our tastes and appetites, has been sought, successfully, by Dobkin, and is embodied in *The Lactation Station Breast Milk Bar*'s preparation, research, interviews, processes of making, videos, installation, tasting performance, publicity materials, and the experience of the audience. Restraint as an aesthetic strategy is still to be explored in more detail, as, I believe, it is very helpful in understanding and appreciating Dobkin's work. Restraint is also something that needs to be further mined in the maternal relation of autophagy and anthropophagy as restraint in relation to the embryo, the fetus, and the infant. The all-consuming status of the maternal body has only recently been theorized and questioned by mothers themselves.[30] If cannibalism appears on the limits of what it means to be human, it is perhaps because we have not yet acknowledged it at the heart of our humanity.

Roy, Probyn, and Dobkin offer new feminist, critical, postcolonial, and anticapitalist readings of anthropophagy as they deconstruct cis-gendered, patriarchal, colonialist, and racist histories and frameworks of cannibalism as a metaphor for ingestion and consumption. The symbolic production of meaning about the worth of others feeds on and is fed by practices of their treatment, their political, social, economic, and cultural value. *The Lactation Station*, enabling this discussion of cannibalism in relation to the maternal body and the maternal self, invites us into this conversation about how the mother tastes.[31]

## Notes

1   Natalie S. Loveless, curator, "New Materialisms: Redux," accessed January 17, 2019, http://newmaternalisms.ca/2016-exhibition-overview.

2   Penny Van Esterik, "Vintage Breast Milk: Exploring the Discursive Limits of Feminine Fluids," *Canadian Theatre Review* 137 (2009): 23.

3   Irina Aristarkhova, "Being of the Breast: Jess Dobkin's 'The Lactation Station Breast Milk Bar,'" in *New Maternalism Redux*, edited by Natalie Loveless (Edmonton: University of Alberta Press, 2017), 78–107. I thank Natalie Loveless for providing me with a reference to another work—*R.A.W. Ass Milk Soap*—where human breast milk is used for a mass product. As in this chapter I focus on Jess Dobkin's project, I am not able to provide an exhaustive survey of other works with breast milk as their primary medium. An excellent resource for that is, for example, R. E. Buller, "Performing the Breastfeeding Body: Lactivism and Art Interventions," *Studies in the Maternal* 8, no. 2 (2016): 14.

4   Charles Reeve, "The Kindness of Human Milk," *Gastronomica: The Journal of Critical Food Studies* 9, no. 1 (2009): 67–68.

5   Jennie Klein, "Review of New Maternalisms: Redux," *Studies in the Maternal* 8, no. 2 (2016): 22.

6   In this paragraph I engage with the psychoanalytic concept of separation, where any caretaker would be occupying the role of the mother: anyone who nurses and takes care is a substitute for the mother, according to the separation anxiety theory. In reconsidering this line of analysis, I do not imply that all mothers are caring and nursing their babies in the same way, or that only mothers (and not fathers, for example) care and nurse. See Irina Aristarkhova, *Hospitality of the*

*Matrix: Philosophy, Biomedicine, and Culture* (New York: Columbia University Press, 2012). Dobkin's performance strongly questions the norms and normalizations about breastfeeding and maternal care, as shown by me in Aristarkhova, "Being of the Breast"; also see R. E. Buller, R. E. "Performing the Breastfeeding Body: Lactivism and Art Interventions." *Studies in the Maternal* 8, no. 2 (2016): 1–15. Here the mother is an inclusive and expansive subject position.

7   A special issue of *Studies in the Maternal*, edited by E. Marchevska and V. Walkerdine, provides an excellent overview of the current state of creative practice that develops these questions (*Studies in the Maternal* 8, no. 2 [2016]). The contributions by R. E. Buller and Natalie Loveless are especially relevant here, as well as Andrea Liss's book *Feminist Art and the Maternal* (Minneapolis: University of Minnesota Press, 2008).

8   Robin Cook, *25 Placenta Recipes—Easy and Delicious Recipes for Cooking with Placenta* (Amazon Digital Services, 2013) and Kati DiBenedetto, *DIY Placenta Edibles: Smoothies + Tincture + Chocolate* (Amazon Digital Services, 2014) are two examples.

9   See my chapter on biomedical sciences in Aristarkhova, *Hospitality of the Matrix*.

10  I am grateful to Parama Roy for sharing her work and for the generous exchange of ideas and comments on this chapter.

11  Parma Roy, *Alimentary Tracts: Appetites, Aversions, and the Postcolonial* (Durham, NC: Duke University Press, 2010), 191–92.

12  Sara Suleri, quoted in Roy, *Alimentary Tracts*.

13  Another example is a reference to cannibalism in Marianna Meneses Romero's extensive discussion of Mirian Simun's performances. The artist used her breast milk to make cheese for the audience. Marianna Meneses Romero, "Eating Human Cheese: The Lady Cheese Shop (Est. 2011)," *Feast*, n.d., accessed on January 17, 2018, http://feastjournal.co.uk/article/eating-human-cheese-the-lady-cheese-shop-est-2011/.

14  My interest here is beyond anthropological debates over whether such cannibalism has ever taken place, or was a product of Western racist imagination and poor research. It would suffice to note that I am using the term as I am interested in exploring the connection between human and nonhuman here, and press further the very connotation of savagery the Spanish colonial term implied, which will be mentioned later in this text. Today, as far as the practice or cases of eating human flesh are concerned, a more accepted term is anthropophagy, to avoid the sensationalism and racism of the former term defining this practice. For further discussion on anthropological debates, see William Arens, *The Man-Eating Myth: Anthropology and Anthropophagy* (New York: Oxford University Press, 1979), and G. Obeyesekere, "Review of the Anthropology of Cannibalism: (L. R. Goldman)," *American Ethnologist* 28, no. 1 (2001): 238–40, and other relevant titles from the bibliography at the end of this chapter.

56

15  See Lynn M. Morgan's *Icons of Life: A Cultural History of Human Embryos* (Berkeley: University of California Press, 2009).

16  I thank the editors, Sushmita Chatterjee and Banu Subramaniam, for two important questions, both of which need to be elaborated further, beyond this chapter. First, whether "auto" in self-eating is "sym-phagy" rather than "auto-phagy," if the body is understood as collective symbiosis rather than one, maternal "self"; and second, how postcolonial critique of cannibalism would enhance the arguments presented here. My foregrounding of the maternal role in generation on the one hand, and questioning of the Western conception of the self–other relations on the other, are intertwined in more ways than this chapter's scope allows me to demonstrate.

17  In my previous work I discussed extensively more novel symbiotic and ecological theories of the self (in evo-devo, informational theory of immunity, epigenetic embryology), which are often based on a systems, or symbiotic, approach. I thank the editors and reviewers for suggesting application of such approaches to the question at hand (autophagy and cannibalism). My ideas could indeed be elaborated upon further along the lines of those symbiotic or ecological theories, defining the mother as a porous and unstable biological conglomerate of various bacteria and other living entities, as an organism(s), or even chemically or physically through atoms, quanta, or vitamins and minerals. I expressed my concerns, though, about such definitions of the maternal in Aristarkhova, *Hospitality of the Matrix*.

18  Roy, *Alimentary Tracts*, 193.

19  Roy, *Alimentary Tracts*, 194.

20  "Flavor of my infancy, my mother, still be food: I want my hunger as it always was, neither flesh nor fowl!" Sara Suleri, quoted in Roy, *Alimentary Tracts*, 191.

21  Irina Aristarkhova, "Thou Shall Not Harm All Living Beings: Feminism, Jainism, and Animals," *Hypatia: A Journal of Feminist Philosophy* 27, no. 3 (2012): 636–50.

22  Elspeth Probyn, *Carnal Appetites: FoodSexIdentities* (London: Routledge, 2000), 80.

23  One of the most well known artistic takes on cannibalism is the work of Rick Gibson. He made jewelry out of maternal and embryonic tissue, ate human tonsils and a donated testicle as part of his performances in 1988 and 1989, and tested legal frameworks of cannibalism in several countries where he performed. He was concerned with the limits of consumption and its norms, literally and figuratively. Contemporary artists use their own or others' (including animals') bodily fluids widely and with various intentions. Selected examples relevant here would include various works by Marco Evarristi, Zhu Yu, Zane Cerpina, and Alexander Selvik Wengshoels (I thank Hege Tapio for bringing the last two names to my attention). 57

24  "Jess Dobkin," *Wikipedia*, https://en.wikipedia.org/wiki/Jess_Dobkin.

25  Probyn, *Carnal Appetites*, 83.

26  Probyn, *Carnal Appetites*, 94.

27  Probyn, *Carnal Appetites*, 99.

28  "Restraint" as a concept and practice is also developed by Jains, and is mentioned by Roy in her introduction to *Alimentary Tracts*. This topic is beyond the scope of this chapter, however, but seems promising for future directions of "eating well" discussions.

29  Probyn, *Carnal Appetites*, 88.

30  From the early feminist art of the 1970s (Andrea Liss, *Feminist Art and the Maternal* [Minneapolis: University of Minnesota Press, 2008]) to the more recent community of New Maternalisms, at http://newmaternalisms.ca, the issue of the mother remains with a complicated history both within art and within feminism.

31  In this text I do not have space to discuss other important questions around "eating the mother": the differences and inequalities among mothers, and whether some are "more" food than others; LGBTQ+ parents and how new technologies of IVF and gender fluidity also help question old meanings of maternity and parenting. The topic is explored in my previous work; see Aristarkhova, *Hospitality of the Matrix*, and Aristarkhova, "Being of the Breast." Another important question is how eating the mother relates to "eating the father," also explored further in Parama Roy's *Alimentary Tracts*. I would point out, for example, that in July 2017, a document came from the Vatican in relation to using the gluten-free bread for the Eucharist, as a substitute for the "body of Christ." Gluten-free bread has been declared not suitable (http://www.bbc.com/news/world-europe-40545023).

## Bibliography

Anglo, M. *Man Eats Man*. London: Jupiter Books, 1979.

Arens, William. *The Man-Eating Myth: Anthropology and Anthropophagy*. New York: Oxford University Press, 1979.

Aristarkhova, Irina. "Being of the Breast: Jess Dobkin's 'The Lactation Station Breast Milk Bar.'" In *New Maternalism Redux*, edited by Natalie Loveless, 78–107. Edmonton: University of Alberta Press, 2017.

Aristarkhova, Irina. *Hospitality of the Matrix: Philosophy, Biomedicine, and Culture*. New York: Columbia University Press, 2012.

Aristarkhova, Irina. "Thou Shall Not Harm All Living Beings: Feminism, Jainism, and Animals." *Hypatia: A Journal of Feminist Philosophy* 27, no. 3 (2012): 636–50.

Askenasy, Hans. *Cannibalism: From Sacrifice to Survival*. Amherst, NY: Prometheus, 1994.

Buller, R. E. "Performing the Breastfeeding Body: Lactivism and Art Interventions." *Studies in the Maternal* 8, no. 2 (2016): 1–15. http://dx.doi.org/10.16995/sim.225.

Cook, Robin. *25 Placenta Recipes—Easy and Delicious Recipes for Cooking with Placenta*. Amazon Digital Services, 2013.

Cortés, Hernando. *Five Letters, 1519–1526*. Translated by J. Bayard Morris. New York: W. W. Norton, 1962.

Davies, Nigel. *Human Sacrifice*. New York: William Morrow, 1981.

DiBenedetto, Kati. *DIY Placenta Edibles: Smoothies + Tincture + Chocolate*. Amazon Digital Services, 2014.

Dobkin, Jess. "Performing with Mother's Milk: *The Lactation Station Breast Milk Bar*." In *Intimacy across Visceral and Digital Performance*, edited by Maria Chatzichristodoulou and Rachel Zerihan, 62–73. London: Palgrave Macmillan, 2012.

Dobkin, Jess. "This Is My Work." http://www.jessdobkin.com. Accessed January 30, 2018.

Gibson, Rick. "Making Art That Is Hard to Look At." https://www.rickgibson.net. Accessed January 30, 2018.

Goldman, Laurence R., ed. *The Anthropology of Cannibalism*. Westport, CT: Bergin and Garvey, 1999.

Goldman, Laurence R. *Child's Play: Myth, Mimesis and Make-Believe*. Oxford: Berg, 1998.

Harris, Marvin. *Cannibals and Kings*. New York: Random House, 1977.

Hogg, G. *Cannibalism and Human Sacrifice*. London: Pan, 1962.

"Jess Dobkin." *Wikipedia*. https://en.wikipedia.org/wiki/Jess_Dobkin. Accessed January 30, 2018.

Klein, J. "Review of New Maternalisms: Redux." *Studies in the Maternal* 8, no. 2 (2016): 22. doi:http://dx.doi.org/10.16995/sim.221.

Liss, Andrea. *Feminist Art and the Maternal*. Minneapolis: University of Minnesota Press, 2008.

Loveless, Natalie, ed. *New Maternalisms: Redux*. Edmonton: Department of Art and Design, University of Alberta, 2018.

Marchevska, E., and V. Walkerdine. "Editorial." *Studies in the Maternal* 8, no. 2 (2016): 10. doi:http://dx.doi.org/10.16995/sim.236.

Meneses Romero, Marianna. "Eating Human Cheese: The Lady Cheese Shop (Est. 2011)." *Feast*, n.d. http://feastjournal.co.uk/article/eating-human-cheese-the-lady-cheese-shop-est-2011/. Accessed January 17, 2018.

Mock, Roberta. "'It Turns Out': Jess Dobkin's Puppet Body." In *Caught in the Act: An Anthology of Performance Art by Canadian Women*, edited by Johanna Householder and Tanya Mars. Toronto: YYZ Books, 2006.

Montaigne, Michel de. *Essays*. Translated by J. M. Cohen. Harmondsworth, UK: Penguin, 1958.

Morgan, Lynn M. *Icons of Life: A Cultural History of Human Embryos*. Berkeley: University of California Press, 2009.

Obeyesekere, G. "Review of the Anthropology of Cannibalism: (L. R. Goldman)." *American Ethnologist* 28, no. 1 (2001): 238–40.

Pickering, M. "Cannibalism Quarrel." *New Scientist*, August 15, 1992, 11.

Probyn, Elspeth. *Carnal Appetites: FoodSexIdentities*. London: Routledge, 2000.

Reeve, Charles. "The Kindness of Human Milk." *Gastronomica: The Journal of Critical Food Studies* 9, no. 1 (2009): 66–73.

Roy, Parama. *Alimentary Tracts: Appetites, Aversions, and the Postcolonial*. Durham, NC: Duke University Press, 2010.

Rumsey, Alan. "The White Man as Cannibal in the New Guinea Highlands." In *The Anthropology of Cannibalism*, edited by Laurence R. Goldman. Westport, CT: Bergin and Garvey, 1999.

Sagan, Eli. *Cannibalism: Human Aggression and Cultural Form*. New York: Harper and Row, 1974.

Sahagón, Bernardino de. *Florentine Codex: General History of the Things of New Spain*. 13 vols. Translated by Charles E. Dibble and Arthur O. Anderson. Santa Fe, NM: School of American Research, 1950–82.

Sanday, Peggy Reeves. *Divine Hunger: Cannibalism as a Cultural System*. Cambridge: Cambridge University Press, 1986.

Springgay, Stephanie. "The Lactation Station and a Feminist Pedagogy of Touch." *n.paradoxa: International Feminist Art Journal* 26 (2010): 59–65.

Turner, Christy G., II, and Jacqueline A. Turner. *Man Corn: Cannibalism and Violence in the Prehistoric American Southwest*. Salt Lake City: University of Utah Press, 2011.

Tuzin, D., and Paula Brown, eds. *The Ethnography of Cannibalism*. Washington, DC: Society for Psychological Anthropology, 1983.

Van Esterik, Penny. "Vintage Breast Milk: Exploring the Discursive Limits of Feminine Fluids." *Canadian Theatre Review* 137 (2009): 20–23.

three | JENNIFER A. HAMILTON

# Reindeer and Woolly Mammoths

## THE IMPERIAL TRANSIT
## OF FROZEN MEAT FROM
## THE NORTH AMERICAN ARCTIC

EATING FROZEN FLESH: WOOLLY MAMMOTHS,
REINDEER, AND THE EXPLORERS CLUB ANNUAL DINNERS

Frozen foods is fundamentally an American industry, indigenous to this
country and spurred by American ingenuity.
—E. W. Williams, *Frozen Foods: Biography of an Industry*

IN 2016, THE SCIENCE JOURNAL *PLoS One* published an article with the
provocative title "Was Frozen Mammoth or Giant Ground Sloth Served
for Dinner at The Explorer's Club?" The short answer—according to a DNA
analysis of a serendipitously preserved piece of cooked animal flesh—was
an emphatic no.[1] The dinner in question took place in 1951 courtesy of the
Explorers Club at the Roosevelt Hotel in New York City. Originally formed
in 1904, the Explorers Club is "an international multidisciplinary professional society dedicated to the advancement of field research and the ideal
that it is vital to preserve the instinct to explore."[2] According to its website,
Explorers Club members "have been responsible for an illustrious series
of famous firsts: First to the North Pole, first to the South Pole, first to the
summit of Mount Everest, first to the deepest point in the ocean, first to

the surface of the moon."[3] In addition to these firsts, the club is also well known for its annual dinner (ECAD), where esteemed guests feast on an exotic and eclectic menu, a practice that continues into the present. The club's "instinct to explore" is maintained at these black-tie gastronomical events. Over the years, members have been served other forms of animal flesh including polar bear, wild boar, alligator, lion, and tarantula. As the *Christian Science Monitor* reported about ECAD's 1951 menu, though, the "chief attraction at the smörgåsbord was a morsel of 250,000-year-old hairy mammoth meat,"[4] and it is this menu item for which the Explorers Club is likely most famous. And yet, as a group of Yale graduate students demonstrated in 2016, a chunk of cooked meat (saved and preserved by a guest unable to attend the dinner) was not even labeled *Mammuthus* but rather *Megatherium* (giant sloth). And, according to genomic analysis, the sample was neither giant sloth nor woolly mammoth, but rather run-of-the-mill sea turtle.[5]

The "mammoth" in question at the ECAD in 1951 was said to have come from "Woolly Cove" on Akutan Island in the Aleutian archipelago, in the then-US territory of Alaska. The main dish was said to be courtesy of the "private reserves" of Father Bernard Hubbard—a Jesuit and early geographer known as the "Glacier Priest"—and its refrigerated transport was coordinated by US Navy Captain George F. Kosco. Although we now know that no mammoth was actually served at the dinner, Kosco nevertheless did arrange "for the U.S. Navy to fly king crabs, table settings of arctic vegetation, and glacial ice (for chilling cocktails) back to New York for the dinner at the Roosevelt Hotel."[6] Thus, the "mammoth" was the featured dish in a themed event celebrating the natural cold of the Arctic as well as the technological innovation that could bring such frozen things south.

Three decades before at the Sixteenth Annual Explorers Club Dinner in 1920, in a menu consisting of "Cape Cod Oyster Cocktail," "Chicken Gumbo à la Creole" and "Supreme Chicken," was a new dish, "Reindeer au Stefansson." Named in honor of the club's erstwhile president and famous Arctic explorer, Vilhjalmur Stefansson, the reindeer dish served at the Hotel Savoy was a novelty, a red meat that was not the usual filet mignon of beef. Served at the ECAD every year in 1920, 1921, and 1922, reindeer abruptly disappeared from the menu in 1923, not to make another appearance until the latter part of the twentieth century. While it is not clear which part of the Arctic north the reindeer for these dinners came from, it is likely that the meat traveled by refrigerated ship from the Seward Pen-

62

insula in Alaska, part of a series of shipments of frozen reindeer carcasses made to places south courtesy of the Lomen Reindeer Corporation (LRC).[7] The LRC was a white settler–owned family company, cofounded by Alfred Lomen and his brother Carl, who was later known as the "Reindeer King of Alaska." Carl Lomen, a friend and business associate of Stefansson, also worked closely with many of New York's business elite to raise funds in support of Alaska's burgeoning reindeer industry. The Arctic imaginary of these businessmen—some of whom had been involved in polar exploration themselves and were also members of the Explorers Club—reflected a deep faith in the virtue and potential of US capitalist expansion. As Lomen patriarch and Alaska federal court judge Gudbrand Lomen remarked, reindeer would allow the United States to "reclaim barren wastes and frozen tundras surpassing in extent the empires founded by Alexander the Great and Genghis Khan."[8]

But the story of how reindeer came to Alaska in the first place is a key part of what I call, following Jodi Byrd's theoretical intervention in *The Transit of Empire* (2011), the imperial transit of frozen meat. Reindeer are a domesticated species that developed in Eurasia thousands of years ago and, unlike their wild cousins the caribou, are indigenous neither to Alaska nor to other parts of the North American Arctic. In fact, reindeer were first brought to Alaska in the 1890s, part of a US government scheme to educate and feed Native Alaskans—then widely known as the Eskimo.[9] The reindeer were imported for the exclusive use of Eskimo peoples as a way to "civilize" them by "changing them from mere hunters to herdsmen."[10] Reindeer ownership was originally limited to Alaska Natives, but a legal ambiguity allowed white settlers to enter the industry in 1914. Between 1914 and 1940, the Lomen Reindeer Corporation (later the Northwestern Livestock Corporation) dramatically increased its reindeer holdings and came to dominate the industry. During the 1920s, Stefansson himself was involved in a project to reproduce the Alaskan reindeer experiment in the Northwest Territory in Canada, part of what historian Richard Diubaldo terms his "arctic empire."[11] The story, then, of the imperial transit of frozen meat—specifically how the Lomen Company and others began to ship frozen reindeer carcasses to places like the Savoy in New York City—forms the major narrative thread of this chapter. But it is also read against and through other modes of imperial transit, especially those made possible by polar exploration and US expansion in the Arctic.

63

## Indigeneity and the Transit of Empire: A Brief Note on Method

I begin this chapter focused on these two Explorers Club Annual Dinner menus—the prominent 1951 tale of the woolly mammoth and the less notable 1920s appearance of reindeer meat—to introduce a series of themes that will run throughout this piece. This chapter moves peripatetically through space and time, tracking the transit of empire by following technologies of cold and movements of frozen meat in order to reveal their long entanglements with indigenous peoples, indigenous knowledges, and tropes of indigeneity. Ultimately the story I want to tell here links technologies of freezing with the imperial politics of meat across a variety of spatial and temporal sites. These sites are deeply intertwined with North American settler colonial and imperial imaginaries—especially with the durable politics of indigeneity—all of which are implicated in cultural and moral economies of meat production and distribution. I take inspiration from Byrd's "cacophonous" imaginary, her capacity to link seemingly disparate contexts, in ways that make apparent "how ideas of 'Indianness' have created conditions of possibility for U.S. empire to manifest its intent."[12] Byrd's insight about the centrality of indigeneity to processes of imperialism provides a theoretical orientation for this piece, allowing me to link the literal circulation of frozen meat with discourses of indigenous difference as a key node of indigeneity-imperialism.

I juxtapose this main account of the imperial transit of frozen meat with a series of discrete "interludes." These interludes—short narratives oriented around visual ephemera such as advertisements, political cartoons, broadsides, and other archival illustrations—are intended to be heuristics that emphasize connections among seemingly disparate contexts, especially in terms of marking the centrality of indigeneity, in this case through the figure of the Eskimo, to American empire. As Byrd reminds us, "Transit is slightly provocative, an incomplete point of entry, and its provenance might be more suited to diaspora studies and border-crossings than to a notion such as indigeneity that is often taken as rooted and static, located in a discrete place."[13] This chapter thus explores indigeneity in order to make clear less apparent relationships between menus at the elite Explorers Club in New York City and the Alaska Purchase; between the figure of the Eskimo in the wider American imaginary and the larger infrastructures of freezing and global food supply chains; and between different colonial and imperial processes and regimes.

64

JENNIFER A. HAMILTON

## "Woolly Mammoth and Reindeer,"
## *Hall of the Age of Man*, American Museum
## of Natural History, 1916

In 1916, the American Museum of Natural History (AMNH) in New York City revealed the first panel in a suite of large murals painted by the artist Charles R. Knight for its installation, *The Hall of the Age of Man*. The first panel, "The Reindeer and Mammoth on the River Somme," a collaborative effort directed by paleontologist Henry Fairfield Osborn and paid for by banker J. P. Morgan, shows herds of reindeer and woolly mammoths from the Pleistocene moving over melting snow and through icy water (figure 3.1). *The Hall of the Age of Man*, an ambitious exhibition featuring human and nonhuman fossil remains organized hierarchically in evolutionary terms, was "intended to illustrate what is known the origin, relationships and early history of man . . . and also to show the animals by which he was surrounded in the early stages of existence."[14] The reindeer and woolly mammoths featured in Knight's mural—based in part on "paintings and engravings left by the Crô-Magnon artists"[15]—operated as powerful visual representations of imagined human prehistory.

It is worth focusing briefly on the careers of both Knight and Osborn as a way to contextualize the larger meaning of the panel and to foreshadow some of the connections between the imperial transit of frozen meat and tropes of indigeneity. Biographers Czerkas and Glut write that Knight "was the first and undeniably the greatest artist to re-create, with both scientific accuracy and romantic beauty, creatures and environments of prehistoric eras that no living human being had ever experienced firsthand."[16] Knight's drawings are featured in museums throughout the world and continue to be reproduced in contemporary popular and scientific works. Osborn, curator and later president of the AMNH, was a key proponent of evolutionary theories in the early twentieth century and designed exhibits to promulgate these ideas to an American public.[17] Marianne Sommer argues that under Osborn, AMNH exhibits like *The Hall of the Age of Man* "functioned as a meaning-making machine regarding 'our' evolutionary past."[18] In particular, Osborn was concerned that Knight's murals "evoke the struggle for survival that had driven the history of the species and races and that was

65

3.1 *Woolly Mammoth and Reindeer*, Restoration painting by Charles R. Knight. Source: Research Library, Digital Special Collections, accessed August 18, 2017, http://lbry-web-007.amnh.org/digital/index.php/items/show /42850.

essential for future progress."[19] In his 2002 biography, *Henry Fairfield Osborn: Race and the Search for the Origins of Man*, Brian Regal argues that Osborn, a proponent of Social Darwinism, was a central figure in bringing questions of human evolution into conversation with the reigning racial sciences of the day, "linking human origins to racial hierarchies to support his conclusions on evolution."[20] While Knight and Osborn often clashed, and ultimately their collaboration ended in acrimony, the results of their work continue to circulate widely.

Through representations like the mural in *The Hall of the Age of Man*, both the reindeer and the woolly mammoth—the key nonhuman figures in this chapter—are symbolically overdetermined by racialized linkages to evolutionary hierarchies. Their prehistoric association with the cold and ice provides a kind of "natural" link with Arctic indigenous peoples, a link I explore more later on in the chapter. It is important to note that Knight and Osborn's collaboration was completed at a time when particular imaginaries of the United States' Arctic north were key to polar exploration, imperialist expansion, and increasing militarization. Throughout the first two decades of the twentieth century, Euro-American expeditions to the circumpolar north were ubiquitous, and these expeditions were covered extensively in the media, especially in the mainland United States. It was also at a time when museums like the AMNH and the Smithsonian were actively collecting human remains and artifacts from so-called primitive peoples, especially from the Arctic and peoples known as the Eskimo, material necessary for the development of the field of "Eskimology" to anthropology and other associated

66

sciences.[21] As artists and scientists speculated about the evolution of mankind in Europe, representations of contemporary inhabitants of the Arctic north—peoples still "frozen in time" as they existed in the land of ice and snow—reflected deeply held beliefs about the primitive nature of Eskimos.

## The Imperial Transit of Frozen Meat: Cold Transit, Frozen Flesh

The stories that are told about cold and the global trade in meat they enabled are also part of the transit of empire. Scholars like Hannah Landecker[22] and Joanna Radin[23] make the point that artificial cold allows for the detachment of flesh from the body and its circulation in novel ways in global circuits of scientific and capitalist exchange.[24] This chapter looks at the imperial transit of meat from the Arctic to places south. Such transit requires a different kind of narrative, one that accounts for the centrality of Arctic exploration, colonization, and imperialism to the conditions of meat production, consumption, and distribution.

Earlier stories of nineteenth- and early twentieth-century explorers eating the defrosted flesh of extinct creatures, especially mammoth and other prehistoric mammals, abound. In 1872, the *New York Times* reported on some French explorers claiming to have lived for a time "entirely on mammoth meat, broiled, roasted and baked."[25] In another example, an article in a 1937 issue of *Popular Mechanics* claimed: "Not long ago, Vilhjalmur Stefansson, famous explorer, gave a dinner party and served as feature course a cut of meat taken from the frozen carcass which had been incased in tundra ice of North Siberia probably for hundreds of thousands of years. The meat was well flavored, edible, and digestible."[26]

Such apocryphal accounts capture something of the imperial imaginary that runs through them. As scholar Hiʻilei Julia Hobart notes, the advent of cold storage technologies in the nineteenth century allowed for the development of a global supply chain wherein meat could originate from one place, be dressed in another, and be eaten in a third.[27] Such cold potentialities, potentialities that allowed for the freezing of flesh and its subsequent defrosting, produced novel modes of consumption, including "experiments in meat eating" by elite men who "anchored [such experiments] to their masculinity by tempting safety, challenging technology, and pushing the boundaries of shelf life."[28]

The modern production and consumption of more mundane frozen animal flesh in warmer climes has its origins in the nineteenth century, part of a larger politics of empire. As historian Rebecca Woods contends, "The ability to control, produce, and claim ownership over cold was a matter of imperial economics and the politics of colonialism, as well as a challenge to ontologies of matter in its various states."[29] In her discussion of the development of the frozen meat trade between Britain and its antipodean colony of New Zealand in the 1880s, Woods focuses on the overproduction of sheep that marked a key moment in the political economy of the island. After the large-scale dispossession of Aboriginal lands at the hands of the British colonial government, much of New Zealand was put in the service of agricultural production. In particular, white settlers worked sheep ranches, and by the latter part of the nineteenth century these ranches produced far more fresh meat than ranchers could sell locally. How to preserve and transport lamb and mutton in a global marketplace necessitated new technologies, including the development and construction of artificial cold storage facilities and modes of transportation. Yet even after some of the necessary infrastructure to safely freeze and transport food transnationally was in place, Woods notes that the British public expressed wariness at frozen foods, especially meat: "Frozen meat at first met 'with suspicion.' . . . People could not be persuaded that it was, to say the least, palatable."[30] Thus, it also became necessary to establish a market for frozen meat that could compete with its more local, fresh counterpart; consumers needed to be convinced of its safety, quality, and value.

The woolly mammoth also makes an appearance in this particular transit of empire. As Woods remarks, the nineteenth-century discovery of prehistoric animals such as mammoths preserved by the cold offered a kind of frozen imaginary to Victorian Britons. People were surprised and inspired that "deep cold could arrest decay almost indefinitely,"[31] and this in turn spawned new visions of cold and possible technological interventions. As novel cold technologies and infrastructures of refrigeration developed and metropolitan palates adjusted, the production and consumption of frozen meat became commonplace, so much so that by the time of the Explorers Club Dinner in 1951, dinner guests did not balk at eating defrosted flesh that was thought to be thousands of years old.

These earlier experiments in freezing and later consuming animal flesh ultimately spawned an entire global industry wherein frozen foods travel all over the globe.[32] The conditions of possibility of frozen meat are rooted in imperial histories and constituted through circuits of empire. Early twentieth-century reindeer meat from Alaska is no exception. The transformation of a small government program designed to govern Alaska Natives into a large-scale industry dominated by white settler Alaskans in part results from the intensification of scientific approaches to reindeer herding, the scaling up of meat production and processing, and the construction of infrastructures of cold storage, allowing for the safe and potentially lucrative transportation of reindeer meat to the southern United States. Yet the story of "Reindeer au Stefansson" is also the larger story of experimentation in the Arctic north itself, experimentation made possible by multiple transits of empire. The reindeer itself can be understood in part as "a tool of northern colonization,"[33] and the cold as a site of technoscientific imaginings. In particular, the appropriation of "natural cold" by the Lomen Reindeer Corporation in Alaska is also a key part of the imperial transit of frozen meat, an appropriation told through triumphant narratives of modernity and one that disregards the centrality of indigenous epistemologies and technologies to the development of cold storage infrastructures.

## "Our New Senators": The Alaska Purchase, 1867

Any genealogy of "Reindeer au Stefansson" and the imperial transit of frozen reindeer meat needs to account for how the land now known as the state of Alaska and its peoples came under the domain of the US empire. In 1867, only two years after the end of the US Civil War, the US government signed a treaty to purchase Alaska from the Russian Empire for just over US\$7 million. The Alaska Purchase, also popularly known as "Seward's Folly" and "Seward's Icebox," after Secretary of State William H. Seward, was only the first in a series of late nineteenth- and early twentieth-century territorial expansions that marked the onset of the formal age of US imperialism. One of the main concerns expressed in the press at the time was that the US government was overextending itself, especially in deciding to govern yet another indigenous population at a time of great upheaval, and especially because of ongoing conflicts with American Indian groups in the western part of the continent. As an editorial in *Harper's Weekly* argued: "The advantage of obtaining a large territory with a population of Esquimaux is certainly not very striking, even with the added control of the fisheries and the fur trade. . . . Undoubtedly, also, it is our 'manifest destiny' ultimately to rule the continent . . . but before we enlarge our borders let us thoroughly organize our present possessions."[34]

In another popular periodical, *Frank Leslie's Weekly*, an unattributed cartoon ran in April 1867, the month following the Alaska Purchase. The satirical cartoon—entitled "Our New Senators"—shows Seward bowing to the two newest members of the US empire: an Eskimo and a penguin (figure 3.2).

OUR NEW SENATORS.

3.2 "Our New Senators," unattributed cartoon, *Frank Leslie's Weekly*, April 1867.

The caption reads: "My dear Mr. Kamskatea, you really must dine with me. I have some of the very finest tallow candles and the lovliest [*sic*] train oil you ever tasted, and my whale's blubber is exquisite—and pray bring your friend Mr. Seal along with you. The President will be one of the party."

Mr. Kamskatea, the Eskimo, wearing snowshoes and holding a speared fish, is considerably darker than either Seward or President Johnson and looks rather sinister as he stands next to an outsized penguin. The cartoon implies the absurdity of having these creatures—the primitive human and the non-human penguin—be the newest quasi-citizens of post–Civil War America. The invitation to the Eskimo—through the Alaska Purchase—to enter into the pinnacle of civilization, embodied by Seward and Johnson with their long coats and top hats, seems doomed to fail. The implication of the cartoon is that the Eskimo—like the penguin—is incapable of being civilized. Questions of whether or not Native North American peoples had the capacity to extend beyond their putative savagery or barbarism—and under what

70

conditions—were central to nineteenth-century colonial discourses; such questions variously preoccupied a range of settler actors including government officials, missionaries, scientists, bureaucrats, and entrepreneurs.

What I highlight here is the imaginary welcome dinner as an example of meat and its relationship to indigeneity. Meat—the "exquisite" whale blubber—and other animal by-products like tallow and train (whale) oil become the sardonic proving ground of civilization. They reference various evolutionary schema that treat different lifeways, especially in terms of the production and consumption of food, as steps in an evolutionary hierarchy. The association of the Eskimo with earlier stages of human evolution through reference to "savage" practices—like the ingestion of whale blubber, the consumption of raw fish, and the failure to properly discern between (human) person and (nonhuman) animal (hence Mr. Seal's invitation to dinner)—marks him as "frozen in time." Closely associated with the Arctic in general, and Alaska Native peoples in particular, the trope of being frozen in time is both long-standing and ubiquitous; it persists into the present day.[35]

In 1867, the potential for civilizing the Eskimo was still very much an open question in the eyes of settler states. Article III of the treaty with Russia (1869) distinguishes between "inhabitants of the ceded territory" (i.e., non-Native Russians and other expatriates) and the "uncivilized native tribes." The former could choose to return to Russia within three years or to be "admitted to the enjoyment of all the rights, advantages, and immunities of citizens of the United States"; indigenous Alaskans, however, were an "exception," "subject to such laws and regulations as the United States may, from time to time, adopt in regard to aboriginal tribes of that country." Thus, the policies and practices of settler colonialism in the mainland United States provided a key context for experiments in ruling the newly acquired territory of Alaska. How best to civilize the Native Alaskan population and how to put the land to the best use were paramount concerns.

Historians often mark a formal shift from policies and practices of settler colonialism (in what is now "the lower forty-eight" of the United States) to those of imperialism. Yet Alaska operated as a site for both.[36] In the larger context of US imperialism, especially the annexation of Hawai'i in 1898 and the acquisition of formerly Spanish possessions—Puerto Rico, Guam, and the Philippines—in the Spanish-American War, Alaska was a defining site in the development of imperialist policy and "laid the foundation for overseas imperialism in the decades that followed."[37] In particular, Alaska was vital to the United States' growing commercial and military interests in the Pacific but was also imagined as a boon to the homeland, especially in terms of its potential for food production. Alaska was at one point considered to "have agricultural possibilities of highest order"[38] and was widely promoted as having settlement potential for white Americans.[39] The Alaska Purchase is thus a key moment in the transit of empire, linking "internal colonialism with overseas imperialism," simultaneously representing "a continuation of earlier U.S. expansionism while marking a transition to a growing emphasis on global commercial empire."[40]

---

## INTERLUDE II

## "Don't Be an Esquimaux": Indigeneity, Meat, and American Advertising

In the latter part of the nineteenth century, the Chicago-based meatpacking company Libby, McNeill & Libby released a series of trade cards designed by lithographers Shober & Carqueville. The card (figure 3.3) shows two dead white men lying on the ground, one with an arrow poking out of his chest, while two Indians raid a box filled with cans of Libby's cooked corned beef and a third stands guard. The caption reads, "Heap Good."

Trade cards, similar in size and scope to baseball cards, were brightly illustrated advertisements widely distributed to customers, retailers, and industry representatives to promote particular companies and products. At the time the "most ubiquitous form of advertising in America," trade cards were enormously popular and collectible in the 1880s and 1890s, and were used to introduce new products to consumers as well as to convince these consumers of the products' necessity, utility, and appeal.[41] Racialized imagery featured heavily in trade cards and other advertising materials, reflecting broader social, political, and economic preoccupations and apprehensions in industrializing post–Civil War America.[42] The figure of the "Indian" in particular has long been a central trope in the American imaginary and "certain representations dating to the earliest colonial encounters have been remarkably persistent."[43] At a time of ongoing armed conflict among US soldiers, white settlers, and indigenous peoples resisting encroachment on their territories in the West, the "Heap Good" trade card reflects popular ideas and concerns about American Indians including ongoing anxieties around their potential for assimilation into "civilized" society. Especially important is that the Indians appear to have no interest in the domesticated

72

3.3 Libby, McNeill & Libby's trade card for cooked corned beef with caption "Heap Good," ca. 1880. Credit: The Warshaw Collection of Business Americana, NMAH, Smithsonian Institution.

oxen yoked to the wagon, opting instead for the ease of the canned corned beef, with the implication that they are perhaps "skipping over" the agricultural stage of evolution and moving right into industrial capitalism.

The opening line of a 1904 Grape-Nuts cereal advertisement in the national magazine *Good Housekeeping* reads as follows: "Dullness, is a racial characteristic of the only people who do not cook their food, viz-the Esquimaux" (figure 3.4). The ad goes on to explain that cooking is in fact "a stage in pre-digestion," a process that allows for the energy normally needed for the digestion of food to be "economized for Intellectual effort," rather than being wasted on a "cruder diet." The creator of Grape-Nuts, C. W. Post, was well known for making pseudoscientific and unproven health claims in his marketing materials.[44] Yet the specific focus on the "Esquimaux" and his "racial characteristic[s]" reminds us of the centrality of "eating as a trope and technology of racial formation during the first 130 years of the U.S. republic."[45]

In another advertisement from the early twentieth century, this one for Crisco vegetable shortening circa 1922, a dark-skinned Eskimo child in a parka reaches over the shoulder of a white child and steals a candle from his birthday cake (figure 3.5). The copy reads: "Young Eskimos relish tallow

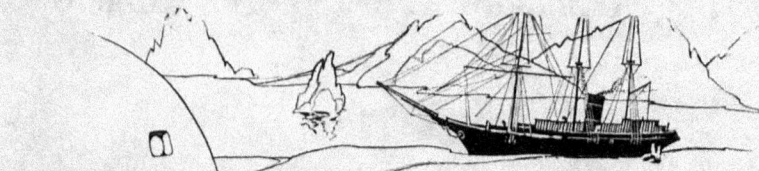

## DON'T BE AN ESQUIMAUX

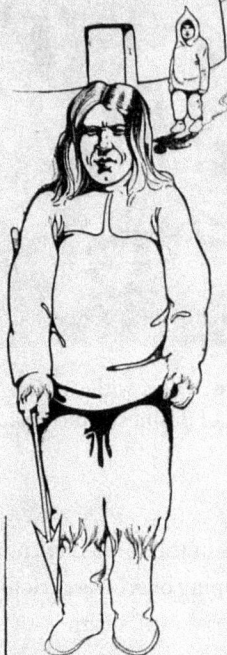

DULLNESS, is a racial characteristic of the only people who do not cook their food, viz-the Esquimaux.

Cooking is simply a stage in pre-digestion. The more pre-digested a food is, before it is eaten, the less energy will it take from Brain-power, during the after process of digestion.

Why do you feel "dull" after a heavy dinner?

Every bit of steam taken away from the engines of a Ship, on a winter voyage, to heat the state-rooms, is so much loss of speed which she might have made, in warmer weather, with the same boilers, and the same Coal consumption.

Digestion is work, just like sawing wood, or thinking out a knotty problem.

The energy put into it can be economized for Intellectual effort, by the liberal use of "Grape-nuts" instead of cruder diet.

Not half the food we eat, is ever fully digested, nor entirely assimilated so that there is no danger of your Liver "getting out of practice" through the use, of pre-digested "Grape-nuts."

The Postman doesn't forget how to walk, merely because he rides home on a street car, when he is tired.

"Grape-nuts" is Wheat, with its Energy-producing Starch, and its Brain-building Phosphates, pre-digested beyond the Liver stage, ready for prompt assimilation and superior Brain work.

A Government analysis proves it to be eighteen times readier for assimilation than Oatmeal, and thrice as dextrinated as the average Wheat food.

This analysis will be sent free on request.

# Grape-Nuts

3.4 "Don't Be an Esquimaux," Grape-Nuts advertisement, *Good Housekeeping*, 1904.

Young Eskimos relish tallow candle fat. But for civilized little stomachs – digestible Crisco – Nature's vegetable shortening. Mothers, avoid any indigestible fat.

for FRYING      for SHORTENING      for CAKE-MAKING

3.5 "But for Civilized Little Stomachs," Crisco vegetable shortening advertisement, ca. 1922.

candle fat. But for civilized little stomachs—digestible Crisco—Nature's vegetable shortening. Mothers avoid any indigestible fat."[46] Again, the preference for vegetable shortening over rendered animal fat—tallow—becomes the proving ground for civilization, and the figure of the Eskimo—the eater of raw flesh—serves as a foil for the cultured metabolism of white America.

The Grape-Nuts and Crisco advertisements are but two examples of what Shari Huhndorf calls "the stunning number of images and artifacts circulating in American society during this period,"[47] and are powerful demonstrations of what Ann Fienup-Riordan calls "Eskimo Orientalism."[48] As in the political cartoon "Our New Senators" (figure 3.2), settler imaginaries of indigenous production and consumption of animal protein are closely linked to notions of civilization and evolution.

What these advertisements all reveal is the centrality of meat to narratives of indigeneity and their attendant tropes of civilization, evolution, and progress. These artifacts also mark key moments in the imperial history of the United States: while the colonization of the western part of the country through white settlement continued, the United States' imperialist project was ramping up, most notably beginning with the Alaska Purchase in 1867. As Huhndorf notes in her discussion of Alaska and its role in "remaking Native America," "the emerging imperial order relied on social hierarchies and ideologies developed during continental expansion to support new national aspirations."[49] Such national aspirations include the continuing doctrine of manifest destiny—the belief in the righteousness and inevitability of US dominance in the Americas.

## From Hunters to Herders: Sheldon Jackson and the Alaska Reindeer Service

In the introduction to his 1954 autobiography *Fifty Years in Alaska*, Carl J. Lomen writes: "I am no Santa Claus, but reindeer became my business."[50] Although the notion of Santa having reindeer can be dated at least to the previous century, the specific American mythology can at least be partly attributed to a savvy marketing campaign undertaken by the Lomen Reindeer Company beginning in 1923. As a way to market reindeer meat to the mainland United States, the Lomen Company created an advertising campaign organized around Santa and his reindeer and coordinated with Macy's department stores to promote products made from reindeer meat and skins in places like New York City.[51]

Understanding the emergence of this mythology necessitates a discussion of the rise and fall of the reindeer industry in Alaska during the territory's early history. In the decades immediately following the Alaska Purchase in 1867, questions of how to govern Native Alaskans in the United States' newest territory became a major concern for the federal government. In 1885, missionary and Presbyterian minister Sheldon Jackson was appointed general agent of education for Alaska, giving him a sweeping federal mandate that extended beyond the formal schooling of children. For a complex series of reasons, including whether or not Alaska Natives could be legitimately classified as "Indians" and thus fall under the purview of the Indian Office, the Bureau of Education was the "only federal agency with jurisdiction to administer federal Indian policy and native services in Alaska."[52] Thus, Jackson's mandate included all "uncivilized native tribes," and it is in this context that Jackson created the Alaska Reindeer Service (ARS), a program that would become his enduring legacy in the region.

Prior to his time in Alaska, Jackson had spent a decade as a missionary among Indian groups in the American West, and so was part of a larger reformist movement that sought to "civilize" indigenous peoples through a variety of governance projects.[53] As historian Stephen Haycox notes, Jackson was "an unexceptional representative of the late nineteenth-century Indian reform movement in the United States," one who "accepted accul-

76

turation as the best solution to the problems of continuing Indian warfare and the inexorable advance of white settlement."[54]

Jackson and other settler Americans of the time believed that Alaska Natives were starving, principally as a result of large-scale Euro-American hunting and fishing enterprises that decimated stocks, leaving Alaska Natives without sufficient food for subsistence. While the accuracy of this view has been challenged by historians,[55] it nevertheless provided an impetus for Jackson and his peers to use reindeer to change Eskimos from "hunters to herders":

> To do this will give the Eskimo as permanent a food supply as the cattle of the Western plains and sheep of New Mexico and Arizona do the inhabitants of those sections. It will do more than preserve life—it will preserve the self-respect of the people and advance them in the scale of civilization. It will change them from hunters to herders. It will also utilize the hundreds of thousands of square miles of moss-covered tundra of arctic and subarctic Alaska and make those now useless and barren wastes conducive to the wealth and prosperity of the United States.[56]

While technically the same species (*Rangifer tarandus*), reindeer and caribou are different animals with distinct behaviors. Although, as historian Roxanne Willis notes, their differences "are largely those of history rather than biology,"[57] caribou tend to be larger and have never been domesticated, while reindeer are smaller and were domesticated thousands of years ago on the continent of Asia. As Willis argues, the different histories of reindeer and caribou "collided at a very particular time and place: 21 September 1891, in Western Alaska," when agents of the United States government imported sixteen reindeer purchased from Chukchi herders in Siberia.[58] The following year, when Jackson and his coworkers brought another 171 reindeer to Alaska, they also brought four Chukchi herders from Siberia to help train the Eskimo, and to help transform them "from hunters to herders."[59]

The ARS was intended to improve the land in, and the people of, the United States' newest territory: "to reclaim and make valuable vast areas of land otherwise worthless; to introduce large, permanent, and wealth-producing industries where none previously existed; to take a barbarian people on the verge of starvation and lift them up to a comfortable self-support and civilization."[60] Reindeer were seen as a vehicle to transform "vegetation into meat . . . necessary to support the Eskimos," to turn "useless land" into productive land, and to civilize the Native peoples in Alaska.[61]

77

## "The Three Races of Man and His Associates during the Age of Evolution," 1904, and *Types of Mankind,* 1854

In a broadside from around 1904, "The Three Races of Man and His Associates during the Age of Evolution," the anonymous author opines that "three distinct races have been developed from the animal creation by the act of destiny," and that "each has been colored according to their merits" (figure 3.6). Broadsides, a printed form of notice or announcement, were popular in the United States from the sixteenth through the nineteenth centuries and were displayed in public places as part of larger conversations and debates. "The Three Races of Man" divides humankind into three distinct races, each descended from a different son of Noah: Japheth, Shem, and Ham. The perspective of the broadside and the "Three Races of Man" is exemplary of polygenism, "the idea that human racial variation could be explained as the result of separate creation, rather than genesis from one primordial pair, which led to a belief in the separation of species."[62] Central to this polygenist argument was that nonhuman animals—the "Associates" of Man—were equally reflective of these divisions. The first column of the broadside, under "the testimony of Japheth" or the white race, reads as follows: "The highest, cleanest and most useful class of animals are those associated with the White Race while there is also the greatest contrast in their physical propensities, and nearest mental relationship if so trained. For instance, the nobility of the horse, faithfulness of the dog, shrewdness of the fox, indominatable persistency of the wolf, intelligence of the bear, usefulness of the cow, sheep, swine and reindeer."

In linking the biblical story of Noah's three sons—Japheth, Shem, and Ham—with the polygenist story of the evolution of mankind, the broadside rehearses prevalent tropes in late nineteenth- and early twentieth-century racial science including the development of distinct racial typologies and the ranking of these typologies along evolutionary lines. Each race—white, red, and black, respectively—possesses immutable characteristics, and each is associated with particular fauna representative of these characteristics. "The Three Races of Man" exhibits two prevalent features of late nineteenth- and early twentieth-century racial science: (1) the cultural per-

78

3.6 "The Three Races of Man and His Associates during the Age of Evolution,"
1904. Source: Library of Congress.

vasiveness of scientized notions of race and racialized notions of science, and (2) the centrality of nonhuman animals to notions of race and associated processes of colonization and imperialism.[63] One can hear rhetorical echoes of Sheldon Jackson's argument for the importation of reindeer to Alaska in the "usefulness of the cow, sheep, swine and reindeer."

Fifty years earlier, in their 1854 volume *Types of Mankind*, Josiah Nott and George Gliddon published what is likely one of the most famous representations of nineteenth-century racial science: a tableau entitled "Types of Mankind" (figure 3.7). Based on a written sketch by biologist and geologist Louis Agassiz, the tableau reproduces images from a variety of natural history sources to make a visually powerful argument about the different races of humankind and their associated flora and fauna. The "Types of Mankind" tableau is divided into eight sections, each column headed by a drawn profile of an individual racial type, organized by geographical origin: 79

3.7 "Tableau to Accompany Prof. Agassiz's 'Sketch'—Nott & Gliddon's Types of Mankind," 1854.

Arctic, Mongol, European, American, Negro, Hottentot, Malay, and Australian. Nott, Agassiz, and Gliddon, part of the American school of what would eventually become anthropology,[64] were also polygenists, and their belief in the distinct origins and faunal associations of the races permeates the tableau.

Agassiz wrote to Nott and Gliddon in 1853, noting that his "general remarks upon natural relations of the human family and the organic world surrounding" were delivered "in the hope that it may call the attention of naturalists to the close connection there is between the geographical distribution of animals and the natural boundaries of the different races of man."[65] Of particular importance in thinking about transits of empire and the larger politics of race and indigeneity is Agassiz's discussion of the "Arctic" column: "Within the limits of this fauna we meet a peculiar race of men, known in America under the name of Esquimaux. . . . This race, so well known since the voyage of Capt. Cook and the arctic expeditions of England and Russia. . . . The uniformity of their characters along the whole range of the arctic seas forms one of the most striking resemblances which these people exhibit to the fauna with which they are so closely connected."[66] The Arctic column in the tableau includes drawings of the "Esquimaux" (figure 3.8) and the "Reindeer" (figure 3.9), drawings reproduced from earlier eighteenth- and nineteenth-century sources. Like "The Three

80

3.8 Detail of Esquimaux, "Tableau to Accompany Prof. Agassiz's 'Sketch'—Nott & Gliddon's Types of Mankind," 1854.

3.9 Detail of Reindeer, "Tableau to Accompany Prof. Agassiz's 'Sketch'— Nott & Gliddon's Types of Mankind," 1854.

Races of Mankind," the "Types of Mankind" also has a narrative about racial types and reindeer, although instead of the "Race of Japheth," reindeer in Nott and Gliddon's tableau are closely allied with the "Esquimaux." Yet it is clear that the 1904 broadside refers to domesticated reindeer—of a kind with other livestock such as swine, cows, and sheep—as the proper domain of the race of Japheth (the white race). In his written sketch, Agassiz makes a special point of emphasizing that "even the reindeer is not domesticated" among the Arctic type of man in North America and clearly refers to what we now know as the caribou.[67]

The juxtaposition of the "Types of Mankind" with "The Three Races of Mankind" makes clear not only the durability of racial science but also reveals the centrality of domestication to ideas of race and evolution, ideas that are reproduced in Jackson's desire to transform Alaska Native peoples "from hunters to herders." Such representations are bound in important ways to questions of civilization: Who is capable of being civilized and under what circumstances?

## From the Alaska Reindeer Service
## to the Lomen Reindeer Corporation

By the turn of the twentieth century, Alaska's development potential was of growing interest to white entrepreneurs in both the US government and private enterprise, domains that often overlapped in terms of ideas, practices, and personnel. The reindeer industry was seen as a particularly good possibility for economic development in the territory. Sheldon Jackson, for instance, believed that he could teach Alaska Natives not only to be "civilized" but also "to be successful capitalists—and develop Alaska's sluggish economy along the way."[68] As former government reindeer agent and entrepreneur Miner Bruce noted in 1899: "There is little doubt that the reindeer industry will in the near future assume considerable proportions, and private companies will embark in the business of raising this animal in these regions for commercial purposes, the same as stock-raising is followed in the grazing regions in many of the States of the Union."[69]

Similarly, G. H. Grosvenor, publisher of *National Geographic* and Explorers Club medal winner, wrote in a 1903 report to the Smithsonian: "The time is coming when Alaska will have great reindeer ranches like the great cattle ranches of the southwest, and they will be no less profitable."[70] In early 1914, *National Geographic* magazine published in full the annual report of Franklin K. Lane, secretary of the interior under President Woodrow Wilson.[71] Entitled "The Nation's Undeveloped Resources," the report focused on areas where public lands were not being used to their full potential, especially in terms of resource extraction and infrastructural development. In particular, Lane opined that Alaska represented the "largest body of unused and neglected land in the United States" and that this "vast and unsurpassed asset lies almost undeveloped."[72] Yet, according to Lane, "the one constructive thing" done by the government since the Alaska Purchase "was the importation of reindeer for the benefit of the Eskimo."[73]

Among this group of white men, reindeer herding was seen as an overwhelmingly positive solution to the problems of governance among Native Alaskans. As Susan Schulten points out in her discussion of the making of *National Geographic*, the magazine's content was provided by "men working for the government who directly witnessed—and aided—the nation's political and economic expansion."[74] Schulten argues that while privately owned and operated, *National Geographic* functioned as another arm of the US government, devoted to the "twin goals of internationalism: expanding trade and native uplift."[75]

Newspapers and magazines of the period speculated widely about the potential of reindeer herding in Alaska, but also portrayed Eskimos as an impediment to capitalist development. Reindeer in Alaska became increasingly associated with whiteness as the industry scaled up in the early part of the twentieth century. In ways that echo the racialized discourses found in the preceding interlude, settler Alaskans claimed reindeer for themselves. As the same USDA scientists cited above argue in their report, "it is evident that the development of the reindeer industry requires white supervision."[76] Carl Lomen later wrote in his autobiography that the Eskimo lack the "instinct" for reindeer herding, at least relative to the Lapps, who "far [surpass] the Eskimo in the affection they have for the reindeer."[77] Reindeer—unlike their wild counterpart the caribou, the naturalized associate of the Eskimo—operate simultaneously as a civilizing vehicle for Alaska Natives and as the proper domain of whites, justifying white settler encroachment on the reindeer industry.

The ARS was originally intended exclusively for Alaska Native peoples; non-Natives in Alaska were expressly prohibited from purchasing breeding deer as a protection against white encroachment on the industry. Due to a series of changes in administrative personnel—including Jackson's retirement in 1907—and the importation of Lapp (Sami) herders from Scandinavia to replace Chukchi herders returned to Siberia, reindeer herding ceased to be the exclusive domain of Alaska Natives. As a result, in 1914 the Lomen brothers were able to exploit what Willis calls a "small but powerful loophole in the bureau's herding policy"[78] and to purchase 1,200 reindeer. Although the formation of the Lomen Reindeer Corporation had the support of government officials, especially in the Department of the Interior, Lomen's entrance and ultimate dominance of reindeer herding and meatpacking on the Seward Peninsula was not without controversy. Historian Margaret Lantis calls this the beginning of "a new and very troubled period in the reindeer industry."[79] From 1914 until the late 1930s, the Lomens expanded their reindeer business and came to dominate the industry; reindeer sold well in the south, and many Native Alaskans became laborers for the LRC.

Yet early twentieth-century attempts to create a sustained US market in Alaska reindeer meat were ultimately failures.[80] The LRC was hit hard by the stock market crash in 1929 and the ensuing Depression. Pressure from the beef industry in the US resulted in some unfavorable trade policies, and in 1937 Congress passed the Reindeer Act, which again limited ownership of reindeer herds in Alaska to Native peoples. In 1938, the federal government arranged to purchase all of the LRC's remaining reindeer for use by Alaska Natives, and by 1940 the Lomens were no longer part of the reindeer business. As Carl Lomen lamented in 1954, "I found them to be dependable and faithful servants of man. . . . It was man, not the reindeer, who generated my woes."[81] And by the time of the Explorers Club dinner in 1951, we now know that the frozen meat on the menu was not mammoth, but neither was it reindeer: "By 1952, domestic reindeer had disappeared from the entire Arctic Slope of Alaska."[82]

## Imperial Transit on Ice

To conclude this discussion, I briefly explore how experiments that partly form the modern frozen foods industry form another node in the imperial transit of meat. In particular, I demonstrate the centrality of indigenous knowledge to the development of cold technologies in the early part of the twentieth century. Modern frozen foods like fish sticks and TV dinners would not exist without the development of technologies of fast freezing, technologies credited to the innovations of American Clarence Birdseye, eponymous founder of Birds Eye Frozen Foods. Birdseye, known as the "man who brought the North Pole South,"[83] famously attributed the idea for his technology of flash freezing to his time spent observing ice fishing among the Inuit in Labrador.[84] According to Birdseye, during his initial stay in Labrador in 1912, he noticed that Inuit ice fishers used the extremely cold subzero air to immediately freeze the fish as they pulled them from the ice and would later carefully thaw them in water, preserving their freshness. As Birdseye himself recounted in a 1941 article in *The Beaver*, the magazine of the Hudson's Bay Company, he "knew nothing of the virtues of quick freezing . . . and couldn't, in fact, have told a refrigeration compressor from a condenser."[85] "But that first winter I saw natives catching fish in fifty below zero weather which froze stiff almost as soon as they were taken out of the water. Months later, when they were thawed out, some of these fish were so fresh that they were still alive!"[86]

According to Kurlansky, Birdseye, who had registered over two hundred patents at the time of his death in 1956, was driven "to ponder on the science of freezing" and "spent endless time reflecting on things that would have barely registered in most minds."[87] Yet multiple historical sources about Labrador suggest Birdseye's "discovery" of fast freezing came from learning about what was common knowledge in the area and indeed identify the Inuit fisherman who taught Birdseye as Garland Lethbridge.[88]

84

Lethbridge is not mentioned in Kurlansky's biography and, to my knowledge, Birdseye never mentions his specific contribution in writing. What I want to emphasize here is that Kurlansky's narrative of Birdseye's inventions follows a familiar trope of dismissing Inuit freezing technologies as outside the realm of any systematic empirical knowledge (science); rather, they belong to the realm of the natural, available for discovery by settler Americans.

As part of the expansion of their reindeer business, the Lomen brothers also became interested in indigenous technologies of "natural cold," especially underground chambers called "ice cellars" (*sigluaq* in Iñupiat), vertical shafts with chambers dug into the permafrost. Such ice cellars have been used by Alaska Natives for over a thousand years, especially although not exclusively for food storage.[89] Not unlike Birdseye's "observation" of Inuit ice fishers in Labrador at around the same time, the Lomen Company "organized a prospecting expedition to look for suitable conditions for natural cold storage."[90] Cold in this formulation is another "natural" Arctic resource available for exploitation: "Realizing the great advantage natural cold storage would give the industry, we made plans for very extensive work on a plant as soon as the winter season opened. The Lomens could thank Mother Nature for her kindness for she not only supplied free fodder for the animals the year round, but now she was ready to furnish a refrigerating system that would run itself and require no fuel."[91]

As environmental historian Stephen Bocking notes, indigenous knowledge has often been "viewed as anecdotal and non-quantitative, more folklore than data, failing to meet standards of scientific evidence and reasoning."[92] This has been particularly true in the Arctic, especially when one considers the intensive scientific experimentation that marks various enterprises—anthropological, developmental, exploratory, and entrepreneurial, for example—enterprises made possible by colonial and imperial transits that unfold over centuries and continue into the present.[93]

### Conclusion: Reindeer and Woolly Mammoths

In 1986, the state legislature named the woolly mammoth as the state fossil of Alaska, an ode to an "animal that was the largest and one of the most prevalent animals in the state but whose remains are now found only as fossils." Hanging in a front window in the third-floor "trophy room" of the Explorers Club headquarters in New York City is a mammoth tusk. Charles Knight's mural is still prominently displayed in the American Museum of

Natural History, and the characterization of Alaska Native peoples as "frozen in time" persists in many anthropological, scientific, and popular discourses. Santa's reindeer (*R.t. saintnicolas magicalus*) are a listed species on the website of the Alaska Department of Fish and Game. Domesticated reindeer remain in Alaska and attempts to recover something of the industry's early twentieth-century success are ongoing. In this chapter, I have traced how seemingly disparate phenomena—woolly mammoths and reindeer, canned meat and breakfast cereal, racial science and its nonhuman familiars—operate as nodes in the imperial transit of frozen meat. Like Byrd, I too "want to imagine cacophonously, to understand that the historical processes that have created our contemporary moment have affected everyone at various points along their transits with and against empire."[94] Tracing these phenomena makes apparent connections among imperialism, colonialism, and indigeneity in the North American Arctic. I have juxtaposed the more linear narrative of Alaska's reindeer industry with a series of interludes demonstrating the entanglements of technologies of cold with the imperial politics of race and indigeneity.

Since 1951, there have been no reports of mammoth meat being served at any Explorers Club events, although rumors of its consumption in secret continue to circulate widely. Nor has "Reindeer au Stefansson" made a return to twenty-first-century ECAD menus. Yet in April 2017, only a couple of months before I began writing this piece, the ECAD served reindeer and rabbit sausage, part of a "cold weather themed menu . . . very careful not to include anything endangered," representing "the eating habits of the world's colder dwelling humans."[95] Like the 1920s ECAD dinners hosted by Stefansson, it is not entirely clear where the reindeer served at the 2017 dinner came from. Norway? Canada? Possibly Alaska? Although beyond the scope of this chapter, I suggest that the answer to this question is equally constituted through other transits of empire.

Returning to the epigraph at the beginning of the chapter from American frozen foods entrepreneur E. W. Williams, I argue the imperial transit of frozen meat demonstrates that Williams's claim that the frozen foods industry is "indigenous" to America is perhaps more accurate than he thought.

## Notes

1 Jessica R. Glass et al., "Was Frozen Mammoth or Giant Ground Sloth Served for Dinner at the Explorers Club?" *PLoS One* 11, no. 2 (2016): e0146825. doi:10.1371/journal.pone.0146825.

JENNIFER A. HAMILTON

2 Explorers Club, "About the Club," accessed December 29, 2017, https://explorers.org/about/about_the_club.

3 Explorers Club, "About the Club."

4 Henry B. Nichols, "Mammoth Appetites Explore a . . . Mammoth," *Christian Science Monitor*, January 17, 1951, 3.

5 Glass et al., "Was Frozen Mammoth or Giant Ground Sloth Served for Dinner at the Explorers Club?"

6 Glass et al., "Was Frozen Mammoth or Giant Ground Sloth Served for Dinner at the Explorers Club?"; see also Nichols, "Mammoth Appetites Explore a . . . Mammoth."

7 Stefansson's own writings suggest that the Lomen Reindeer Corporation provided the reindeer for the Explorers Club dinners: "The winter of 1920–21 the Alaska firm, Lomen and Company, of Nome, shipped to the United States sixteen hundred reindeer carcasses which were sold to the best clubs and hotels for prices between three and four times as high as corresponding cuts of beef." Vilhjalmur Stefansson, *The Northward Course of Empire* (New York: Harcourt, Brace, 1922), 58.

8 Cited in Preston Jones, *Empire's Edge: American Society in Nome, Alaska, 1898–1934* (Fairbanks: University of Alaska Press, 2007), 127.

9 I use the term *Eskimo* here to encompass a diverse group of indigenous peoples whose traditional territories traverse the contemporary nation-states of the United States, Canada, Greenland, and Russia. The term Eskimo is and continues to be controversial and imprecise, but I reproduce it here because it was the preferred term of missionaries, bureaucrats, entrepreneurs, anthropologists, and explorers during the late nineteenth and early twentieth centuries. This usage is reflected in the archival history of the reindeer industry and in representations of generic "Eskimos" in advertisements and other ephemera from this era.

10 John C. Cantwell, "Alaska and the Reindeer," *The Californian* 3 (1893): 259.

11 Richard Diubaldo, *Stefansson and the Canadian Arctic* (Montreal: McGill-Queen's University Press, 1999).

12 Jodi A. Byrd, *The Transit of Empire: Indigenous Critiques of Colonialism* (Minneapolis: University of Minnesota Press, 2011), xvii.

13 Byrd, *The Transit of Empire*, xv–xvi.

14 Henry Fairfield Osborn, W. K. Gregory, and George Pinkley, *The Hall of the Age of Man* (New York: American Museum of Natural History, 1925), 5.

15 Osborn et al., *The Hall of the Age of Man*, 30.

16 S. M. Czerkas and D. F. Glut, *Dinosaurs, Mammoths, and Cavemen: The Art of Charles R. Knight* (New York: E. P. Dutton, 1982), 1.

17 Marianne Sommer, *History Within: The Science, Culture, and Politics of Bones, Organisms, and Molecules* (Chicago: University of Chicago Press, 2016).

18 Sommer, *History Within*, 21.

19 Sommer, *History Within*, 86.

87

20  Brian Regal, *Henry Fairfield Osborn: Race and the Search for the Origins of Man* (Aldershot, UK: Ashgate, 2002), xv.

21  See, for example, Igor Krupnik, *Early Inuit Studies: Themes and Transitions, 1850s–1980s* (Washington, DC: Smithsonian Institution, 2016).

22  Hannah Landecker, *Culturing Life: How Cells Became Technologies* (Cambridge, MA: Harvard University Press, 2007).

23  Joanna Radin, *Life on Ice: A History of New Uses for Cold Blood* (Chicago: University of Chicago Press, 2017).

24  See also Joanna Radin and Emma Kowal, *Cryopolitics: Frozen Life in a Melting World* (Cambridge, MA: MIT Press, 2017).

25  Cited in Cecil Adams, "Prehistoric Meat Up," *Washington City Paper*, September 12, 2007.

26  Charles Morrow Wilson, "The Electric Age in Food," *Popular Mechanics*, 1937.

27  Hiʻilei Julia Hobart, "Mammoth and Other Frozen Meats," *Harvard Design Magazine* 43 (2016). See also Rebecca J. H. Woods, "From Colonial Animal to Imperial Edible: Building an Empire of Sheep in New Zealand, ca. 1880–1900," *Comparative Studies of South Asia, Africa and the Middle East* 35, no. 1 (2015): 117–36; Rebecca J. H. Woods, "Nature and the Refrigerating Machine: The Politics and Production of Cold in the Nineteenth Century," in *Cryopolitics: Frozen Life in a Melting World*, edited by Joanna Radin and Emma Kowal, 89–116 (Cambridge, MA: MIT Press, 2017).

28  Hobart, "Mammoth and Other Frozen Meats."

29  Woods, "Nature and the Refrigerating Machine," 90–91.

30  Woods, "Nature and the Refrigerating Machine," 102.

31  Woods, "Nature and the Refrigerating Machine," 96.

32  For example, Kostas Gavroglu, *History of Artificial Cold, Scientific, Technological and Cultural Issues* (Dordrecht: Springer, 2014); Jonathan Rees, *Refrigeration Nation: A History of Ice, Appliances, and Enterprise in America* (Baltimore: Johns Hopkins University Press, 2013).

33  Andrew Stuhl, *Unfreezing the Arctic: Science, Colonialism, and the Transformation of Inuit Lands* (Chicago: University of Chicago Press, 2016), 64.

34  "The Russian Treaty," *Harper's Weekly*, April 13, 1867, 226.

35  Robert P. Wheelersburg, "*National Geographic* Magazine and the Eskimo Stereotype: A Photographic Analysis, 1949–1990," *Polar Geography* 40, no. 1 (2017): 35–58, doi:10.1080/1088937X.2016.1257659.

36  Shari M. Huhndorf, *Mapping the Americas: The Transnational Politics of Contemporary Native Culture* (Ithaca, NY: Cornell University Press, 2009).

37  Shari M. Huhndorf, "Colonizing Alaska: Race, Nation, and the Remaking of Native America," in *Mapping the Americas*, edited by Shari M. Huhndorf (Ithaca, NY: Cornell University Press, 2009), 32.

38  C. C. Georgeson, "The Possibilities of Alaska," *National Geographic* 13, no. 3 (1902): 81.

39 See also James R. Shortridge, "The Collapse of Frontier Farming in Alaska," *Annals of the Association of American Geographers* 66, no. 4 (1976): 583–604.

40 Huhndorf, "Colonizing Alaska," 30.

41 Robert Jay, *The Trade Card in Nineteenth-Century America* (Columbia: University of Missouri Press, 1987), 3. See also Margaret E. Hale, "The Nineteenth-Century American Trade Card," *Business History Review* 74, no. 4 (2000): 683–88, doi:10.2307/3116471; Jennifer M. Black, "Corporate Calling Cards: Advertising Trade Cards and Logos in the United States, 1876–1890," *Journal of American Culture* 32, no. 4 (2009): 291–306.

42 Kyla Wazana Tompkins, *Racial Indigestion: Eating Bodies in the 19th Century* (New York: NYU Press, 2012).

43 Pauline Turner Strong, *American Indians and the American Imaginary: Cultural Representation across the Centuries* (Boulder, CO: Paradigm, 2013), 1.

44 Scott Bruce and Bill Crawford, *Cerealizing America: The Unsweetened Story of American Breakfast Cereal* (Boston: Faber and Faber, 1995), especially chapter 3.

45 Tompkins, *Racial Indigestion*, 2.

46 Roy Dickinson, "When McConnachie Helps," *Printer's Ink Monthly* 5, no. 5 (1922): 25.

47 Shari M. Huhndorf, "Nanook and His Contemporaries: Imagining Eskimos in American Culture, 1897–1922," *Critical Inquiry* 27, no. 1 (2000): 126, doi:10.1086/449001.

48 Ann Fienup-Riordan, "Preface: Eskimo Orientalism," in *Freeze Frame: Alaska Eskimos in the Movies* (Seattle: University of Washington Press), 1995.

49 Huhndorf, "Colonizing Alaska," 46.

50 Carl J. Lomen, *Fifty Years in Alaska* (New York: D. McKay, 1954), 27.

51 Lomen, *Fifty Years in Alaska*.

52 Stephen Haycox, "'Races of a Questionable Ethnical Type': Origins of the Jurisdiction of the US Bureau of Education in Alaska, 1867–1885," *Pacific Northwest Quarterly* 75, no. 4 (1984): 156.

53 Stephen W. Haycox, "Sheldon Jackson in Historical Perspective: Alaska Native Schools and Mission Contracts, 1885–1894," *Pacific Historian* 28, no. 1 (1982): 18–28.

54 Haycox, "Sheldon Jackson in Historical Perspective," 19.

55 For example, Roxanne Willis, "A New Game in the North: Alaska Native Reindeer Herding, 1890–1940," *Western Historical Quarterly* 37, no. 3 (2006): 277–301; Bathsheba Demuth, "More Things on Heaven and Earth: Modernism and Reindeer in Chukotka and Alaska," in *Northscapes: History, Technology, and the Making of Northern Environments*, edited by Dolly Jørgensen and Sverker Sörlin, 174–94 (Vancouver: UBC Press, 2013).

56 Sheldon Jackson, *Introduction of Domestic Reindeer into Alaska* (Washington, DC: US Government Printing Office, 1896).

57 Willis, "A New Game in the North," 279.

58  Willis, "A New Game in the North," 279.

59  Jackson, *Introduction of Domestic Reindeer into Alaska*, 10.

60  Sheldon Jackson, *Report on Education in Alaska* (Washington, DC: US Government Printing Office, 1896), 1438.

61  Sheldon Jackson, *Annual Report on Introduction of Domestic Reindeer into Alaska*, vol. 14 (Washington, DC: US Government Printing Office, 1905), 130.

62  Adam Dewbury, "The American School and Scientific Racism in Early American Anthropology," *Histories of Anthropology Annual* 3, no. 1 (2007): 121.

63  See, for example, Virginia DeJohn Anderson, *Creatures of Empire: How Domestic Animals Transformed Early America* (New York: Oxford University Press, 2006).

64  Dewbury, "The American School and Scientific Racism in Early American Anthropology," 121–47.

65  Cited in Josiah C. Nott and George R. Gliddon, *Types of Mankind: Or, Ethnological Researches, Based upon the Ancient Monuments, Paintings, Sculptures, and Crania of Races, and upon Their Natural, Geographical, Philological, and Biblical History* (Philadelphia: J. B. Lippincott, Grambo, 1854).

66  Nott and Gliddon, *Types of Mankind*, lxi.

67  Nott and Gliddon, *Types of Mankind*, lxi.

68  Willis, "A New Game in the North," 287.

69  Miner W. Bruce, *Alaska: Its History and Resources, Gold Fields, Routes and Scenery* (New York: G. P. Putnam's Sons, 1899), 87.

70  Gilbert Hovey Grosvenor, "Reindeer in Alaska," *National Geographic* 14, no. 4 (1903): 127.

71  Franklin K. Lane, "The Nation's Undeveloped Resources," *National Geographic* 25, no. 2 (1914): 183–228.

72  Lane, "The Nation's Undeveloped Resources," 185, 186.

73  Lane, "The Nation's Undeveloped Resources," 186.

74  Susan Schulten, "The Making of the *National Geographic*: Science, Culture, and Expansionism," *American Studies* 41, no. 1 (2000): 6.

75  Schulten, "The Making of the *National Geographic*," 15.

76  Isaac Andre Seymour Hadwen and Lawrence J. Palmer, *Reindeer in Alaska* (Washington, DC: US Government Printing Office, 1922), 69.

77  Lomen, *Fifty Years in Alaska*, 49.

78  Willis, "A New Game in the North," 293.

79  Margaret Lantis, "The Reindeer Industry in Alaska," *Arctic* 3, no. 1 (1950): 28.

80  See, for example, Lantis, "The Reindeer Industry in Alaska," 27–44; Willis, "A New Game in the North."

81  Lomen, *Fifty Years in Alaska*, 57.

82  Stuhl, *Unfreezing the Arctic*, 62.

83  Nan Ickeringill, "Food News: 30 Years of Freezing," *New York Times*, March 7, 1960, 22.

84  Mark Kurlansky, *Birdseye: The Adventures of a Curious Man* (New York: Doubleday, 2012); Clarence Birdseye, "The Birth of an Industry," *The Beaver*, September 1941, 24–25.

85  Birdseye, "The Birth of an Industry," 24.

86  Birdseye, "The Birth of an Industry," 24.

87  Kurlansky, *Birdseye*, 117.

88  For example, David William Zimmerly, *Cain's Land Revisited* (St. John's, NL: Institute of Social and Economic Research, 1975); Lynne D. Fitzhugh, *The Labradorians: Voices from the Land of Cain* (Guilford, CT: Breakwater Books, 1999), 186.

89  Kelsey E. Nyland et al., "Traditional Iñupiat Ice Cellars (SIĠLUAQ) in Barrow, Alaska: Characteristics, Temperature Monitoring, and Distribution," *Geographical Review* 107, no. 1 (2017): 143–58.

90  Lomen, *Fifty Years in Alaska*, 81.

91  Lomen, *Fifty Years in Alaska*, 82.

92  Stephen Bocking, "Indigenous Knowledge and the History of Science, Race, and Colonial Authority," in *Rethinking the Great White North: Race, Nature, and the Historical Geographies of Whiteness in Canada* (Vancouver: UBC Press, 2011), 39; see also Candis Callison, *How Climate Change Comes to Matter: The Communal Life of Facts* (Durham, NC: Duke University Press, 2014); Andrew Baldwin, Laura Cameron, and Audrey Kobayashi, *Rethinking the Great White North: Race, Nature, and the Historical Geographies of Whiteness in Canada* (Vancouver: UBC Press, 2011); Stuhl, *Unfreezing the Arctic*; Stuhl, "The Experimental State of Nature"; Chris Cuomo, Wendy Eisner, and Kenneth Hinkel, "Environmental Change, Indigenous Knowledge, and Subsistence on Alaska's North Slope," *Scholar and Feminist Online* 7, no. 1 (2008).

93  For example, Igor Krupnik, *Early Inuit Studies: Themes and Transitions, 1850s–1980s* (Washington, DC: Smithsonian Institution, 2016).

94  Jodi A. Byrd, *The Transit of Empire: Indigenous Critiques of Colonialism* (Minneapolis: University of Minnesota Press, 2011), xxxix.

95  Jennifer Baughman and Ronnie Davis, "Explorers Club Gala 2017," *Great Performances Blog*, April 20, 2017, http://www.greatperformances.com/blog/explorers-club-gala.

## Bibliography

Adams, Cecil. "Prehistoric Meat Up." *Washington City Paper*, September 12, 2007.

Anderson, Virginia DeJohn. *Creatures of Empire: How Domestic Animals Transformed Early America*. New York: Oxford University Press, 2006.

Baldwin, Andrew, Laura Cameron, and Audrey Kobayashi, eds. *Rethinking the Great White North: Race, Nature, and the Historical Geographies of Whiteness in Canada*. Vancouver: UBC Press, 2011.

Baughman, Jennifer, and Ronnie Davis. "Explorers Club Gala 2017." *Great Performances Blog*, April 20, 2017. http://www.greatperformances.com/blog/explorers-club-gala.

Birdseye, Clarence. "The Birth of an Industry." *The Beaver*, September 1941, 24–25.

Black, Jennifer M. "Corporate Calling Cards: Advertising Trade Cards and Logos in the United States, 1876–1890." *Journal of American Culture* 32, no. 4 (2009): 291–306.

Bocking, Stephen. "Indigenous Knowledge and the History of Science, Race, and Colonial Authority." In *Rethinking the Great White North: Race, Nature, and the Historical Geographies of Whiteness in Canada*, edited by Andrew Baldwin, Laura Cameron, and Audrey Kobayashi, 39. Vancouver: UBC Press, 2011.

Bruce, Miner W. *Alaska: Its History and Resources, Gold Fields, Routes and Scenery*. New York: G. P. Putnam's Sons, 1899.

Bruce, Scott, and Bill Crawford. *Cerealizing America: The Unsweetened Story of American Breakfast Cereal*. Boston: Faber and Faber, 1995.

Byrd, Jodi A. *The Transit of Empire: Indigenous Critiques of Colonialism*. Minneapolis: University of Minnesota Press, 2011.

Callison, Candis. *How Climate Change Comes to Matter: The Communal Life of Facts*. Durham, NC: Duke University Press, 2014.

Cantwell, John C. "Alaska and the Reindeer." *The Californian* 3 (1893): 259–72.

Cuomo, Chris, Wendy Eisner, and Kenneth Hinkel. "Environmental Change, Indigenous Knowledge, and Subsistence on Alaska's North Slope." *Scholar and Feminist Online* 7, no. 1 (2008).

Czerkas, S. M., and D. F. Glut. *Dinosaurs, Mammoths, and Cavemen: The Art of Charles R. Knight*. New York: E. P. Dutton, 1982.

Demuth, Bathsheba. "More Things on Heaven and Earth: Modernism and Reindeer in Chukotka and Alaska." In *Northscapes: History, Technology, and the Making of Northern Environments*, edited by Dolly Jørgensen and Sverker Sörlin, 174–94. Vancouver: UBC Press, 2013.

Dewbury, Adam. "The American School and Scientific Racism in Early American Anthropology." *Histories of Anthropology Annual* 3, no. 1 (2007): 121–47.

Dickinson, Roy. "When McConnachie Helps." *Printer's Ink Monthly* 5, no. 5 (1922): 24–26.

Diubaldo, Richard. *Stefansson and the Canadian Arctic*. Montreal: McGill-Queen's University Press, 1999.

Explorers Club. "About the Club." https://explorers.org/about/about_the_club. Accessed December 29, 2017.

Fienup-Riordan, Ann. "Preface: Eskimo Orientalism." In *Freeze Frame: Alaska Eskimos in the Movies*. Seattle: University of Washington Press, 1995.

Fitzhugh, Lynne D. *The Labradorians: Voices from the Land of Cain*. Guilford, CT: Breakwater, 1999.

Gavroglu, Kostas. *History of Artificial Cold, Scientific, Technological and Cultural Issues*. Dordrecht: Springer, 2014.

Georgeson, C. C. "The Possibilities of Alaska." *National Geographic* 13, no. 3 (1902): 81–85.

Glass, Jessica R., Matt Davis, Timothy J. Walsh, Eric J. Sargis, and Adalgisa Caccone. "Was Frozen Mammoth or Giant Ground Sloth Served for Dinner at The Explorers Club?" *PLoS One* 11, no. 2 (2016): e0146825. doi:10.1371/journal.pone.0146825.

Grosvenor, Gilbert Hovey. "Reindeer in Alaska." *National Geographic* 14, no. 4 (1903): 127–49.

Hadwen, Isaac, Andre Seymour, and Lawrence J. Palmer. *Reindeer in Alaska.* Washington, DC: US Government Printing Office, 1922.

Hale, Margaret E. "The Nineteenth-Century American Trade Card." *Business History Review* 74, no. 4 (2000): 683–88. doi:10.2307/3116471.

Haycox, Stephen W. "'Races of a Questionable Ethnical Type': Origins of the Jurisdiction of the US Bureau of Education in Alaska, 1867–1885." *Pacific Northwest Quarterly* 75, no. 4 (1984): 156–63.

Haycox, Stephen W. "Sheldon Jackson in Historical Perspective: Alaska Native Schools and Mission Contracts, 1885–1894." *Pacific Historian* 28, no. 1 (1982): 18–28.

Hobart, Hi'ilei Julia. "Mammoth and Other Frozen Meats." *Harvard Design Magazine* 43 (2016).

Huhndorf, Shari M. "Colonizing Alaska: Race, Nation, and the Remaking of Native America." In *Mapping the Americas*, edited by Shari M. Huhndorf, 25–70. Ithaca, NY: Cornell University Press, 2009.

Huhndorf, Shari M. *Mapping the Americas: The Transnational Politics of Contemporary Native Culture.* Ithaca, NY: Cornell University Press, 2009.

Huhndorf, Shari M. "Nanook and His Contemporaries: Imagining Eskimos in American Culture, 1897–1922." *Critical Inquiry* 27, no. 1 (2000): 122–48. doi:10.1086/449001.

Ickeringill, Nan. "Food News: 30 Years of Freezing." *New York Times*, March 7, 1960.

Jackson, Sheldon. *Annual Report on Introduction of Domestic Reindeer into Alaska*, vol. 14. Washington, DC: US Government Printing Office, 1905.

Jackson, Sheldon. *Introduction of Domestic Reindeer into Alaska.* Washington, DC: US Government Printing Office, 1896.

Jackson, Sheldon. *Report on Education in Alaska.* Washington, DC: US Government Printing Office, 1896.

Jay, Robert. *The Trade Card in Nineteenth-Century America.* Columbia: University of Missouri Press, 1987.

Jones, Preston. *Empire's Edge: American Society in Nome, Alaska, 1898–1934.* Fairbanks: University of Alaska Press, 2007.

Krupnik, Igor. *Early Inuit Studies: Themes and Transitions, 1850s–1980s.* Washington, DC: Smithsonian Institution, 2016.

Kurlansky, Mark. *Birdseye: The Adventures of a Curious Man.* New York: Doubleday, 2012.

93

Landecker, Hannah. *Culturing Life: How Cells Became Technologies*. Cambridge, MA: Harvard University Press, 2007.

Lane, Franklin K. "The Nation's Undeveloped Resources." *National Geographic* 25, no. 2 (1914): 183–228.

Lantis, Margaret. "The Reindeer Industry in Alaska." *Arctic* 3, no. 1 (1950): 27–44.

Lomen, Carl J. *Fifty Years in Alaska*. New York: D. McKay, 1954.

Nichols, Henry B. "Mammoth Appetites Explore a . . . Mammoth." *Christian Science Monitor* January 17, 1951, 3.

Nott, Josiah Clark, and George R. Gliddon. *Types of Mankind: Or, Ethnological Researches, Based upon the Ancient Monuments, Paintings, Sculptures, and Crania of Races, and upon Their Natural, Geographical, Philological, and Biblical History*. Philadelphia: Lippincott, Grambo, 1854.

Nyland, Kelsey E., Anna E. Klene, Jerry Brown, Nikolay I. Shiklomanov, Frederick E. Nelson, Dmitry A. Streletskiy, and Kenji Yoshikawa. "Traditional Iñupiat Ice Cellars (SIĠLUAQ) in Barrow, Alaska: Characteristics, Temperature Monitoring, and Distribution." *Geographical Review* 107, no. 1 (2017): 143–58.

Osborn, Henry Fairfield, W. K. Gregory, and George Pinkley. *The Hall of the Age of Man*. New York: American Museum of Natural History, 1925.

Radin, Joanna. *Life on Ice: A History of New Uses for Cold Blood*. Chicago: University of Chicago Press, 2017.

Radin, Joanna, and Emma Kowal, eds. *Cryopolitics: Frozen Life in a Melting World*. Cambridge, MA: MIT Press, 2017.

Rees, Jonathan. *Refrigeration Nation: A History of Ice, Appliances, and Enterprise in America*. Baltimore: Johns Hopkins University Press, 2013.

Regal, Brian. *Henry Fairfield Osborn: Race and the Search for the Origins of Man*. Aldershot, UK: Ashgate, 2002.

"The Russian Treaty." *Harper's Weekly*, April 13, 1867, 226.

Schulten, Susan. "The Making of the *National Geographic*: Science, Culture, and Expansionism." *American Studies* 41, no. 1 (2000): 5–29.

Shortridge, James R. "The Collapse of Frontier Farming in Alaska." *Annals of the Association of American Geographers* 66, no. 4 (1976): 583–604.

Sommer, Marianne. *History Within: The Science, Culture, and Politics of Bones, Organisms, and Molecules*. Chicago: University of Chicago Press, 2016.

Stefansson, Vilhjalmur. *The Northward Course of Empire*. New York: Harcourt, Brace, 1922.

Strong, Pauline Turner. *American Indians and the American Imaginary: Cultural Representation across the Centuries*. Boulder, CO: Paradigm, 2013.

Stuhl, Andrew. "The Experimental State of Nature: Science and the Canadian Reindeer Project in the Interwar North." In *Ice Blink: Navigating Northern Environmental History*, edited by Brad Martin and Stephen Bocking, 63–102. Calgary: University of Calgary Press, 2017.

Stuhl, Andrew. *Unfreezing the Arctic: Science, Colonialism, and the Transformation of Inuit Lands*. Chicago: University of Chicago Press, 2016.

Tompkins, Kyla Wazana. *Racial Indigestion: Eating Bodies in the 19th Century*. New York: NYU Press, 2012.

Wheelersburg, Robert P. "*National Geographic* Magazine and the Eskimo Stereotype: A Photographic Analysis, 1949–1990." *Polar Geography* 40, no. 1 (2017): 35–58. doi:10.1080/1088937X.2016.1257659.

Williams, E. W. *Frozen Foods: Biography of an Industry*. Boston: Cahners, 1970.

Willis, Roxanne. "A New Game in the North: Alaska Native Reindeer Herding, 1890–1940." *Western Historical Quarterly* 37, no. 3 (2006): 277–301.

Wilson, Charles Morrow. "The Electric Age in Food." *Popular Mechanics*, June 1937.

Woods, Rebecca J. H. "From Colonial Animal to Imperial Edible: Building an Empire of Sheep in New Zealand, ca. 1880–1900." *Comparative Studies of South Asia, Africa and the Middle East* 35, no. 1 (2015): 117–36.

Woods, Rebecca J. H. "Nature and the Refrigerating Machine: The Politics and Production of Cold in the Nineteenth Century." In *Cryopolitics: Frozen Life in a Melting World*, edited by Joanna Radin and Emma Kowal, 89–116. Cambridge, MA: MIT Press, 2017.

"Woolly Mammoth Given State Honor." *Daily Sitka Sentinel*, April 28, 1986, 8.

Zimmerly, David William. *Cain's Land Revisited*. St. John's, NL: Institute of Social and Economic Research, 1975.

# Beefing Yoga

## MEAT, CORPOREALITY, AND POLITICS

TO THINK WITH MEAT involves invoking corporeal politics on many levels: the politics of disgust, decay, death, life, appetite, and frenzy, and multiple sensory entanglements, as well as the politics of sight, smell, sound (maybe the silence of death, or the sizzle of meat over hot coals), and touch. Working with meat's myriad corporeal frames and affects, I would like to draw our attention to two kinds of politics: beef bans in India and the seemingly disparate politics of yoga. The first signals Hindu nationalism, which pits Hindus against Muslims, with widespread violence against Muslims. The second invokes well-being, harmony, and a unity of mind, body, and people. So think with me of frenzied cow protection groups driving Muslim families out of villages and towns in India, men patrolling the borders of villages and towns in India to make sure that no one consumes beef or slaughters cows, and a renewed sense of masculine responsibility to protect the motherland against contamination and impurity. Now think of a different scenario. Imagine a scene of men and women in white stretching their bodies, breathing in and out—a reinvigorated feeling of embodiment alongside evolving vistas of corporeal connections with bodies around them. The yoga-practicing body is about corporeal extension, making sure muscles, arms, limbs, chest, and stomach are unified with breath and sensation. In addition, the unceasing spread of yoga through the world marks its transnational corporeal outreach. Placing beef bans in India and the highly visible spread of yoga in the same frame means recognizing the curious amalgamation of the national and transnational, violence and peace, and the craft of politics, which brings together food, health rituals, patriotism, nostalgia, trade, foreign policy, and myriad other interactors into play with each other to create citizen-subjects. Discerning stratagem and the craft of politics through meat's body politics is thus a central endeavor.

This essay endeavors to work through the messy politics of meat through two recent corporeal overtures: the beef bans in different parts of India and the emphasis by the Indian government on yoga as foreign policy. Both stances have various intricacies, and there are long histories that predate their contemporary manifestations. However, what insights might we generate by reading these two phenomena as entangled, intertwined complexities? Understandably, there is no dearth of investigations into yoga or the genealogy of food histories in India. However, maybe there is a need to read histories and events concomitantly, as interactive body politics or insidious "trans-corporeality," as coined by Stacy Alaimo, to understand not only how we are all globally interdependent, but also how this interaction is a condition of state rule and governability. While recent conversations on corporeality and the porous nature of bodies and beings hinge on underscoring shared vulnerabilities in the Anthropocene and/or under neoliberal political economies, I interrogate another dimension to this politics. What about trans-corporeality as explicit political manipulation, fabricated and actively framed to make us breathe in and out in unison? In the context of India, how does thinking about the "cow as mother" and violent cow protection vigilance muddy our understanding of interactive corporeality?

Situating meat at the heart of government politics, I move through this essay wondering at curious (and oftentimes very violent) trajectories of events that make us think anew about our frames of analysis. I grapple with European and Indian texts on body politics, selected texts that help us imagine politics. In addition, while I stress maneuvers by governments and stratagems behind policy measures, I am reminded incessantly of the incalculable and uncontrollable, unlikely offshoots. Think for instance of a cow that eats meat, climbs stairs, and perhaps, could do yoga. However, before moving toward this incalculable cow, I would like us to think about politics within its corporeal framing.

Politics is entangled within a curious body-maze. While somatophobia underlines many aspects of politics because of the emphasis on reason and a disembodied mind, a human body, and particularly a male body, frames varied imaginations of politics. For instance, the references to muscles, brains, legs, and arms, coordination between body parts, and an autonomous body define much of liberalism's protocol on government and governed subjects. Liberalism's rights-based framing has a fleshy arterial enclosing that works in tandem with its contractual logic. Humans need the state to protect their private property and bodies, and humans are represented in the body of the state. Flesh and blood as connection and kinship, and blood as a symbol of sacrifice and patriotism are just some commonplace visual and material motifs to signify belonging to a political community and state.[1] Thus, in many ways, meat is integral to politics in imagining functioning regulations through the state. We could argue that meat as corporeal politics legitimizes governing and being governed when the state exists as a public embodiment of citizen representation and bodies residing within a political territory remain responsive to protocols of rule. Thus, following body politics as a model for governing, I interrogate the beef ban in India and India's renewed emphasis on yoga. I see these two broad policy measures as translations of body politics that can help us understand varied entanglements of politics, economics, identity, and cultural history. Boldly and adventurously, I bracket the corporeal politics of beef and yoga together as "meat" to theorize on national and transnational body politics. What do beef and yoga as meat tell us about a transnational body politic?

I frame political bodies through the prism of meat to understand their precarity, culpability, and animacy. Understanding the stratagem of politics means recognizing how bodies are acted upon and act, a negotiation of resources and power, and how certain bodies are incessantly precarious, vulnerable, and subjects to power. A recognition of culpability and responsibility is often seen as outside of discourses on precarious bodies, as if precarity functions outside of responsibility and is a monolithic vulnerability. I think it is important to add an understanding of culpability to precarity, to recognize that through an understanding of intersectionality, certain bodies are always more vulnerable than others. Mel Y. Chen's theorization of "animacy" adds to our understanding of culpability and precarity by undoing static conceptions of living and dead. By instilling the idea of bodies as complexly interactive, animacies lays the ground for understanding levels and layers of precarity and culpability. Framing politics through translations of precarity, culpability, and animacies means reckoning with the craft of politics, a creation of bodies as meat to work within the body politic. I will draw my analysis of body politics further in succeeding sections.

98

Here I emphasize its centrality in understanding the beef bans and spread of yoga as mischievous trans-corporeality, a concomitant policy measure sanctioned by the Indian government and politics, which works on bodies as meat even when ostensibly banning specific manifestations of it within the body politic.

A reckoning with mischievous trans-corporeality enables us to discern concomitant politics that are often read as separate and dissimilar. Widespread commentary from India underlines the violence in the beef bans as they are targeted against Muslims; on the other hand, yoga is often invoked as a mechanism to spread peace, whether for individual bodies or for communities. Also, while the beef bans are ostensibly about food, and yoga about health rituals, it is important to discern how our parameters of what is food and optimum health are framed on political exigencies and intertwine in intimate ways. Moreover, while the beef bans pertain to national and subnational politics, the politics of yoga delineated in this essay highlights its transnational orbit. Often read as disparate events with very different politics, my essay seeks to interrogate the overlapping politics that undergird the corporeal politics of both, and thus my essay moves through the following trajectory. I interweave my analysis of the beef bans and yoga with reference to texts like Thomas Hobbes's *Leviathan*, Machiavelli's *The Prince*, and Wendy Doniger's analysis of creation forms in ancient Indian texts, alongside other works. These reminders of the myriad traditions using the human body as the basis for politics are indispensable in situating the beef bans and of yoga in their explicit corporeal politics. An analysis of the beef bans and spread of yoga signals the overlapping contours of the national and transnational, the impetus to frame a family of purity and traditional virtues, ensconced through communal lines. While framing the stratagems and political maneuvers that frame both, I want us also to reckon with the spill-overs and unlikely effects of political actions, whereby it becomes impossible to erect a holistic frame to encase the varied translations of practices. I draw from Mahasweta Devi's "Non-Veg Cow" in the conclusion of this paper to underline the border-spilling ramifications of strategies that fail to be contained. For instance, how do we account for the multifarious health benefits of yoga to varied constituencies, even when we critique its political genealogy? In an effort to draw out complexities, the next section draws out details about the beef ban and yoga to situate their context and location.

99

## A Brief Glimpse at Yoga and the Beef Ban

Today yoga is everywhere: in India, around the world, in local yoga studios, TV, gyms, adorning Kashi cereal boxes, and also visibly present through dedicated yoga spaces within international airports such as in San Francisco and Chicago. From scalding reports in Indian newspapers about the government's intention to make yoga compulsory for all schools and colleges, to debates about secularism and apprehensions about yoga's genealogy in Hinduism, to hybrid yoga, lunchtime yoga, goat yoga, naked yoga, and all kinds of yoga . . . yoga truly is everywhere. Even as we notice its pervasive sway, and its interaction with forms of identity in specific ways—for instance, the able-bodied whiteness of most yoga studios—I am confronted with a curious cultural commodity, or even just simply body postures, worked by specific bodies in myriad ways, oftentimes with health benefits, but which invokes cultural nostalgia and "Orientalism" in full force. The trouble with yoga does not begin or end with the outside consuming India pose by pose, albeit the consumption happens in different modes such as patronage of yoga gurus by white women, how Indian gurus sell yoga as a pure system of ancient body practices, and the framing of yoga as a symbol of multiculturalism. Yoga is also used as embodied feminist and queer pedagogy in conversations on sustainable health practices. Indeed, there are many aspects to the politics of yoga. Let us add to the list by seeing the usage of yoga by India as its currency to be the cultural ambassador to the rest of the world. International Yoga Day is celebrated all around the world under the auspices of the Indian government, and Indian Prime Minister Narendra Modi declared yoga the "biggest mass movement in the world" as he joined thousands of people in public demonstration of yoga poses in Chandigarh, India, on June 21, 2016.[2]

BBC News announced that "650 of India's 676 districts participat[ed]" and "35,000 officials, soldiers and students attend[ed] the main event on Rajpath in Delhi, including PM Narendra Modi."[3] A sea of people in white clothes practicing yoga has become the visual reference point for the amazing popularity of this body regimen in India and abroad. As people in India and elsewhere stretch their bodies and muscles, breathe in and out, connect with themselves, and truly experience embodiment in a thoughtful manner, yoga becomes intriguing corporeal politics as a strategic political initiative and feel-good foreign policy mechanism. It is not a coincidence that Narendra Modi, during his address to the US Congress on his fourth visit to the United States, referred to yoga three times, democracy seven

SUSHMITA CHATTERJEE

times, and equality twice.[4] Not that word frequency gauges parameters of importance, but the absence or presence of words does delineate at least a resonance. When addressing the US Congress, Modi says, "our links overcame history's hesitations."[5] And one such link is yoga.

Alongside the spread and popularity of yoga, we read and hear about beef bans in different parts of India. Maharashtra and Haryana were the first two states in India to ban the slaughter of cows. Cow slaughter laws were extended to bulls and oxen, and these were also considered offenses to be met with a prison term. These bans have spread quickly to other states in India. It is important to note, as Manil Suri points out, that these are not new laws but have been in place pending legislative enactment for twenty years.[6] The rise of the Bharatiya Janata Party (BJP), with its Hindu base, has accelerated the tempo of these bans through India, and there are only a few exceptions to the rule. Muslims are the worst hit, along with poor people and workers in slaughterhouses and leather factories. All kinds of violence have accompanied these beef bans, such as unemployment for workers from leather factories, harassment of Muslim families, Muslim people being driven out of villages, attacks against people suspected of eating beef, and other escalating forms of violence.

Cow slaughter is variously attributed to Muslims and British rule; it is seen as an alien imposition on India's pristine cultural history, notwithstanding the lack of credibility in most such stories. What it displays is a certain political framing of purity, noncontamination, and insulation of the Hindu body from the vices of eating the flesh of the cow, seen as sacrosanct mother and life-giver. Ironically, it is to be noted that India is one of the largest exporters of beef in the international market, and some states (such as Punjab) have an exemption to their beef laws with regard to the export of beef. "Beef" itself is defined in India with dangerous ambiguity, whereby the meats of cow, buffalo, bullock, and ox are all variously read as included or excluded in the ban, with varied repercussions on the people accused of animal slaughter. Overall, it is significant to note that the issue is "political," with no consistent policy historically or in contemporary times as to the meaning of beef, the root of its evil, or even a complete ban when noting that its economics trumps religious concerns when exporting it outside the Hindu nation.

Moreover, the affective politics of meat-eating has complicated meaning plays in different parts of Indian society. Parvis Ghassem-Fachandi writes with reference to central Gujarat: "In central Gujarat, the substance of meat in its production and consumption not only provides an idiom for stigmatizing the Muslim but also channels visceral and affective expression. Meat . . . both is a tempting taste and can be experienced as disgust, anxiety, and hate; in both senses, it enables stigma to become corporeal. At the same time, meat also indexes intimate questions of sexuality and renunciation, *himsa* and *ahimsa* (violence and nonviolence), sacrifice and incorporation—features of substantial importance in contemporary identity formation in Gujarat."[7]

Ghassem-Fachandi's work showcases the messy coagulation of disgust, anxiety, hate, sexuality, violence, and sacrifice in meat's corporeal logic within a specific Hindu segment of Indian society. The body politics with reference to the eating of meat involves passionate affective impulses through which the meat-eating body is starkly demarcated and sequestered from the non-meat-eating body. As forbidden appetite, dirty, immoral, and sexual, meat-eating frames the "other" and defines that which needs to be violently effaced in order to keep together a sense of self and pure community. Clearly working with a logic of borders and defined boundaries, elucidated through constant media reports of Hindu men beating and driving Muslim families out of their homes, villages, and towns if they are suspected of consuming beef or storing any part of the dead animal's body, the beef ban is about violent definition and containment of bodies.

So what does the increasing attention to yoga and the simultaneous beef ban tell us about meat as body politics within a state-defined and transnational frame? What are some insights we can gather to understand the politics of meat as it travels the world? In an attempt to work through this intriguing companionship, the emphasis on yoga and the beef ban, I turn next to certain selected formulations of body politics that help us imagine the genealogy of state and government. I use selected texts, an eclectic mix from different times and contexts, to emphasize the incessant strategy to use the body as a motif for politics and stability. Also, noting that when Dipesh Chakrabarty writes about the constructed nature of "the European intellectual tradition" as "an imaginary entity," he lucidly points out: "In unravelling the necessary entanglement of history—a disciplined and institutionally regulated form of collective memory—with the grand narratives of rights, citizenship, the nation-state, and public and private spheres, one cannot but problematize 'India' at the same time as one dismantles 'Europe.'"[8] Chakrabarty's analysis situates discourse within power hierarchies and the "entanglement of history," for example, through colonialism and postcolonialism, whereby it becomes necessary to move beyond pristine formulations of India or Europe and to think about shared genealogies of the state in India and Europe. Thus, we note that despite differences in time periods and philosophical trajectories, political theory repeatedly frames its treatises on state, governance, and resistance on the human body, which is never an inclusive paradigm, as a brief analysis of Hobbesian body politics demonstrates.

Working toward an understanding of varied entanglements between bodies, nations, and politics, I will move toward an analysis of beef and yoga as body politics—national and transnational—with the last section of my paper examining the transnational politics of meat through concepts such as trans-corporeality. Throughout the essay, I will call attention to insidious political mechanisms that work with a strange logic of selective appropriation. For instance, why is yoga spawning onto all forums for domestic and foreign policy, and not something else like curry, which is also a moving cultural idiom? What accounts for the strange companionship of these two political maneuvers, with one ostensibly linked to peace and well-being, and the other clothed explicitly with duress and violent repercussions? Is it an uncanny coincidence that a specific yoga posture is called "cow pose"? Moreover, what do we learn from the common linguistic origin of the terms *yoga* and *yoke*, used to restrict cows and oxen? If yoga implies an expansion and freeing of the body and breath, an embodied enlargement, how do we reconcile its companionship with restriction, control, and discipline—ironically, the intimate play of freedom and discipline in the embodied body practicing yoga, and the protection of cows through vigilant nationalism? Maybe an understanding of the framings of body politics would help situate the importance of these two corporeal maneuvers before we move toward their complications.

## The State and Body Politics

This section identifies and problematizes the recurring reference to body politics in political treatises. Easily recognizable theories on state and politics emphasize the contours of politics based on a healthy human body. Muscles, joints, nerves, flesh, and productive meat constitute the state and form an inextricable part of the politics of governance. Thus, fathoming the politics of yoga and the beef bans necessitates paying attention to our formulations of body politics and its frames of recognition. A perfect synchronization and balance of muscles, posture, and our breath constitute yoga's positioning. Concomitantly, the beef bans intend to keep certain bodies pure and outside sacrilegious contamination through beef-eating, as a cow is seen as holy mother and its flesh is much more than simply dead meat. In an effort to think about social policies through actual bodies and their exclusions, let us turn first to Thomas Hobbes's body politics.

Hobbes's *Leviathan* offers a graphic visualization of liberalism's body politics. Hobbes writes:

> For by art is created that great LEVIATHAN called a COMMONWEALTH, or STATE (in Latin CIVITAS), which is but an artificial man, though of greater stature and strength than the natural, for whose protection and defence it was intended; and in which *sovereignty* is an artificial soul, as giving life and motion to the whole body; the *magistrates* and other *officers* of judicature and execution, artificial *joints*; *reward* and *punishment* (by which fastened to the seat of the sovereignty every joint and member is moved to perform his duty) are the *nerves*, that do the same in the body natural; the *wealth* and *riches* of all the particular members are the *strength*; *salus populi* (the people's safety) its *business*.[9]

Hobbes's body politics defines the needs of English political society after the Puritan revolution and establishment of the Republic. Hobbes draws out why subjects need rule and the state by framing a somatic technology for state rule. The subjects and functionaries of the state all perform indispensable roles, as described by the quote above. For example, the magistrates form the artificial joints, and the wealth of its subjects is the strength of the body. The Hobbesian body politics also describes the contract between the ruler and the subjects. Encrypted within the body of the ruler, the bodies and wealth of the subjects are protected and vice versa. The body for politics works with a reciprocal logic of obedience bartered for protection. This imagination also draws out a firm border for the state as body, as natural community, and as cohesive fraternity, or "fratriarchy," as coined by Jacques Derrida.[10]

Moira Gatens, in "Corporeal Representation in/and the Body Politic," draws our attention to Hobbes's artificial man created by natural man to free himself from nature and women.[11] As Gatens points out, the masculine Leviathan, composed of all the many men, "incorporates" and "regulates" women's bodies as women are invisible in this visual trope.[12] In addition, the fabric of unity permits the disavowal of differences. As Gatens writes, "The metaphor functions to restrict our political vocabulary to one voice only: a voice that can speak of only one body, one reason, and one ethic."[13] Gatens's thought-provoking essay delineates the exclusions to a conceptualization of politics through the frame of "a" body that marginalizes, excludes, and renders invisible the voices of dissonance and dissidence.

Here it is important to state that Hobbes's project is just one example of a long and varied trajectory in political thought to legitimize governing, governability, homogeneous communities, and the state with reference to the prototypical human body. For example, in the *Politics*, while arguing for the "natural" status of the city-state, Aristotle writes about how the "whole is necessarily prior to the part. For if the whole body is dead, there will no longer be a foot or a hand, except homonymously, as one might speak of a stone 'hand' (for a dead hand will be like that); but everything is defined by its TASK and by its capacity."[14] There are obvious differences between Hobbes's and Aristotle's body politics, starkly demarcated by differences in space and time, but rather than delve into the specificities of the individual projects, here I would like to emphasize the centrality of the body in political imagination as criterion for inclusion and exclusion. Singularity, unity, wholeness, harmony, synchronization, and control define the body recognized by politics, excluding different genders, races, nationalities, and disabilities. I have started this essay with broad strokes and selective examples to signify the recurring motif of body politics, as well as to emphasize the logic of exclusion. Thus, exclusions, eradications, and avoidances, rather than inclusion, formulate the body logic in defining the city-state, Leviathan, or statecraft.

In a similar vein, another widely recognizable treatise on politics and the craft of government, Machiavelli's *The Prince*, describes how the ruler should maintain his political rule by treating symptoms immediately. As Machiavelli writes, "In the beginning the disease is easy to cure, difficult to diagnose; but, after a while, if it has not been diagnosed and treated early, it becomes easy to diagnose and hard to cure."[15] Many forms of yoga follow a similar logic in being advertised as bodily practices that enable disease prevention and strengthening of the body. It is no coincidence that able nationalism safeguards the body politics and protects it from "diseases," whether seen as invasions, seditions, uprisings, death, or decay. The human body in Hobbes's, Aristotle's, and Machiavelli's works helps craft politics and maintain rule and stability.

Describing creation forms in Hindu mythology, Wendy Doniger draws our attention to the body of man: "The primeval Man is not changed into the various forms of life: rather, he is those forms, always."[16] Describing man or *purusa* from the *Rig Veda*, Doniger describes how he has many eyes, heads, and feet: "All creatures make up a quarter of him; three quarters are the immortal in heaven."[17] The descriptions frame the coming into being of bodies out of chaos, a unified corporeality that can work in cohesion. Mortal and immortal bodies coalesce, and man and the universe are woven through a cosmic cycle of unity out of fragmentation. Thus, through different traditions of thought—*Rig Veda*, Greek history, Italian Renaissance, Puritan revolution, and others—the human body as a stubborn leitmotif for politics weaves it way through varied ideological trajectories, despite many differences in the hierarchy of elements making up the body, its ends, or even its purpose. Thinking with Donna Haraway, "It matters what matters we use to think other matters with; it matters what stories we tell to tell other stories with; it matters what knots knot knots, what thoughts think thoughts, what descriptions describe descriptions, what ties tie ties."[18] Working with the body as something that provides a prism to politics, defines its inclusions and exclusions, its somatic technology, its biopower in terms of security regimes, that which "ties tie ties," moves us to understand that the body is politics, and politics is a body. For example, the body is politics, as efficiently summed up in the radical feminist proclamation that the "personal is political"; and politics is a body in terms of citizenship rights, entitlements of speaking a common language, or the many appeals to "belonging." The territorial definitiveness of being a body with/in politics seems to proclaim nations and nationalisms as of common blood, kinship groups, and/or language groups. What about transnationalism and the messy entanglements through different bodies? How do we work toward uncovering a transnational body politic and understanding the "knots which knot knots" in an intensely interconnected world of strictly defined and shifting borders?

Appeals to politics that affirm differences and democracy often posit heterogeneous movements and the "multitude" as an antithesis to the unitary composition of the Leviathan. Michael Hardt and Antonio Negri describe the "multitude" as "an open, inclusive concept" that recognizes changes in the global economy.[19] Responding to shifts in trade and labor movements, the "multitude" to Hardt and Negri is very different from "the people," with connotations of a unitary and singular identity.[20] The multitude does have a "common," which allows communication, an idea that Hardt and Negri further develop in the last book of their trilogy, *Commonwealth*. They write, "This biopolitical production and its expansion of the common is one strong pillar on which stands the possibility of global democracy today."[21] Therefore, one can discern how unitariness and heterogeneity are in constant play when thinking about global economics and politics. Contrary to the *Leviathan*, the multitude works with heterogeneous differences and through spiraling labor networks. However, in common action and communications lies the possibility for democracy. Indeed, a creative "assemblage" infuses global and transnational thinking in our contemporary moment. Indistinct togetherness often defines subversive activism, and biopolitical productions waltz with/in geopower to create possibilities for labor, bodies, health regimes, thought, and activism.

Here I would like to apply such thinking to overall imaginations of unity and coherence depicted through imaginary frames of the human body. The body cements politics through an imaginative "meat," which, through perfect synchronization within itself, is able to ensure stability and life. Muscles, veins, head, and feet are all aspects of our political corporeal imagination. A body composed of meat, and of functioning or productive meat, is given the recognition of life and it/they become political actors. Of course, the qualifier of "productive" is framed within dominant normative discourses. Those without recognition as productive citizens, or simply as "meat," remain outside a state-informed body politics without concomitant rights and representation. Even when laboring within the state, for example, as workers in slaughterhouses, bodies as meat remain residual and outside frames of representation. As Judith Butler points out in *Frames of War*, "to be a body is to be exposed to social crafting and form, and that is what makes the ontology of the body a social ontology."[22] Therefore, the way meat is framed determines its social ontology. This manner of looking at meat as already omnipresent in all matters of state and government, but with varying degrees of recognition, representation, and legitimacy, would continue and differ from the arguments of many who write about meat in juxtaposition to life and living. For instance, Carol Adams, in *The Sexual Politics of Meat*, writes, "Animals' lives precede and enable the existence of meat. If animals are alive they cannot be meat."[23] I argue instead that government and discipline presuppose meat, and differences in what Butler calls "social ontology" determine the status of the meat and its political prowess. Therefore, by framing the conversation on meat through the politics of governmentality, I want us to think of dead and alive as frames posited through state-based politics of recognition and representation. Certain bodies are never socially alive, and others never dead in their seething presence through all social policies and practices.

Moreover, my thinking on meat is inspired by recent conversations on entangled matter, intertwined futures, and the impossibility of keeping conversations and materialisms separate and distinct.[24] Writing on "trans-corporeality" under "exposed" conditions, Stacy Alaimo describes it as "a new materialist and posthumanist sense of the human as perpetually interconnected with the flows of substances and the agencies of environments."[25] Graphically describing "shell on acid" and naked environmental protests, Alaimo develops a vibrant analysis of various constitutions—human, marine, plants, habitats—producing "incommensurable grids of vulnerability" with "no position outside."[26]

Working with trans-corporeality through realms of environmentalism, activism, and political imagination, Alaimo delivers an interesting addition to conversations on corporeal politics and governments. In some ways, Hobbes's *Leviathan*, with the many bodies forming sovereignty and the basis for government, bodies interacting and interdependent, could be read as an early visualization of a perverse political trans-corporeality. Without undermining the importance of working with trans-corporeality as the basis for thinking anew the Anthropocene and climate change, I wonder about how we can write about hierarchies of trans-corporeality whereby some bodies are affected more quickly than others, some penetrations are pleasure and protest, while others could be assault and colonialism, all the while keeping in mind that indeed there is "no position outside." Thinking about meat through the discourse on trans-corporeality renders it porous and shifting, in constant mutation, and within shifting grounds. How does an understanding of trans-corporeality change or shift our thinking of state and governments? How do we visualize the movement from corporeal politics to trans-corporeal politics in our understanding of nations and transnationalism, keeping in mind labor migrations, refugees, and shifting borders?

To answer these overly ambitious questions, let us turn back to the beef bans in India and the increasing emphasis on yoga as part of India's diplomatic overtures to the rest of the world. Both these issues have a national and transnational context. The beef ban is currently at work in most parts of India, with very few exceptions.[27] All of northern India is covered by the prohibition of cow slaughter, and punishment can extend up to ten years of imprisonment. The laws are spelled out in detail, but with considerable variance between states. For example, in Uttar Pradesh it is illegal to store or transport beef except within closed containers, which are reserved for consumption by foreigners only. Haryana, on the other hand, prohibits any kind of storage or sale of beef products, even in canned form. It also has laws against the killing of disabled or diseased cows. The bans have led to widespread violence against Dalits, poor people, and Muslims, where even the faintest shadow of suspicion leads to assault, murder, a public demonstration of the culprits being made to drink cow urine and dung, and various other atrocities. A new cadre of *gau rakshaks* (cow protectors) are constantly vigilant to protect cows, and as Snigdha Poonam writes, they are "in holy war against everyone whose culture approves the killing of the blessed bovine—Muslims, Christians, Hindu outcastes."[28] No wonder, an editorial column in *The Times of India* titled "Trumpji ka birthday" questions whether the Hindu Sena were missing the "real beef about Trump" while celebrating his birthday with gusto in Delhi: "where's the beef burger?"[29] In other words, why was an organization that supports cow protection celebrating Trump and his frequently noted affection for burgers and steak?

Concomitantly, there is another widespread movement in Indian society: pressures to make yoga compulsory in schools and colleges, the widespread acknowledgment of the uses of yoga as a pristine cultural asset to fight many ills of modernity such as obesity and illnesses, and the use of yoga as diplomacy and power leverage in foreign policy. It would be an error to claim that yoga has existed separate from state-bound politics in India, with a rudimentary example being Indian postage stamps with yoga postures—a markedly state-sanctioned stamp on yoga. Sarah Strauss writes about postage stamps honoring Vivekananda and Sivananda, as well as expensive stamps depicting hatha yoga issued for the global market in the 1990s.[30] Recently, the emphasis on yoga has accelerated tremendously. The Narendra Modi government has established a yoga ministry, and schools and colleges throughout the country have been strongly encouraged to add yoga to their curriculum.[31] Celebrated and owned as a cultural asset to fight the stresses and maladies of modernity and the West, yoga is increasingly used by the Indian government as "soft power," or "the ability to get what you want through attraction rather than coercion or payments."[32] Whether eating dinner with US President Barack Obama or speaking to reporters in Australia, the use of yoga as diplomacy and political bridge has been incessantly signaled by Narendra Modi.[33]

What kind of transnational body politics do these two postures constitute? How do they intertwine to compose transnational trans-corporeality?

### Beef and Yoga as Body Politics: National and Transnational

Thinking about beef as body politics has many co-complicating frames. Carol Adams would say, for instance, that beef per se is the "dead" meat of a cow. However, its meaning and its alive/dead designation changes as we move through space, belief systems, and cultural sciences. Not all spaces look at beef as "dead" meat. In fact, the cow as mother in Hindu nationalist politics can never really be dead or mortally alive; it exists as the repository of pure consciousness for pristine nationalism, morality, and masculinity. A cow in Hindu nationalist politics is certainly "more than human" in a very literal way. Any injury to the cow is seen as an injury to aggressive Hindu masculinity, constituting what Parama Roy calls "gastroaesthetics," where ethics and its translational style coagulate in a "philosophy of bodily administration."[34] Roy's analysis refers to Gandhi's vegetarianism, the politics of ahimsa, celibacy, and issues connected to self-representation, leadership style, and other matters, and highlights the connections between these seemingly disparate issues. Moreover, the politics of gastroaesthetics provides a valuable prism to visualize Haryana's militia of gau rakshaks, where consuming cow's milk becomes the measure of one's commitment to the cause. Snigdha Poonam describes the routine of belonging to a gau rakshak clan: "Wake up at 4, wash your clothes, join the prayers, lift weights in the gym, eat pure vegetarian food and drink milk."[35] In other words, the gau rakshak mode of aggressive, stylized masculinity works with proactive body administration as seen in exercise regimes, milk consumption, and vegetarianism. Eating beef in this context is akin to consuming one's mother, as seen in the milk-drinking son's violent vigilance about cow slaughter.

Roy's gastroaesthetics frames an important aspect of individual corporeal surveillance with its associated values of purity, sanctity, and the abhorrence of alterity. Ghassem-Fachandi's use of the phrase *visceral nationalism* picks up on this affective politics of corporeality, where the sight of meat inspires immediate gut-level repugnance, disgust, and horror toward those who consume meat, slaughter animals, or even store meat in their homes.[36] Thus, one can state that the body politics associated with the beef bans is one of extreme affective individualism, felt in somatic reactions and in personal body training. This individualism works with strict boundaries and border control regarding keeping people either inside its realm of purity or outside it. The individualism is also aggressively expansive, with the modus operandi of killing people who are different, and/or castigating them as unclean and impure because they eat beef. Thus, this nationalistic individualism extends into "communities of belonging," as seen in cow protection armies, state-level bans implemented by political parties, and the threading of these bans through Hindu-majority states all over India. Ironically, this aggressive, national corporeal politics of beef has arisen alongside the notion of vegetarianism as a global signifier of ahimsa (nonviolence); as

Ghassem-Fachandi writes, "the doctrine of ahimsa and the figure of Gandhi have become the most successful spiritual exports out of India into the global marketplace of ideas."[37] Linking Hindus through a diasporic global family, public vegetarianism situates a corporeality ostensibly based on food choice saturated with ideas of morality, religion, and righteousness.

The public nature of these issues, beef ban and the spread of yoga, is an important and interesting detail to note. Writing about yoga in modern India, Joseph Alter points out, "Yoga, a profoundly antisocial form of self-discipline . . . occupies an important place, and defines an explicitly public space, in the modern world of medicine, self-help therapy, and public health."[38] Thousands of bodies practicing yoga is a recurrent visual image seen throughout the world on International Yoga Day. But there are many other public displays of these body practices. Chandrima Chakraborty writes about Swami Ramdev's popularity in India and abroad, through televised public yoga lessons screened daily.[39] The public nature of these body practices establishes what Chakraborty terms "an imagined, somatic community."[40] Thinking with the gist of the term *yoga* as "union," one discerns a curious unity through individual body reflexes and strengthening, as well as the fabrication of communities of yoga practitioners as very visible public performance.[41] Group yoga and partnered yoga bring with them a different conception of unity and somatic consciousness; however, the public nature of these practices remains an interesting interjection toward comprehending yoga's corporeal politics.

Yoga has very often been positioned as a cure for the effects of Western modernity, whether by Vivekananda or Ramdev. Vivekananda's presentation of yoga to the Western world in 1893 in Chicago is considered a landmark in the spread and marketing of yoga to the Western world.[42] To repeat an often-quoted statement from Vivekananda, "You will be nearer to God through football than through the *Bhagwad Gita*," reflects the emphasis on bodybuilding and reclaiming masculinity.[43] Oftentimes, celibacy accompanies the emphasis on yoga. Ramdev, for instance, maintains a strictly vegetarian diet and publicly declares that he has never had sexual affairs.[44] The non-meat-eating male body who practices yoga becomes the symbol of health, spiritual prosperity, and the epitome of true Indianness. How is it that the bodily practice of yoga, originally intended to serve as a cure for Western modernity, has gathered such presence in the West? Why does the West eagerly consume a product that should serve to cure it from itself? 111 Ironies proliferate when thinking about the beef ban and yoga propaganda. As transnational mechanisms, both policy initiatives work within multiple tensions of purity and contamination, self-discipline and sociality, and self and other. The corporeality of the beef ban and yoga practices extend from body to body, creating intimate communities of connection, often of violence. It is impossible to restrict these two practices to individual bodies or even to simply attribute to them a bordered corporeality; rather, like waves in motion, bodies intermingle to create further widening of these practices—an incessant spread.

## The Transnational Politics of Meat

Stacy Alaimo draws her conception of trans-corporeality separate from Gail Weiss's "intercorporeality" when she writes, "My term 'trans-corporeality' suggests that humans are interconnected not only with one another but also with the material interchanges between body, substance, and place."[45] In *Exposed*, Alaimo invites us to think "disanthropocentrically" by submerging our thinking in the dense entanglements of co-constitution and intertwined futures between and through bodies and different materialisms.[46] Thinking with interactive materialisms, trans-corporeality emphasizes the connections between flesh and place, "dissolving shells," plastic pollution, and the "sheer exuberance of more-than-human sexualities and genders."[47] Alaimo's emphasis on trans-corporeality carries resonance for this project in its attempt to connect seemingly disparate practices and intentions. Fitness instructors, yoga mats, specific spaces, cow protection armies, and other seemingly related and unrelated objects coalesce through their intentional use by governments and other bodies. Bodies in unison, whether we are thinking about the thousands of people on yoga mats, or the frenzied crowd singling out Muslim locales and families for their consumption of beef, trans-corporeality rings a macabre note when viewed through a transnational prism.

In an uncanny rearticulation of liberalism's body politics, Ramdev describes "Mother India" in the follow way: "The head is the Himalayas, the hands are Rajasthan and Bengal, the legs are Kanyakumari."[48] Mother India is certainly not a feminized Leviathan; rather, as goddess and extra-human, the mother's body needs to be protected by defining its territory and clearly delineating borders. Besides being a mapping of pristine nationalism, this description also underwrites a corporeality born of many bodies and regions, communities that can move together; Mother India is geopolitics imagined in a complete symphony. The feminized motherland and masculine body politic are a curious amalgam in portraying nationalism's sleight

112

of hand whereby women need to be protected as material signifiers of community honor, but the masculine body politic overwrites masculine corporeal conditions in all aspects of statecraft. Corporeality frames nationalisms and their imaginings through invocations of the motherland and the masculine duty to protect her from external assaults. However, while corporeal body politics has firm territorial framings, an emphasis on the trans-corporeal highlights intimate entanglements and the impossibility of perfect containment.

Reckoning with Alaimo's concept of trans-corporeality and its important messages, I would like to travel with it in reference to manipulated corporeal and trans-corporeal bodies and politics. Her conception of trans-corporeality understands common vulnerability and connections, noting significantly, "the human is always the very stuff of the messy, contingent, emergent mix of the material world."[49] Alaimo's analysis of toxic bodies serves as an excellent example of the unpredictable nature of material conglomerations under contemporary capitalism, where human bodies are rendered toxic with high concentrations of harmful chemicals.[50] Further, by discussing environmental racism—"the pancreas under capitalism," "the proletarian lung"—Alaimo draws out the "trans-corporeal networks causing harm."[51] The analysis emphasizes economic inequality and its ramifications on material bodies. Pushing this analysis through the terrain of politics, I ask: What about contrived, projected trans-corporeality used to further cement unequal power relations and hierarchies? How is trans-corporeality being used by governments and in foreign policy to create more borders for certain people? While we are all messily co-constituted, why are some people affected more than others are by increasingly blurred boundaries? I remain troubled by these questions in an attempt to work through the entangled politics of beef and yoga. Understanding the simultaneous impulse to contain bodies and maintain borders, as seen in the beef ban and communalism, alongside the emphasis on spreading corporeal practices across borders, as illustrated by yoga, gets to the heart of the tension of transnationalism in our contemporary times. Invoking trans-corporeality with transnationalism helps us discern the manifold political cartographies of changeable bodies and borders.

This essay has been an endeavor to bring an analysis of yoga alongside the recent beef bans in India to point out the strategic political calculations that underwrite both maneuvers. The beef bans and the urgent framing of yoga as a remedy for modernity's evil repercussions signal toward pure bodies, flexible bodies, virile masculinity, and uncontaminated geopolitics.

113

Understanding the "trans" in transnationalism—as described by Aihwa Ong as "moving through space or across lines, as well as changing the nature of something"—I have highlighted the stratagems behind evolving "communities of belonging" based on the beef ban and yoga-practicing bodies.[52] To describe the present historical moment, Ong emphasizes "flexible citizenship," which tells us that under conditions of late capitalism and globalization, "individuals as well as governments develop a flexible notion of citizenship and sovereignty as strategies to accumulate capital and power."[53] Flexibility, repositioning, and relocations signal political economy's and subjects' endeavors to profit maximally under it. The changing natures of family, identity, and self are an immediate corollary. The fluid body that can practice yoga, the expansion of breath and depth, the loosening of the body through disciplined practices, herald this age of flexible citizenship. Cow protection armies, Hindu youth drinking milk and vowing to defend the body politic of Mother India from the sacrilegious contamination of India's beef-eating populace signify the flexing of citizenship norms under duress and scripted within motions of violence. These trans-corporeal and transnational political overtures work with predictability and calculation, as well as unpredictability, emotional fervor, and incalculable effects and lines of spread and seepage. Let us turn finally to a yogic cow to decipher the need to grapple with baffling exigencies of moments and the movements beyond frames of knowledge-making.

I conclude by invoking Mahasweta Devi's "Non-Veg Cow," not with the aim of offering a solution, but taking seriously Donna Haraway's injunction to "stay with the trouble." Haraway writes, "staying with the trouble requires learning to be truly present, not as a vanishing pivot between awful or edenic pasts and apocalyptic or salvific futures, but as mortal critters entwined in myriad unfinished configurations of places, times, matters, meanings."[54] Haraway's words add layers to my understanding of trans-corporeality, with its emphasis on being "truly present" and engaging with time and space as "unfinished" projects with myriad meaning-plays. Mahasweta Devi's cow works for me as a wily agent of trans-corporeality to highlight its incalculable corporeal configurations. This story, "Nyadosh, the Incredible Cow," first appeared in a children's magazine called *Sandesh* in 1976. Devi narrates, through Paramita Banerjee's translation: "In Cock and Bull Stories, cows climb trees; but my mother's cow actually climbed all the way up to the first floor and loved eating fish and meat."[55] This delightful story tells us about an extremely opinionated cow who chewed her way through English grammar books and many other school textbooks belong-

114

ing to the author and her family. However, Nyadosh, the cow, soon turned toward a carnivorous diet after she was inadvertently fed banana leaves with leftover pieces of fish still clinging to them.[56] Nyadosh also had a taste for climbing stairs, going to the terrace, and drinking date palm juice, which left her a little bit drunk and embellished her gait with a swagger.[57] Her mother's cow, rather than cow as mother, left an indelible impression on the author's mind. I choose to continue my introspection with this story as it helps me twist the many knots that make our narratives of entanglements. Events, bodies, and places often move with unprecedented frames and surprising processes. If a cow eats meat, how does that subvert our understanding of the cow as simply meat? This yogic cow refused to be relegated to "a" place. Without undermining the violence associated with the beef bans, I want us to think about this story as "staying with the trouble," thinking creatively about cross-border transactions, and simply noting the irony of our own creations. This blasphemous imagination of the cow eating meat troubles definitions and narratives of absolute containment. Participating in the economy of meat, Nyadosh riddles our attempts to forge any definitiveness, and instead we remain swimming within fleshy narratives and incongruent offshoots that override any stratagem.

## Acknowledgments

Many thanks to the participants of the Meat seminar in IRWG, University of Michigan–Ann Arbor, for great feedback and generative conversations. I am very grateful to Diane Mines, Banu Subramaniam, stef shuster, Jill Ehnenn, and Ellen Lamont for reading drafts of this essay and for helpful suggestions.

## Notes

1  See, for example, Jacques Derrida, *The Politics of Friendship*, translated by George Collins (London: Verso, 2005).

2  "India's Yoga-Loving PM Joins Millions Marking International Yoga Day," *The Telegraph*, June 21, 2016, accessed December 26, 2017, http://www.telegraph .co.uk/news/2016/06/21/indias-yoga-loving-pm-joins-millions-marking -international-yoga/.

3  "India Yoga: PM Narendra Modi Leads Thousands in Celebration," *BBC News*, June 21, 2015, accessed on December 26, 2017, http://www.bbc.com/news/world -asia-india-33212949.

4 Chidanand Rajghatta, "Udta India: Once Rebuffed, Modi Flies New Delhi Closer to America," *Times of India*, June 10, 2016, 16.

5 "Our Links Overcame History's Hesitations," *Mumbai Mirror*, June 9, 2016, 12.

6 Manil Suri, "A Ban on Beef in India Is Not the Answer," *New York Times*, April 17, 2015, accessed on December 26, 2017, https://www.nytimes.com/2015/04/18/opinion/sunday/manil-suri-a-ban-on-beef-in-india-is-not-the-answer.html?_r=0.

7 Parvis Ghassem-Fachandi, "The Hyperbolic Vegetarian: Notes on a Fragile Subject in Gujarat," in *Being There: The Fieldwork Encounter and the Making of Truth*, edited by John Borneman and Abdellah Hammoudi (Berkeley: University of California Press, 2009), 80.

8 Dipesh Chakrabarty, *Provincializing Europe: Postcolonial Thought and Historical Difference* (Princeton, NJ: Princeton University Press, 2000), 5, 43.

9 Thomas Hobbes, *Leviathan: With Selected Variants from the Latin Edition of 1668*, edited by Edwin Curley (Indianapolis, IN: Hackett, 1994), 3.

10 Derrida, *The Politics of Friendship*.

11 Moira Gatens, "Corporeal Representation in/and the Body Politic," in *Cartographies: Poststructuralism and the Mapping of Bodies and Spaces*, edited by Rosalyn Diprose and Robyn Ferrell (Sydney: Allen & Unwin, 1991), 80.

12 Gatens, "Corporeal Representation in/and the Body Politic," 81.

13 Gatens, "Corporeal Representation in/and the Body Politic," 81. In addition, Wendy Brown argues that the liberal state is "socially masculine": "its discursive currencies are rights rather than needs, individuals rather than relations, autogenesis rather than interdependence, interests rather than shared circumstances." Wendy Brown, *States of Injury: Power and Freedom in Late Modernity* (Princeton, NJ: Princeton University Press, 1995), 184.

14 Aristotle, *Politics*, translated by C. D. C. Reeve (Indianapolis, IN: Hackett, 1998), 4.

15 Niccolò Machiavelli, *The Prince*, in *Selected Political Writings*, edited by David Wootton (Indianapolis, IN: Hackett Publishing Company, 1994), 11.

16 Wendy Doniger, *Hindu Myths* (London: Penguin, 1975), 27.

17 Doniger, *Hindu Myths*, 27.

18 Donna J. Haraway, *Staying with the Trouble: Making Kin in the Chthulucene* (Durham, NC: Duke University Press, 2016), 12.

19 Michael Hardt and Antonio Negri, *Multitude: War and Democracy in the Age of Empire* (New York: Penguin, 2004), xiv–xv.

20 Hardt and Negri, *Multitude*, xiv.

21 Hardt and Negri, *Multitude*, xvi.

22 Judith Butler, *Frames of War: When Is Life Grievable?* (London: Verso, 2009), 3.

23 Carol J. Adams, *The Sexual Politics of Meat: A Feminist-Vegetarian Critical Theory* (New York: Bloomsbury, 2015), 20–21.

SUSHMITA CHATTERJEE

24 Jane Bennett, *Vibrant Matter: A Political Ecology of Things* (Durham, NC: Duke University Press, 2010); Mel Y. Chen, *Animacies: Biopolitics, Racial Mattering, and Queer Affect* (Durham, NC: Duke University Press, 2012).

25 Stacy Alaimo, *Exposed: Environmental Politics and Pleasures in Posthuman Times* (Minneapolis: University of Minnesota Press, 2016), 112.

26 Alaimo, *Exposed*, 188. Alaimo writes about the prolific incidence of naked protests and the significance of naked protesting bodies. As she writes, "Baring their bodies to the elements, they practice an ethics of exposure, which sets aside the fortification of the 'I' in favor of the embrace of the multiple, the inter-twined, the sensate" (78). Alaimo writes about the increasingly acidic content of the oceans, which dissolves the shells of marine animals; she writes, "The design of the shells, the spirals that swirl with a continual, smooth transformation between what is inside and what is outside, suggests the contemplation of our own bodies as intertwined with our surroundings" (163).

27 "Beef Row: Where It Is Illegal and What the Law Says," *Indian Express*, July 27, 2016, accessed on December 26, 2017, http://indianexpress.com/article/india/india-news-india/beef-madhya-pradesh-video-cow-vigilantes-gau-rakshaks-2938751/.

28 Snigdha Poonam, "The Cult of the Hindu Cowboy," *Granta*, December 9, 2016, accessed April 2, 2017, https://granta.com/cult-hindu-cowboy/, 2.

29 Sagarika Ghosh, "Trumpji ka birthday," *Times of India*, June 20, 2016.

30 Sarah Strauss, "'Adapt, Adjust, Accommodate': The Production of Yoga in a Transnational World," *History and Anthropology* 13, no. 3 (2002): 236.

31 Sanjay Kumar, "International Yoga Day Sparks Controversy in India," *The Diplomat*, June 20, 2015, http: //thediplomat.com/2015/06/international-yoga-day-sparks-controversy-in-india/.

32 Matt Wade, "Yoga Diplomacy," *Sydney Sun-Herald*, September 11, 2016, 29.

33 Wade, "Yoga Diplomacy."

34 Parama Roy, *Alimentary Tracts: Appetites, Aversions, and the Postcolonial* (Durham, NC: Duke University Press, 2010), 76.

35 Poonam, "The Cult of the Hindu Cowboy," 6.

36 Ghassem-Fachandi, "The Hyperbolic Vegetarian," 81.

37 Ghassem-Fachandi, "The Hyperbolic Vegetarian," 81.

38 Joseph S. Alter, *Yoga in Modern India: The Body between Science and Philosophy* (Princeton, NJ: Princeton University Press, 2004), 8.

39 Chandrima Chakraborty, "The Hindu Ascetic as Fitness Instructor: Reviving Faith in Yoga," *International Journal of the History of Sport* 24, no. 9 (2007): 1181.

40 Chakraborty, "The Hindu Ascetic as Fitness Instructor," 1181.

41 Alter, *Yoga in Modern India*, 10.

42 Strauss, "Adapt, Adjust, Accommodate."

43 Chakraborty, "The Hindu Ascetic as Fitness Instructor," 1176.

44 Chakraborty, "The Hindu Ascetic as Fitness Instructor," 1177.

45  Alaimo, *Exposed*, 77.

46  Alaimo, *Exposed*, 8.

47  Alaimo, *Exposed*, 42.

48  Chakraborty, "The Hindu Ascetic as Fitness Instructor," 1181.

49  Stacy Alaimo, *Bodily Natures: Science, Environment, and the Material Self* (Bloomington: Indiana University Press, 2010), 11.

50  Alaimo, *Bodily Natures*, 18.

51  Alaimo, *Bodily Natures*, 28, 31.

52  Aihwa Ong, *Flexible Citizenship: The Cultural Logic of Transnationality* (Durham, NC: Duke University Press, 1999), 4.

53  Ong, *Flexible Citizenship*, 6.

54  Haraway, *Staying with the Trouble*, 1.

55  Mahasweta Devi, *Our Non-Veg Cow and Other Stories*, translated by Paramita Banerjee (Calcutta: Seagull, 2000), 7.

56  Devi, *Our Non-Veg Cow and Other Stories*, 12.

57  Devi, *Our Non-Veg Cow and Other Stories*, 14.

## Bibliography

Adams, Carol J. *The Sexual Politics of Meat: A Feminist-Vegetarian Critical Theory.* New York: Bloomsbury, 2015.

Alaimo, Stacy. *Bodily Natures: Science, Environment, and the Material Self.* Bloomington: Indiana University Press, 2010.

Alaimo, Stacy. *Exposed: Environmental Politics and Pleasures in Posthuman Times.* Minneapolis: University of Minnesota Press, 2016.

Alter, Joseph S. *Yoga in Modern India: The Body between Science and Philosophy.* Princeton, NJ: Princeton University Press, 2004.

Aristotle. *Politics.* Translated by C. D. C. Reeve. Indianapolis, IN: Hackett, 1998.

"Beef Row: Where It Is Illegal and What the Law Says." *Indian Express*, July 27, 2016. http://indianexpress.com/article/india/india-news-india/beef-madhya-pradesh-video-cow-vigilantes-gau-rakshaks-2938751/. Accessed December 26, 2017.

Bennett, Jane. *Vibrant Matter: A Political Ecology of Things.* Durham, NC: Duke University Press, 2010.

Bost, Suzanne. "Practicing Yoga/Embodying Feminism/Shape-Shifting." *Frontiers* 37, no. 2: 191–210.

Brown, Wendy. *States of Injury: Power and Freedom in Late Modernity.* Princeton, NJ: Princeton University Press, 1995.

Butler, Judith. *Frames of War: When Is Life Grievable?* London: Verso, 2009.

Chakrabarty, Dipesh. *Provincializing Europe: Postcolonial Thought and Historical Difference.* Princeton, NJ: Princeton University Press, 2000.

SUSHMITA CHATTERJEE

Chakraborty, Chandrima. "The Hindu Ascetic as Fitness Instructor: Reviving Faith in Yoga." *International Journal of the History of Sport* 24, no. 9 (2007): 1172–86.

Chen, Mel Y. *Animacies: Biopolitics, Racial Mattering, and Queer Affect.* Durham, NC: Duke University Press, 2012.

Derrida, Jacques. *The Politics of Friendship.* Translated by George Collins. London: Verso, 2005.

Devi, Mahasweta. *Our Non-Veg Cow and Other Stories.* Translated by Paramita Banerjee. Calcutta: Seagull, 2000.

Doniger, Wendy. *Hindu Myths.* London: Penguin, 1975.

Gatens, Moira. "Corporeal Representation in/and the Body Politic." In *Cartographies: Poststructuralism and the Mapping of Bodies and Spaces*, edited by Rosalyn Diprose and Robyn Ferrell, 79–87. Sydney: Allen and Unwin, 1991.

Ghassem-Fachandi, Parvis. "The Hyperbolic Vegetarian: Notes on a Fragile Subject in Gujarat." In *Being There: The Fieldwork Encounter and the Making of Truth*, edited by John Borneman and Abdellah Hammoudi, 77–112. Berkeley: University of California Press, 2009.

Ghosh, Sagarika. "Trumpji ka Birthday." *Times of India*, June 20, 2016.

Haraway, Donna J. *Staying with the Trouble: Making Kin in the Chthulucene.* Durham, NC: Duke University Press, 2016.

Hardt, Michael, and Antonio Negri. *Multitude: War and Democracy in the Age of Empire.* New York: Penguin, 2004.

Hobbes, Thomas. *Leviathan: With Selected Variants from the Latin Edition of 1668.* Edited by Edwin Curley. Indianapolis, IN: Hackett, 1994.

"India Yoga: PM Narendra Modi Leads Thousands in Celebration." *BBC News*, June 21, 2015. http://www.bbc.com/news/world-asia-india-33212949. Accessed December 26, 2017.

"India's Yoga-Loving PM Joins Millions Marking International Yoga Day." *The Telegraph*, June 21, 2016. http://www.telegraph.co.uk/news/2016/06/21/indias-yoga-loving-pm-joins-millions-marking-international-yoga/. Accessed December 26, 2017.

Kumar, Sanjay. "International Yoga Day Sparks Controversy in India." *The Diplomat*, June 20, 2015. http://thediplomat.com/2015/06/international-yoga-day-sparks-controversy-in-india/.

Machiavelli, Niccolò. *Selected Political Writings.* Edited by David Wootton. Indianapolis, IN: Hackett, 1994.

Ong, Aihwa. *Flexible Citizenship: The Cultural Logic of Transnationality.* Durham, NC: Duke University Press, 1999.

Poonam, Snigdha. "The Cult of the Hindu Cowboy." *Granta*, December 9, 2016. https://granta.com/cult-hindu-cowboy/. Accessed April 2, 2017.

Probyn, Elspeth. *Eating the Ocean.* Durham, NC: Duke University Press, 2016.

Roy, Parama. *Alimentary Tracts: Appetites, Aversions, and the Postcolonial.* Durham, NC: Duke University Press, 2010.

Strauss, Sarah. "'Adapt, Adjust, Accommodate': The Production of Yoga in a Transnational World." *History and Anthropology* 13, no. 3 (2002): 231–51.

Suri, Manil. "A Ban on Beef in India Is Not the Answer." *New York Times*, April 17,
2015. https://www.nytimes.com/2015/04/18/opinion/sunday/manil-suri-a-ban
-on-beef-in-india-is-not-the-answer.html?_r=0. Accessed December 26, 2017.

Wade, Matt. "Yoga Diplomacy." *Sydney Sun-Herald*, September 11, 2016, 29.

# Eating after Chernobyl

## SLOW VIOLENCE AND
## REINDEER CONSUMPTION
## IN THE POSTNUCLEAR AGE

The right to food is the right to have regular, permanent, and unrestricted access, either directly or by means of financial purchases, to quantitatively and qualitatively adequate and sufficient food corresponding to the cultural traditions of the people to which the consumer belongs, and which ensure a physical and mental, individual and collective, fulfilling and dignified life free of fear.[1]

IN THE EARLY MORNING HOURS of April 26, 1986, one of the world's worst industrial disasters occurred at the Chernobyl nuclear facility located in Ukraine about twenty kilometers south of the border with Belarus. At the time of the accident, the plant had four working reactors (units 1, 2, 3, and 4). At the time, operators were running a test on an electric control system of unit 4. The accident purportedly occurred because of a combination of basic engineering deficiencies in the reactor and the faulty actions of the operators.[2] Though the damage was primarily in the immediate environs in Ukraine and Belarus, the passage of time and the effects of slow violence saw particles of radioactive chemicals drift as far away as Scandinavia, where they landed and were absorbed into the soil. Indeed, the radioactive cloud that emanated from the reactor dispersed a variety of radioactive materials over large portions of Europe. Most notable among the radioactive materials were iodine and cesium radionuclides. A report released in 2005 by the Chernobyl Forum[3] clarifies that radioactive iodine-131 has a short half-life (eight days) and more or less disintegrated in the immediate aftermath of the disaster. More pernicious, however, was the fallout of radioactive cesium-137, which has a significantly longer half-life (thirty years) and remains measurable in soils and some foods in many parts of Europe far removed from the immediate environs of the actual disaster.[4]

The Chernobyl Forum report notes that in the aftermath of the accident, high levels of radioactive cesium were found within the forest ecosystems. Of note in the report is the following: "The high transfer of radio cesium in the pathway lichen-to-reindeer meat-to-humans has been demonstrated again after the Chernobyl accident in the Arctic and sub-Arctic areas of Europe. The Chernobyl accident led to high contamination of reindeer meat in Finland, Norway, Russia and Sweden and caused significant problems for the indigenous Sami people."[5]

That cesium-137 particles migrated from the epicenter of the nuclear disaster to affect the food and ecosystem of the Sami people is of crucial importance. In this chapter I examine the effects of slow violence on the destruction of indigenous forms of eating by looking at the case of how the radioactive fallout from Chernobyl has slowly been eroding a way of life among the Sami people. The Sami of Norway typically live in bitterly cold conditions, herding reindeer, both for economic survival and as part of an embedded cultural tradition. Indeed, harvesting reindeer meat for consumption is part and parcel of this indigenous group's way of life.

At the same time that nuclear and environmental disaster has slowly eroded the Sami way of life, the growing popularity of New Nordic cuisine and its showcasing of Nordic ingredients has meant that reindeer meat appears more frequently in top-rated restaurants in Scandinavia. Chef Magnus Nilsson, for instance, explains the appearance of reindeer blood pancakes in his cookbook, noting: "Reindeer blood pancakes reveal, for example, that the Sami people of northern Scandinavia live in a cold, unforgiving landscape. They needed to make use of every part of the animal, including its blood." Rene Redzepi's world-renowned Noma features "sous vide reindeer shoulder served with celery root rolled in hay ashes and a wild herb gel." The appearance of reindeer on both Nilsson's and Redzepi's menus is not accidental. Rather, it is the strategic effort to follow the 2004 "Nordic Food Manifesto," a ten-point plan, signed by twelve chefs, that articulates how the transnational Nordic regions of Scandinavia can work to raise awareness of Nordic cuisine and put the region on the gastronomic world map, promote the common food culture, and build on the qualities of the Nordic region, while emphasizing that local foods are pure, simple, and safe.

In this chapter, I consider several interrelated issues—the complex relationship among meat consumption, culinary appropriation, indigeneities, and environmental justice—to offer a way to think through the complicated meanings of eating "exotic" and "local" meat in the context of postnuclear violence. Throughout, I emphasize that it is important to identify the land-based origins of meat, but, as revealed by research on slow violence post-Chernobyl, neither food studies nor environmental studies has fully grappled with what it means to acknowledge that so-called exotic meats are more than simply ways to satiate one's desire for adventure or the new. Rather, I suggest that the entangled genealogies of eating reindeer meat in Scandinavia must be understood through the slow violence of the fallout (literal and metaphorical) of nuclear disaster and the simultaneous gentrification of indigenous food and lifeways as part of the move to create nationalist haute cuisine. In this context, my chapter deliberately begins with the local before moving to the global. I start my inquiry at a very local site, a grocery store at which I regularly shop near my home in Cincinnati, Ohio. I consider how so-called exotic meats are marketed and packaged for local consumers. I then consider how exotic meats are sold in the purportedly more cosmopolitan setting of London's Borough Market for tourists interested in adventurous eating. I follow this with an examination of how reindeer meat has started to appear on menus in what has come to be known as New Nordic cuisine. I conclude with a discussion of what it means to think about consuming "exotic" meats within the framework of "adventurous" eating versus eating reindeer as a practice of everyday life and how, ultimately, we need to think about the emergence of one form of exotic meat, reindeer, in the context of its local emergence in the contaminated lands of the Sami, the indigenous peoples of Scandinavia.

## From Porkopolis to London

In Jungle Jim's, my local gourmet grocery store in Cincinnati, Ohio (imagine a store with the square footage of a Costco but with a range of vegetables, fruit, meat, cheeses, nonperishables, liquor, frozen foods, and so much more imported from almost every corner of the world); one of the prize

123

attractions for shoppers is a barely noticeable but significant refrigerator in the meat section of the store. In an impressively large six-compartment refrigerator, above which is the sign "Exotic Meats From around the World: Alligator, Buffalo, Elk, Guinea Foul [*sic*], Kangaroo, Ostrich, Venison, and Wild Boar Bacon," is a veritable cornucopia of meats for the so-called adventurous eater. The shelves are lined with imported meats like ground yak, camel, rabbit, and kangaroo (see figure 5.1). On occasion, I have found snake meat. Alligator meat is a staple, as is the increasingly non-exotic goat. My use of the word "exotic" draws from Lisa Heldke's definition: "uncustomary parts of customary animals (i.e. parts of cows, pigs or chickens not often eaten by Euro Americans); animals that are familiar to food colonizers but not normally eaten by them (e.g. cats, dogs, bear) and unfamiliar wild or game animals (antelope, zebra, civet). Two significant subcategories of exotic animals are those whose consumption involves some form of danger (the fugu fish which can poison its eater if it is not prepared properly); and rare or endangered animals."[6] To this, one can add meat that forms part of the diet of many ethnic or national groups (alligator in Florida and Louisiana, guinea pig/*cuy* in Ecuador and Peru, puffin in Iceland, reindeer in Scandinavia, seal in Montreal, and so forth).

On their website, Jungle Jim's describes this as the section where they stock an unrivaled selection of meats: "our selection is unmatched. From duck feet to cow tongues and more. In addition to the steaks and lamb chops you might expect to find, we offer several types of exotic meats including kangaroo, rabbit, alligator and more." The placement of this particular meat refrigerator is notable for the ways in which it produces a spectacle around certain kinds of meat while reinforcing discourses of normative eating practices. Meat outside of the triad of chicken-pork-beef (with the seasonal addition of lamb and turkey) are markedly exotic. They carry a novelty value and appeal to adventurous eaters, who are more likely to gawk at the meat within the freezer than they are to purchase the meats. Because these meats are safely ensconced within the space of Jungle Jim's, a well-known grocery store within the greater Cincinnati area, people will flock to see, and occasionally purchase, these meats. When I have purchased the seemingly less exotic meats such as goat, kangaroo, or yak, I have often been met with questions from cashiers and curious onlookers alike, such as, "Are you going to eat that?" (yes); "How do you cook it?" (do I really have the time to answer this?); and my favorite, "Doesn't it taste weird?" (no comment).

This kind of fascination with the exotic, however, is almost entirely absent in local and ethnic grocery stores that cater to immigrant populations.

124

5.1 Exotic meat freezer in Jungle Jim's, Cincinnati, Ohio.

Cincinnati's CAM Asian market, for instance, carries similar meat products and a much higher proportion of offal and trash fish. Yet there is no tourist-like gaze placed on the food here, where the patrons are by and large members of Cincinnati's Asian American community, for whom chicken feet, pig's blood, cow's tail, tripe, and pork intestines form an integral part of many everyday cuisines. To draw an example from a much larger city, London's Borough Market, a wholesale and retail market in Southwark, is arguably the biggest and most diverse food market in the city. Hidden in the maze-like structure of the market is the Exotic Meat Company. On their website they note: "The Exotic Meat Company is best known for the ostrich fillets, steaks, tenderloins and meat products produced at its own Gamston Wood ostrich farm in north Nottinghamshire. But the exoticism doesn't end there. The stall also sells kangaroo, water buffalo, springbok, kudu, bison, zebra, impala and crocodile, along with biltong, huge ostrich eggs and feather dusters. The stall's hot food grill serves burgers and steak sandwiches, utilizing many of these unlikely meats." With its proximity to

125

several popular London tourist spots, notably the Tate Modern, Shakespeare's Globe, and the London Eye, Borough Market draws a crowd of tourists at all times of the day. In addition to the onlookers are those who will buy the slider-sized portions of exotic burgers.

I begin with this somewhat lengthy trail through the retail landscape of what are called exotic meats as a means of entering into a conversation about the larger cultural, social, and ecological implications of eating reindeer so as to set a context for where and how the consumption of "exotic" meats differs radically from normatively constructed meat. Part of the appeal of consuming (leaving aside the question of whether one actually ingests the meat) these kinds of meat has to do with the novelty value of eating and procuring such meats from venues like the ones I have described above in Cincinnati and London. The more open-minded one is, the more likely one is to consume difference, or so the popular logic goes. To eat the flesh of traditionally non-domesticated animals that are also not endangered can come to signify a kind of ethos of being ecologically responsible while also publicly engaging in acts that display one's capacity to push one's palate to the extreme. Although eating meat has traditionally been thought of as a masculinized activity, meat, as Heldke notes, is often constructed as "macho food." Yet there is a growing movement to disarticulate meat-eating from masculinity. Niamh Shield's blog "Eat Like a Girl" revels in the pleasures of food and meat-eating, and a 2009 campaign for Hardee's featured *Top Chef* host and model Padma Lakshmi devouring their signature thick meaty burger with relish.[7] And yet we are also at a critical moment when the foodie is all too aware of the ethics of eating meat; knowing the provenance of food—especially when it comes to so-called exotic meats—is as important, often, as consuming the meat itself. The Exotic Meat Company notes, for instance, that all their food is sustainably produced and that no endangered species are ever served on their menus. As these two examples illustrate, prime importance is placed on one's sense of adventure via an appeal to the visual. A well-curated refrigerator or display case in a gourmet grocery store can appeal to one's palatal urges while also normativizing meats. In addition, the absence of an image of the whole animal, either because the meat comes packaged in a nonthreatening box or because it is packaged in Styrofoam and Saran Wrap and made to resemble ground meat, is no more threatening than ground beef. Consumers are thus trained to rely on their sense of the visual to place these exotic meats squarely within the realm of the palatable. They cease to be the megafauna that are beloved and believed to carry more intrinsic value than animals that we recognizably eat as meat in the West—pigs, cows, and hens, which we euphemistically call pork, beef, and chicken to mask their animal origins. They have in a sense been culturally deodorized to eliminate traces of any excessive hint of unfamiliarity.

In this context, what one sees is culturally sanitized. Within the recent movement to raise meat ethically, a high premium has been placed on the visual and what we as consumers can see happening when it comes to how our food is produced. What we see happening in abattoirs and poultry farms has been removed far from public view; at the same time the farm-to-table movement has made clear why consumers need to be aware of where foods come from. At the forefront of this movement is the writer Michael Pollan, who has argued strenuously for being fully involved in every aspect of meat preparation. For Pollan, it is more important to know where one's food comes from than it is to advance particular diets that focus around eliminating animals from one's diet.

In his much-lauded *Omnivore's Dilemma*, Pollan devotes an entire chapter in his section on the pastoral to the act of slaughtering chickens at Polyface Farm, where proprietors Joel and Daniel Salatin slaughter some hundreds of chickens six times a month. As he narrates it, Pollan decides on this occasion to immerse himself fully in the act of killing chickens: "Nobody was insisting I personally slaughter a chicken, but I was curious to learn how it was done and to see if I could bring myself to do it. The more I'd learned about the food chain, the more obligated I felt to take a good hard look at all of its parts. It seemed to me not too much to ask of a meat eater, which I was then and still am, that at least once in his life he take some direct responsibility for the killing on which his meat-eating depends."[8]

As the chapter progresses, he develops the narrative about how the chickens are slaughtered, ostensibly in an effort to lay bare the process by which animals become meat; the chapter, after all, is titled "The Glass Abattoir." Pollan is removing the veil of secrecy from around meat production to allow his readers to see exactly how meat comes to be. And if his aim is not to convert eaters or even persuade them to become vegetarians, it is largely focused on rendering visible what consumers may not be able to see, or out of willful ignorance choose not to see. Embedded in the logic of the latter, that consumers willfully choose not to see, is the idea that if Pollan can lay bare the processes through which he partakes in the act of slaughtering an animal, with the end goal of consuming that animal, consumers will also think more deeply about the kinds of meat they choose to consume. At heart, then, is the notion that people would choose better cuts of meat "if only they knew" better what they were putting into their bodies. But I want to expand on the notion on what "knowing better" means. In an ontological sense, how can one know better? What are the classed and racialized implications of knowing better? How has this logic swept into so much of the farm-to-table movement and led to romanticization of certain kinds of meat-raising practices? Julie Guthman in particular has noted the pervasiveness of this logic in Pollan's writings and media appearances. As she notes, the phrase "if people only knew where their food was coming from" resonates strongly in the alternative food movements of which Michael Pollan is at the forefront. Guthman develops this line of thinking, noting: "The phrase warrants additional parsing. Who is the speaker? Who are those that do not know? What would they do if they only knew? Do they not know now? When pushed, the subjects of this rhetoric argue that such an unveiling of the American food supply would necessarily trigger a desire for local, organic food and people would be willing to pay for it. Then, so the logic goes, the food system would be magically transformed into one that is ecologically sustainable and socially just."[9]

But what happens in instances of meat consumption when one cannot entirely see how the animal is reared or guarantee its safety because of far less containable threats to the ecosystem? What happens when there is a limit to what is knowable in terms of ecological degradation? Pollan's scenario, after all, is one that still imagines that animals are raised within a pastoral economy where the farmer can coexist with the animal and carefully control the ecosystem within which the animal lives before it is slaughtered—humanely or otherwise—to become meat. Pollan's scenario is one that imagines that the local can be bound both temporally and spatially, and that the conditions of production have no epistemological limits. But what happens, as in the case of the reindeer-herding Sami, where the local has been gradually devastated by transnational environmental risk and the ability to fully know what is happening is vastly limited because of corporate and national interests that collude to cover up massive industrial disasters? For the animals that are truly free-ranging in the Arctic regions and where the animals have gradually been poisoned by radioactive contamination for over thirty years, and for the communities that rely on herding animals in order to procure meat for sustenance, a different kind of threat altogether rears its head. To explore this in further detail, I turn now to the case of consuming reindeer meat and the emergence of New Nordic cuisine.

## New Nordic Cuisine

I ate reindeer moss at Noma, deep-fried, spiced with cèpes, and deliciously crisp. It was the third of twenty-three appetizers and tasting dishes I ate that night, the first being a hay parfait—a long infusion of cream and toasted hay, into which yarrow, nasturtium, chamomile jelly, egg, and sorrel and chamomile juice were then blended.[10]

In the first few years of the twenty-first century, we have seen the global emergence of New Nordic cuisine. The most well-known exemplar of this is Rene Redzepi and his world-renowned Noma, which opened in 2003 in Copenhagen to mixed critical reviews and ushered in an era of New Nordic cuisine. Briefly, Redzepi used the restaurant as a place to emphasize the local foods of the region, "running west from Finland through Scandinavia and across the North Atlantic to the Faroes, Iceland, and Greenland—and using them to evoke and, in the end, re-imagine and refine a common culture of rye grains, fish, fermentation, salt, and smoke, inherited from farmers and fishermen."[11] A strong proponent of eating local, Redzepi urges consumers to eat foraged foods. Within this worldview, the exotic is presented as normal fare at the same time that it is the "exotic" value of the local that often drives demand for his particular take on New Nordic cuisine. In various interviews and in his cookbooks, Redzepi extols the virtue of eating reindeer moss, even reindeer meat, but nowhere in his paean to foraging or the local does he attend to the possibility that the food he is serving might be radioactive or bring attention to the ways in which reindeer moss and reindeer meat have steadily become unavailable to the Sami, even though they inhabit the region that Noma purports to celebrate. Rather, reindeer is presented, as it is in this recipe in a tongue-in-cheek manner, as something that one can eat if one were to open one's mind to the possibility of eating more exotic meats.

### Reindeer with Celeriac and Wild Herb Gel

"Shoot reindeer in back yard. Slice 200g of meat from the shoulder and the loin and preserve the hide. Vacuum-pack the shoulder and cook for three hours at 84C. Poke it and cook for a further three hours at 87C. Blend the loin with celeriac very quickly (no longer than 3.7 seconds) then put in thermomixer and add to the shoulder and poach for 14 minutes at 68C. Boil up the reindeer hooves and wild herbs into a glue and stick the hide back on."[12]

At the same time, these are obviously not recipes the lay cook will be able to prepare at home. The paradox of the foods that he cooks are that they are at once indelibly local and obviously exotic. After all, Redzepi's cookbook is not particularly interested in teaching home cooks how to prepare foods at home; simply put, it would be too difficult for the home cook to work with this very localized form of reindeer meat or reindeer moss. Apart from the fact that most of the ingredients will not be available to most readers and home cooks, even those in Scandinavia, the techniques are far too complex for the average home cook. Rather, this is a high-end version of what you do when you go to a store like Jungle Jim's in Cincinnati or Borough Market in London to seek out novel experiences. One might foray into looking into the exotic meat freezer but stop short of purchasing the meat or imagining them as suitable ingredients for the home cook. Cooking with ingredients such as reindeer moss or reindeer meat is attributed to the individuated forms of genius of these chefs.[13]

Though Noma closed the doors to its Copenhagen restaurant at the end of 2016, its thirteen-year run did much to put New Nordic cuisine on the global map. And yet at no point in the embracing of the local did the restaurant engage significantly in any public debate about what it means to forage safely amid ecologically risky zones. As such, a much-sanitized version of what it means to eat reindeer meat emerges while wholly submerging any possible conversation about the vital link between ecology, indigenous peoples' rights, and food safety. Certainly, the missionary impulses enacted in the alternative food spaces and practices, albeit entirely high-end ones, created by Redzepi resonate strongly with the rhetoric of "if they only knew" that is inherent in Pollan's privileging of foraging and the local.

## Sami People and Settler Colonialism

Though eating reindeer meat is not new per se, its appeal on a global scale and its appearance on the menu of critically acclaimed restaurants is a relatively new phenomenon. Along the northern swathes of Scandinavia that are home to the Sami people, herding and eating reindeer is a practice that dates back several centuries. Over the centuries the Sami have developed sophisticated techniques for reindeer herding. Adapting their strategies as nomadic hunters who sought mainly to fulfill immediate needs for food, herds are now often semi-domesticated, with feeding places and migration routes controlled by humans and subject to international breeding programs. In large part, this practice has developed to ensure a consistent supply of meat for the future.[14] A community that is considered to be the northernmost indigenous people of Europe, the Sami (who inhabit an area of the Arctic that encompasses part of northern Norway, Sweden, Finland, and Russia's Kola Peninsula) are the only indigenous people of Scandinavia recognized and protected under the international conventions on indigenous people. The Sami are estimated to live across 400,000 square kilometers, with the highest concentration in Norway. Though they live transnationally, some critics argue that they have a relatively "homogeneous identity, although their local cultures and languages vary."[15] "Reindeer herding has long been the main source of livelihood for the Sami people. Additionally, the practices of reindeer herding vary from country to country. Whereas Norway and Sweden restrict the practice to ethnic Sami, this restriction is not in place in Finland.[16] With the onset of modernity, and increasing pressure from the various nation-states in which Sami lands are located to assert the right to extract and develop minerals and set up renewable energy projects in the Sápmi region, only about 10 percent of the Sami remain active in reindeer herding.[17] Nevertheless, the practice remains an important part of the Sami way of life. As Castro and colleagues note, "despite the growing shift in livelihood practices, the Sami and their relations with reindeer have special significance in terms of spirituality and cultural identity. As a result, it is not only about physical sustenance, but also about maintaining a ceremonial role as well as emotional bondage, that makes up the entities that are implicated in reindeer-herding practices."[18]

Lest one romanticize the Sami as apolitical indigenous peoples of the world, it is worth noting that in early 2017 the Sami were very highly visible on the international stage because of their activism around capitalism and settler colonialism. The most visible manifestation of this came to light in March 2017, when "in an act of international solidarity between indigenous peoples, the Sami parliament in Norway persuaded the country's second largest pension fund to withdraw its money from companies linked . . . to the project to build the 1,900 km Dakota Access oil pipeline across six US states."[19] Their commitment to thinking about environmental justice thus is not limited to their specific lands, but also extends to a global understanding of how mineral and industrial exploitation can have devastating impacts on people and indigenous lands.

But even with careful measures in place to safeguard the rights of the Sami and their access to their lands and the practice of reindeer herding, a larger question emerges concerning the long-term survival of both the Sami and the reindeer. Related to this, one might ask: How safe is it for

131

the Sami to eat reindeer meat given the transnational risk that the Chernobyl nuclear disaster posed and continues to pose? Though the majority of the reindeer that the Sami herd are seemingly far away from Ukraine, the epicenter of the Chernobyl disaster, the particles of radioactive cesium-137 that were unleashed into the atmosphere on April 26, 1986, did not stay put in time or place. While the damage was primarily in the immediate environs, the passage of time and the effects of slow violence saw particles of the radioactive chemicals drift as far away as the Arctic Circle, where they were subsequently absorbed into the soil. Traces of the radioactive isotope showed up in the food chain because of the ease with which it is absorbed by the gypsy mushroom and lichen (or reindeer moss, as is it known locally) that is a major part of the diet of the local reindeer population. The fallout from Chernobyl and its deleterious impact on the ecosystem of the Sami people is a paradigmatic instance of what Rob Nixon describes as slow violence. Discussing Chernobyl, Nixon describes the difficulty of ascertaining the full impact of the nuclear fallout. Because chemical disasters over the course of time are "spectacle deficient,"[20] they "may range from the cellular to the transnational and (depending on the specific character of the chemical or radiological hazard) may stretch beyond the horizon of imaginable time."[21]

It is this notion of imagined time that I wish to press further; for many of the Sami herders whose livelihoods depend on working with reindeer, it is outside the scope of imaginable time to conceive that a disaster that occurred in 1986 continues to wreak havoc on the natural environment in 2020. Within this logic, the Sami fall out of the imagination of prevailing economic and political interests because of the inherent difficulty in establishing that the Sami people and their lands fall within the scope of toxic suffering.[22] Though Nixon rightly points out that Chernobyl "received far more sustained attention in the Western media [and that] because of Chernobyl's proximity to Western Europe it was perceived as an ongoing transnational threat to 'us' rather than a purely national threat,"[23] it bears mentioning that only some aspects of the Chernobyl story were imagined to be a legible risk. Moreover, an alternative narrative to Nixon's emerges if we take seriously the searingly powerful narratives that emerge from Svetlana Alexievich's *Chernobyl Prayer*, a collection of oral testimonies from people who were affected by the Chernobyl disaster. Through a series of monologues, it becomes clear that many among the local community adjacent to Chernobyl were aware of the immediate risk of consuming contaminated meat. At the same time, many individuals knew their option was either to suffer a slow death through consuming contaminated meat, or a more immediate one through starvation. Even with the world's seeming attention on Chernobyl, the individual communities in and around Pripyat, Ukraine, were rendered invisible, or simply judged to be of no value by the Soviet government. As Lyudmila Dmitrievna Polyanskaya, a village schoolteacher, narrates to Alexievich: "The panic during those first days: some rushed to the pharmacy and bought up stocks of iodine. Some people stopped visiting the market to buy milk and meat, especially beef. In our family, we stopped trying to be economical and bought more expensive sausage hoping that meant it was made from safe meat. We soon found out, though, that they were deliberately adding contaminated meat to expensive sausage. Their logic was that, as it was expensive, people would buy only a little of it and eat less. We had no protection."[24]

At a more official level, a former chief engineer at the Institute for Atomic Energy, Belarus Academy of Science, confesses to Alexievich, "After the first tests, it became clear that what we were dealing with was not meat but radioactive waste.... Every piece of information had become a secret at precisely the time when short-lived elements were emitting maximum radiation." He continues to describe sausages and eggs randomly tested from stores as radioactive waste, and when asked why silence persisted in the face of experts having the knowledge, he responds, "we stayed still and obeyed orders because we were under Party discipline."[25] The engineer's response, then, is one that suggests knowledge was readily available; bureaucratic measures to file reports were followed, but ultimately, other goals were deemed more important. Simply having the knowledge was not enough to stop people from producing or consuming contaminated food.

In her invaluable ethnographic account of life in the shadow of Chernobyl, Adriana Petryna takes up this question about having knowledge about food being contaminated—the idea of "knowing better"—versus persisting in purportedly risky behaviors such as willfully consuming contaminated food or remaining within zones of contamination. Despite locals having knowledge that cesium-137 particles transfer from the soil into local foodstuffs like milk, berries, mushrooms, fish, and potatoes, and despite the availability of filtering devices to reduce the radioactive content of food, many local inhabitants refuse to change their consumption practices.[26]

Similarly, the transnational risk posed to the indigenous communities of Northern Europe had largely been side-stepped or simply ignored. In the immediate aftermath of the Chernobyl disaster, much of the Sami people's way of life came under attack because of the threat to the reindeer population. According to Radio Free Europe/Radio Liberty, "Reindeer meat is a mainstay in the Scandinavian diet. The meat from one reindeer currently fetches around $400 for the Sami herders. But only if the deer isn't too radioactive to eat." Notably, this is not a new development; many of the reindeer first became radioactive around 1986. During periods of rain or snow, radioactive dust, absorbed by lichen and mushrooms, would find its way into the ground and eventually groundwater. With continued and consistent contamination of the land and groundwater, cesium levels have remained at higher than acceptable levels, making it not only unsafe for the Sami to consume reindeer but impossible to ethically herd and sell reindeer as a sustainable form of meat. In essence, their access to safe meat and their livelihood, a basic human right to safe food, as noted in the epigraph to this chapter, was put into crisis.

With few venues to advocate for their rights, the plight of the Sami has been all too easy to ignore on the global stage. And yet the case of persistent meat contamination remains an all too eerie reminder of the long-term effects of industrial disasters.

## Conclusion

To reiterate, meat is seen as coming from the land, but in the case of research on Chernobyl, neither food studies nor environmental studies has fully grappled with what it means to acknowledge that so-called exotic meats are more than simply ways to satiate one's desire for adventure or the new. As in the case of the Sami, whose very livelihood depends on having safe and uncontaminated meat, it becomes necessary to consider (as suggested in the epigraph to this chapter) when and how access to safe, nonirradiated meat is a basic human right. The question, ultimately, is less whether it is ethical or adventurous to eat reindeer or not but to consider how the slow violence and the fallout from Chernobyl are not just a localized threat but that has devastating impacts on the immediate environs, as Svetlana Alexievich so brilliantly captures in her series of interviews, but a transnational one that has already begun to change the way the Sami people live within their environment. In this context, the invisibility of the Sami's plight and the concomitant plight of the reindeer is all too noticeable in the fetishizing of the local in Redzepi's and Nilsson's attempts to capitalize on the cultural value of New Nordic cuisine. Merely widening one's horizons to consider reindeer acceptable to the palate is not enough;

134

rather, one must remain vigilant about knowing the terms on which the meat is made accessible and inaccessible because of the continued effects of transnational environmental slow violence.

## Notes

1 Hilal Elver, "Special Rapporteur on the Right to Food," Office of the High Commissioner for Civil Rights, n.d., accessed August 13, 2017, https://www.ohchr .org/EN/Issues/Food/Pages/FoodIndex.aspx.

2 According to one report, "The safety systems had been switched off, and the reactor was being operated under improper, unstable conditions, a situation which allowed an uncontrollable power surge to occur. This power surge caused the nuclear fuel to overheat and led to a series of steam explosions that severely damaged the reactor building and completely destroyed the unit 4 reactor. The explosions started numerous fires on the roofs of the reactor building and the machine hall, which were extinguished by fire-fighters after a few hours. Approximately 20 hours after the explosions, a large fire started as the material in the reactor set fire to combustible gases. The large fire burned during 10 days. Helicopters repeatedly dumped neutron-absorbing compounds and fire-control materials into the crater formed by the destruction of the reactor and later the reactor structure was cooled with liquid nitrogen using pipelines originating from another reactor unit." "Chernobyl Nuclear Accident," GreenFacts, n.d., accessed November 17, 2017. https://www.greenfacts.org/en/chernobyl/l-2/o -what-happened-chernobyl.htm#o.

3 The Chernobyl Forum is the name of a group of UN agencies, founded on February 3–5, 2003, at the IAEA (International Atomic Energy Agency) Headquarters in Vienna, Austria, to scientifically assess the health effects and environmental consequences of the Chernobyl disaster and to issue reports on its environmental and health effects. It includes nine member organizations: the IAEA, FAO (Food and Agriculture Organization), OCHA (United Nations Office for the Coordination of Humanitarian Affairs), UNDP (United Nations Development Programme), UNEP (United Nations Environment Programme), UNSCEAR (United Nations Scientific Committee on the Effects of Atomic Radiation), WHO (World Health Organization), the World Bank, and the governments of Belarus, Russia, and Ukraine.

4 "Chernobyl's Legacy: Health, Environmental and Socio-Economic Impacts, and Recommendations to the Governments of Belarus, the Russian Federation and Belarus," Chernobyl Forum, 2006, accessed July 15, 2017, https://www.iaea.org /sites/default/files/chernobyl.pdf, 10.

5 "Chernobyl's Legacy," 25.

6 Lisa Heldke, *Exotic Appetites: Ruminations of a Food Adventurer* (London: Routledge 2003).

7 Laura Wright's somewhat limited reading of this advertisement suggests that it can only work for a masculine gaze, presupposing that a woman enjoying a meaty burger, and a woman of color at that, is somewhat of an anomaly. If it were to happen, Wright seems to suggest, it must necessarily be denying agency or pleasure. Laura Wright, *The Vegan Studies Reader: Food Animals and Gender in the Age of Terror* (Athens: University of Georgia Press, 2015), 120. A more interesting reading of the Hardee's commercial can be found in the drag performance enacted by Vidur Kapoor, wherein drag is utilized to bring attention to the pleasure and excesses in Padma Lakshmi's performance. See "Vidur Kapur as Padma Lakshmi in a Western Bacon Thick Burger Ad," *YouTube*, July 4, 2009, accessed July 10, 2017, https://www.youtube.com/watch?v=9c3KEAql5zE.

8 Michael Pollan, *The Omnivore's Dilemma: A Natural History of Four Meals* (New York: Penguin 2007), 231.

9 Julie Guthman, "'If They Only Knew': Color Blindness and Universalism in California Alternative Food Institutions," *Professional Geographer* 60, no. 3 (2008): 387–97.

10 Jane Kramer, "The Food at Our Feet: Why Is Foraging All the Rage?," *New Yorker*, November 21, 2011, accessed August 13, 2017, http://www.newyorker.com/magazine/2011/11/21/the-food-at-our-feet.

11 Kramer, "The Food at Our Feet."

12 John Crace, "Noma: Time and Place in Nordic Cuisine by Rene Redzepi," *The Guardian*, November 22, 2010, accessed July 17, 2017, https://www.theguardian.com/books/2010/nov/22/noma-nordic-cuisine-rene-redzepi.

13 One can also explore in detail the work of Magnus Nilsson, who also specializes in New Nordic cuisine. His restaurant Faviken, located in Jarpen, Sweden, is a sixteen-seat restaurant listed as among the best in the world. Like Redzepi, Nilsson focuses on local ingredients and techniques that include foraging.

14 Damian Castro, Kamrul Hoosain, and Carolina Tytelman, "Arctic Ontologies: Reframing the Relationship between Humans and Rangifer," *Polar Geography* 39, no. 2 (2016): 102.

15 Castro et al., "Arctic Ontologies," 101.

16 Castro et al., "Arctic Ontologies," 101.

17 "Land and Resource Rights Are Key to Sami People's Self-Determination, UN Rights Expert Says," UN Office of the High Commissioner for Human Rights, August 28, 2015, accessed August 9, 2017, https://www.ohchr.org/EN/NewsEvents/Pages/DisplayNews.aspx?NewsID=16361&LangID=E.

18 Castro et al., "Arctic Ontologies," 101–2.

19 Rachel Fixsen, "Sami People Persuade Norway Pension Fund to Divest from Dakota Access," *The Guardian*, March 17, 2017, accessed July 15, 2017. https://www.theguardian.com/us-news/2017/mar/17/sami-dakota-access-pipeline-norway-pension-fund-divest.

20 Rob Nixon, *Slow Violence and the Environmentalism of the Poor* (Cambridge, MA: Harvard University Press, 2011).

21  Nixon, *Slow Violence and the Environmentalism of the Poor.*

22  See Adriana Petryna, *Life Exposed: Biological Citizens after Chernobyl* (Princeton, NJ: University Press, 2002).

23  Nixon, *Slow Violence and the Environmentalism of the Poor.*

24  Svetlana Alexievich, *Chernobyl Prayer: Voices from Chernobyl, a Chronicle of the Future* (London: Penguin, 2016), 223.

25  Alexievich, *Chernobyl Prayer*, 202.

26  Petryna, *Life Exposed*, 85–86.

## Bibliography

Alexievich, Svetlana. *Chernobyl Prayer: Voices from Chernobyl, a Chronicle of the Future*, Translated by Anna Gunin and Arch Tait. London: Penguin, 2016.

Castro, Damian, Kamrul Hossain, and Carolina Tytelman. "Arctic Ontologies: Reframing the Relationship between Humans and Rangifer." *Polar Geography* 39, no. 2 (2016): 98–112.

Chapple, Amos, and Wojtek Grojek. "Chernobyl's Reindeer: The Norwegian Herders Still Living in the Shadow of Nuclear Disaster." Radio Free Europe/Radio Liberty, n.d. https://www.rferl.org/a/chernobyls-reindeer/27575578.html#. Accessed November 7, 2017.

"Chernobyl Nuclear Accident." GreenFacts, n.d. https://www.greenfacts.org/en/chernobyl/l-2/0-what-happened-chernobyl.htm#0. Accessed November 17, 2017.

"Chernobyl's Legacy: Health, Environmental and Socio-Economic Impacts, and Recommendations to the Governments of Belarus, the Russian Federation and Belarus." Chernobyl Forum, 2006. https://www.iaea.org/sites/default/files/chernobyl.pdf. Accessed July 15, 2017.

Crace, John. "Noma: Time and Place in Nordic Cuisine by Rene Redzepi." *The Guardian*, November 22, 2010. https://www.theguardian.com/books/2010/nov/22/noma-nordic-cuisine-rene-redzepi. Accessed July 17, 2017,

Elver, Hilal. "Special Rapporteur on the Right to Food." UN Office of the High Commissioner for Civil Rights, n.d. https://www.ohchr.org/EN/Issues/Food/Pages/FoodIndex.aspx. Accessed November 17, 2017.

Fixsen, Rachel, "Sami People Persuade Norway Pension Fund to Divest from Dakota Access." *The Guardian*, March 17, 2017. https://www.theguardian.com/us-news/2017/mar/17/sami-dakota-access-pipeline-norway-pension-fund-divest. Accessed July 15, 2017.

Guthman, Julie. "'If They Only Knew': Color Blindness and Universalism in California Alternative Food Institutions." *Professional Geographer* 60, no. 3 (2008): 387–97.

Heldke, Lisa. *Exotic Appetites: Ruminations of a Food Adventurer*. London: Routledge, 2003.

Kramer, Jane, "The Food at Our Feet: Why Is Foraging All the Rage?" *New Yorker,* November 21, 2011. https://www.newyorker.com/magazine/2011/11/21/the -food-at-our-feet. Accessed August 13, 2017.

Nixon, Rob. *Slow Violence and the Environmentalism of the Poor.* Cambridge, MA: Harvard University Press, 2011.

Petryna, Adriana. *Life Exposed: Biological Citizens after Chernobyl.* Princeton, NJ: Princeton University Press, 2002.

Pollan, Michael. *The Omnivore's Dilemma: A Natural History of Four Meals.* New York: Penguin, 2007.

Wright, Laura. *The Vegan Studies Project: Food, Animals and Gender in the Age of Terror.* Athens: University of Georgia Press, 2015.

138

# Romancing the Pig

## A QUEER CRIP TALE FROM BARBECUE TO XENOTRANSPLANTATION

What I have shown here written on the motions of the heart I am the more emboldened to present to your Majesty, according to the custom of the present age, because almost all things human are done after human examples, and many things in a King are after the pattern of the heart. . . . Here, at all events, best of Princes, placed as you are on the pinnacle of human affairs, you may at once contemplate the prime mover in the body of man, and the emblem of your sovereign power.
—William Harvey, *De Motu Cordis* (1628), addressed to King Charles I

Today, pig is as much king on the Southern table as when I took my first bites of juicy pork roast with sweet potatoes, fried salty country ham with red-eye gravy, and pickled pig's feet.
—James Villas, *Pig: King of the Southern Table* (2010)

WHAT DO DISCOURSES SURROUNDING THE ENTHUSIASM for authentic barbecue in the US South and the hopes and fears sparked by xenotransplantation suggest about how "the other white meat" figures at the frontier of race, gender, science, and empire? In what follows, I offer a critically queer crip analysis of the pig as a biopolitical site of the reproduction and management of the borders of race, gender, sexuality, nation, and species. Specifically, I explore the queer crip entanglements of barbecue and of xenotransplantation as sites where the bodies of pigs are incorporated into human bodies and imperial imaginaries with debilitating consequences for those who are the most marginalized. I do so in order to consider how assumptions about queerness/normalcy and disability/ability inform the persistence of violence at the heart of empire. My focus on romancing the pig aims to get to the heart of the matter about the materialization of the pig as a site of a transnational politics of meat that circulates beneath the skin, distinguishing between self and other in discourses of health, disability, and belonging.

The connections between barbecue and xenotransplantation explored in this project enlist queer crip as a critical method for thinking differently about bodies, minds, identities, normalization, and other categories, processes, and experiences that affect lives and life chances. A queer crip method thinks on and against the boundaries that distinguish between categories, critically attending to the forces of inclusion and exclusion that stabilize, normalize, and naturalize them. A queer crip method opens possibilities for thinking in undisciplined ways about the meaning, significance, and mutually constitutive relation between queerness, disability, barbecue, and xenotransplantation.

While acknowledging the importance and even necessity of identity, queer crip analysis is critically attuned to the forces of normalization that shape and secure binaries, including but not limited to ability/disability, normal/abnormal, and human/animal. A queer crip approach offers an expansive conception of queerness and disability, moving beyond identities and practices that conform to more conventional conceptions of what it means for a body-mind or practice to be queer and/or disabled.[1] More than a mere combination of two fields or identity categories, a queer crip framework of analysis offers a critical perspective on queerness and disability as entangled historical, cultural, political, and material sites of various mutually constitutive forms of exclusion and transformative possibilities.

Important to queer crip theory has been its reconception of disability as a site of resistant subjectivities and imaginaries and new possibilities of being in the world.[2] In her discussion of queer crip analysis, Nirmala Erevelles cautions against celebrations of the transformative potential of disability that deflect from ongoing disabling continuities between historical and contemporary globalized violence.[3] As Erevelles persuasively argues,

140

transforming ableist conceptions of disability (from a site of negative lack to a site of creative, resistant ways of being in and knowing the world) must also reckon with globalized material violence that disproportionately targets marginalized, oppressed groups. Otherwise, such celebrations falsely universalize the global elite's embodied experiences of disability. In other words, the historical and social contextualization of disability is crucial to the critical project of reconceiving disability. As Erevelles argues, a critically queer crip analysis must foreground how ableism is at the heart of the violent, transnational, hierarchal context in which the meanings of disability are matters of life and death.[4] Thus, understanding the becoming that disability is involves exposing and grappling with "the structural violence embedded deep within the fleshy body."[5]

In this chapter, I build on Erevelles's understanding of what it means to think transnationally and critically about disability and offer a queer crip perspective on the transnational politics of meat, focusing on histories and structures of violence that inform two sites where the pig becomes meat—US Southern barbecue and xenotransplantation. Rather than primarily focus on meat as a site for the production of disability—whether in humans or animals—I focus on some of the ways ableist transnational ontologies and epistemologies[6] shape how the pig becomes meat. The queer crip approach to barbecue and xenotransplantation proposed here considers how anxieties, knowledge, and ignorance in the context of settler colonialism and imperialism are materialized in the flesh and heart of the pig and generate abstract celebrations of hybridity that normalize and naturalize empire's ideologies and practices. This approach reframes disability's relation to meat: from thinking exclusively about disabled workers, eaters, and animals (though this is certainly important) to thinking about meat as a materialization of ableism, a site of incorporation that reinforces the norm of the ableist pure body-mind at the heart of empire. A culture of empire is constituted, in part, by metaphorical and material practices of incorporation—a simultaneous consumption, pathologization, and assimilative erasure of threatening difference. Incorporation is a site where empire's ontological and epistemological vulnerabilities and anxieties are managed by backgrounding (or relegating to the past) imperialist and settler colonial violence and foregrounding hybridity as one of its accomplishments.

To become meat is to become matter in place, which for the pig involves, as Lynda Birke explains, a process of purification-transformation from dirt or source of pollution to food: that which can be incorporated into the body in order to sustain it.[7] That said, conventional culinary tales about the pig erase the violence of historical encounters that are inseparable from the boundary crossings that inform movements and transformations of pork products, cuisines, and culinary knowledge. The transformative promise of hybridity is also a prominent theme in discussions about xenotransplantation. The possibility of saving human lives with donor organs from genetically engineered pigs is a tale of heroic Western science at the frontier of biomedical research; and the human–pig hybrid organs of xeno science are celebrated for their promise of new insight into what it means to be human.[8] As David K. C. Cooper and Robert P. Lanza point out, the transplantation of pig organs into human bodies requires "humanized pigs."[9] The queer crip tale I present in this chapter critically intervenes in both these romanticized notions of hybridity, foregrounding the historical and structural violence that shapes an ableist transnational politics of meat beneath the skin. Here I will focus on how pigs become meat, that is, how they become incorporated into human imaginaries, bodies, and hearts— symbolically and materially.[10]

The pig is not only a hybrid body, it is also a frontier body. Left by ships as a promised food source for settler-colonizers, pigs are at the heart of both highly experimental scientific research and of white Southern nostalgia for imagined purity and authenticity. Ambiguities abound in the concept of the frontier, a concept that has important affective ties to senses of identity and belonging.[11] In the imaginary of empire, the frontier is a site of anxiety in the face of porous and thus vulnerable borders.[12] In what follows, I consider some of the ways in which such anxieties about frontiers inform discourses surrounding the threat presented by the incorporation of the pig into human bodies and imaginaries. At the imagined frontier of experimental science and the culinary encounter that produced barbecue, transnational porcine politics is characterized by a temporality[13] that reaches simultaneously toward the past and future. The queer crip method developed here considers how this particular form of reaching toward the past and future is a romanticized normalization of violence at the heart of ableist ontologies (e.g., the purity of self, body, and nation) and epistemologies (e.g., practices of historical forgetting and ignorance) that structure the becoming-meat of the pig.

Rather than a counter-ableist approach, this project's queer crip approach reframes what it means to think about how empire is central to ableist structures that circulate in/as meat. The quest for authentic US Southern barbecue and the quest for sufficiently humanized transgenic pigs are biopolitical sites for the management of anxiety about vulnerability and

142

belonging that are central to ableist, heteronormative, and settler colonial imaginaries. While xeno scientists endeavor to "fool" the human immune system into accepting that which is "foreign" (e.g., a pig's heart) as self (i.e., human),[14] and the US culinary scene seems to be going hog wild for "authentic" Southern barbecue, pigs are weaponized in anti-Semitic and Islamophobic hate crimes that cast Jewish people and Muslims as foreigners who do not belong.[15] I contend that the heightened anxieties that come together in the figure of the pig are informed by and reinforce a "eugenic logic"[16] oriented toward the elimination of disability and all marked as impure, inauthentic, and foreign. The nostalgia that characterizes the defense of authentic barbecue and xenotransplantation imagines a past and future purged of threatening, destabilizing difference.

## Pigs, Politics, and Ethics

Often the proposed solution to the ethical dilemma regarding what we should eat is to clean up our ontologies in order to more clearly distinguish between beings more properly categorized as food and beings more properly categorized as subjects, living beings that should not be eaten.[17] In short, as is consistent with the mainstream alternative food movement in the United States, regardless of one's particular stance on eating animals, the solution is to purify one's diet and thus one's body. For vegetarians and vegans, meat is a category mistake, a euphemism that masks the moral harm of slaughtering nonhuman animals for human consumption, and the reason most often given against eating meat is that the animal in question has some characteristic that humans deemed "normal" possess. Similarly, eager to defend their work as ethical, many xeno scientists place pigs and nonhuman primates in different moral categories based on evolutionary proximity, perceived differences in intelligence, and the public perception of pigs as farm animals raised for food.[18] Claims about the moral significance of differences between pigs and nonhuman primates ground the presumed greater moral acceptability of replacing nonhuman primates with pigs in xeno research. However, the moral significance of species difference is hotly debated. While many may assume that pigs are "less intelligent" than human beings, there are studies that offer evidence of a degree of pigs' intelligence that supports a presumption that they are autonomous.[19]

143

From a disability studies perspective, the emphasis on intelligence and other characteristics deemed natural and normal for human beings reflects the ableist logic prevalent in philosophical discussion about disabled people's quality of life, as well as the moral considerability of nonhuman animals.[20] In her discussion of "romancing the meat," Sunara Taylor critiques the ableism that informs the new meat movement's critique of vegetarianism and veganism. As she points out, members of the new meat movement defend the consumption of meat from animals that are raised humanely on sustainable, small farms, and they accuse vegetarians and vegans of romanticizing nature by ignoring the violence that is an intrinsic part of it.[21] Taylor proposes a cripping of animal ethics that, in part, entails a reconceptualization of what is considered humane. As she puts it, "[C]ommodifying and slaughtering animals for food is not natural or righteous—even if it's done on a small family farm or in a factory system designed to minimize cruelty."[22] Romanticism, Taylor contends, is a charge more justifiably directed at defenders of the new meat movement who ignore the interdependencies of all forms of life in their rush to naturalize violence.

Ethical concerns about what one should eat are important, and discussions about them have done a great deal to call attention to the deplorable treatment of animals on factory farms. Nonetheless, when it comes to eating in the context of empire, complex complicities are not resolved by adopting a more "pure" eating practice. In fact, as Parama Roy argues, eating as a scene of purification has itself been a site of violence, a way to secure boundaries against the threat of a contaminating other.[23] While I share Taylor's concerns about the specific form of romanticism with which she is concerned, I wonder what might come into view if we orient ourselves differently in discussions of food, asking different questions about how meat in general and the pig in particular have been romanced.


Bad Romance and the Search for the True 'Cue

As John Shelton Reed quips, "Southern barbecue is the closest thing . . . in the U.S. to Europe's wines or cheeses."[24] While there are many people for whom the word barbecue is a verb meaning to cook outside on a grill, barbecue in the US South is both a verb and a noun.[25] As a verb, to barbecue means to cook meat low and slow over smoldering hardwood coals. Barbecue, as John Edge puts it, is "a marriage of smoke, time, meat, and sauce."[26] While people can and do barbecue beef, mutton, chicken, and tofu, barbecue in the US South is a word most often synonymous with the pig. The pervasive image of smiling, dancing pigs on signs at barbecue restaurants all over the South makes this association abundantly clear. How did the pig come to occupy this prized place? What does it mean to understand the US South as the "real" home of barbecue?[27] What is true 'cue?

From a queer crip perspective, the longing for authentic barbecue is a form of romance as purity campaign; and the culinary incorporation that constitutes the romance surrounding authentic US Southern barbecue is, I contend, another site of dispossession. In culinary dispossessions, a privileged group appropriates agricultural and culinary knowledge and skill and declares it their own. Here I focus on two forms of purification involved in the desire for authentic US Southern barbecue: (1) nostalgia about the plantation and frontier past that erases the presence of African and Indigenous culinary knowledge; and (2) able-nationalist efforts to rehabilitate both barbecue as a site of multicultural eating that heals national wounds of racist violence and the pig as a healthy source of protein.

So strong is some people's love for barbecue that they have started the Campaign for Real Barbecue. Established in 2013, its mission is "to preserve authentic North Carolina barbecue as a significant element in the culture of the South."[28] Restaurants that continue the tradition of cooking pork over hardwood coals can receive a certificate of authenticity from the Campaign for Real Barbecue. The meaning of these efforts cannot be reduced to individual intentions, but must be understood within the historical context of racism, settler colonialism, and imperialism that continues to resonate in the region. Furthermore, current equations of eating pork with that which is authentically Southern conceptualize the Southern as that which does not include people for whom eating pork is culturally taboo, such as Muslims. As Shannon Sullivan argues, the heart and stomach are sites of racialization and the management of white ignorance.[29]

While Sullivan's analysis importantly emphasizes the history of white refusal to eat with African Americans, I suggest that ableist white ignorance, in the form of romanticized notions of the past and its relation to the present, is also sustained through selective historical eating with others enacted in romancing barbecue and, thus, the pig. For example, nostalgic, romanticized notions of barbecue tend to ignore the fact that barbecue's place in Southern cuisine is an effect of "Africanizing" the US diet through "cultural blending and cultural resistance."[30] The distinction between soul food and barbecue works to contain and manage the distinction between Black, Indigenous, and white cuisine by ignoring the fact that without Black and Indigenous culinary knowledge and spices, there would be no Southern barbecue. As Michael Twitty notes, enslaved cooks on plantations brought culinary knowledge to their kitchens and, as a matter of survival and re-sistance, skillfully produced foods that disguised African influences in order to give the appearance that "Europe still had the upper hand."[31] But rather than romanticize these moments of culinary resistance in an effort to cele-brate the culinary hybridity of the South, Twitty contextualizes them within the realities of the violence on the plantation, where the kitchen was also a site of sexual violence against enslaved women.

Locating the home of authentic barbecue in a romanticized notion of the US South also erases its Indigenous roots. Barbecue—both the method and the word—are derived from Spanish interpretations of how Taíno people in the Caribbean roasted meat on wooden frames over fire.[32] Proclaiming barbecue as "authentic" US Southern cuisine shores up the boundaries of a white national identity premised on distinction from and disappearance of Indigenous people. It is also an example of epistemic ignorance. As Charles Mills points out, white ignorance is an epistemic framework for making sense of the world and managing memory; it is not a necessary feature of being white and can be implemented by nonwhites.[33] When it comes to barbecue, the troubling issues surrounding nostalgia aren't reducible to the identities or skin color of the people who love it. The crucial factor is the extent to which the framing of authenticity subordinates or erases African and Indigenous knowledge and culinary skills, as well as the context of set-tler colonial violence in which those skills were honed, that continue to constitute barbecue in order to secure a notion of authentic regional forms of Southern barbecue as purified of its violent roots.

In his analysis of settler time, Mark Rifkin notes, "The colonial violence of settler rule has worked through forced incorporation of Indigenous peoples into the 'domestic' space of the nation," and those incorporations have normalized and universalized a settler colonial spatial and temporal framework by "disappearing" Indigenous people from the present.[34] The search for authentic US Southern barbecue is, I suggest, such a site where the Indigenous and Africanizing foundations of US Southern cuisine are disappeared through their incorporation into a narrative that ultimately subordinates their presence by favoring a progressive narrative of culinary influence that fixes Indigenous and African influences in a past that has been overcome. Romanticized notions of authentic barbecue erase the transnational realities that shape the economic, social, and political con-tours of what is taken to be authentic US Southern cuisine. Romanticized notions of authentic barbecue also enact a culinary mode of disappearance though incorporation in the "domestic" space of the kitchen.

Understood in this way, barbecue becomes authentic US Southern cuisine precisely because its connection to Indigenous and Africanizing foodways and the violence of forcible removal and the plantation system are erased from the romanticized past and thereby incorporated into a whitened cuisine. As Elspeth Probyn points out, "Eating naturalizes colonial, racialized, and ethnic relations . . . and pushes them to the background."[35] More than the heady aroma of a slow-cooked pig, the enthusiastic search for true 'cue or pure, authentic pork is a site where the meaning of a white US national imaginary is forged in the normalization and naturalization of racial and settler colonial hierarchies. Rethinking how the pig comes to matter on the frame over the coals thus reveals a different tale of cooks and conquerors.[36]

Other sites where the pig is romanced in the US national culinary imaginary are able-nationalist efforts to rehabilitate barbecue as an occasion of multicultural community and the pig as a healthy source of meat. In the film based on his recent book *Cooked*, Michael Pollan (unintentionally) reproduces a white settler colonial narrative of barbecue. The film opens with a discussion of cooking with fire in Australia, focusing on an Aboriginal family who have gone into the bush for a weekend of hunting and camping. The film then zeros in on how the meat is cooked: buried in the ground, at the side of the fire, and covered in coals. Pollan's off-camera narrative informs viewers that they are witnessing the first form of barbecue in human cultures, a narrative that has the effect of fixing Aboriginal people and culture in the past, despite the fact that he is talking about an outing by a contemporary Aboriginal family. The film then moves from the Australian outback to a rural area in North Carolina where Pollan meets Ed Mitchell, an African American pit master, and learns how to barbecue whole pigs. Barbecue as site of multicultural unity, in Pollan's account, is a tacit promise to heal wounds created by historical and contemporary racist violence. The pig on the frame promises a rehabilitated, healed future.

But rehabilitation and repair are central to able-nationalist, normalizing inclusions made possible by the creation of disability (or debility)[37] elsewhere.[38] Barbecue in the US South, as Bertram Wyatt-Brown explains, has always been a ritual of "uneven friendship" that both ignores and secures race, class, and gender hierarchies.[39] Pollan's romanticized tale ends with him at his home in Berkeley where he, with the help of a couple of friends, a grill, a fire bowl, and a lot of aluminum foil, manages to improvise a smoke delivery system for cooking a whole pig on his deck. By the end of the film, Southern barbecue, it seems, has brought very privileged, mostly white

147

people together, even vegetarians. The roasted pig in this scene serves as a proxy for a nation that has been repaired and has overcome its racist past through a process of incorporation and culinary dispossession.

Another site of the pig's rehabilitation is its transformation from unhealthy to health food. While pigs have long been associated with impurity, dirt, disability, and poverty, they have more recently become quite trendy among white hipsters. These days, eating high on the hog involves eating everything on the pig, from the snout to the tail. However, this process of transforming pork into health food first involved transforming it into white meat. In 1987, "Pork, the Other White Meat" was introduced as a marketing campaign paid for by the National Pork Council. Rebranding pork as "the other white meat" was designed to persuade health-conscious consumers that, while pigs are known for their nondiscriminating appetites and fat, pork is leaner (and thus more consistent with a heart-healthy diet) than beef. Furthermore, the desire to maintain a sharp distinction between beef as "red meat" and pork as "white" led to efforts to give pork a pale appearance, made possible by a diet that deprives commercially raised pigs of essential nutrients and makes them anemic.[40] In response, heritage pork producers point to research that raises questions about the presumed relationship between eating red meat and heart disease. They counter that red flesh is a sign of healthy pigs, verdant fields, and dense forests—a scene far removed from the realities of toxic air, polluted waters, and deforestation that characterize many rural landscapes in the US South. Regardless of the color of its flesh, pork remains the other white meat: in its production and consumption, pork is constituted as part of a heart-healthy diet for the most privileged at the expense of the debilitation of poor whites and people of color who work in and live near industrial pig farms and pork production facilities that satisfy much of the world's demand for pork.

## Humanized Pigs and the Promise of Xenotransplantation

If so many humans seem willing to accept large-scale pig farming and pork production practices that transform pigs into meat for human consumption, xeno scientists reason, they might be open to incorporating other pig parts—such as hearts and other organs—into the human body as medical treatment or even cure.[41] In her work on the "transplant imaginary" of xeno science, Lesley Sharp observes that the prevalence of industrial pig farming has paved the way for a farm–lab connection that normalizes the use of the pig as subject of scientific research, including the now-central

148

place of the pig in xeno science labs.[42] To realize their dream of xenotransplantation, however, xeno scientists must first conquer the obstacle of the human immune system, which rejects pig organs.[43] Notably, Donna Haraway describes the immune system as "a map drawn to guide recognition and misrecognition of self and other in the dialectics of Western biopolitics. In other words, the immune system is a plan for meaningful action to construct and maintain the boundaries for what may count as self and other in the crucial realms of the normal and the pathological."[44] Building on Sharp and Haraway, in this section I discuss how the possible/promised transgression of self/other, human/porcine boundaries occasioned by xenotransplantation also positions the pig as a site for anxieties about the presumed contagion that would accompany the incorporation of that which is deemed foreign.[45]

In xeno science discourse, the pig serves as a narrative prosthesis in the romantic tale of heroic experimental science and its future promise to eliminate suffering and pain, that is, disability. As David Mitchell and Sharon Snyder contend, disability in literature serves as a narrative prosthesis that supports the ableist, normalizing trajectory of the tale; in other words, as narrative prosthesis, disability in literature is that which is overcome in the ultimate achievement of normalcy.[46] Relatedly, within the romanticized tale of heroic xeno science, the experimental achievement of the monstrous, hybrid body of the humanized pig promises to enable the achievement of normalcy for human transplant recipients. Xeno research promises a future of normalcy through incorporation of the pig as human; the engineering of swine results in body parts that will be accepted as human/same/self by the human immune system.[47]

A major focus of xeno research is figuring out how to "fool" the human immune system "into perceiving foreign tissue as 'self' rather than 'other.'"[48] In their efforts to overcome the obstacle presented by the human immune system, xeno scientists have focused on genetically modifying pigs, producing swine bodies shaped in part by human cells. Their goal is seamless incorporation of pig parts that will not be rejected as foreign by human bodies. However, it is important to reflect on the use and social and political significance of the word *foreign* in discussions of xenotransplantation. In writing about the distinction between native and foreign species in the field of invasive biology, Banu Subramaniam maintains that "so long as the category of 'foreign species' (whatever we may call it) exists in our own minds, it is still limited biologically, relationally, historically, and philosophically to a binary world of natives/aliens. . . . The point is not only the xenophobia

149

that permeates the terms of invasion biology, as some have argued, but also the way natives and aliens are presented as a biologically and ecologically useful binary."[49] As Subramaniam demonstrates, central to the framework of native/alien (and in the case of xeno science, self/human versus foreign/ nonhuman) are anxieties and ambivalences about identity, belonging, and difference—key affective registers animated by the imaginary of empire.[50] The hope that is central in legitimating narratives about xeno science coexists with anxiety about bioinsecurity and moves to secure borders against threatening others.[51] In recognition of this fact, Lesley Sharp uses the term "naturalization," a term that underscores the politics of the production of transgenic pigs.[52] The transformation of the pig from a more evolutionarily distant organism to a "naturalized" human, or from a sort of evolutionary wilderness (or frontier) into civilization (or nation/human) is a process of purification and incorporation into human (and nation).

In the tale of humanized pigs and their parts, the pig serves not only as proxy for the human in general (à la Sharp) but also for queerness and disability. Ironically, another immune system obstacle that xeno scientists face is a swine retrovirus that has been found to be capable of jumping the "species barrier" and infecting human cells: porcine endogenous retroviruses, also called PERVs. PERVs is "the equivalent of HIV" in swine, and while the virus is endemic to the genome of pigs, pigs themselves are, largely it seems, asymptomatic.[53] So it seems that "pervs" have once again been cast in the role of threats to the human immune system, public health, and global biosecurity.[54] As with the use of terms like "foreign" in scientific explanations of phenomena, PERVs circulates, I contend, as much more than a mere acronym. In particular, anxieties about PERVs are historically informed and haunted by the heteronormative, ableist anxieties that gave rise to GRID (gay-related immune deficiency) as an acronym for what later came to be called AIDS (acquired immune deficiency syndrome). AIDS is, as Paula Treichler famously observed, both a disease with real health consequences and an epidemic of signification.[55] Just as the historical and cultural resonances of colonial discourse cannot be disentangled from the use of the word *foreign* in scientific research, so too the historical and cultural resonances of moral panics in response to HIV/AIDS cannot be disentangled from the anxieties about threats to biosecurity presented by the presence of PERVs in pigs. Transgenic pigs and xeno grafts thus figure as queer forms of interspecies intimacy that trouble human–animal boundaries assumed to be natural and fixed. Within heteronormative and ableist imaginaries, the possibility of queer contagion presented by such boundary transgressions

150

leads to anxious efforts to reinforce and protect borders against zoonotic threats. Thus, as a romanced figure in the desire for authentic US Southern barbecue and successful xenotransplantation, the pig becomes meat in frontier imaginaries that shape both nostalgic renderings of cuisine and the promise of science.

## The Future Is Pig Stuff

John Shelton Reed jokes that if you want to find a good, authentic barbecue restaurant, just follow the flies. "You should," he says, "ask what the flies know that you don't."[56] While Reed is talking about the rural Southern locations of what he deems authentic barbecue joints, if we really follow the flies, they will undoubtedly take us to the hog waste lagoons that pepper eastern North Carolina. Where there is shit, there are flies, and eastern North Carolina is awash in hog feces, urine, viruses, hormones, parasites, antibiotic-resistant bacteria, and pharmaceuticals that are used to keep confined pigs healthy enough until it is time to slaughter them.[57] North Carolina is second only to Iowa in global pork production and is home to approximately 8.9 million pigs and 9.8 million humans; in some areas in the eastern part of the state, there are more pigs than people. Whether in the form of the humanized pig parts of xeno researchers' dreams or in the realities of industrial pig farming, the future that unites US Southern barbecue and xeno science is full of pig stuff. In this final section, I offer a queer crip reframing of the messy, violent, debilitating intimacies that are denied in romantic tales of barbecue and xeno science.

Michael Pollan describes barbecue in eastern North Carolina as the most "unreconstructed," pure form of Southern barbecue.[58] He uses the term *unreconstructed* to indicate unchanged, true to tradition, and, thus, authentic. But despite his intended meaning, in the South, the purported home of "true 'cue," his use of the word *unreconstructed* evokes the US Civil War, Reconstruction, the meaning of race, and the legacy and persistence of anti-black racism. Given this historical, social, and political framework, I submit that the real meaning of the "unreconstructed" nature of North Carolina barbecue is realized in the fact that the state's toxic hog waste lagoons are located where mostly poor and Black people live. To keep the lagoons from overflowing, the reddish brown contents are sprayed to fertilize fields. Residents have complained of the nauseating smell, headaches, and respiratory ailments, and they have described the mist of hog waste that permeates everything during spraying—closed doors and windows cannot keep out the odor. In fact, local residents in the area recently filed a lawsuit against Murphy-Brown LLC, the supplier of pigs to Smithfield Foods. Their complaint was that the company's practice of spraying hog waste violated their property rights.[59] In response, the North Carolina legislature passed House Bill 467 in April 2017 to protect farmers (that is, large-scale industrial pork producers) from "nuisance" lawsuits. Governor Roy Cooper vetoed the bill; however, the North Carolina legislature voted to override the governor's veto. The law prevents residents from suing for damages that exceed the value of their property; however, the value of their property is devalued by the spraying and the proximity of their homes to a toxic industry. The law has been heralded by the North Carolina Pork Council as "setting the record straight."[60] To set the record straight in this instance is to ignore the precarity that is produced in the production of authentic US Southern cuisine, that is, true 'cue, pure pork, the other white meat.

Anna Tsing posits that precarity is at the heart of life on a damaged planet,[61] an observation that requires rethinking assumptions about intimacy. Conventional accounts conceive of intimacy as rooted in autonomy and desire to be with another; however, in precarious contexts, so many intimacies are beyond the control of many—for example, the unchosen intimacy with hog waste. To the extent that precarity characterizes relationships between beings and worlds, intimacy is itself quite precarious. Unchosen intimacy with pig waste is a debilitating reality for poor whites and people of color who live near industrial pig farms that supply much of the world's pork. Thus, the white ableist longing for pure, authentic US Southern barbecue not only erases African and indigenous culinary knowledge; it also ignores the debilitating effects of racist and classist geographies that are an enduring legacy of imperialism, slavery, and settler colonialism.

Consider now a different form of intimacy. Perhaps few intimacies can feel as precarious as having the heart of another beat inside one's chest. In fact, many heart transplant recipients report feeling a profound disruption to their sense of self.[62] In describing his own heart transplant, Jean-Luc Nancy described his new heart as a stranger, "a strangeness at the heart of what is most familiar."[63] For Nancy, the most profound sense of his heart as other than himself is expressed in his revelation that "without the limits of sex or ethnicity [his] heart may be the heart of a black woman,"[64] an idea that threatens the boundaries of whiteness and maleness that secure his sense of himself as distinct from an/other. Alternatively, Margrit Shildrick suggests that heart transplants can further awareness of "hybridity as the condition of all forms of embodiment."[65] For his part, Nancy ultimately

152

concludes that the stranger that is his heart is himself. However, contrary to Shildrick's concept of a hybrid body that transforms the self, Nancy's conclusion seems to reflect an incorporation of the other as self that is a central feature of whiteness, cis-heteropatriarchal masculinity, and empire.

What if one's heart is a pig's heart? Could the hybrid bodies promised by xeno science be an occasion for a transformed understanding of what it means to be human and a rejection of toxic anthropocentrisms? That would portend hope for the future indeed; nonetheless, there is at least one reason to be cautious about romantic tales of xeno research. Even though pigs bred for their organs would have to be kept in extremely clean conditions to guard against the possibility of a virus being transferred from them to the humans who receive their organs, pigs raised for biomedical purposes, just like pigs raised for food, would also produce waste. Waste from genetically engineered donor pigs would add to the waste from pigs raised for their meat. Furthermore, recipients of pig hearts might develop a sense of themselves as co-constituted and entwined with nonhuman animals like pigs, but such transformations would be reserved for the global elite who have access to medical care and who wouldn't be made worse off by their proximity to waste generated by farm-lab pig production. Thus, the practices that rehabilitate the lives of some will make those who are most precariously situated sicker. Considered from this perspective, the romance of the pig in xeno science reflects an able-transnationalism that promises health, normalcy, and progress for global elites at the expense of disease and death elsewhere. "Elsewhere" in this sense refers to geographies off the beaten track that deviate from what Mark Rifkin refers to as the straight line of the story of progress and greater inclusiveness.[66] By "elsewhere" I also mean that which ignores or erases the endurance of imperial and settler colonial violence at its heart, violence that seeks to secure boundaries that define belonging.

In the context of a world in which it is not possible to avoid implication in impurity through conscious ethical choice, Alexis Shotwell calls for a practice of memory that resists forgetting histories of colonialism and their continuing world-making resonance in the present.[67] A critically queer crip approach to porcine matters strives to notice and attend to the unavoidable complicities of precarious intimacies in the context of empire. Attending to complicities and precarious intimacies in contexts of imperial and settler colonial violence rejects normalizing desires for purity and rehabilitation and pursues instead a queer crip critical rendering of the messy hybridities that make up bodies and worlds. In questioning the fixity of what is and

153

contextualizing possibilities of being other-wise, such an approach offers not a remedy, but a reckoning.

## Notes

I am grateful to Banu Subramaniam and Sushmita Chatterjee for their helpful feedback on this chapter and for the opportunity to participate in the seminar on meat that they organized at University of Michigan's Institute for Research on Women and Gender. I would also like to thank Jill Ehnenn; the Meat seminar participants; audiences at Yale University, Wake Forest University, and the Society for Phenomenology and Existential Philosophy; and anonymous readers for feedback on this project at various stages.

1   Robert McRuer, *Crip Theory* (New York: New York University Press, 2006); Robert McRuer, *Crip Times: Disability, Globalization, and Resistance* (New York: New York University Press), 22.

2   Fiona Kumari Campbell, *Contours of Ableism: The Production of Disability and Abledness* (London: Palgrave Macmillan, 2001); McRuer, *Crip Theory*.

3   Nirmala Erevelles, *Disability and Difference in Global Contexts: Enabling a Transformative Body Politic* (New York: Palgrave Macmillan, 2011).

4   Erevelles, *Disability and Difference*, 39–40.

5   Erevelles, *Disability and Difference*, 17.

6   See Campbell, *Contours of Ableism*. I am indebted to Fiona Kumari Campbell's argument that disability studies needs to center ableism rather than disability per se in order to advance a more critical, rather than assimilationist, approach to Western neoliberal, ableist norms.

7   Lynda Birke, "The Broken Heart," in *Vital Signs: Feminist Reconfigurations of the Bio/logical Body*, edited by Margrit Shildrick and Janet Price (Edinburgh: Edinburgh University Press, 1998), 209; Mary Douglas, *Purity and Danger: An Analysis of the Concepts of Pollution and Taboo* (London: Routledge, 1966).

8   In her discussion of xenotransplantation, Linda Birke rightly focuses on the "narrative of purification" in which pigs become human in order to assuage mainstream anxieties about contamination from other species. See Birke, "The Broken Heart," 210. In this chapter, I highlight how this normalizing approach to hybridity is also part of the structure of ableism.

9   David K. C. Cooper and Robert P. Lanza, *Xeno: The Promise of Transplanting Animal Organs into Humans* (New York: Oxford University Press, 2000), 44.

10  In her analysis of the heart's biological and cultural meanings, Lynda Birke stresses the importance of a feminist body politics that does not remain at the body's surface. As she points out, imperialism is both exterior to and within the heart. Birke, "The Broken Heart," 198–99, 203–4.

11  Derek Hall, *Land* (Malden, MA: Polity, 2013), 19.

12  Hall, *Land*, 54–55.

154

13  See Sharp's insightful analysis of the temporal longing that is part of the moral framework in which xeno scientists strive to legitimate and secure support for their work. Lesley Sharp, *The Transplant Imaginary: Mechanical Hearts, Animal Parts, and Moral Thinking in Highly Experimental Science* (Berkeley: University of California Press, 2014), 150–54.

14  For more about the xeno scientists' desire to fool the human immune system, see Lesley Sharp, "Monkey Business: Interspecies Longing and Scientific Prophecy in Experimental Xenotransplantation," *Social Text* 29, no. 1 (106) (2011): 45. Sharp's excellent analysis of the pig as proxy for human beings in xeno research informs my thinking about the pig as an affective proxy for anxieties about vulnerability and belonging.

15  For more about how pigs have been weaponized in anti-Semitic and Islamophobic acts, see José Medina, *The Epistemology of Resistance: Gender and Racial Oppression, Epistemic Injustice, and Resistant Imaginations* (New York: Oxford University Press, 2013), 135–45; Mark Hay, "How Islamophobes Weaponize Pork," *Vice.com*, October 12, 2016, accessed September 20, 2017, https://www.cnn.com/2015/12/08/politics/philadelphia-mosque-pigs-head/index.html; Dana Ford, "Pig's Head Left at Philadelphia Mosque," *CNN.com*, December 9, 2015, accessed September 20, 2017, https://www.cnn.com/2015/12/08/politics/philadelphia-mosque-pigs-head/index.html.

16  Rosemarie Garland-Thomson, "The Case for Conserving Disability," *Journal of Bioethical Inquiry* 9, no. 3 (2012): 339–55.

17  Lisa Heldke, "An Alternative Ontology of Food: Beyond Metaphysics," *Radical Philosophy Review* 15, no. 1 (2012): 67–88; Kim Q. Hall, "Toward a Queer Crip Feminist Politics of Food," *philoSOPHIA: A Journal of Continental Feminist Philosophy* 14, no. 2 (2014): 177–96.

18  See, for example, Sharp, *The Transplant Imaginary*, 51–53, 81–84.

19  David Judd and James Rocha, "Autonomous Pigs," *Ethics and the Environment* 22, no. 1 (2017): 1–18.

20  Alison Kafer, *Feminist Queer Crip* (Bloomington: Indiana University Press, 2013); Licia Carlson, *The Faces of Intellectual Disability: Philosophical Reflections* (Bloomington: Indiana University Press, 2010); Sunara Taylor, *Beasts of Burden: Animal and Disability Liberation* (New York: New Press, 2017); and Harriet McBryde Johnson, "Unspeakable Conversations," *New York Times Magazine*, February 16, 2003.

21  Taylor, *Beasts of Burden*, 163.

22  Taylor, *Beasts of Burden*, 177.

23  Parama Roy, *Alimentary Tracts: Appetites, Aversions, and the Postcolonial* (Durham, NC: Duke University Press, 2010).

24  John Shelton Reed, "Barbecue Sociology: The Meat of the Matter," in *Cornbread Nation 2: The United States of Barbecue*, edited by Lolis Eric Elie (Chapel Hill: University of North Carolina Press, 2004), 78.

25  John Shelton Reed, *Holy Smoke: The Big Book of North Carolina Barbecue* (Chapel Hill: University of North Carolina Press, 2008).

26  John Edge, *The Potlikker Papers: A Food History of the Modern South* (New York: Penguin, 2017), 271.

27  Edge, *The Potlikker Papers*, 79.

28  Calvin Trillin, "In Defense of the True 'Cue: Keeping Pork Pure in North Carolina," *New Yorker*, November 2, 2015, accessed September 20, 2017, https://www.newyorker.com/magazine/2015/11/02/in-defense-of-the-true-cue.

29  Shannon Sullivan, *The Physiology of Sexist and Racist Oppression* (New York: Oxford University Press, 2015).

30  Michael W. Twitty, *The Cooking Gene: A Journey through African American Culinary History in the Old South* (Princeton, NJ: Princeton University Press).

31  Twitty, *The Cooking Gene*, 235.

32  Mark Essig, *Lesser Beasts: A Snout to Tail History of the Humble Pig* (New York: Basic Books, 2015), 186; Reed, *Holy Smoke*, 16, 18.

33  Charles Mills, "White Ignorance," in *Race and Epistemologies of Ignorance*, edited by Shannon Sullivan and Nancy Tuana (Albany, NY: State University of New York Press, 2007), 22, 28.

34  Mark Rifkin, *Beyond Settler Time: Temporal Sovereignty and Indigenous Self-Determination* (Durham, NC: Duke University Press, 2017), 2, 6.

35  Elspeth Probyn, *Carnal Appetites: Food, Sex, Identities* (New York: Routledge, 2000), 123.

36  Lizzie Collingham, *Curry: A Tale of Cooks and Conquerors* (New York: Oxford University Press, 2006). In her history of curry, Collingham uncovers the history of invasions that have produced curry. Collingham's account reveals that the quest for an "authentic Indian meal" is never satisfied even as the longing for authenticity continues to whet empire's appetite.

37  Jasbir Puar, *The Right to Maim: Debility, Capacity, Disability* (Durham, NC: Duke University Press, 2017). Here I reference Puar's distinction between disability and debility. Disability, for Puar, is connected to identity-based movements for recognition and rights and consists of those whose lives otherwise approximate norms, making them legible as worthy of recognition. Debility, however, is Puar's term for those whose peripheral body-minds cannot be made legible, rendering them ineligible for consideration and recognition. Such lives are marked for death; they cannot be rehabilitated to fit prevailing norms of the human.

38  David T. Mitchell and Sharon L. Snyder, *The Biopolitics of Disability: Neoliberalism, Ablenationalism, and Peripheral Embodiment* (Ann Arbor: University of Michigan Press, 2015); Puar, *The Right to Maim*.

39  Bertram Wyatt-Brown, "Introduction: The Mind of W. J. Cash," in *The Mind of the South*, by W. J. Cash (New York: Vintage, 1991), xx.

40  Allena, "The Culture of the 'The Other White Meat,'" *Today from Firefly Farms*, July 28, 2015, accessed September 20, 2017, https://todayfromfireflyfarms.wordpress.com/2015/07/28/the-culture-of-the-the-other-white-meat/.

41  Sharp, "Monkey Business"; Sharp, *The Transplant Imaginary*.

42  Sharp, *The Transplant Imaginary*, 80–82.

43  Sharp, "Monkey Business," 44.

44  Donna Haraway, *Simians, Cyborgs, and Women: The Reinvention of Nature* (New York: Routledge, 1991), 204.

45  Lesley Sharp, "Perils before Swine: Bioinsecurity and Scientific Longing in Experimental Xenotransplantation Research," in *Bioinsecurity and Vulnerability*, edited by Nancy N. Chen and Lesley A. Sharp (Santa Fe, NM: School for Advanced Research Press, 2015), 53; Sharp, *The Transplant Imaginary*, 50, 66, 77–78, 163. Sharp points out that opponents often characterize xeno research as "monster science," research that disturbs nature by the creation of transgenic organisms. Nonetheless, despite their different aims, both proponents and opponents of xeno research desire purification. For xeno opponents, nature is presented as pure and in need of protection from contaminating human influences, whereas, for xeno proponents, the crucial task is to purify swine parts so that they will be able to trick the human immune system.

46  David T. Mitchell and Sharon L. Snyder, *Narrative Prosthesis: Disability and the Dependencies of Discourse* (Ann Arbor: University of Michigan Press, 2001).

47  Sharp, "Perils before Swine," 58.

48  Sharp, *The Transplant Imaginary*, 66.

49  Banu Subramaniam, *Ghost Stories for Darwin: The Science of Variation and the Politics of Diversity* (Urbana: University of Illinois Press, 2014), 104.

50  Subramaniam, *Ghost Stories for Darwin*, 117.

51  Sharp, *The Transplant Imaginary*.

52  Sharp, *The Transplant Imaginary*, 65–66.

53  Sharp, *The Transplant Imaginary*, 65–66

54  Sharp, "Perils before Swine." In this essay, Sharp discusses the global biopolitical infrastructure that has emerged to contain risks associated with zoonoses like PERVs.

55  Paula A. Treichler, "AIDS, Homophobia, and Biomedical Discourse: An Epidemic of Signification," in *AIDS: Cultural Analysis, Cultural Activism* (Cambridge, MA: MIT Press, 1987), 32.

56  Reed, "Barbecue Sociology," 82.

57  Sara Peach, "What to Do about Pig Poop? North Carolina Fights a Rising Tide," *National Geographic*, October 30, 2014, accessed September 20, 2017, https://news.nationalgeographic.com/news/2014/10/141028-hog-farms-waste -pollution-methane-north-carolina-environment/.

58  *Cooked*, produced by Alex Gibney, featuring Michael Pollan, Netflix documentary series, aired February 19, 2016.

59  Ken Fine and Erica Hellerstein, "N.C. House Backs Big Pork, Votes to Override Cooper's HB 467 Veto," *Indy Week*, May 10, 2017, accessed September 20, 2017, https://www.indyweek.com/news/archives/2017/05/10/nc-house-backs -big-pork-votes-to-override-coopers-hb-467-veto; Erica Hellerstein, "The N.C.

Senate Overrides Cooper's HB 467 Veto, Hog-Farm-Protection Bill Is Law," *Indy Week*, May 11, 2017, accessed September 20, 2017, https://indyweek.com/news /archives/n.c.-senate-overrides-cooper-s-hb-467-veto-hog-farm-protection -bill-law/; Amy Goodman and Denis Moynihan, "In North Carolina, Pigs Don't Fly but Their Feces Do," *Democracy Now*, May 4, 2017, accessed September 20, 2017, https://www.democracynow.org/2017/5/4/in_north_carolina_pigs_don _t; Sid Shapiro and Vanessa Zboreck, "Bill Would Weaken Neighbors' Ability to Be Compensated in Hog Farm Lawsuits," *News and Observer*, April 1, 2017, accessed September 20, 2017, http://www.newsobserver.com/opinion/op-ed /article142045219.htm; "North Carolina Hog Farms Spray Manure around Black Communities: Residents Fight Back," *Democracy Now*, aired May 3, 2017, accessed September 30, 2017https://www.democracynow.org/2017/5/3/nc _lawmakers_side_with_factory_farms.

60  North Carolina Pork Council, "House Bill 467: Setting the Record Straight," accessed September 20, 2017, http://www.ncpork.org/house-bill-467-setting -record-straight/.

61  Anna Tsing, *The Mushroom at the End of the World: On the Possibility of Life in Capitalist Ruins* (Princeton, NJ: Princeton University Press), 20.

62  Margrit Shildrick, "Visceral Phenomenology: Organ Transplantation, Identity, and Bioethics," in *Feminist Phenomenology and Medicine*, edited by Kristin Zeiler and Lisa Folkmarson Käll (Albany: State University of New York Press, 2014).

63  Jean-Luc Nancy, "L'Intrus," translated by Susan Hanson, *New Centennial Review* 2, no. 3 (2002): 4.

64  Nancy, "L'Intrus," 8.

65  Shildrick, "Visceral Phenomenology," 60.

66  Rifkin, *Beyond Settler Time*.

67  Alexis Shotwell, *Against Purity: Living Ethically in Compromised Times* (Minneapolis: University of Minnesota Press, 2016), 7.

## Bibliography

Allena. "The Culture of the 'The Other White Meat.'" *Today from Firefly Farms*, July 28, 2015. https://todayfromfireflyfarms.wordpress.com/2015/07/28/the -culture-of-the-the-other-white-meat/. Accessed September 20, 2017.

Anderson, Virginia DeJohn. *Creatures of Empire: How Domestic Animals Transformed Early America*. New York: Oxford University Press, 2004.

Birke, Lynda. "The Broken Heart." In *Vital Signs: Feminist Reconfigurations of the Bio/logical Body*, edited by Margrit Shildrick and Janet Price, 197–223. Edinburgh: Edinburgh University Press, 1998.

Campbell, Fiona Kumari. *Contours of Ableism: The Production of Disability and Abledness*. London: Palgrave Macmillan, 2001.

Carlson, Licia. *The Faces of Intellectual Disability: Philosophical Reflections.* Bloomington: Indiana University Press, 2010.

Collingham, Lizzie. *Curry: A Tale of Cooks and Conquerors.* New York: Oxford University Press, 2006.

*Cooked.* Produced by Alex Gibney, featuring Michael Pollan. Netflix documentary series, aired February 19, 2016.

Cooper, David K. C., and Robert P. Lanza. *Xeno: The Promise of Transplanting Animal Organs into Humans.* New York: Oxford University Press, 2000.

Douglas, Mary. *Purity and Danger: An Analysis of the Concepts of Pollution and Taboo.* London: Routledge, 1966.

Edge, John T. *The Potlikker Papers: A Food History of the Modern South.* New York: Penguin, 2017.

Erevelles, Nirmala. *Disability and Difference in Global Contexts: Enabling a Transformative Body Politic.* New York: Palgrave Macmillan, 2011.

Essig, Mark. *Lesser Beasts: A Snout to Tail History of the Humble Pig.* New York: Basic Books, 2015.

Fine, Ken, and Erica Hellerstein. "N.C. House Backs Big Pork, Votes to Override Cooper's HB 467 Veto." *Indy Week*, May 10, 2017. https://www.indyweek .com/news/archives/2017/05/10/nc-house-backs-big-pork-votes-to-override -coopers-hb-467-veto. Accessed September 20, 2017.

Ford, Dana. "Pig's Head Left at Philadelphia Mosque." *CNN.com*, December 9, 2015. https://www.cnn.com/2015/12/08/politics/philadelphia-mosque-pigs-head /index.html. Accessed September 20, 2017.

Garland-Thomson, Rosemarie. "The Case for Conserving Disability." *Journal of Bioethical Inquiry* 9, no. 3 (2012): 339–55.

Goodman, Amy, and Denis Moynihan. "In North Carolina, Pigs Don't Fly but Their Feces Do." *Democracy Now*, May 4, 2017. https://www.democracynow.org /2017/5/4/in_north_carolina_pigs_don_t. Accessed September 20, 2017.

Hall, Derek. *Land.* Malden, MA: Polity, 2013.

Hall, Kim Q. "Toward a Queer Crip Feminist Politics of Food." *philoSOPHIA: A Journal of Continental Feminist Philosophy* 14, no. 2 (2014): 177–96.

Haraway, Donna. *Simians, Cyborgs, and Women: The Reinvention of Nature.* New York: Routledge, 1991.

Hay, Mark. "How Islamophobes Weaponize Pork." *Vice.com*, October 12, 2016. https://www.vice.com/en/article/yvewxb/pork-hate-crimes-muslims-islamo- phobia. Accessed September 20, 2017.

Heldke, Lisa. "An Alternative Ontology of Food: Beyond Metaphysics." *Radical Philosophy Review* 15, no. 1 (2012): 67–88.

Hellerstein, Erica. "The N.C. Senate Overrides Cooper's HB 467 Veto, Hog-Farm-Protection Bill Is Law." *Indy Week*, May 11, 2017. https://indyweek.com/news /archives/n.c.-senate-overrides-cooper-s-hb-467-veto-hog-farm-protection -bill-law/. Accessed September 20, 2017.

159

Johnson, Harriet McBryde. "Unspeakable Conversations." *New York Times Magazine*, February 16, 2003. https://www.nytimes.com/2003/02/16/magazine/unspeakable-conversations.html. Accessed September 22, 2017.

Judd, David, and James Rocha. "Autonomous Pigs." *Ethics and the Environment* 22, no. 1 (2017): 1–18.

Kafer, Alison. *Feminist Queer Crip*. Bloomington: Indiana University Press, 2013.

McRuer, Robert. *Crip Theory*. New York: New York University Press, 2006.

McRuer, Robert. *Crip Times: Disability, Globalization, and Resistance*. New York: New York University Press, 2018.

Medina, José. *The Epistemology of Resistance: Gender and Racial Oppression, Epistemic Injustice, and Resistant Imaginations*. New York: Oxford University Press, 2012.

Mills, Charles. "White Ignorance." In *Race and Epistemologies of Ignorance*, edited by Shannon Sullivan and Nancy Tuana, 13–38. Albany: State University of New York Press, 2007.

Mitchell, David T., and Sharon L. Snyder. *The Biopolitics of Disability: Neoliberalism, Ablenationalism, and Peripheral Embodiment*. Ann Arbor: University of Michigan Press, 2015.

Mitchell, David T., and Sharon L. Snyder. *Narrative Prosthesis: Disability and the Dependencies of Discourse*. Ann Arbor: University of Michigan Press, 2001.

Nancy, Jean-Luc. "L'Intrus." Translated by Susan Hanson. *New Centennial Review* 2, no. 3 (2002): 1–14.

"North Carolina Hog Farms Spray Manure around Black Communities; Residents Fight Back." *Democracy Now*, May 3, 2017. https://www.democracynow.org/2017/5/3/nc_lawmakers_side_with_factory_farms. Accessed September 30, 2017.

North Carolina Pork Council. "House Bill 467: Setting the Record Straight." http://www.ncpork.org/house-bill-467-setting-record-straight/. Accessed September 20, 2017.

Peach, Sara, "What to Do about Pig Poop? North Carolina Fights a Rising Tide." *National Geographic*, October 30, 2014. https://news.nationalgeographic.com/news/2014/10/141028-hog-farms-waste-pollution-methane-north-carolina-environment/. Accessed September 20, 2017.

Pollan, Michael. *Cooked: A Natural History of Transformation*. New York: Penguin, 2014.

Probyn, Elspeth. *Carnal Appetites: FoodSexIdentities*. New York: Routledge, 2000.

Puar, Jasbir. *The Right to Maim: Debility, Capacity, Disability*. Durham, NC: Duke University Press, 2017.

Reed, John Shelton. "Barbecue Sociology: The Meat of the Matter." In *Cornbread Nation 2: The United States of Barbecue*, edited by Lolis Eric Elie, 78–87. Chapel Hill: University of North Carolina Press, 2004.

Reed, John Shelton. *Holy Smoke: The Big Book of North Carolina Barbecue*. Chapel Hill: University of North Carolina Press, 2008.

Rifkin, Mark. *Beyond Settler Time: Temporal Sovereignty and Indigenous Self-Determination*. Durham, NC: Duke University Press, 2017.

Roy, Parama. *Alimentary Tracts: Appetites, Aversions, and the Postcolonial*. Durham, NC: Duke University Press, 2010.

Shapiro, Sid, and Vanessa Zboreak. "Bill Would Weaken Neighbors' Ability to Be Compensated in Hog Farm Lawsuits." *News and Observer*, April 1, 2017. http://www.newsobserver.com/opinion/op-ed/article142045219.html. Accessed September 20, 2017.

Sharp, Lesley. "Monkey Business: Interspecies Longing and Scientific Prophecy in Experimental Xenotransplantation." *Social Text* 29, no. 1 (2011): 43–69.

Sharp, Lesley. "Perils before Swine: Bioinsecurity and Scientific Longing in Experimental Xenotransplantation Research." In *Bioinsecurity and Vulnerability*, edited by Nancy N. Chen and Lesley A. Sharp, 45–64. Santa Fe, NM: School for Advanced Research Press, 2015.

Sharp, Lesley. *The Transplant Imaginary: Mechanical Hearts, Animal Parts, and Moral Thinking in Highly Experimental Science*. Berkeley: University of California Press, 2014.

Shildrick, Margrit. "Visceral Phenomenology: Organ Transplantation, Identity, and Bioethics." In *Feminist Phenomenology and Medicine*, edited by Kristin Zeiler and Lisa Folkmarson Käll, 47–68. Albany: State University of New York Press, 2014.

Shotwell, Alexis. *Against Purity: Living Ethically in Compromised Times*. Minneapolis: University of Minnesota Press, 2016.

Subramaniam, Banu. *Ghost Stories for Darwin: The Science of Variation and the Politics of Diversity*. Urbana: University of Illinois Press, 2014.

Sullivan, Shannon. *The Physiology of Sexist and Racist Oppression*. New York: Oxford University Press, 2015.

Taylor, Sunara. *Beasts of Burden: Animal and Disability Liberation*. New York: New Press, 2017.

Treichler, Paula A. "AIDS, Homophobia, and Biomedical Discourse: An Epidemic of Signification." In *AIDS: Cultural Analysis, Cultural Activism*, edited by Douglas Crimp, 31–70. Cambridge, MA: MIT Press, 1987.

Trillin, Calvin. "In Defense of the True 'Cue: Keeping Pork Pure in North Carolina." *New Yorker*, November 2, 2015. https://www.newyorker.com/magazine/2015/11/02/in-defense-of-the-true-cue. Accessed September 20, 2017.

Tsing, Anna. *The Mushroom at the End of the World: On the Possibility of Life in Capitalist Ruins*. Princeton, NJ: Princeton University Press, 2015.

Twitty, Michael W. *The Cooking Gene: A Journey through African American Culinary History in the Old South*. New York: Amistad, 2017.

Wyatt-Brown, Bertram. "Introduction: The Mind of W. J. Cash." In *The Mind of the South*, by W. J. Cash, vii–xli. New York: Vintage, 1991.

161

# On Being Meat

## THREE PARABLES ON SACRIFICE AND VIOLENCE

THIS CHAPTER IS AN ENDEAVOR to think about the relations between human subjects and nonhuman ones, in the context of interspecies sacrifice in particular and of interspecies violence in general. As we know, animal sacrifice and carnivory are perhaps the most consequential and ethically freighted instances of interspecies violence and/or interspecies sacrifice. At the same time, and notwithstanding the licensed or normative carnivory that prevails in the majority of human societies, along with the practice of ritual or cultic animal sacrifice in several, a global history of thinking about dietary ethics and interspecies obligations has called the logic of violence against animals strongly to account. Such thought seeks the sacrifice of animal sacrifice, whether for secular-instrumental or ritual purposes, and an unthinking or at least rethinking of the animal as killable.[1] At the most ethically exigent bound of their carnivorous and sacrificial abolitionism, advocates for the sacrifice of animal sacrifice provide scenarios for a reversed template of sacrifice: human obligation to the nonhuman and self-sacrifice on its behalf in place of the familiar, often normative, sacrifice of the animal to human (and supernatural) interests. I investigate some of these scenarios of normative and reverse sacrifice as a route into the knotty philosophical and ethical entailments of carnivory, vegetarianism, and self-sacrifice.

How do texts of carnivorous or sacrificial advocacy map the material and moral process though which animals become imaginable as meat? Conversely, how do abolitionist advocates imagine the forms of violence and nonviolence, injury and care that are at stake when humans sacrifice themselves or offer up their bodies for the protection or nurture of animals? I enter these questions by deploying three parabolic instantiations, drawn from early modern England and from ancient Indic materials and contemporary Indian ones, of the ethics of carnivorous consumption and the abjuration of carnivory. These encompass the domains of literature, religious narrative, and contemporary anthropology/lived practice. I begin with Ben Jonson's famous country house poem of 1616, "To Penshurst." This is a preeminent example of what has been described as "an exceedingly carnivorous genre," notable for the ways in which it dramatizes the willing sacrifice of fish and fowl for the benefit of the lord of the manor.[2] A text such as this can be juxtaposed instructively with a variety of narratives of ethical extremity—here drawn from the subcontinental context—in which the bodies of humans are sacrificed to sustain nonhuman animal life. Hence the second of my parables is drawn from Indian Buddhist narrative literature (especially the Jatakas, accounts of the Buddha's past lives), which is full of instances of what has been identified as *dehadana*, the gift of one's body, either in whole or in part, to rescue a recipient—often an animal recipient—from death or disability.[3] Such instances of self-dismemberment or self-sacrifice are seen as exemplifying in the most spectacular degree the virtue of generosity, the highest-ranked among Buddhist virtues or "perfections." The third parabolic instance is drawn from stories told of the Bishnoi of western India. For them the conservation of animal and arboreal life constitutes a key plank of their religious observance, so much so that numerous Bishnoi have been killed protecting wildlife and trees against poachers and fellers of trees.

Not so much a work of comparison, this essay is a thought exercise in imagining carnivory in relation to instances, real and imagined, of what is a little more rare: human edibility and human self-sacrifice, especially on behalf of the nonhuman. Taken together, these three parabolic instances of other-sacrifice and self-sacrifice furnish an occasion to meditate upon "extreme" forms of charity or hospitality, which involve a kind of a giving without reserve and beyond reason, to the point of abjuring in favor of an other any property right of the subject in its own body, or any right to abstain from injuring or sacrificing this body. These parables of multi- or interspecies sacrifice also permit us to pose some critical questions: Is the "willing" self-sacrifice of animals a mystification of their status as killable, as mere meat? What is the place of violence in the sacrifice of animal sacrifice? What is at stake in the translation of a (living) human (or superhuman) body into meat or food? Might the rendering of human (or superhuman) bodies into meat or food represent a reversal of a familiar hierarchy of anthropocentric and carnivorous privilege, permitting the emergence of an ethics not wholly governed by anthropocentrism? Or is self-sacrifice, or the deliberate, uncoerced rendering of oneself into meat, itself a singular mode of consolidating or enhancing anthropocentric or superhuman privilege? As the following sections will demonstrate, the answers to these questions are the very reverse of straightforward.

## Beasts: The Lives and Deaths of Animals

While animal sacrifice has featured in many of the world's major religions, the sacrifice of animal sacrifice has marked both Judaism and Christianity for close upon two millennia. Sacrifice, described in great prescriptive detail in the Book of Leviticus, had come to be centralized in the temple at Jerusalem by various kings and high priests. After the destruction of the Second Temple in Jerusalem in 70 CE by the Romans, sacrifice could no longer be practiced, and it came to be replaced by prayer and Torah study as the basis for religious life. Sacrifice came eventually to be seen as a relic of a past that was contaminated by proximity to pagan polytheistic Canaanitism in the ancient Near East; Maimonides argued, for instance, that sacrificial laws were inessential and expendable in light of such an accommodation to the exigencies of pagan proximity.[4] Even the invocation of sacrifice during prayer could be fraught. On occasion, post–Second Temple Judaism's prayers for the building of a Third Temple at Jerusalem demonstrate some discomfort with the notion of a renewal of sacrifice; as Kimberley Patton notes, "recent versions of some modern reform, reconstructionist and even conservative Jewish *siddurim* suppress the traditional Orthodox prayers, found in the seventeenth blessing of the *Amida*, for the rebuilding of the Temple and the renewal of the sacrificial cult."[5] Such a posture derives some of its inspiration from the criticism of sacrifice by the prophets Isaiah, Jeremiah, Amos, Hosea, and Micah, who denounced ritual acts that were disaggregated from righteous conduct and obedience to the God of Israel. Hence, says Jill Robbins, "there arises the emphasis on the relation between the *outer* form of sacrifice and the *inner* attitude, which will become especially important in the New Testament and the Christian context."[6] In

164

general it may be averred that Christian theology reads Christianity as the movement from the public cult of the blood sacrifice of animals to the self-sacrifice of Christ, and thus as the sacrifice of sacrifice itself in its archaic, ritual, and bodily forms. Christian sacrifice is predicated upon the establishment of a reconceptualized, sublimated order of inward or spiritualized sacrifice, which achieves its distinctness and ethical superiority in contrast with its gory original. "The history of Western onto-theology [is] thus read," says Hent de Vries, "as the unfolding of a generalized transubstantiation of broken bodies and spilt blood."[7] Once Christianity was established as the official religion of the Roman Empire in the fourth century CE, animal sacrifices were abolished by repeated imperial edicts. This abolition functioned as part of the state's Christianizing effort and was at the same time an attack upon the pagan cults that undertook animal sacrifice and competed with the new religion.[8]

The turn away from animal sacrifice, though, did not necessarily entail vegetarianism as a general law of ethical conduct. Animal sacrifice may have been viewed in a Jewish and Christian modern world order as a barbaric religious reflex—a view that assumed the status of common sense through much of the Christian world—but animals were not encompassed in the prohibition against killing.[9] Vegetarianism may have been normative in Eden, but after the Deluge, the Noachide covenant licensed carnivory as a concession to human sinfulness. There were occasions, such as Lent, on which abstention from flesh was enjoined upon the lay faithful as penance for sin. And in the late ancient world and in the medieval era, several anchorites and members of religious orders practiced an ascetic discipline that involved fasting and abstention from carnivory. But these practices were grounded not so much in a consideration for animal welfare as in the sense that meat, as a paradigmatically "hot" food, engendered carnal desires.[10] Hence it may be asserted that to a significant degree the nonsacrificial killing of animals passed into the realm of religious indifference. Most influential Christian theologians and ethicists of the ancient and medieval worlds defended carnivory on the grounds of the superiority of human reason, which could permit of no fellowship with irrational animals. For the Augustine of the *City of God*, "When we say 'Thou shalt not kill,' we do not understand this of the plants, since they have no sensation, nor of the irrational animals that fly, swim, walk, or creep, since they are dissociated from us by their want of reason, and are therefore by the just appointment of the Creator subjected to us to kill or keep alive for our own uses."[11] Aquinas's synthesis of Aristotelian and Augustinian notions of natural hierarchy

165

also permitted the instrumental use of animals by humans; cruelty against the brute creation did not encompass killing, and was lamentable primarily because it might be a stepping-stone to cruelty against humans.[12] The slaughter of an animal was thus (what Derrida has named) a noncriminal putting to death of a living being, and the human entitlement to animal flesh, whether for the table or the hunt or any other purpose, largely unassailable. Though humans could be and sometimes are subject to this allowable, noncriminal putting to death, it is the animal that has functioned most often as the paradigmatic instance of what Donna Haraway calls "killable" life.

To all intents and purposes this human entitlement to animal flesh seems to be flaunted to spectacular effect in the country house (or estate) poem of the seventeenth century. Indeed, the genre constitutes a touchstone in discussions of carnivory in early modern England. It reworks materials from many sources, including the Greco-Roman classical myth of the golden age in which virtuous men lived in harmony with a benevolent earth that gave copiously and spontaneously of its bounty without the necessity of the compulsion, labor, or suffering that belongs to the less metallically blessed ages plagued by struggle, lack, ostentation, and monetary exchange. This hyperbolical offering, as emblematized in the *sponte sua* (on one's own accord) topos, is part of an economy simultaneously agricultural and moral. As deployed by Hesiod, Virgil, and Martial, it encompasses most orders of the living, including vegetables, animals, and men (the last category made up of slaves, tenants, farmers, neighbors, and guests).[13] "From vegetable to overlord," says William McClung, "each component of the estate willingly does that which must be done, finding, indeed, fulfillment of identity in performing the act."[14] There were other, less august sources of inspiration for the country house poem in addition to these classical ones. Visions of animals offering themselves up for human tables also belong to a medieval European peasant vision of gastronomic excess emblematized in the myth of Cockaigne, though in the medieval instance they come ready-cooked and instantly available for consumption. In seventeenth-century poetry, however, such a vision is repurposed from its origins in peasant populist fantasy and recycled to serve the celebration of aristocratic hospitality.[15]

Hence, in a poem like "To Penshurst," Jonson's panegyric to the preternatural perfection of Robert Sidney, Lord Lisle's estate, the poet magnifies the natural bounties of the manor's woodlands, river, ponds, orchards, and gardens, which provide timber, game animals and domestic ones, fish, and fruit in uncoerced and inexhaustible plenty. Among the most notable lines in the poem are those in which nonhuman creatures of all kinds offer themselves, first dutifully and then with increasing enthusiasm, as oblations to an exceptionally worthy lord:

> The painted partridge lies in every field,
> And, for thy mess, is willing to be killed.
> And if the high-swol'n Medway fail thy dish,
> Thou hast thy ponds, that pay thee tribute fish,
> Fat aged carps that run into thy net,
> And pikes, now weary their own kind to eat,
> As loath the second draught or cast to stay,
> Officiously at first themselves betray;
> Bright eels that emulate them, and leap on land
> Before the fisher, or into his hand.[16]

The sheer extravagance of these lines has inspired no small measure of critical attention; whether approving or appalled, critics have felt that the lines are the very opposite of anodyne. Some describe them as instances of Jonson's "witty hyperbole," characteristic of the emblematic mode used to describe human regulation of nature's bounty in the georgic mode.[17] Other critics have found the conceit troubling for a variety of reasons. Raymond Williams famously insists on the political and interpretive value of reading the lines naturalistically rather than typologically, remarking that "this natural order is simply and decisively on its way to table."[18] And Peter Remien notes the ways in which these lines about willing self-sacrifice involve more than nonhuman animals; they find an echo later in the poem in the description of humble tenants offering gifts of food, sometimes through their "ripe daughters, . . . whose baskets beare / An emblem of themselves, in plum, or peare." The celebration of carnivorous abundance at aristocratic tables thus does not leave the flesh of the lower orders unscathed, figuratively speaking; "they illuminate," he says, "the tenuous distinction between Penshurst's personified fish and its consumable humans."[19] Carnivory in this poem is not predicated, in ways we usually take for granted, upon the human–animal distinction alone, nor upon an injunction against the consumption of human flesh; it is predicated, rather, upon the distinction between the seigneur and other forms of life, including human ones, that are open to being consumed symbolically or literally.

At the same time, as Remien notes, if some humans are not nonconsumable, the poet's strategy of personifying the animals that are metamorphosing into meat—they are rendered as volitional agents choosing in a quasi-human fashion to offer their bodies up—suggests that they are not entirely distinct from humans either. There is, therefore, some tension between the vision of "absolute dominion" represented by animal life entirely subsumed to human ends and the moral decision of the pheasant that is "willing to be kill'd."[20] What is also worth noting about the poem is the poet's conspicuous reluctance to avow that animals that are intended for the table are put to the knife. Despite Jonson's focus on his own gluttony, the guests' (including the poet's) scenes of feasting on "beer and bread and . . . wine" are not as carnivorous as one might expect from the earlier lines on the animal bounty at hand.[21] Though the poem has brief references to hunting, the rituals of gift-giving prevail over those of blood and slaughter, which move discreetly offstage.[22] Such hesitations and occlusions about killing and carnivory suggest that Jonson's poem hesitates to treat nonhuman lives purely as objects that can be translated into meat without compunction, even as it *also* naturalizes a human right to nonhuman animal flesh.

Jonson's reluctance to speak of bloodletting is best understood perhaps not so much in terms of normative carnivory but in terms of the logic of a putatively superseded religious sacrifice, in which the sacrificial animal is not simply instrumental or anonymous or mere meat—if meat can ever be such. Patton accentuates the fact that animals picked for sacrifice were generally seen as the most perfect specimens of their kind. In the Jewish, Greek, Roman, and Vedic worlds of antiquity, "animals [were] seen as active subjects from start to finish in the sacrificial process, . . . whose cooperation [was] essential to the efficacy of the ritual."[23] In their celebrated work on sacrifice, Henri Hubert and Marcel Mauss note that "excuses were made for the act that was about to be carried out, the death of the animal was lamented. . . . Its pardon was asked before it was struck down. The rest of the species to which it belonged were . . . entreated not to avenge the wrong about to be done to them in the person of one of their number."[24]

This ambivalence in many religious traditions, even about *religiously* sanctioned violence against the animal thus seeks to distinguish sacrifice from murder and to establish it, rather, as a form of symbolic or ritual nonviolence; death in such a scheme is a transit into a more elevated sphere. In India, the Vedic vision of the world was governed by (what would come later to be known as) *matsyanyaya* (the law of the fishes), in which bigger fish devour little fish. Far more remorseless than the *scala naturae* or the Great Chain of Being that we see elaborated in "To Penshurst," matsyanyaya, or the Vedic law of the jungle, is "a hierarchically ordered sequence of Chinese boxes, or better, Indian stomachs."[25] But even in the prevegetarian

168

universe of these Vedic texts, it was important to believe that the sacrificial animal did not bleed or suffer or cry out, and one way to establish this was to strangle the victim rather than dispatch it by other means. "When an animal offering is put to death in the Vedic *pasubandha* or animal sacrifice," says Kathryn McClymond, "the texts focus on the priests stopping breath, not on drawing blood."[26] It might be useful to recall here the etymological association of cruelty with spilled blood in Latin, as Derrida has underlined;[27] Hubert and Mauss underline the care taken to control the effusion of the blood of the sacrificed.[28] A similar association of cruelty with the shedding of blood clearly extends to religio-cultural contexts other than the Judeo-Christian or the Greco-Roman, and here includes the Vedic one.

The ritual of securing the consent of the animal chosen for sacrifice is also critically important for its religious efficacy; it cannot be bypassed. The sprinkling of water on the animal's head in the burnt animal offering of the ancient Greek *thusia* or the ancient Israelite *qorban 'ola*, so that it seems to nod in acquiescence, was an important part of the ritual.[29] In hunting societies, too, as established by Jonathan Z. Smith, it was crucial to imagine that the animal—"a gift from the 'Master of the Animals,' . . . [and] a visitor from the spirit world"—was not slain by the hunter's weapon or initiative but offered itself up freely in exchange for a strict ceremonial recognition of its dignity and singularity.[30] All sacrifice is thus nothing but self-sacrifice; a coerced sacrifice is a contradiction in terms, and no sacrifice at all. In addition, the language of the Vedic texts uses a series of rhetorical substitutions for killing and death, often asserting not just that the animal had acquiesced in his own sacrifice but occasionally even urging on the sacrificial animal that what he was to undergo was not death at all. Hence, in the hymn of the horse sacrifice in the *Rig Veda*, the horse is addressed in the following terms: "Let not the ax do lasting harm to your body. . . . You do not really die through this, nor are you harmed. You go to the gods on paths pleasant to go on."[31]

That the conditions for this idealized sacrifice or hunting are impossible to meet commonsensically or empirically is not in doubt. But to dismiss these conditions as rank hypocrisy or incoherence or contradiction is also to miss some of the more interesting aspects of sacrificial thought. Smith comments usefully on the way in which sacrificial or hunting ritual partakes of a kind of theater, staging or vivifying rather than abolishing the ethical tensions inherent in these acts. "Ritual," says he, "provides the means for demonstrating that we know what ought to have been done. . . . It provides an occasion for reflection and rationalization on the fact that what ought to have been done was not done."[32] The sponte sua topos in "To Penshurst," in which animals take the initiative in becoming meat for the aristocratic table, may be said, then, to partake of this orchestration of discrepancy between prescription and practice that Smith claims is a major function of (sacrificial and hunting) ritual. Through the very flamboyance of its images of nonhuman creatures flocking to the table in nonreciprocal surrender, Jonson ensures that matters of unequal life and unequal death remain front and center in the reader's experience.

## Bodhisattvas: Incarnation, Excarnation

The sponte sua topos of the Latin poetry of antiquity and of the seventeenth-century country house poem dramatizes a sacrificial economy that depends upon the flesh of animals, whether as killable life or as willing sacrifice—though, as we have seen, there is a not inconsiderable degree of ambiguity in Jonson's poem about the ethics of animal death. In contrast to the country house poem and its classical antecedents, however, there are other traditions in which the flesh and blood of humans (or highly enlightened humans) is sacrificed to sustain nonhuman animal life, sometimes, though not necessarily always, in conditions of ethical extremity. In the subcontinent, the ethos of devouring of the Vedic period came eventually to be overtaken by increasingly normative sanctions against both the religious sacrifice of animals and carnivory. In its place arose an ethos of vegetarianism and nonviolence (ahimsa), especially for Brahmins, that sought to break the chain of alimentary violence and to urge forms of eating that were not predicated upon the deliberate slaughter of animals. There is some dispute about the origins of this vegetarianism and nonviolence. Some scholars have argued that the Hindu doctrine of ahimsa was an outgrowth of the limits on sacrificial violence in the Vedic texts.[33] Others have argued that the ahimsaic turn constituted a non-Vedic and anti-Brahmanical revolution in values, receiving a decisive impetus from the heterodox teachings and activities of the world-renouncing traditions of the *sramanas* (ascetics), who rejected the authority of the Vedas, with their emphasis on ritual and blood sacrifice.[34] These sramanas, later known as Jains and Buddhists, became increasingly influential starting in the sixth century BCE.

It is perhaps not surprising, then, that one of these heterodox traditions placed tremendous importance upon the *obverse* of animal sacrifice, in the form of the Jataka tale in Buddhist narrative literature. This genre features the legends of the Buddha in his previous Bodhisattva incarnations—

170

whether as a man, or, less frequently, a deity, or a higher animal—and instantiates through his phenomenal actions the various "perfections" (or *paramitas*) that go into the making of his buddhahood.[35] Of the various perfections needed to attain to attain buddhahood, the *dana-paramita* (the "perfection of generosity") is the most highly prized. "Gift-giving of various sorts, in fact, may well be the single most popular subject of Indian Buddhist narrative literature, taken as a whole," notes Reiko Ohnuma, and tales that illustrate this quality recur with great frequency among the Jatakas and the Avadanas (religious biographies of monastics and lay disciples).[36] One recurrent example of a generosity that gives out of pure altruism and without any expectation of reciprocity is the Bodhisattva's bodily self-sacrifice, in which he gives away all or part of his body—flesh, head, blood, marrow, eyes, feet, and ears—to all manner of beneficiaries. These stories constitute an important subgenre that Ohnuma has christened dehadana (gift of the body) tales. Over and over again, the Bodhisattva gives away his life or parts of his body (and, on at least one famous occasion, his wife and children), sometimes to save a single being, or multiple other beings, from death, disability, hunger, or thirst, and sometimes simply because this gift is requested of him.[37] Often, this experience of excarnation is the necessary portal to incarnation as the Buddha.

The tales are well known. In the fourth-century *Jatakamala* (Garland of Jatakas) of Aryasura, the King Shibi, for instance, is so addicted to almsgiving that he falls into discontent when beggars' needs are met, and begins to long for occasions when his limbs might be demanded of him. So when he is asked for the gift of an eye by a blind old Brahman, he responds joyfully by giving him both of his, and reducing himself to blindness.[38] In the *Avadanasataka* 31, the virtuous king Padmaka commits suicide and is reborn as a giant *rohita* fish, so that his subjects, suffering from an epidemic, might consume its flesh and be saved. In other stories, the kings Candraprabha and Sarvamdada give away their heads to malicious Brahmans who ask for them, and King Maitribala effects a conversion to Buddhism of five anthropophagous *yakshas* (tree spirits, usually demonic and violent) by allowing them to feed upon his flesh and blood. Rupavati, one of the rare female incarnations of the Buddha in a prior life, sacrifices her breasts to a famished new mother trying to eat her infant, and is transformed into the man Rupavata as a reward. And so on.

Like the Latin georgics and the seventeenth-century country house poem, there are some Jataka tales that feature animals that sacrifice themselves eagerly to save humans from distress or simply to comply with human desires, no matter how malevolent. There are tales of six-tusked elephants who either lose their lives willingly by giving away their tusks to evil queens or more mundane ones who kill themselves to provide food for lost and hungry travelers, just as there are even more famous tales of rabbits who practice self-immolation in an endeavor to offer hospitality to visiting Brahmans. Almost without exception, these heroically self-sacrificing animals are not animals qua animals but prior incarnations of the illustrious being who eventually is born as Siddhartha Gautama, or the Buddha.

Thus, where gifting and self-sacrifice in the country house poem flow upward on the Great Chain of Being, from hierarchical inferiors, whether animal or human, to hierarchical superiors, in the instance of the Jatakas they flow downward, from the Bodhisattva to various lesser forms of being, whether human, demonic, or animal. Perhaps more notably, there are several important instances where the Bodhisattva in his human births undergoes suffering or death in order to nurture or save the lives of nonhuman animals. In one of the most famous of these, the Shibi Jataka, the king finds himself torn between competing responsibilities to two different orders of nonhuman life. When a dove being chased by a hawk finds refuge with him, he can neither give up the dove to its predator nor withhold its fleshly diet from the bird of prey. In order to be just to both, he offers enough flesh from his own body to equal the weight of the dove. But no matter how much flesh the king parts with, it falls short of the weight of the dove on the scales. Finally, reduced to bone and sinew, the king climbs onto the scale himself, at which point dove and hawk reveal themselves as deities seeking to test the extent of his concern for the welfare of others, especially the lowliest of others.[39]

In another famous tale, the prince Mahasattva, coming across a tigress who has recently given birth and is driven by hunger and thirst to contemplate devouring her own cubs, leaps off a cliff and falls dead before the tigress so that she might eat him. In another version of this tale, in the *Suvarnaprabhasa*, the Bodhisattva has to work harder still to turn his body into consumable meat for the starving animal; finding that she is too weak to avail herself of his gift, he cuts his throat with a bamboo creeper so as to assist in her feeding.[40] In other examples, the merchant's son Sattavara pities the hungry birds of prey in the cremation grounds, and feeds them upon pieces of his flesh and his eyes until he expires. King Shibi, having exhausted his generosity to his human subjects, extends his care to the smallest and most noxious of living creatures; creating several wounds in his body, he feeds fleas and mosquitoes upon his blood. These are outdone by King Ambara, who "gives away to various recipients his feet, eyes, ears, genitals, flesh, blood, and hands [in addition to giving away his kingdom, wife, and children]. His ministers dump his mutilated body into a charnel ground, where the remainder is devoured by flies, mosquitoes, dogs, jackals, and vultures." Not content with this, he aspires to become "a mountain of flesh" so that "whatever beings have flesh for food and blood for drink [might] come eat [his] flesh and drink [his] blood."[41] This body is an inexhaustible somatic resource, an aggregation of boundlessly divisible and proliferating parts that allow him to give endlessly and never be used up in his endeavor to be a host to an infinity of hungry others. In many of the tales we are invited to linger not just on the inconceivable munificence of the sacrifice but also on the properties of his flesh. It is, we are told, the best kind of meat, pleasing to the palate, therapeutic in its properties, and capable of furnishing its eaters with both metaphysical and alimentary gifts.

In all these transactions, the enlightened being who is the Bodhisattva offers gifts that are composed simultaneously of flesh and spirit. Without a doubt his self-sacrifice is an allegory of the immeasurable gift of Buddhist *dharma* (law, teaching), inasmuch as it is a sacrifice of the bloody animal sacrifice demanded by Brahmanical ritual. But the sacrifice is never only allegorical, and it certainly is never nonviolent. It emphatically is a sacrifice of the flesh; in fact, the violence that the Bodhisattva's body endures, extremely and repeatedly, is irreducible in this sacrifice of sacrifice.

What is evident in all these stories is that the Bodhisattva is marked by a certain heroism of generosity that gives extravagantly and without calculation to all who might request a gift or plead for protection, and frequently out of compassion alone, without any request being made. Such instances of self-dismemberment or self-sacrifice are seen as paradigmatic acts of generosity, extraordinary not only for their sheer excessiveness but because they are given in such profusion and even so preposterously to the malicious, the frivolous, and the utterly lowly. That said, it should be remembered that the Bodhisattva's death or self-mutilation is not prompted by any sense of the radical equality of all forms of life, or of all beings, or of any confusion of categories among low and high, worthy and unworthy. The recipients of such generosity, in other words, are not superiors (or even cognates or intimates) for whom sacrifices are usually made but beings of often markedly inferior status. Among these are beings that Ohnuma describes as "pitiful" recipients—those animals (or humans driven to near-animality by the experience of desperate hunger or thirst)—who are in dire straits but

173

who are, generally speaking, not petitioners for the Bodhisattva's gifts of his body or his life.[42]

Such gifting is an anomaly within Indic religious traditions, where gifts are soteriological investments by householders, who constitute the paradigmatic donors. Gifts are expected to be directed upward toward religious elites, such as renunciants and Brahman males, who are considered superior to donors and thus the most worthy of esteem and generosity. "Moral action is illustrated," says Maria Heim, "by the imagery of sowing or planting good deeds in the world which in turn yield produce or fruits . . . one plants the seed of a good action in a suitable field of a recipient which yields, often exponentially, the fruits of one's effort."[43] Gifts given to inferior or unworthy recipients—that is to say, gifts prompted by altruism and pity rather than by what Heim has named "an ethics of esteem"—are invested with less merit and thus are gifts thrown away, as it were. Such aneconomic gifts as the ones named above flow not from mere mortals or householders but from exceptional and more-than-human beings like Bodhisattvas, who stand outside the reciprocities and calculations involved in gift-giving in its usual transactional forms. In fact, notes Ohnuma, the Bodhisattva goes out of his way to seek out recipients who are "unworthy," unable in any way to enter into relations of reciprocity with him; only through such a gulf between himself and the objects of his sacrifice is his status as the beau ideal of generosity made spectacularly manifest. This asymmetry between subject and object of sacrifice speaks powerfully to the question of who can undertake the responsibility of sacrifice. If sacrifice is a burden it surely is also an entitlement, to be assumed by the most exceptional of beings, rather than being open to all. Only one who owns himself absolutely and is unbound to others can undertake such an act; that is to say, only he can make that gift of his body and/or life to another that is entailed in self-sacrifice.

It should be noted that animals, in a Buddhist world view, have souls as much as humans do, and they are sentient beings deserving of human and superhuman regard and protection. They are particularly deserving of compassion because they inhabit a near-hellish world of violence, suffering, lack of freedom, and religious ignorance. But they are also definitively inferior to humans ontologically. To be born a nonhuman animal is to be unfortunate in one's birth; it is to be condemned to limited rationality and self-control, as well as vulnerability to suffering and exploitation.[44] Generally speaking, a human incarnation is required for the practice of virtue and the attainment of enlightenment; moreover, it is primarily actions undertaken in a human birth that have any kind of karmic significance.[45] It should come as no surprise, then, that so many of the heroic or articulate animal actors in the dehadana tales in the Jatakas are either Bodhisattvas in their animal incarnations or gods in animal disguise—the latter part most often assumed by Shakra (Indra in Sanskrit), who is continually testing the Bodhisattva's capacity for compassion. But what is surely also worth noting are the many instances when the animal objects of the Bodhisattva's self-sacrifice are animals qua animals—not shape-shifting gods, not animal votaries of the Buddha, and not prior incarnations of eminent human disciples. Quite often, moreover, they are predatory creatures or noxious, polluting, or contemptible ones—such as tigresses, vultures, jackals, dogs, mosquitoes, and maggots—who do not normally inspire pity and whose actions cannot be made serviceable for human ends. In fact, in the version of the tigress tale in the *Divyavadana* 32, the Bodhisattva distinguishes himself from his companions precisely because of his willingness to make a sacrifice they consider unreasonable and excessive: "'I can sacrifice myself for the sake of a mere animal.'"[46]

This early Buddhist vision of the sacrifice of the body for nonhuman beneficiaries might appear to function as a challenge to modes of thought instantiated, albeit quite ambiguously, in the world of a poem like "To Penshurst." In the latter, being a human, at least of the masculine and status-privileged persuasion, might be seen to entail the fantasy of an unbreachable corporeal integrity. In such an order, the violence and injury involved in eating meat was meant, typically, to proceed in a single, nonreversible direction, with the human at the head of an alimentary or sacrificial chain; the maintenance of an alimentary apartheid between predator and prey, the edible and the nonedible, was crucial to human superiority over the nonhuman world. At the same time, Christian theology and aesthetics delighted in reminding puffed-up humans of the body's vulnerability to death, decay, and consumption; medieval European funerary art and poetry were at considerable pains to horrify their living human viewers with reminders that they were food for worms.[47] In such a scheme, a recognition of one's bodily vulnerability and one's finitude (rather than one's bodily integrity and autonomy) could be an approach to a recognition of one's own animality and one's bodied companionship with the rest of mortal creation. If we allow ourselves to be thought of and consumed (usually but not always posthumously) as food, we might be able to see eating and bodily dependence as disseminated across a multitude of hungry mouths and bellies. Our bodies exist at a crossroads where our appetites encounter those of others who are not necessarily there by invitation. Who eats and who gets eaten can then be flexibly contingent rather than unyieldingly predictable. This, I hasten to add, is not a nonviolent process for the most part; the consumption of (human or nonhuman) flesh by hungry others is generally a bloody, asymmetric, and nonvoluntaristic business. But it is generally thought capable of breaching at a symbolic level anthropocentric claims of invulnerability and self-sufficiency.

We would be mistaken, however, in imagining that an openness to thinking of one's flesh as meat for consumption guarantees a divestiture or even an unsettling of one's human or superhuman ascendancy or autonomy. Rather, the Jataka tales make clear that the Bodhisattva's buddhahood is augmented and consolidated by such an action; it is a distancing from rather than an approach to somatic vulnerability and limitation. As we know from Kaja Silverman's virtuosic discussion of T. E. Lawrence's "reflexive masochism" in *The Seven Pillars of Wisdom*, virile leadership can be constituted through the competitive assumption of pain and suffering to a degree that leaves all others behind. Lawrence's heroism, she notes, often seems to inhere in his inordinate capacity for enduring pain, to the point that "the one who heaps the greatest pain upon himself diminishes those around him."[48] The live excarnation that the Bodhisattva undergoes in being reduced to a carapace of bone and sinew in the story of King Shibi is, if anything, an emblem of his divestiture of softness or penetrability, of anything that might leave him with soft spots as it were. His life or essence or aura is not extinguished by any means by the eradication of his flesh, nor does the act establish his killability in the way an animal's slaughter usually does in a carnivorous order. Rather, rendering himself into meat paradoxically distances him from the precarious status of mortal flesh and blood, signaling his mastery over the vulnerability of the flesh and over death. He is enriched, in other words, by his willingness and his capacity to turn himself into meat, while those who partake of the gift of his flesh are not so much consumers exercising alimentary privilege as they are subordinate recipients of charity. In several of the stories, in fact, he not only qualifies for reincarnation as the Buddha but, in addition, regains his body in a perfected and superhuman form as a result of his willingness to turn it into meat. This body comes to be transformed into something incomparably rare, value-laden, and transcendent precisely through being given or thrown away as meat for animal mouths.

176

## Bishnois: Altruistic Dying, Altruistic Suckling

My third and final parable of self-sacrifice and violence comes from the biophilic practices of the Bishnoi community of western Rajasthan in India. Unlike the two previous models of sacrifice, it features neither a mythological realm nor transcendent subjects. Its subjects are emphatically inhabitants of a this-worldly sphere, even though they have attained near-mythic status in the annals of indigenous environmentalism. Unlike the Bodhisattva, whose self-sacrifice derives its value from being sui generis and not susceptible of imitation by ordinary mortals, the Bishnoi practice forms of self-sacrifice that are disseminated across significant numbers of ordinary people. It is worth pondering if their more democratic practices of sacrifice on behalf of animals and trees might displace anthropocentric privilege in a way not available in the supernatural heroism of the Jataka tales.

In recent decades scholars and environmental activists have come to take a strong interest in this community for what seems to be an unusually eco-friendly form of religious practice. The Bishnoi constitute a small Hindu Vaishnavite sect resident in a few western and northern states of India, but most densely concentrated in the Thar Desert of western Rajasthan. They have gained a reputation over nearly three centuries, but most especially since the mid-1990s, of being zealous custodians of the desert biome. They are known for organizing protests to demand the implementation of wildlife protection laws in India, and sometimes have sacrificed their own lives to keep trees and wild creatures from harm. They have captured public attention through sensational stories and images of women breastfeeding orphaned fawns, as well as through their capture in 1998 of Bombay film star Salman Khan in the act of poaching the endangered black buck and chinkara (Indian gazelle).

The fifteenth-century founder of the sect, Guru Jambheshwar (or Jamboji), is supposed to have been moved by the experience of an extended drought that exacted a terrible toll in terms of tree felling and animal death. This is said to have inspired his twenty-nine principles of morality and conduct, which include a ban on hunting and the felling of trees, a vegetarian diet, the filtering of water and milk, noninjury to minute life forms, adherence to rules of purity and restricted commensality, a ban on castrating bulls, and a commitment to ahimsa. Eight of these rules pertain to the preservation of animals and trees.[49] In keeping with the syncretic and reformist trends of the many *bhakti* (theistic, devotional) sects that emerged in northern, eastern, and western India from the fifteenth through the seventeenth centuries, Bishnoism owed debts to Brahmanical Hinduism as well as Islam. In the 1891 census in Marwar, Bishnois were classified as Muslims, notes Pankaj Jain, though since the partition of the subcontinent in 1947 they have become emphatically Hinduized, and they reject the notion of Muslim influence on their doctrine or practice.[50] In fact, in the current juncture of quasi-fascist Hindu majoritarianism and the Bishnois' achievement of upward caste mobility, Muslims are despised and avoided as "impure" (putatively because of their practice of carnivory).[51]

Of the twenty-nine rules, those enjoining protection of trees and nonhuman animals have historically been most zealously implemented. One of the most famous events in the Bishnoi narratives involves the mass martyrdom in 1730 of 363 people in the village of Khejarli. These Bishnoi—a group of 294 men and 69 women, led by Amrita Devi—are said to have laid down their lives to prevent the chopping down of the sacred *khejri* trees ordered by Abhay Singh, the Rajput ruler of Jodhpur. The news of this massacre apparently shocked the king into instituting punishments against those who cut trees or killed animals in Bishnoi territories. (The commemoration of this massacre has been, since 1978, one of the most important events in the Bishnoi calendar.) The event is commonly glossed as an act of environmental resistance, though it might equally have been a form of resistance to the supremacy of Rajput rulers.[52] In any event, Bishnoi villages have been described as extraordinarily rich in plant and animal life, in stark contrast to the barren landscapes of the Thar Desert. Visitors describe near-visionary Bishnoi landscapes as a this-worldly enactment of a peaceable kingdom in which antelopes, gazelles, peacocks, and other animals move without fear among their human friends and protectors, and are provided with water, feed, and ground to graze. The Bishnoi have also been far more effective at stopping poaching than the state agencies tasked with the protection of wildlife.

The Bishnoi live in rural areas as farmers and settled pastoralists, and many are quite prosperous, being well supplied with tractors and motorcycles. There are many who are settled in urban areas and employed as civil servants, forest officers, lawyers, business people, and politicians; writing in 1985, Kailash Sankhala and Peter Jackson remark that Bishnois have been chief ministers of the states of Rajasthan and Haryana.[53] While the rules about the protection of nonhuman life forms seem geared quite emphatically toward rural living, several of those settled in cities also seek to nurture animal life.

The legend of the Khejarli massacre continues to be an inspiration to Bishnois in the present day. Men are particularly active in chasing and tack-

178

ling poachers, and dozens are said to have lost their lives in consequence. Animal victims of human violence are ceremonially buried, sometimes near the humans who have died trying to save them.[54] Bishnois describe themselves as duty bound, even compelled, to offer protection at any cost to trees and animals that they see as uniquely vulnerable in ways that no human is. According to Alexis Reichert's ethnography, they are not necessarily given to the kind of sentimentality that one often associates with animal protection (notwithstanding the sentimental mode of the genre of newspaper or video reportage about them).[55] They are driven, rather, by a certain sense of urgency, a sense of past and ongoing holocausts of animal and arboreal lives, that compels them to leave their homes and fields at night, and to hurl their often unarmed bodies at poachers and powerful figures armed with guns—and to do this repeatedly despite the toll in human deaths. Salman Khan's lawyer provides a diagnostic of the Bishnoi that, despite its obvious callousness and defensive obtuseness, has details worth noting. He implies that there is something obviously irrational about their passionate commitment to nonhuman welfare; the Bishnoi, he says, are "people whose attraction to wildlife—even worship of it—twists their thinking."[56] In fact, an obsessive, unsleeping commitment, giving of itself without limit and beyond reasonableness, seems the hallmark of Bishnoi self-sacrifice on behalf of the nonhuman. In its unreasonableness it seems to resonate with the model of dehadana; it has to be extravagant, or it is not the kind of gift that counts as sacrifice. But unlike dehadana, and unlike the early modern Great Chain of Being, it is not predicated on the animal's inferiority; according to all existing ethnographic reports, the Bishnoi believe and affirm, rather, that the value of the life of a black buck or a gazelle is greater than their own human lives.

As Derrida reminds us, the true gift is impossible within the circularity of an exchange economy, whether monetary or symbolic. The circle for him is figurally and definitionally central to any notion of the economic: "[E]conomy implies the idea of exchange, of circulation, of return. . . . The figure of the circle . . . stands at the center of any problematic of *oikonomia*, as it does of any economic field: circular exchange, circulation of goods, products, monetary signs or merchandise, amortization of expenditures, revenues, substitution of use values and exchange values."[57] The gift proper cannot be part of this circular, self-interested, self-absorbed, self-regarding logic of economy; it must "interrupt" or "suspend" it. In fact, says Derrida, "if the figure of the circle is essential to economics, the gift must remain *an-economic*."[58] Logically the gift cannot be thought except in its relation to an exchange economy; but while it cannot be radically outside such an economy it is other to it or holds it in abeyance. And if economy proper is predicated upon a logic of scarcity, and the saving and calculation this entails, giving is a nonutilitarian principle of infinite expenditure, of exceeding the economic or calculative relations between persons. As Derrida notes in *The Gift of Death*, true giving is "beyond economy," and indeed must involve the "sacrifice of economy" itself.[59] In risking and frequently sacrificing their lives for animals in a fashion that most would see as inordinate, the Bishnoi would seem to fulfill the conditions of Derrida's aneconomic giving, especially since their acts (unlike those in the Jataka tales) occur outside any horizon of spiritual reward or exaltation.

It is important to note that such willingness to die for trees and animals is not necessarily a gentle affair. Sankhala and Jackson are perceptive about recognizing the fiercely martial and violent ethos that underlies the sacrifices. They liken the mass sacrifice/massacre of 1730 to the acts of Rajput warriors and women in wartime conditions against Muslim opponents, when men are said to have fought to the death and women committed themselves en masse to the flames rather than submit to capture at the hands of religious antagonists.[60] The vegetarianism and their activism on behalf of the nonhuman are not governed by ahimsaic principles. Some poachers have been lynched, while others have been beaten so badly that they were unable to walk again.[61] This theme of violence, including killing, in the defense of the biome is a constant in accounts of the Bishnoi; they are proud, says Reichert, of their reputation as rough defenders of their lands and its most valued nonhuman forms.[62]

Women are less active than men in running down poachers; their task is that of offering food and grain to birds and animals, and nurturing the injured among them, in a conventionally gendered division of the labors of care and protection. On occasion their own bodies constitute the source of nourishment. They have attracted a good deal of attention for breastfeeding orphaned fawns on occasion; in fact, such pictures of breastfeeding are among the most iconic and widely reproduced images worldwide of Bishnoi devotion to nonhuman welfare.[63] In a striking inversion of stories of children raised by wolves—stories widely associated with the subcontinent in the nineteenth and early twentieth centuries—newspaper articles and videos show pictures of fawns being breastfed along with human babies. In other pictures, we see fawns being rocked in cloth cradles.[64] The iconography of these photographs (and of the text accompanying them) is reminiscent of classical Roman as well as Christian models of charity, which instantiate with great literalism the milk of human kindness in the form of altruistic lactation. Breastfeeding is the sphere in which the putative givens of female biology can become the ground of female virtue, the more remarkable in this case for being directed to an other-than-human object. On the one hand, milk is the one bodily fluid that is supposedly designed to function as a gift without return, sustaining the life of another. The Cixous of *The Newly Born Woman* affirms this maternal gift or "feminine economy" as a rebuke to "modern assumptions of possessive individualism and conditions of scarcity."[65] But this maternal milk is often also presumed to circulate within relatively constrained circuits of intimacy or sociality—circuits that are usually governed by an idea of natural limits.[66] What happens, then, when the movement of this quasi-occult fluid crosses the species barrier, and what ideas of kinship come to be rethought when the overflowing human breast goes to sustain those outside its presumably natural orbits and boundaries? Bishnoi mothers in these articles and videos describe the fawns as their children, and younger Bishnoi use a similar language of kinship: "'My parents have never differentiated between a baby deer and me. We are one family and it is in our religion to protect them.'"[67] Both Bishnoi men and Bishnoi women emphatically reject the carnivorous logic of sacrifice and, it seems, human supremacism. But Bishnoi women, unlike Bishnoi men, can offer a gift of the flesh without the forms of death and injury that male heroism seems to require. Their breastfeeding is both the fulfillment of nature while also in excess of it, in being extended as an overflow to vulnerable nonhuman recipients.

Nonetheless it is worth taking a slightly closer look at the gift or sacrifice of the body that is involved in the breastfeeding of the orphaned fawn. The following story is told about Kiran Bishnoi, who rescued and breastfed a three-month-old fawn, and whose image is featured in Rajesh Bedi's book of photographs on Rajasthan: "She had walked up to some two kilometres [to collect firewood] when she saw this chinkara baby being attacked by dogs. The dogs had already killed the mother. Kiran was all alone but somehow managed to save the animal and shooed away the dogs. It was a long distance, so she couldn't have possibly carried the wood and the chinkara together, so she had to throw away all the wood she had collected."[68] Bringing it home, she offers it a bottle but to little effect. She then offers the fawn her breast, which is eagerly received. Thereafter her six-month-old daughter and the fawn are fed simultaneously. Kiran Bishnoi goes out of her way to emphasize the similitude between human and animal infants in her eyes: "I treated her like my own child. I felt for her the same affection that

I felt for my daughter." The two are even assigned matched names—Pooja (worship) and Aarti (religious ritual, a component of pooja). When the fawn grows older, she is released into the open near the Bishnoi ashram, where her human foster parents see her from time to time over subsequent years.

The story, with its tale of the nursing mother's multiple sacrifices and gifts—of difficult-to-find firewood, of breast milk, and of equal, hospitable, generous love—is a moving one, and full of a parabolic simplicity. That it is an emblematic story is made clear by some of the final details of the story. We are told that Kiran Bishnoi is "a role model for many in her village," and that her photograph has found a place both in the veterinary hospital in Jodhpur and in seventh-grade school textbooks in the state. What does this pedagogy of protection, love, and exemplarity tell us about responsibility and hospitality in a multispecies universe? It is worth noting that though this is a woman's story of altruistic breastfeeding, it is also a story of valor and struggle, more commonly the domain of men. Kiran Bishnoi has managed, despite being by herself and far from home, to rescue the fawn from the dogs that have killed its mother and that seek to attack the fawn in turn. The human–animal drama thus involves more than human and gazelle. It involves at least three species that we know of: humans, chinkara gazelles, and dogs. If this story sounds somewhat familiar, it is because we have encountered a version of it already, though with some important differences. It has a triangle reminiscent of the story of King Shibi, caught between the competing claims of dove and hawk. In this version of the story, though, the dogs as carnivores have no claim upon the gazelles that they have hunted, presumably for food; nor is an alimentary/fleshly substitute offered to them in the manner of the Jataka tales. The chinkara fawn is rescued and fed, but this must happen by transforming her status as meat for the dogs, who remain unfed (at least on her flesh). The Bishnoi fable demonstrates that no commitment to nonhuman life can be entirely open-ended, or indeed without cost. The Bishnoi may be willing to die for some animals, and to breastfeed others. But their commitment to all nonhuman life forms is strictly noncomparable. Like the human world, the nonhuman world is encompassed by the logic of caste hierarchy; the abandonment of human supremacism involved in sacrifice on animals' behalf does not entail a turn away from the hierarchies of caste where Bishnois (and, indeed, many other communities in the subcontinent) are concerned. Some trees, like the khejri, and some animals, like the black buck, chinkara, and peacock, are highly valued for their "purity"; in fact, the black buck is seen as a manifestation of the Guru Jambheshwar. They are worth the sacrifice

182

of human life. Dogs and pigs, on the other hand, are despised as polluting, as they are over much of the subcontinent. Along with poachers (and occasionally Muslims), the latter fill the role of pariahs or antagonists in the tense Bishnoi morality play of multispecies cohabitation. Dogs are associated in Hindu texts with Dalits, who are presumed by caste Hindus to eat dogs, which in turn are carnivorous, when they are not disgustingly promiscuous eaters.[69] There is an implicit assumption that in the animal kingdom, too, the vegetarians are superior to the carnivores; the former are revered while the latter are tolerated at best, even by a community that is willing to die for or to suckle vulnerable animals.

The Bishnoi case may instantiate the paradoxical logic or structure of sacrifice itself—that there is no responsibility toward one being without a betrayal of all others. As Derrida notes in his meditations on Kierkegaard on the Abrahamic sacrifice, we are responsible not to one Other but to an innumerable host of others. Under such conditions, every act of ethical decision making, every response to the call of an other who makes an ethical appeal to us, every act of fidelity or commitment to one sacrificial beneficiary constitutes an inescapable betrayal of all others—human, animal, or divine—who can demand sacrifice of one.[70] At the same time, and as an entailment of this inescapable dialectic of fidelity and betrayal, we must be wary of domesticating the irreducible alterity of the absolute other; the other must in the last instance be a radically undetermined rather than an already known and anticipated figure who has prior and legible claims upon the subject of sacrifice. Thomas Keenan notes that responding to the call of the other must of necessity be attended by an experience of *strangeness* rather than any form of familiarity or recognizability; to hear a familiar call is to be exempt from needing to hear the call at all. Thus, Keenan avers, "the call remains irreducibly different, alien, addressed to us . . . but 'like someone else's mail.'"[71] The Bishnoi case, responding invariably in a caste-marked way to the appeal of the herbivorous, high-caste gazelle over that of the marauding, carnivorous wild dog, might suggest the limits of circumscribing all too clearly and unequivocally the identity of the other for whom or which one is willing to sacrifice oneself.

Taken together, these three parables on meat epitomize the dilemmas and paradoxes of sacrifice and self-sacrifice, killability and consumability, hospitality and exclusion. Even Jonson's poem of putatively carnivorous naturalization demonstrates how far from simple or natural is the process of establishing the status of animal bodies as meat. Meat is not, in this poem, a simple matter of consumption, nor is it incorporated unproblematically

183

within anthropocentric hierarchies of privilege. But if Jonson's poem suggests in its details that anthropocentric privilege rests upon uncertain ground, the examples that showcase human or superhuman sacrifice *for* rather than *of* the animal attest that such privilege is not easily banished or superseded either. The Bodhisattva's virile self-sacrifice on behalf of non-human beneficiaries seems on occasion to be prompted as much by his own yearning for sacrifice as by the needs of those to whom he offers his flesh or other parts of his body. In any event, it is his capacity to render himself as meat that seals him in his status as an enlightened being, translated above mere mortals like animals or even other humans. In contrast, Bishnoi forms of sacrifice for and nurture of the animal, especially in the everyday form of suckling, seem to be exempt from the logics of human supremacism and heroic spiritual elevation. Yet even such a hospitable vision of interspecies care is not without its caste-marked limits, given its hierarchies of (pure) vegetarian animals worth saving and (impure) carnivorous ones that must be guarded against.

The point of such an exercise in parabolic concatenation is not necessarily to establish hierarchies of nonanthropocentric virtue, or indeed to proclaim that all endeavors at guarding against anthropocentric hierarchy must necessarily meet their limits. That the latter is true is undeniable; yet knowing this does not exempt us from striving toward this goal. At the same time, what constitutes a departure from anthropocentrism needs always to be subject to skeptical investigation. The point of examining both the scenarios of naturalized carnivory and those of anticarnivorous advocacy is to develop a certain modesty about presuming too quickly that we know what the meanings are of meat, anthropocentric privilege, or the sacrifice of animal sacrifice.

## Notes

1 Donna Haraway, *When Species Meet* (Minneapolis: University of Minnesota Press, 2008), 80. For a complex elaboration of the affects attached to killing and killability, see Bhrigupati Singh and Naisargi Dave, "On the Killing and Killability of Animals: Nonmoral Thoughts for the Anthropology of Ethics," *Comparative Studies of South Asia, Africa and the Middle East* 35, no. 2 (August 2015): 232–45.

2 Peter Remien, "'Home to the Slaughter': Noah's Ark and the Seventeenth-Century Country House Poem," *Modern Philology* 113, no. 4 (May 2016): 507.

3 The Jataka tales were composed over many centuries. They may be found in an assortment of Buddhist texts, the largest and most famous of which is the

*Jātakatthavannanā* or *Jātakatthakathā* (Commentary on the Jātaka), a Pāli-language Theravāda collection of almost 550 stories from the fifth century CE. Naomi Appleton, "Jataka," *Oxford Research Encyclopedia of Religion*, accessed February 7, 2019, oxfordre.com/religion.

4  Jill Robbins, "Sacrifice," in *Critical Terms for Religious Studies*, edited by Mark C. Taylor (Chicago: University of Chicago Press, 1998), 286.

5  Kimberley Patton, "Animal Sacrifice: Metaphysics of the Sublimated Victim," in *A Communion of Subjects: Animals in Religion, Science, and Ethics*, edited by Paul Waldau and Kimberley Patton (New York: Columbia University Press, 2006), 392 (italics in original).

6  Robbins, "Sacrifice," 287 (italics in original).

7  Hent de Vries, *Religion and Violence: Philosophical Perspectives from Kant to Derrida* (Baltimore: Johns Hopkins University Press, 2002), 201. Though the pre–Second Temple sacrificial order that is superceded with the emergence of Christianity is orchestrated primarily around animal sacrifice, it may also on rare occasions admit the possibility of human sacrifice, as the stories of Abraham and Isaac and of Jephthah and his daughter underline.

8  David Grumett and Rachel Muers, *Theology on the Menu: Asceticism, Meat and Christian Diet* (London: Routledge, 2010), 108.

9  Grumett and Muers note that rituals of animal sacrifice persisted in some, primarily Orthodox, Christian communities into the twentieth century (*Theology on the Menu*, 109–15).

10  Grumett and Muers, *Theology on the Menu*, 5, 8–11.

11  Augustine, *City of God*, translated by Marcus Dods (Peabody, MA: Hendrickson Publishers, 2009), 31.

12  On Augustine, and especially Aquinas, on nonhuman animals, see Karl Steel, *How to Make a Human: Animals and Violence in the Middle Ages* (Columbus: Ohio State University Press, 2011), chapter 3 and passim. For a consideration of the more theriophilic dimensions of the three great Abrahamic religions, see Kimberley C. Patton, "'He Who Sits in the Heavens Laughs': Recovering Animal Theology in the Abrahamic Traditions," *Harvard Theological Review* 93, no. 4 (October 2000): 401–34.

13  William A. McClung, *The Country House in English Renaissance Poetry* (Berkeley: University of California Press, 1977), 7–17.

14  McClung, *The Country House in English Renaissance Poetry*, 118.

15  Robert Applebaum, *Aguecheek's Beef, Belch's Hiccup, and Other Gastronomic Interjections* (Chicago: University of Chicago Press, 2006), 118–36.

16  Ben Jonson, "To Penshurst," ll. 29–38, in *Ben Jonson and the Cavalier Poets*, edited by Hugh McLean (New York: W. W. Norton, 1974), 22. Also see the following lines from Thomas Carew's "To Saxham": "The Pheasant, Partiridge, and the Larke, / Flew to thy house, as to the Arke. / The willing Oxe, of himselfe came / Home to the slaughter, with the Lambe, / And every beast did thither bring / Himselfe, to be an offering. / The scalie herd, more pleasure tooke, / Bath'd in

thy dish, then in the brooke: / Water, Earth, Ayre, did all conspire, / To pay their tributes to thy fire" (164).

17 Alastair Fowler, "Country House Poems: The Politics of a Genre," *The Seventeenth Century* 1, no. 1 (1986): 8. The word "painted" invites us to read these lines about animals turning themselves into meat as an analogue to nature morte/still life painting; the genre assumed ostentatious form in the large-format game pieces of seventeenth-century Flemish painters such as Frans Snyders, Jan Fyt, and Jan Weenix. I thank Irina Aristarkhova for suggesting this possibility to me.

18 Raymond Williams, *The Country and the City* (New York: Oxford University Press, 1973), 30.

19 Remien, "'Home to the Slaughter,'" 519.

20 Erica Fudge, *Animal* (London: Reaktion, 2002), 77.

21 On Jonsonian gluttony, see Bruce T. Boehrer, "Renaissance Overeating: The Sad Case of Ben Jonson," *PMLA* 105, no. 5 (October 1990): 1071–82.

22 See, in contrast, Robert Herrick's "The Hock Cart," which draws attention to the animal flesh that features largely in the Earl of Westmoreland's largesse, or to Jonson's own "Inviting a Friend to Supper," which is not shy about enumerating the carnivorous attractions of his table.

23 Patton, "Animal Sacrifice," 393.

24 Henri Hubert and Marcel Mauss, *Sacrifice: Its Nature and Function*, translated by W. D. Halls (Chicago: University of Chicago Press, 1964 [1898]), 33.

25 Brian K. Smith, "Eaters, Food, and Social Hierarchy in India: A Dietary Guide to a Revolution in Values," *Journal of the American Academy of Religion* 58, no. 2 (1990): 177. "Meat is indeed the best kind of food," proclaims the Satapatha Brahmana, quite unreservedly (cited in Smith, "Eaters, Food, and Social Hierarchy in India," 197). Also see Francis Zimmerman, *The Jungle and the Aroma of Meats* (Berkeley: University of California Press, 1987), for the "violent therapeutics" of the Ayurveda. In a later period—most notably in the era of Kautilya's *Arthashastra*, the treatise on statecraft composed and redacted between the second century BCE and the third century of the Christian era—matsyanyaya became an emblem of ungoverned, prepolitical life, where might established right.

26 Kathryn McClymond, "Death Be Not Proud: Reevaluating the Role of Killing in Sacrifice," *International Journal of Hindu Studies* 6, no. 3 (December 2002): 226 (italics in original).

27 Huber and Mauss, *Sacrifice*, 34.

28 Huber and Mauss, *Sacrifice*, 34.

29 Patton, "Animal Sacrifice," 396.

30 Jonathan Z. Smith, "The Bare Facts of Ritual," *History of Religions* 20, nos. 1–2 (August–November 1980), 120.

31 Wendy Doniger, *The Hindus: An Alternative History* (New York: Penguin, 2009), 115–16.

32  Smith, "The Bare Facts of Ritual," 125.

33  See, for instance, J. C. Heesterman, "Non-Violence and Sacrifice," *Indologica Taurinensia* 12 (1984): 119–27.

34  Smith, "Eaters, Food, and Social Hierarchy in India," 197. Uma Chakravarti has an account of the antagonism between sramanas and Brahmans in early Buddhist literature; see "Renouncer and Householder in Early Buddhism," *Social Analysis: The International Journal of Anthropology*, No. 13 (May 1983): 70–83.

35  Reiko Ohnuma, "Jataka," in *Encyclopedia of Buddhism*, vol. 1, edited by Robert E. Buswell Jr. (New York: Thomson Gale, 2004), 400–401.

36  Reiko Ohnuma, *Bodily Self-Sacrifice in Indian Buddhist Literature* (Delhi: Motilal Banarsidass, 2007), 141.

37  Interestingly, the usual criticism of extreme asceticism in Buddhist soteriological practice coexists with the exaltation of extreme self-punishment in the pursuit of dehadana.

38  By Ohnuma's reckoning, some 20 percent of the Pali Jatakas feature the Buddha in a prior male animal incarnation; these run the gamut from lion and elephant to pig, dog, vulture, and mouse. Reiko Ohnuma, *Unfortunate Destiny: Animals in the Indian Buddhist Imagination* (New York: Oxford University Press, 2017), 42–43, 183–85. In these anthropomorphic incarnations the Bodhisattva speaks, reasons, and acts like a perfected human being.

39  When the tale is told in the Hindu epic the *Mahabharata*, King Shibi first offers the hawk "a steer, a boar, a deer, or even a buffalo" in exchange for the dove, and does not proffer his own flesh until challenged to do so by the hawk. Vyasa, "King Shibi Saves the Dove from the Hawk," *Norton Anthology of World Religions*, vol. 1, edited by Jack Miles et al. (New York: W. W. Norton, 2015), 171–72. This may be an indication of the more wavering commitment to ahimsa against nonhuman life in Hinduism, or it might index the difference in genre between the Jataka tale and the Hindu epic.

40  Har Dayal, *The Bodhisattva Doctrine in Buddhist Sanskrit Literature* (Delhi: Motilal Banarsidass, 1970 [1932]), 183.

41  Ohnuma, *Bodily Self-Sacrifice*, 279, 82–84. Another famous non-Jataka tale of tenderness toward nonhuman life involves the Mahayana monk Asanga, who attained enlightenment by demonstrating compassion to an animal. Unsuccessful at a twelve-year period of meditation, he emerges from his cave to encounter an old dog with a suppurating wound infested with maggots. Wishing to relieve the dog but unwilling to cause harm to the maggots, he cuts off a piece of flesh from his own thigh and transfers the maggots to it, using his tongue to effect the transfer. As a result of this, he is rewarded with a vision of the future Buddha Maitreya. See Robert Thurman, "Introduction," in *Tsong Khapa's Speech of Gold in the Essence of True Eloquence: Reason and Enlightenment in the Central Philosophy of Tibet*, translated by Robert Thurman (Princeton, NJ: Princeton University Press, 1984), 28–29.

42  Ohnuma, *Bodily Self-Sacrifice*, 54.

43  Maria Heim, *Theories of the Gift in South Asia: Hindu, Buddhist, and Jain Reflections on Dana* (New York: Routledge, 2004), 40. Many scholars of Indic thought and South Asian anthropology have described the anonymous, asymmetrical, and unreciprocated forms of giving involved in some varieties of dana. But while the donor's gifts are unreciprocated by the recipient, there is a general understanding that this is treasure laid up in heaven; a return will come from elsewhere. For the many different aspects of this argument, see Jonathan Parry, "The Gift, the Indian Gift, and the 'Indian Gift,'" *Man* 21, no. 3 (September 1986): 453–73; Gloria Goodwin Raheja, *The Poison in the Gift: Ritual, Prestation, and the Dominant Caste in a North Indian Village* (Chicago: University of Chicago Press, 1988); James Laidlaw, "A Free Gift Makes No Friends," *Journal of the Royal Anthropological Institute* 6, no. 4 (December 2000): 617–34.

44  Reiko Ohnuma, "Animal Doubles of the Buddha," *Humanimalia* 7, no. 2 (2016): 3–4.

45  Ohnuma, *Unfortunate Destiny*, xiii.

46  Ohnuma, *Bodily Self-Sacrifice*, 126. Sacrificing one's flesh for animals, especially birds, is not unknown in the Jain and (Hindu) Shaiva traditions; for the latter, see Carl Olson, "The Saiva Mystic, Self Sacrifice, and Creativity," *Religion* 10, no. 1 (1980): 32, 33. But a discussion of this is outside the scope of this chapter.

47  Karl Steel, "Abyss: Everything Is Food," *postmedieval* 4, no. 1 (2013): 93–104. Also see his blog posts, especially "Man Is the Pasture of Being, Part 2: Sky Burial, Mostly Persian," July 26, 2015, https://medievalkarl.com/2015/07/26/man-is-the-pasture-of-being-part-2-sky-burial-mostly-persian/, and "Man Is the Pasture of Being 3: Mandeville in Tibet, at Long Last," August 8, 2015, http://www.inthemedievalmiddle.com/2015/08/man-is-pasture-of-being-3-mandeville-in.html, for a comprehensive account of medieval European knowledge about sky burial (accessed September 30, 2016).

48  Kaja Silverman, *Male Subjectivity at the Margins* (New York: Routledge, 1992), 327. Ladwig describes the renowned Bodhisattva Vessantara—he who proves his fitness for reincarnation as the Buddha by giving away his wife and children—as "a sort of Buddhist Ubermensch who increasingly moves away from the 'justice of commoners,' which according to Nietzsche is based on the principle of reciprocity." Patrice Ladwig, "Emotions and Narrative: Ethical Giving and Ethical Ambivalence in the Lao Vessantara Jataka," in *Readings of the Vessantara Jataka*, edited by Steven Collins (New York: Columbia University Press, 2016), 67.

49  Pankaj Jain, *Dharma and the Ecology of Hindu Communities: Sustenance and Sustainability* (Farnham, UK: Ashgate, 2011), 59. Some of the rules, especially those pertaining to the filtration of water and milk to prevent the ingestion of minute life forms below the threshold of visibility, appear to be indebted to the norms of Jain practice.

50  Jain, *Dharma and the Ecology of Hindu Communities*, 52–56.

51 Alexis Reichert, "Sacred Trees, Sacred Deer, Sacred Duty to Protect: Exploring Relationships between Humans and Nonhumans in the Bishnoi Community" (MA thesis, Department of Classics and Religious Studies, University of Ottawa, 2015), 100–102. In contemporary India, religious and caste bigotry is often couched in imputations of "impure" dietary practices.

52 R. J. Fisher, *If Rain Doesn't Come: An Anthropological Study of Drought and Human Ecology in Western Rajasthan* (Sydney: Manohar, 1997), 69–70.

53 K. S. Sankhala and Peter Jackson, "People, Trees and Antelopes in the Indian Desert," in *Culture and Conservation: The Human Dimension in Environmental Planning*, edited by Jeffrey A. McNeely and David Pitt (London: Croom Helm, 1985), 209.

54 Franck Vogel and Benoit Segur, *The Bishnoi* [documentary] (Gedeon Programmes, 2011); Reichert, "Sacred Trees, Sacred Deer, Sacred Duty to Protect," 76.

55 Reichert, "Sacred Trees, Sacred Deer, Sacred Duty to Protect," 24.

56 Barry Bearak, "Nature-Loving Indians Turn Poachers into Prey," *New York Times*, November 29, 1998.

57 Jacques Derrida, *Given Time: 1. Counterfeit Money*, translated by Peggy Kamuf (Chicago: University of Chicago Press, 1992), 6 (italics in original).

58 Derrida, *Given Time*, 7 (italics in original).

59 Jacques Derrida, *The Gift of Death*, translated by David Wills (Chicago: University of Chicago Press, 1995), 95.

60 Sankhala and Jackson, "People, Trees and Antelopes in the Indian Desert," 208. Rajputs are members of (mostly Hindu) patrilineal clans of western and central India.

61 Sankhala and Jackson, "People, Trees and Antelopes in the Indian Desert," 208; Sanjoy Hazarika, "Sect in India Guards Desert Wildlife," *New York Times*, February 2, 1993.

62 Reichert, "Sacred Trees, Sacred Deer, Sacred Duty to Protect," 24. Narayan notes, "Young men from the community have even formed vigilante groups with names like 'Commando Force' and 'Tiger Force' to protect the animal from poachers." Krishna Narayan, "Who Killed One of India's Wildlife Commandos?," *Nova*, January 20, 2016, http://www.pbs.org/wgbh/nova/next/nature/vigilante-conservation/.

63 The Bishnoi are not by any means the only human community to engage in the practice of interspecies suckling. See James Serpell, *In the Company of Animals* (Cambridge: Cambridge University Press, 1996 [1986]), 61–65, for anthropological evidence of several such communities around the world in the nineteenth and twentieth centuries.

64 On the other hand, an ethnography of the multispecies world that the Bishnoi inhabit suggests that these are anomalous rather than common practices, resorted to when more conventional methods of feeding have proved unavailing.

189

Reichert, "Sacred Trees, Sacred Deer, Sacred Duty to Protect," 66. But there is no doubt that they have occurred in several instances.

65  Alan D. Schrift, "Logics of the Gift in Cixous and Nietzsche: Can We Still Be Generous?," *Angelaki* 6, no. 2 (August 2001): 113–23.

66  This is not to deny the widespread use of wet-nursing, which suggests that maternal milk has been, and continues to be, a commodity in the marketplace. I am speaking rather to the fetishistic meanings commonly attached to human maternal milk once eighteenth-century reformers such as Jean-Jacques Rousseau championed exclusive maternal breast-feeding as paradigmatic of enlightened female domesticity. See Irina Aristarkhova's essay in this volume for an account of the questions that are raised when human breast milk comes to circulate outside the restricted economies of mothers and their biological children.

67  See, for instance, Charnamrit Sachdeva, "'I Breastfeed Deer Because They Are Like My Own Children': The Bishnoi Mothers Who Use Their Own Breast Milk to Rear Wild Fawns," *Daily Mail*, April 29, 2016, http://www.dailymail.co .uk/news/article-3564005/I-breastfeed-deer-like-one-family.html, and Shailaja Tripathi, "A Woman and a Baby Chinkara," *The Hindu*, August 16, 2013, http:// www.thehindu.com/features/metroplus/society/a-woman-and-a-baby-chinkara /article5029062.ece.

68  Tripathi, "A Woman and a Baby Chinkara." The speaker is Kiran Bishnoi's husband, Shyam Sunder Bishnoi.

69  Wendy Doniger, *On Hinduism* (New York: Oxford University Press, 2014), 488.

70  Derrida, *The Gift of Death*, 68–70.

71  Thomas Keenan, *Fables of Responsibility: Aberrations and Predicaments in Ethics and Politics* (Stanford, CA: Stanford University Press, 1997), 28.

## Bibliography

Applebaum, Robert. *Aguecheek's Beef, Belch's Hiccup, and Other Gastronomic Interjections*. Chicago: University of Chicago Press, 2006.

Appleton, Naomi. "Jātaka." *Oxford Research Encyclopedia of Religion*. doi:10.1093/ acrefore/9780199340378.013.18. Accessed February 7, 2019.

Aryasurya. "Sibi." In *Once the Buddha Was a Monkey: Aryasurya's Jatakamala*, translated by Peter Khoroche, 10–17. Chicago: University of Chicago Press, 1989.

Augustine. *City of God*. Translated by Marcus Dods. Peabody, MA: Hendrickson, 2009.

Bearak, Barry. "Nature-Loving Indians Turn Poachers into Prey." *New York Times*, November 29, 1998. https://www.nytimes.com/1998/11/29/world/nature -loving-indians-turn-poachers-into-prey.html. Accessed March 10, 2017.

Boehrer, Bruce T. "Renaissance Overeating: The Sad Case of Ben Jonson." *PMLA* 105, no. 5 (October 1990): 1071–82.

Chakravarti, Uma. "Renouncer and Householder in Early Buddhism." *Social Analysis: The International Journal of Anthropology*, no. 13 (May 1983): 70–83.

Derrida, Jacques. *The Gift of Death*. Translated by David Wills. Chicago: University of Chicago Press, 1995.

Derrida, Jacques. *Given Time: 1. Counterfeit Money*. Translated by Peggy Kamuf. Chicago: University of Chicago Press, 1992.

Derrida, Jacques. "Psychoanalysis Searches the State of Its Soul: The Impossible Beyond of a Sovereign Cruelty." In *Without Alibi*, translated by Peggy Kamuf, 238–80. Stanford, CA: Stanford University Press, 2002.

De Vries, Hent. *Religion and Violence: Philosophical Perspectives from Kant to Derrida*. Baltimore: Johns Hopkins University Press, 2002.

Doniger, Wendy. *The Hindus: An Alternative History*. New York: Penguin, 2009.

Doniger, Wendy. *On Hinduism*. New York: Oxford University Press, 2014.

Fisher, R. J. *If Rain Doesn't Come: An Anthropological Study of Drought and Human Ecology in Western Rajasthan*. Sydney: Manohar, 1997.

Fowler, Alastair. "Country House Poems: The Politics of a Genre." *Seventeenth Century* 1, no. 1 (1986): 1–14.

Fudge, Erica. *Animal*. London: Reaktion, 2002.

Grumett, David, and Rachel Muers. *Theology on the Menu: Asceticism, Meat and Christian Diet*. London: Routledge, 2010.

Haraway, Donna. *When Species Meet*. Minneapolis: University of Minnesota Press, 2008.

Har Dayal. *The Bodhisattva Doctrine in Buddhist Sanskrit Literature*. Delhi: Motilal Banarsidass, 1970. (Originally published 1932.)

Heesterman, J. C. "Non-Violence and Sacrifice." *Indologica Taurinensia* 12 (1984): 119–27.

Heim, Maria. *Theories of the Gift in South Asia: Hindu, Buddhist, and Jain Reflections on Dana*. New York: Routledge, 2004.

Herrick, Robert. "The Hock Cart, or Harvest Home: To the Right Honourable Mildmay, Earle of Westmorland." In *The Poetical Works of Robert Herrick*, edited by L. C. Martin, 101–2. Oxford: Oxford University Press, 1956.

Hubert, Henri, and Marcel Mauss. *Sacrifice: Its Nature and Function*, translated by W. D. Halls. Chicago: University of Chicago Press, 1964. (Originally published 1898.)

Jain, Pankaj. *Dharma and the Ecology of Hindu Communities: Sustenance and Sustainability*. Farnham, UK: Ashgate, 2011.

Jonson, Ben. "Inviting a Friend to Supper." In *Ben Jonson and the Cavalier Poets*, edited by Hugh McLean. New York: W. W. Norton, 1974.

Jonson, Ben. "To Penshurst." In *Ben Jonson and the Cavalier Poets*, edited by Hugh McLean. New York: W. W. Norton, 1974.

Keenan, Thomas. *Fables of Responsibility: Aberrations and Predicaments in Ethics and Politics*. Stanford, CA: Stanford University Press, 1997.

Ladwig, Patrice. "Emotions and Narrative: Ethical Giving and Ethical Ambivalence in the Lao Vessantara Jataka." In *Readings of the Vessantara Jataka*, edited by Steven Collins, 53–80. New York: Columbia University Press, 2016.

Laidlaw, James. "A Free Gift Makes No Friends." *Journal of the Royal Anthropological Institute* 6, no. 4 (December 2000): 617–34.

McClung, William A. *The Country House in English Renaissance Poetry*. Berkeley: University of California Press, 1977.

McClymond, Kathryn. "Death Be Not Proud: Reevaluating the Role of Killing in Sacrifice." *International Journal of Hindu Studies* 6, no. 3 (December 2002): 221–42.

Narayan, Krishna. "Who Killed One of India's Wildlife Commandos?" *Nova*, January 20, 2016. http://www.pbs.org/wgbh/nova/next/nature/vigilante -conservation/. Accessed March 15, 2017.

Ohnuma, Reiko. "Animal Doubles of the Buddha." *Humanimalia* 7, no. 2 (2016).

Ohnuma, Reiko. *Bodily Self-Sacrifice in Indian Buddhist Literature*. Delhi: Motilal Banarsidass, 2007.

Ohnuma, Reiko. "Jātaka." In *Encyclopedia of Buddhism*, vol. 1, edited by Robert E. Buswell Jr., 400–401. New York: Thomson Gale, 2004.

Ohnuma, Reiko. *Unfortunate Destiny: Animals in the Indian Buddhist Imagination*. New York: Oxford University Press, 2017.

Olson, Carl. "The Śaiva Mystic, Self Sacrifice, and Creativity." *Religion* 10, no. 1 (1980): 31–40.

Parry, Jonathan. "The Gift, the Indian Gift, and the 'Indian Gift.'" *Man* 21, no. 3 (September 1986): 453–73.

Patton, Kimberley. "Animal Sacrifice: Metaphysics of the Sublimated Victim." In *A Communion of Subjects: Animals in Religion, Science, and Ethics*, edited by Paul Waldau and Kimberley Patton, 391–405. New York: Columbia University Press, 2006.

Patton, Kimberley. "'He Who Sits in the Heavens Laughs': Recovering Animal Theology in the Abrahamic Traditions." *Harvard Theological Review* 93, no. 4 (October 2000): 401–34.

Raheja, Gloria Goodwin. *The Poison in the Gift: Ritual, Prestation, and the Dominant Caste in a North Indian Village*. Chicago: University of Chicago Press, 1988.

Reichert, Alexis. "Sacred Trees, Sacred Deer, Sacred Duty to Protect: Exploring Relationships between Humans and Nonhumans in the Bishnoi Community." MA thesis, Department of Classics and Religious Studies, University of Ottawa, 2015. https://ruor.uottawa.ca/bitstream/10393/32877/1/Reichert_Alexis _2015_thesis.pdf. Accessed May 2, 2017.

Remien, Peter. "'Home to the Slaughter': Noah's Ark and the Seventeenth-Century Country House Poem." *Modern Philology* 113, no. 4 (May 2016): 507–29.

Robbins, Jill. "Sacrifice." In *Critical Terms for Religious Studies*, edited by Mark C. Taylor, 285–97. Chicago: University of Chicago Press, 1998.

Sachdeva, Charnamrit. "'I Breastfeed Deer Because They Are Like My Own Children': The Bishnoi Mothers Who Use Their Own Breast Milk to Rear Wild

Fawns." *Daily Mail*, April 29, 2016. http://www.dailymail.co.uk/news/article
-3564005/I-breastfeed-deer-like-one-family.html. Accessed March 20, 2017.

Sankhala, K. S., and Peter Jackson. "People, Trees and Antelopes in the Indian
Desert." In *Culture and Conservation: The Human Dimension in Environmen-
tal Planning*, edited by Jeffrey A. McNeely and David Pitt, 205–10. London:
Croom Helm, 1985.

Schrift, Alan D. "Logics of the Gift in Cixous and Nietzsche: Can We Still Be Generous?" *Angelaki* 6, no. 2 (August 2001): 113–23.

Serpell, James. *In the Company of Animals*. Cambridge: Cambridge University
Press, 1996. (Originally published 1986.)

Silverman, Kaja. *Male Subjectivity at the Margins*. New York: Routledge, 1992.

Singh, Bhrigupati, and Naisargi Dave. "On the Killing and Killability of Animals:
Nonmoral Thoughts for the Anthropology of Ethics." *Comparative Studies of
South Asia, Africa and the Middle East* 35, no. 2 (August 2015): 232–45.

Smith, Brian K. "Eaters, Food, and Social Hierarchy in India: A Dietary Guide to a
Revolution in Values." *Journal of the American Academy of Religion* 58, no. 2
(1990): 177–205.

Smith, Jonathan Z. "The Bare Facts of Ritual." *History of Religions* 20, nos. 1–2
(August–November 1980): 112–27.

Steel, Karl. "Abyss: Everything Is Food." *postmedieval* 4, no. 1 (2013): 93–104.

Steel, Karl. *How to Make a Human: Animals and Violence in the Middle Ages*. Columbus: Ohio State University Press, 2011.

Steel, Karl. "Man Is the Pasture of Being, Part 2: Sky Burial, Mostly Persian." July 26,
2015. https://medievalkarl.com/2015/07/26/man-is-the-pasture-of-being-part
-2-sky-burial-mostly-persian/. Accessed September 30, 2016.

Steel, Karl. "Man Is the Pasture of Being 3: Mandeville in Tibet, at Long Last." August 8, 2015. http://www.inthemedievalmiddle.com/2015/08/man-is-pasture
-of-being-3-mandeville-in.html. Accessed September 30, 2016.

Thurman, Robert. *Tsong Khapa's Speech of Gold in the Essence of True Eloquence:
Reason and Enlightenment in the Central Philosophy of Tibet*. Translated by
Robert Thurman. Princeton, NJ: Princeton University Press, 1984.

Tripathi, Shailaja. "A Woman and a Baby Chinkara." *The Hindu*, August 16, 2013.
http://www.thehindu.com/features/metroplus/society/a-woman-and-a-baby
-chinkara/article5029062.ece. Accessed March 20, 2017.

Vogel, Franck, and Benoit Segur. *The Bishnoi* [documentary]. Gedeon Programmes,
2011.

Vyasa. "King Shibi Saves the Dove from the Hawk." In *The Norton Anthology of
World Religions*, vol. 1, edited by Jack Miles et al., 171–72. New York: W. W.
Norton, 2015.

Williams, Raymond. *The Country and the City*. New York: Oxford University Press,
1973.

Zimmerman, Francis. *The Jungle and the Aroma of Meats*. Berkeley: University of
California Press, 1987.

# "I Hide in Plain Sight"

## FOOD AND BLACK MASCULINITY IN VINCE GILLIGAN'S *BREAKING BAD*

SCHOLARSHIP FOCUSING ON MEN, masculinity, and food, when theorized, tends to focus on white males.[1] Very little, if any, analyzes the ways in which African American men perform gender and/or masculinity. When popular culture is the primary vehicle of representations, images of African American men tend to lean toward illustrating them as lazy, criminal, always unintelligent, evil, dangerous, and otherwise wholly bad in every way. This means of stereotypically presenting African American men most likely is the impetus for why I was caught off guard by a question about the role of Gus in Vince Gilligan's AMC blockbuster, *Breaking Bad*. When initially asked, I had to ponder because, though I was familiar with the television series, I had not thought about Gus's character in any serious way. Quizzically, I responded, "To what, exactly, are you referring when you ask about Gus?" He responded, and I'm paraphrasing here, "well, he sells chicken and he's a black man."[2] Perhaps it was because I was primarily focused on the show's dramatic content that I missed this obvious relevance to my research. Or maybe it is that African American consumption of chicken tends to be pervasive in popular culture. Either way, it was missed by me and quite certainly many others as this form of African American male entrepreneurship was all but "hidden in plain sight" throughout the series.

This paper maintains that Vince Gilligan's choice to use chicken as the bedrock for developing Gus's character is not simply happenstance. It is an interesting decision. Because of the stereotypes surrounding African Americans and chicken, the element of suspicion about Gus and his illegal activities in the underground drug economy are greatly reduced. While questions are often asked about Gus's sexuality in online discussions, interviews, and so on—speculation to which Gilligan repeatedly says he "[intentionally] leaves it open for interpretation"—few, however, if any, have questioned or made reference to Gilligan's choice to having Fring be a fried chicken entrepreneur.[3] And why would they? African Americans have long histories with the "gospel bird," so much so that it is taken for granted and effectively able to be used. I further argue in this chapter that when coupled with performances of black respectability politics, Gus's character is fully able to succeed in his real endeavor—the drug trade. This discussion, then, explores the nexus of meat (chicken), black masculinity, and respectability politics as a locus for African American male invisibility in the underground economy.

## Eating One's Way through *Breaking Bad*

*Breaking Bad*, which aired from 2008 to 2013 on AMC, is a crime drama about Walter White, mild-mannered chemist turned methamphetamine dealer. In this tale of protagonist turned antagonist, White, after learning he has lung cancer, decides the best way to provide for his family and ensure their financial future is to produce a chemically pure form of the drug. Together with a former student, Jesse Pinkman, Walter White begins producing meth and, in the process, transforms himself into a semi-ruthless alter-character named Heisenberg in order to fit into the criminal underground economy. The series is full drama and part comedy, at times lending itself to aspects of believability. This is achieved in no small part due to the inclusion of families and myriad aspects of everyday life.

One of these features of the everyday is eating. As with any television or film production that takes us into the lives and relationships of families, food is bound to have a central role. Yet it is its ubiquity and its "just thereness" that makes it easy to overlook.[4] Los Pollos Hermanos, the chicken restaurant, is as pervasive a character in the series as its owner Gustavo Fring, to whom we are introduced in season 2, episode 11 ("Mandala"). Once Gus is brought onto the show, we see multiple elements of the eatery—containers, cups, background scenes of the diner. The Los Pollos Hermanos franchise is the most popular chicken restaurant in the Southwest. Loosely translated as "the Chicken Brothers," the restaurant was founded by Gus and his friend/"brother"/possible lover, Max Arciniega, who is killed early in the show. The eatery is there throughout the show even when no central action is taking place therein. Even a member of Walter White's family recognizes the frequency with which chicken makes its appearance, remarking at one point, "Why don't we ever get Chinese?" (212, "Phoenix"). Gus's character is almost always associated with acts of chicken procurement, production, and consumption, making the food as critical an actor as the humans.

As I have detailed in most of my publications, African American histories with chicken have been long and intricate. In *Building Houses out of Chicken Legs: Black Women, Food, and Power*, I have demonstrated some of the ways that chicken—both the bird and the food—have played multiple roles in the lives of African Americans from the slavery era to the present. It has provided food and been a source of income for many families—especially for those in the rural South. Like other forms of cultural production—clothing, music, and dance, for example—a food like chicken has been used over time to shape a distinctive African American culture. It has helped women (and men) define and exert themselves in racist and hostile environments. While I acknowledge the negative interpretations of black culture associated with chicken imagery, my analysis tends to focus on the ways black women (and men) have forged their own self-definitions and relationships to the bird. In so doing, African Americans sometimes have used chicken to defy conventional representations of blackness and gender identity, as well as to exercise influence through food preparation and distribution. Through an analysis of Gus Fring's engagements with food in *Breaking Bad*, another example of this phenomenon emerges for consideration.

A Cautious Man . . .

Gustavo Fring (played by actor and director Giancarlo Esposito) is cast in the role of the black Hispanic[5] in the television series. Esposito, who is self-declared Italian and African American, plays the part of a Chilean who ultimately crosses the border to America in search of a better life. Toward the end of season 2 (211, "Mandela"), Gus, the primary person of color in *Breaking Bad*, is introduced through Walter White's lawyer Saul, because White and his partner Jesse are incompetent when it comes to meth distribution. Saul admonishes them that they need someone disciplined and methodical and thus suggests Gus, with the caveat that it will be difficult because Fring is "a cautious man."

The next day, Mr. White orders food and sits all day in Los Pollos Hermanos hoping to meet the new distributor. At one point in the day, Jesse, Walter White's young partner, arrives, obviously very high. But the businessman never makes an appearance. Mr. White eventually leaves, only to return alone the next day hoping still to meet the potential new partner. He orders more food and waits. Time passes to no avail. Late in the day, after most of the patrons have left, White happens to look wearily and angrily out the restaurant window. Against the darkness of the fading evening sun, he sees the visage of Gus across the room busily wiping down tables. Perhaps sensing he is being watched or hoping for the attention, Gus straightens up, folds the dishtowel, and stares straight at White. A realization dawns on White and he races to the food counter sensing the person he has been waiting for has been in his midst the entire time. As he approaches the counter Gus says, "Can I help you, sir?" "Diet Coke, please," responds White. When Gus moves to refill the soda, White says, "And five minutes of your time." This gives Gus a slight pause.

In the next clip, Gus approaches White and says, "What can I do for you," maintaining the veneer of the consummate customer service provider. Walter White tells him to have a seat . . . and after a moment quickly adds, "please." After convincing Fring to sit down with him in order to hear his pitch, Walter says, "I would like to know why you wouldn't meet with me yesterday." Fring demurs, answering, "I'm sorry, I'm not following," and proceeds to tell White he is confusing him with someone else.[6] After a brief look back over his shoulder, Fring very humorously says to White in the jovial, well-rehearsed tone of someone who has taught his employees well, "Sir, if you have a complaint, I suggest you submit it through our email system. I would be happy to refer you to our website." White presses on, amused but undeterred, saying to Fring: "I was told that the man I would be meeting with is very careful. A cautious man. I believe we're alike in that way. . . . If you are who I think you are, you should give me another chance." As White is talking, the camera is focused on Gus's face, which quickly but subtly changes. Registering a blank look that is described as "[Gus's] trademark cold calculation"[7] stare, Gus says: "I don't think we're alike at all, Mr. White. You are not a cautious man at all. Your partner is late and he was high." After White acknowledges this, Gus goes on to say, "You have poor judgment. I can't work with someone with poor judgment." Walt steadfastly assures him that his product is the best there is and they both stand to gain

197

a lot of money. When asked why Mr. White associates with Jesse, White indicates that not only can he trust the young minion, but also, he "does what I say." Gus prepares to leave but not before responding that he will be in touch if he decides to work with the two. Gus turns again to leave the table but then turns back to say, "You can never trust a drug addict."

I detail this scene at length for several reasons. One, it is interesting that this discussion occurs in the chicken restaurant. Food spaces often serve as masking arenas for difficult conversations. In this way, they can be contested culinary spaces, or what Denis Byrne refers to as "nervous landscapes." A landscape can be nervous when a multiplicity of powers and identities are introduced, and homogeneity and hegemony are disrupted, giving rise to a form of nervousness. It is the way of thwarting systematic power that ushers in the anxiety and concern lending itself to a nervous landscape.[8] At Los Pollos Hermanos, Gus makes the landscape nervous. Walter White goes looking for a distributor, only to find that he has been sitting, unaware, with the drug king for days. Gus clearly controls the scenario, though White has the product to be distributed. Moreover, while Walter sees the man in the window/mirror and feels they are alike, Gus strongly rebukes such a comparison, refusing to be conjoined, despite his dealing with the white power structure embodied by Walter White. On the other hand, in that scene we are compelled to feel for White because he desperately needs Gus's help. He is, after all, dying and doing all of this to provide for his wife, son, and soon to be born daughter. Gus has no excuse. He is simply a drug dealer disguised as a businessman—thus, the social order is restored.

Though Fring and White go on to form a lethal business partnership, this scene also should be noted for the Janus-faced ways in which Fring operates. He goes from being agreeable and mild-mannered to "placid savagery," according to Matt Grant. Grant continues, "It is his unexcitable demeanor when enraged that makes him unpredictable and highly volatile to be around, and that's exactly what you want in a good antagonist: never knowing what he is going to do next. When Gus threatens, you know he means it. Recall the reserved venom with which he offers his ultimatum to Walter in the middle of the desert, after [Gus] has successfully trained Jesse [Pinkman] to be his cook in order to cut Walter out of the equation: 'If you try to interfere, this becomes a much simpler matter. I will kill your wife. I will kill your son. I will kill your infant daughter.'"[9] Gus is ever mindful of the privilege with which White—his name implies it all—moves. White, like Fring, often is able to get away with murder—literally and figuratively.

Unlike Fring, however, White does not have to use stereotypes to hide. Instead, his race and class are the cloaks that shield him from suspicion.

## The Unsuspected Negro: Gus Fring and Black Respectability Politics

In his restaurant, Gus is nothing if not customer service–oriented. He is charming, amiable, and charismatic to all he serves. As a philanthropist, he is heavily involved in giving to numerous charities, including the antidrug efforts of the Albuquerque Drug Enforcement Agency. To all appearances, Gus is your everyday, average "Joe." He is well-groomed and soft-spoken. He moves slowly and deliberately, with calculated gestures; thus, he is nothing short of a properly controlled black man. This control extends to his material possessions. Gus is conservative in his choices, driving a Volvo station wagon, for instance. Patrick George explains: "A Volvo wagon is the perfect choice for this guy. It's a nice car, fitting for a successful guy like him, and a sensible, safe choice. But it's not going to draw any attention from the feds. If you're going to be a large-scale drug distributor, a Volvo wagon is a much better choice than a Maybach."[10] He has a comfortable home and an eclectic palate—one that embraces his Chilean roots. He is fastidious in his dress, and careful and thoughtful with his tongue. And, perhaps most importantly, Gus is employed—not only as a laborer, but also as an entrepreneur—at a fast-food chain and also his laundry facility—even though both are a front for his larger economic enterprise—meth distribution.

These appearances are everything to Gus, and they have to be in order for him to fly well under the radar. Given all of these material accoutrements and his performances of respectability with regard to demeanor and character attributes, Andrew Howe maintains, "other than the color of his skin, Fring is generally portrayed as a sort of mainstream white character."[11] Howe goes on to indicate,

> Fring is a well-rounded character with interesting and complex motivations. He is not at all the addicted, violent, shallow stereotype of an over-the-top Latin American drug kingpin à la Tony Montana or Tuco Salamanca. The fact that Fring is black also establishes an interesting aspect of Latino identity not often referenced in popular culture. During the sixteenth through nineteenth centuries, the Middle Passage brought African slaves not only to the eastern shores of North America, but also to Brazil and the Caribbean, as well as a few Central American nations

199

such as Panama. The "Black Hispanic" is rarely portrayed in American depictions of Latinos, and the choice of Esposito for the role of Fring introduced complexity to the series' racial depictions.[12]

While I mostly agree with Howe's observations, it must be noted that while Gilligan is deconstructing one kind of stereotype, he is reinforcing others—the violent, criminalized black man who is associated (regardless of the capacity) with chicken. This latter point seems to be driven home several times throughout the series as Gus is constantly referred to as "the chicken man."[13]

Despite these occasional offhand comments, Gus is presented as an anomaly. He is considered the epitome of a "respectable Negro." Unlike most African American men who are naturally assumed to take part in the criminal underworld, Gus is able to evade suspicion—at least for a while. Scholars of visual media have well noted that portrayals of African Americans in popular culture tend to follow an insidious set of stereotyped scripts. Men, for example, according to film historian Donald Bogle, tend to fall under the category of the ever-loyal Uncle Tom; the unreliable, lazy coon; or, the hypersexualized buck.[14] In *Scripting the Black Masculine Body*, Ronald Jackson II makes a similar argument in responding to the early twentieth-century question, "How does it feel to be a problem?," which was asked by scholar and activist W. E. B. Du Bois. Jackson responds, "Black bodies were inscribed with a set of meanings, which helped to perpetuate the scripter's racial ideology. Through these scripts, race gradually became its own corporeal politics." As Jackson further explains, these narratives that socially assigned black bodies to an "underclass" had their origins in the institutions of "slavery and the mass media."[15]

Anticipating Jackson, in *Building Houses Out of Chicken Legs*, I demonstrate how these "scripts" extended to cultural products like food. I further argue stereotypes and images that sought to denigrate African American men, women, and children's foods, as chicken and watermelon were—and continue to be—pervasive. In the blog post, "Black Lives Matter, Even in Food Justice," I discuss how African Americans are today still stereotyped with chicken and watermelon. I cite the incident in 2009 when President Obama won the presidential election and the then mayor of Los Alamitos, California, Dean Grose, sent out an email depicting the South Lawn of the White House planted with watermelons instead of the decorations that normally adorned the grass in preparation for the annual Easter Egg Roll. The title accompanying the post read, "No Easter egg hunt this year."

200

Countless memes circulated showing the president's name in relation to chicken.

What these scripts (and images) reveal is that Black bodies in the United States are still very much inscribed with and socially constructed by race meanings and representations, thus rendering them politicized. Black bodies in their visual and cultural difference have been deemed insufficient, incapable, inferior, and unruly. From slavery to the present, representatives of state power—slavemasters, police, and other representatives of the state imbued with the authority to regulate behaviors and enforce order—have sought to control African American minds, bodies, and spirits because they always have been considered outside the bounds of civility and morality.

Against this historical backdrop, I read the character of Gus Fring as an "unsuspected" Negro. (Here, I deliberately use Negro to signal back to a historical moment when the politics of respectability was in its prime, hence the New Negro.)[16] Turn-of-the-twentieth-century black middle- and elite-class ideology maintained that there was a proper way to do (a thing), to say (a thing), and to wear (a thing). These rules, known as the politics of respectability, were devised largely to police the actions of other blacks—most especially ex-slaves (and/or their descendants) who were migrating from the South. With the backing of the state and the support of ordinary blacks who believed in their efficacy, these rules—then and now—regulated black conduct. At the turn of the twentieth century, the philosophy was that proper conduct was necessary for uplifting the race. By correcting the "bad" traits of the black poor, it was believed that the black race would be seen as "acceptable" and "good," worthy, if you will, of full citizenship.

In his essay "The Rise of Respectability Politics," Frederick Harris explains that today this practice "has now evolved into one of the hallmarks of black politics in the age of Obama, a governing philosophy that centers on managing the behavior of black people left behind in a society touted as being full of opportunity."[17] Fring's character is always aware of this politics, and thus all of it is used—the grooming, the acquiescence, the graceful manner, and most of all the sale of chicken to hide his participation in the lethal trade in meth. This was a shrewd deployment on the part of Gilligan—whether intentional or not—because it reveals modern-day sensibilities of many African Americans who work the underground economy. As Harris explains, "In an era marked by rising inequality and declining economic mobility for most Americans—but particularly for black Americans—the twenty-first-century version of the politics of respectability works to

201

accommodate neoliberalism. The virtues of self-care and self-correction are framed as strategies to lift the black poor out of their condition by preparing them for the market economy."[18] Three food episodes will help bring home my point.

## Eating Black Respectability

### THE TRICKSTER

Gus performs black respectability politics so well that it makes him palatable—almost literally—to his customers, to his local community, and most importantly, to the state (represented by the Drug Enforcement Agency). In episode 308, "I See You," Hank Schrader, DEA agent and Walter White's brother-in-law, is in the hospital clinging to life after an attack that was unknowingly orchestrated by Gus. Gus learns that one of the assassins is also in the hospital, having sustained a major injury to his knees during the attempt. This, of course, poses a problem for Gus because his identity as the orchestrator can easily be revealed. To allow time for his henchman, Mike, to get onto the hospital floor undetected, slip pass the police, and get into the room to kill the assassin, Gus personally delivers Los Pollos Hermanos fried chicken to the throng of police who are standing vigil and keeping guard. One of the detectives is talking with Walter White about Hank's bravery during the attack when he is told the chicken has arrived. With glee and delight he says to White, "Food's here—you like Pollos Hermanos? The owner is a big supporter of the DEA." Not just a DEA supporter, Gus is also a charmer, telling Marie, Hank's wife, "Men like your husband are the thin blue line between us and these animals." To further his charade, he offers a $10,000 reward for information leading to an arrest in this unfortunate incident. Gus's goodwill and the meat delivery prove to be just the distraction that is needed so that Mike can sneak into the hospital room and kill the shooter.

Gus's role here as trickster should not be overlooked. Trudier Harris describes the role:

> By definition, tricksters are animals or characters who, while ostensibly disadvantaged and weak in a contest of wills, power, and/or resources, succeed in getting the best of their larger, more powerful adversaries. Tricksters achieve their objectives through indirection and mask-wearing, through playing upon the gullibility of their opponents. In other words, tricksters succeed by outsmarting or outthinking their

opponents. In executing their actions, they give no thought to right or wrong; indeed, they are amoral. Mostly, they are pictured in contest or quest situations, and they must use their wits to get out of trouble or bring about a particular result.[19]

Gus uses chicken to stroke the egos and fill the stomachs of the powerful law enforcers, all while stealthily eliminating any ties to his violence and treachery. But they are not just any police force—this is the DEA. There is a game of one-upmanship taking place here. He is "sticking it to the man." The "man" being Walter White, the DEA, and their representative, Hank. He is also sticking it to the drug hierarchy establishment because the assassins are the nephews of one his archenemies and are a part of the cartel that twenty years earlier killed his partner Max.

Thus, while wearing the mask of the respectable businessman, Gus is carrying out with ruthless aplomb the work he deems necessary to maintain his cover and also climb the ladder as drug kingpin. While everything else is going on, Gus talks with Juan Bolsa, a high-level member of a competing drug cartel. Juan suspects that Gus set up Hank and also the twin brother hitmen, "the cousins." Juan warns Gus that he is onto him and thus will reckon with him. Unbeknownst to Juan, however, Gus has also set him up to be killed while his home is surrounded by Mexican *federales*. By the end of this episode, Walter White has learned that Gus knew all along that White was related to a DEA agent. Whispering to Gus, Walt asks, "You knew my brother-in-law was DEA?" Gus not only tells Walter White that he investigates everyone with whom he works, but he also tells him—"I hide in plain sight, same as you."

On these kinds of maneuverings, Harris remarks: "True tricksters manipulate the mask. . . . They are in control of that manipulation, and they never forget that their motives and objectives are antithetical to those of the persons against whom their trickery is directed."[20] Gus's deployment of trickery differs somewhat from the enslaved African American who intended to "outwit ol' massa" in order to gain a modicum of power. But it is similar in that he sought to level the playing field of social and economic inequality in America and succeeded in doing so for a small period of time. One could argue that he is a con artist more than a representative of the African American folk hero. But, to be sure, inherent in both is a streak of amorality and often violence.

203

In the beginning of the episode immediately following the extension of Gus's largesse to the DEA agents, we are shown a commercial for the Los Pollos Hermanos chain. As the camera pans, we are told of the chain's likely mythical history and the secret to its success.[21] The camera cuts to the bright blue of crystal meth in Walter and Jesse's lab, with the resulting drug being transported to Gus's chicken farm. There we find another of Gus's henchmen, Victor, overseeing the groups of women sorting and packaging the product into plastic bags, which are then carefully submerged into containers of chicken fry batter. From the windows of the warehouse, we see Gus carefully looking after the trucks that leave his processing plant for distribution (309, "Kafkaesque").

Shortly after this scene, Walter White arrives for a meeting with Gus to "lay all his cards on the table." As they sit and talk in the stark room of the trailer across from one another at a large, bare table, Walter thanks Gus for protecting him because White believes (rightly) that he was the actual target of the hitmen cousins instead of Hank. White ultimately leaves the conversation relieved and elated, with an open-ended multimillion-dollar deal from Gus.

The importance of this scene is not in the conversation or the deal that was made. Gus sits completely erect and expressionless as White talks on about his speculations that he was almost in harm's way and that Gus orchestrated the hit to take over the meth trade in the Southwest. The room is large, bland, and bare except for the table and other office miscellany. It appears cold and relatively devoid of any life except for three interesting items on the table—two large carafes of coffee and a small platter of crudités— carrots and what appears to be celery, olives, and the like. The same décor appears in an earlier episode (303, "I.F.T.") when Gus meets with members of the cartel. It is an odd choice of food to have, especially alongside coffee.

There is no dip for the vegetables, nor are there any additives (cream or sugar) for the coffee. For that matter, there are no utensils, plates, or napkins. The food and drink are most likely merely serving the role of a minimalist prop in the overall scheme of showing hospitality and some measure of warmth. They further serve to prop up Gus's persona as a man of respectability and one who shows proper social graces. For sure, one can drink whatever she/he might like with such an appetizer but from the standpoint of food pairing, most often the choice is some kind of wine. To the unknowing, such a presentation might go unnoticed or unremarked upon. But for the food-knowing, such a display might be read as a culinary

204

misstep. This analysis suggests that this performance is just that—a show—and a further demonstration of Gus's desire to define himself as respectable.

This performance is tucked between two culinary scenes that bookend (311, "Abiquiu," and 409, "Bug"). These two vignettes are significant because not only do they take place at Gus's house, but they also involve the same Chilean *paila marina* or fish stew. It is here, in his home, during these illustrations that we really see Gus perform. From the moment Walter White approaches Gus's palatial home in his upper-middle-class neighborhood, we are confronted with several creature comforts. Gus's home is complete with lovely photographs and paintings, faux foliage, well-constructed furniture, and even children's toys. The kitchen represents that of a gourmand—marble countertops, cabinets full of different kinds of glasses, state-of-the-art cookware, a cutlery block set, an oil and vinegar cruet, multiple bottles of wine, the requisite coffee pot, and a large canister of candies. Dish towels and designer hand soap line the first set of sinks. Everything that is needed is in place but seemingly well-used, as well as the cutting block on which Gus has begun chopping a variety of vegetables—cilantro; green, red, and orange peppers; and garlic cloves. With jazz music playing in the background, Gus welcomes Walter White by telling him that he is preparing a fish stew. He says, "Sounds like a cliché but it's just like my mother used to make." Gus goes on to add: "This is a Chilean dish that I love, but I never get to make it. The kids won't eat it. You know how that is." Walter White asks Gus, "Why did you invite me here?" To this, Gus replies, "We work together, why not break bread together? Now, the garlic?" With this matter-of-fact reply he hands White a butcher knife. After Walter looks at his reflection in the blade (and without washing his hands), he begins chopping thinly.

The dinner consists of the stew, a green salad, crusty bread, and white wine—a relatively perfect pairing, unlike the crudités and coffee. Admiring his near perfect meal, Gus takes a sip and says, "Mm." He then launches into a brief soliloquy about the transformation of mere ingredients into an "amalgam." He says, "Taken separately, these ingredients alone don't remind me of anything. I mean not very much at all. But in this precise combination the smell of this meal instantly brings you back to my childhood." This is an interesting statement by Gus because we know very little about his early life.[22]

This is a beautifully scripted scene because it appeals to the sense of sight, while we can imagine taste, touch, smell, and hearing. And it is enlightening for the way in which it reveals how commensality can unveil the

205

intersections of culture, food, and memory and the ways in which, as Gus recalls, food evokes our deepest memories. There is a lot tied up in this meal. If we consider that at some point Gus not only planned on the invitation but also had to shop for ingredients (assuming he did not already have the combination on hand), then there is a great deal of effort expended on his hospitality. The fact that most of it was probably as much of a ruse as the stories he tells about the founding of Los Pollos Hermanos and even about cooking for the "kids" indicates the lengths to which he will go to maintain his appearance as an upstanding moral citizen.

It is quite possible that the stew/soup evoked powerful memories of Gus's childhood. It is equally possible that said childhood was fraught with power struggles, particularly if he grew up in Chile under the regime of Augusto Pinochet. So when Gus casually tells Walter he wishes that someone had advised him how to be rich because it is easy to be poor, Gus may very well be thinking of his early life and the ways in which he and his partner Max trusted the cartel leaders enough to go to them and try to entice them to buy their meth. This encounter came at great cost to Gus because not only was Max killed but also it was the only time he admits to being truly terrified. It may, in fact, have helped shape him into the cold-blooded Janus-faced person he is—one who can cook a homemade stew as casually as he can slit your throat with a box cutter (401, "Box Cutter"). All of these thoughts may well have been in play, prompted by the meal and the memories it engendered, when Gus issues the coup de grâce with a direct stare and a tentative smile: "Never make the same mistake twice."

There are several contrasts to be made between dinner with Walter White and dinner with Jesse. Though the scenes begin almost identically with the two men arriving at Gus's home, Jesse arrives in dark jeans, a T-shirt, and sneakers. White arrives in a suit jacket. Once inside, it is Jesse's job to try to poison the soup with niacin. But he is unable to do so, most likely out of fear. Gus does not ask Jesse to slice garlic or otherwise touch any of the food. Jesse is invited because Gus learned from his hitman Mike that Jesse "has questions." Gus acknowledges what Mike has conveyed to him and says, "We'll eat first, then we will talk." To this, Jesse replies, "Right on!" The dinner meeting is further differentiated by the tone of the meal. While the repast between Gus and White was cordial and gentlemanly, speaking of memories and longing/belonging, dining with Jesse takes on a sinister tone when Gus says, "I know you have concerns." Almost immediately, Jesse becomes sarcastic, referencing a shooting that occurred at Gus's chicken farm the previous day, while he was on site. With his hands folded neatly in front of him, Gus responds: I have invited you into my home, prepared food so we can sit and talk, discuss what's going on in this business, our business, like men. I will explain what is happening, but first, I need you to answer one question for me, can you cook Walter's formula? Jesse becomes indignant, responding, "What?" After Gus rephrases and repeats the question, Jesse replies: "No. Why? You're asking me if I can cook Mr. White's crystal? Without him? Me? The junkie loser you were about to waste and dump in the desert a month ago? This is your plan, huh? Invite me in your house. . . . Make whatever this is . . . , be my buddy and make me feel important, then get me to keep cooking for you after you kill Mr. White? You wanna—You wanna talk like men? Let's talk like men. You kill Mr. White, you're gonna have to kill me too!" To this Gus calmly replies, "That is not what I asked you." After telling Jesse he would explain how working with and for the cartel had become "untenable" and thus he needed Jesse's help, Gus again repeats, "Now, if you would answer the question. . . ."

Again, a great deal is going on in this scene, not least of which is an overt power and privilege play. It is no secret that Gus does not like or respect Jesse. He makes this clear from the outset when meeting Walter White as he admonishes him never to trust a junkie. His feelings notwithstanding, in an earlier scene (401, "Box Cutter") Jesse witnesses Gus coming to the lab where he and Mr. White cooked meth, Gus donning one of the orange protective suits that are used in the lab when cooking meth, and coolly and coldly grabbing another of his henchmen, Victor, and slicing his neck with a box cutter. For maximum visual effect, Gus pulls back Victor's neck so blood squirts all over Jesse and Walter White, all while Gus looks at them. Finally, Gus lets go of Victor, calmly washes his face and hands, changes back into his street clothes, and prepares to leave. Before doing so, he turns back to Jesse and Walter, saying, "Well? Get back to work." Despite the savagery with which Gus carries out the murder, Jesse is disaffected. This, perhaps, is why he feels secure in his privilege, despite his low totem pole position, to dismiss Gus while in his host's home. Jesse's reference to Gus's home-cooked fare as "whatever this is" with a dismissive wave of his hand further illustrates how white, male privilege gives rise to perceptions of power. This is also despite Jesse's youth or being in the presence of one of the most merciless drug lords in the Southwest. In short, Gus's displays of respectability or masculinity are no match for Jesse's whiteness.

Jesse's rejection of Gus's hospitality was, in many ways, a game of chicken. Who will blink first and who will have the last word? Jesse thinks he has the upper hand over Gus because the drug dealer needs the producer and his

207

partner Walter White. But we see Gus weighing this and other perspectives in the performance of his bodily gestures, facial responses, and tone of voice.

Unlike the air of relaxation that seemed to permeate when Gus and Walter were eating, almost from the onset, the air is tense during Jesse's meal. The camera pans out to show a clearly uncomfortable Jesse fidgeting at the table. Whether because he is alone in Gus's presence, he is unfamiliar with fine dining, or what have you, it is an unsteady culinary event. When Jesse defiantly asks, "What am I doing here?," Gus tries to be reassuring by admonishing Jesse that he is a guest in Gus's home. When he tells Jesse that they are going to discuss their business affairs like men, it is ironic because Gus's slight emphasis on the word "men" suggests he believes Jesse is anything but. Gus then leans in slightly, and a bit anxiously, to ask if Jesse can cook the formula without Walter White. But when Jesse launches into his tirade about being a "junkie loser," Gus calmly stops eating and folds his hands in front of his plate, listening closely, his face again slightly reflecting impatience. And as Jesse is telling Gus that he cannot kill Walter White without also killing him, the camera pans to close-up on Gus's face as he says, "That is not what I asked you." With rapid speech, Gus goes on to tell Jesse that he really needs his help, implying that White cannot be involved in this part of the business for his own safety. Gus concludes with a final, "Now, if you would answer the question," while the camera provides a sidelong view of his body and the tension that has set in his face as he deals with Jesse as one would a moody child. One can see the limits of Gus's good graces being tested.

Conclusion

Through this examination, I hoped to demonstrate how a food like chicken holds a great deal of power in its myriad interpretations. This is particularly the case where African Americans are concerned. In the examples discussed here, chicken is used to shield as much as it is used to highlight Gus's blackness, his masculinity, and his performances of respectability. On the one hand, Gus's character uses a food/a meat often associated with African Americans to conceal his illegal activities. On the other hand, it is this very concealment that allows him seemingly to defy conventional representations of blackness and to exercise influence (albeit illegal) through food preparation and distribution.

# Notes

1 Alice Julier and Laura Lindenfeld, "Mapping Men onto the Menu: Masculinities and Food," *Food and Foodways* 13, nos. 1–2 (2005): 1–16. In particular see Fabio Parascecoli, "Feeding Hard Bodies: Food and Masculinities in Men's Fitness Magazines," *Food and Foodways* 13, nos. 1–2 (2005): 17–37; Jeffrey Sobal, "Men, Meat, and Marriage: Models of Masculinity," *Food and Foodways* 13, nos. 1–2 (2005): 135–58.

2 This conversation between Jürgen Martschukat and myself took place in 2013 while I was visiting Erfurt University in Germany to provide a lecture and workshop on African American foodways.

3 In a Reddit conversation with actor Giancarlo Esposito, "Food Villain" asks about the possibility of Gus being "homosexual." Esposito maintains, "There was never any indication at all that Gus had any homosexual tendencies, other than episode 408. And I personally believe that nothing is ever black and white. . . . I had long discussions with Vince Gilligan that it shouldn't be pointed up either way (and he agreed). And the audience should have to decide." This position has been maintained by Gilligan in other interviews. See Giancarlo Esposito, "I Am Actor Giancarlo Esposito, and I Play Gus on the Show Breaking Bad," *Reddit*, January 10, 2012, accessed April 1, 2017, https://redd.it /oazow.

4 Unlike the long-running hit mobster series *The Sopranos*, where James Gandolfini's character, Tony Soprano, drew attention to food consumption as part of his Italian culture, it is much more understated, though omnipresent, in *Breaking Bad*.

5 Andrew Howe writes on this point in his essay "Not Your Average Mexican: *Breaking Bad* and the Destruction of Latino Stereotypes." He explains that by making Esposito's character a Chilean, Gilligan furthers the "complexity of border politics" by illustrating that Mexicans are not the only ones seeking a new life by coming to the United States. In *Breaking Bad: Critical Essays on the Contexts, Politics, Style, and Reception of the Television Series*, edited by David Pierson (Lanham, MD: Lexington, 2012), 92.

6 Vince Gilligan, Karen Moore, Dave Porter, Bryan Cranston, Anna Gunn, R. J. Mitte, Aaron Paul, Dean Norris, Betsy Brandt, and Raymond Cruz, *Breaking Bad*, Season 2, Episode 11, "Mandala" (Culver City, CA: Sony Pictures Home Entertainment, 2010).

7 Matt Grant, "The Case for Gustavo Fring as the Greatest Villain in Television History," *Popmatters*, August 21, 2013, accessed October 5, 2016, http://www .popmatters.com/feature/174332-go-home-walter-gustavo-fring-as-the-greatest -villain-in-television-h/.

8 For more on contested culinary spaces, see Psyche Williams-Forson, *Building Houses out of Chicken Legs: Black Women, Food, and Power* (Chapel Hill: University of North Carolina Press, 2006), 109. Also see Denis Byrne, "Nervous

Landscapes: Race and Space in Australia," *Journal of Social Archaeology* 3, no. 2 (2003): 169–93.

9 See Episode 411, "Crawl Space," *Breaking Bad*; Grant, "The Case for Gustavo Fring as the Greatest Villain in Television History."

10 Patrick George, "Why Breaking Bad Has the Best Cars on Television Right Now," *Jalopnik*, February 2, 2013, accessed October 5, 2016, http: //jalopnik.com /5980961/why-breaking-bad-has-the-best-cars-on-television-right-now.

11 Howe, "Not Your Average Mexican," 87–102.

12 Howe, "Not Your Average Mexican," 92.

13 I am thankful to Monica White for lending this perspective to the analysis.

14 Donald Bogle, *Toms, Coons, Mulattoes, Mammies, and Bucks: An Interpretive History of Blacks in American Film* (New York: Viking, 1973).

15 Ronald Jackson II, *Scripting the Black Masculine Body: Identity, Discourse, and Racial Politics in Popular Media* (Albany: State University of New York Press, 2006), 90. See also Psyche Williams-Forson, "Black Lives Matter Even in Food Justice," *Food, Fatness and Fitness*, January 5, 2016, http://foodfatnessfitness .com/author/psyche-williams-forson/.

16 My reference plays off the term *New Negro*, which was coined in the late nineteenth century and popularized by Alain Locke during the Harlem Renaissance. The concept of the New Negro was seen invariably "as men and women (but mostly men) of middle-class orientation who often demanded their legal rights as citizens, but almost always wanted to craft new images that would subvert and challenge old stereotypes. An all-encompassing term, it "insisted on so many spheres at self-definition, self-expression and self-determination, a striving after what Locke called 'spiritual emancipation.'" See Henry Louis Gates, "The Trope of a New Negro and the Reconstruction of the Image of the Black," *Representations* 24 (Fall 1988): 131.

17 Frederick C. Harris, "The Rise of Black Respectability Politics," *Dissent*, winter 2014, accessed June 12, 2016, https://www.dissentmagazine.org/article/the-rise -of-respectability-politics/.

18 Harris, "The Rise of Black Respectability Politics."

19 Trudier Harris, "The Trickster in African American Literature," TeacherServe, National Humanities Center, February 15, 2018, http://nationalhumanitiescenter .org/tserve/freedom/1865–1917/essays/trickster.htm.

20 Harris, "The Trickster in African American Literature."

21 A similar apocryphal narrative is told by Gus to his employees after the hitmen cousins appear at the restaurant on consecutive days. In the prequel, *Better Call Saul* (403, "Sabrosito"), Gus gathers his employees together and in response to the question, "Mr. Fring, who were those guys?," tells the starry-eyed youth that they tried to extort money from him when he opened his first restaurant. They returned for more, but Gus empathically said no. "This is America. Here, the righteous have no reason to fear. Here, those men have no power. And when they saw that I had no fear of them, they ran like the cowards they are back

across the border. They will not return. We will move on from this. My friends, I promise you that together, we will prosper." This pro-America motivational speech was followed by applause.

22  We are told that Gus comes from Chile and immigrated to the United States. There is some suggestion that he was well connected in the Pinochet regime. See "Gustavo Fring." *Fandom*, n.d., accessed February 1, 2018, http://breakingbad.wikia.com/wiki/Gustavo_Fring; see also Episode 408, "Hermanos."

## Bibliography

Bogle, Donald. *Toms, Coons, Mulattoes, Mammies, and Bucks: An Interpretive History of Blacks in American Film.* New York: Viking, 1973.

Byrne, Denis. "Nervous Landscapes: Race and Space in Australia." *Journal of Social Archaeology* 3, no. 2 (2003): 169–93.

Esposito, Giancarlo. "I Am Actor Giancarlo Esposito, and I Play Gus on the Show Breaking Bad." *Reddit*, January 10, 2012. https://redd.it/0azow. Accessed April 1, 2017.

Gates, Henry Louis. "The Trope of a New Negro and the Reconstruction of the Image of the Black." *Representations* 24 (1988): 129–55.

George, Patrick. "Why *Breaking Bad* Has the Best Cars on Television Right Now." *Jalopnik*, February 2, 2013. http://jalopnik.com/5980961/why-breaking-bad-has-the-best-cars-on-television-right-now. Accessed October 5, 2016.

Gilligan, Vince, Peter Gould, Nina Jack, Diane Mercer, Bob Odenkirk, Jonathan Banks, Rhea Seehorn, Patrick Fabian, Michael Mando, Michael McKean, Arthur Albert, and Dave Porter. *Better Call Saul*, Season 3. New York: AMC Network, 2017.

Gilligan, Vince, Karen Moore, Dave Porter, Bryan Cranston, Anna Gunn, R. J. Mitte, Aaron Paul, Dean Norris, Betsy Brandt, and Raymond Cruz. *Breaking Bad*, Season 2. Culver City, CA: Sony Pictures Home Entertainment, 2010.

Grant, Matt. "The Case for Gustavo Fring as the Greatest Villain in Television History." *Popmatters*, August 21, 2013. http://www.popmatters.com/feature/174332-go-home-walter-gustavo-fring-as-the-greatest-villain-in-television-h/. Accessed October 5, 2016.

"Gustavo Fring." *Fandom*, n.d. http://breakingbad.wikia.com/wiki/Gustavo_Fring. Accessed February 1, 2018.

Harris, Frederick C. "The Rise of Black Respectability Politics." *Dissent*, winter 2014. https://www.dissentmagazine.org/article/the-rise-of-respectability-politics. Accessed June 12, 2016.

Harris, Trudier. "The Trickster in African American Literature." TeacherServe, National Humanities Center, February 15, 2018. http://nationalhumanitiescenter.org/tserve/freedom/1865-1917/essays/trickster.htm.

Howe, Andrew. "Not Your Average Mexican: *Breaking Bad* and the Destruction of Latino Stereotypes." In *Breaking Bad: Critical Essays on the Contexts, Politics, Style, and Reception of the Television Series*, edited by David Pierson, 87–102. Lanham, MD: Lexington, 2012.

Jackson, Ronald, II. *Scripting the Black Masculine Body: Identity, Discourse, and Racial Politics in Popular Media*. Albany: State University of New York Press, 2006.

Julier, Alice, and Laura Lindenfeld. "Mapping Men onto the Menu: Masculinities and Food." *Food and Foodways* 13, nos. 1–2 (2005): 1–16.

Parascecoli, Fabio. "Feeding Hard Bodies: Food and Masculinities in Men's Fitness Magazines." *Food and Foodways* 13, nos. 1–2 (2005): 17–37.

Sobal, Jeffrey. "Men, Meat, and Marriage: Models of Masculinity." *Food & Foodways* 13, nos. 1–2 (2005): 135–58.

Williams-Forson, Psyche. "Black Lives Matter Even in Food Justice." *Food, Fatness and Fitness*, January 5, 2016. http://foodfatnessfitness.com/author/psyche-williams-forson/.

Williams-Forson, Psyche. *Building Houses out of Chicken Legs: Black Women, Food, and Power*. Chapel Hill: University of North Carolina Press, 2006.

nine | NEEL AHUJA

# On Phooka

## BEEF, MILK, AND
## THE FRAMING OF ANIMAL CRUELTY
## IN LATE COLONIAL BENGAL

TO BEGIN AN EXAMINATION OF the intersection of the politics of species and food in India, it is necessary to inquire historically into the unique status of bovine-derived foods in public culture. Both taboos against beef consumption and veneration of the cow and its milk have been central to the construction of Hindu identity as national identity. Despite the purported secularism of the Indian state, the persistent wielding of specific caste Hindu traditions as inviolable cultural norms has resulted in such practices of dietary prohibition and veneration being constructed as core "indigenous" food practices. Yet despite robust historical study of the colonial proliferation of cow protection riots and related attempts by Hindu nationalists to prevent cow slaughter, why has historical work on cows and bovine-derived foods in India focused less centrally on the issue of cow veneration and the resulting social meanings and regulatory practices related to milk production? My provisional suggestion in this essay is that dairy regulation was a site at which the colonial state could resolve contradictory social meanings attached to animal suffering in food production, particularly as colonial officials attempted to introduce a specific scopic regime of colonial humanitarian reform. Witnessing the bestiality of the reproductive management of the cow in dairy production allowed for a particular vision of both human sovereignty and animal welfare, a vision that reinforced the colonial state's centrality in policing the borders of species. And although this scopic re-gime was an imposition of the colonial state, it succeeded in taking advantage of the gendering of colonial difference such that Hindu and Muslim nationalists accepted the resulting settlement that dairying should be subject to colonial animal welfare policing even if prohibitions on slaughter remained out of bounds politically. The effects of this colonial resolution of controversies over bovine-derived food products has ramifications for India's postindependence politics of species up to the present, as renewed right-wing cow protectionist violence rehearses the racial, caste, and gender dynamics of the fundamental differentiation of beef and milk within public culture.

## Gau Mata, Cow Protection, and
## the Ideological Division of Milk and Beef

By the time print capitalism arose in India in the 1880s, the cow was domesticated as a threatened figure for the emergent Indian nation.[1] Following growing state attempts to monitor and regulate caste and religious custom, the expansion of print communications allowed colonial surveillance to become more deeply ingrained in sites of identity formation. If nationalist sentiment concerning the cow initially seemed to be concentrated among the higher castes and landowning classes, the polemicists of Hindu revival in the late nineteenth century increasingly engaged broader constituencies in developing a public discourse concerning the endangered cow. As such, "a considerably expanded section of Hindu and Muslim 'communities' was affected by the reports and rumors of the period," especially as colonial officials began to anticipate local conflicts over the ownership, transport, or slaughter of cows, pigs, and other animals significant to ritual sanctification or prohibition.[2] At this time, when the British Raj was governed by an unelected class of colonial elites, the colonial archive (the collection of governing documents and memoranda of the various departments of the Raj) began recording widespread evidence of riots in cities and towns across northern India. Cow protection became a primary site at which organized Hindu nationalists resisted the authority of the state and contested the social distribution of goods and rights.

There is a significant and growing historical literature on the rise of the cow protection movement at the end of the nineteenth century, which situates the movement's violent tactics within the context of the rise in religious revivalism; transformations in communication, transport, and agri-

214

culture; the declining wealth and power of small landowners; and changing dynamics of caste formation.[3] The rise of cow protection during the reign of the Raj anticipates the postindependence species politics aligned with the Hindu nationalist movement, realized most spectacularly in the 1966–67 cow protection riots.[4] This cow protectionist current has recently redoubled in India under the Hindutva rule of Bharatiya Janata Party (BJP) Prime Minister Narendra Modi and the launch of a national cow vigilante umbrella organization, the Bharatiya Gau Rakshak Dal, in 2012. Since 2014, gau rakshaks have engaged in widespread mob violence against Muslims and Dalits aimed at suppressing the beef trade and spurring political support for policies such as a national ministry of cow protection.[5]

As documented by historians of Hindu nationalism, beef has long been the target of an indigenizing nationalist discourse that situated the alimentary traditions of the colonized within a nostalgic, historically dubious paradigm of Vedic vegetarianism.[6] It should be no surprise, then, that the Indian colonial archive queries the social meaning and economic significance of the rendering of animals into meat, with a focus on beef as a material nexus for social fragmentation and mobilizations against colonial sovereignty. However, the fact that attempts to restrict the exploitation of bovines for meat in India coincided with the proto-industrial expansion of the exploitation of bovines for milk suggests limits of a critique of cow protection focused primarily on the politics of beef and animal slaughter. It reveals the ideological nature of the language used to distinguish bovine species as well as bovine-derived food products. The distinction between meat and dairy products in India indicates not only a material differentiation of commoditized extracted flesh (meat) from commoditized extracted fluid (milk), but also a manner of distinguishing the taboo on consumption of animal-derived commodities produced by slaughter (non-veg) from the normalization and, in the case of dairy, the sanctification of products produced by reproductive management (veg). Such distinctions aim to conceal the political economy that incorporates the commodity chains of both beef and milk into the machinery of mass animal killing. The gendered distinctions between cow, ox, and bull, as well as the species distinction between cattle and water buffalo, further complicate efforts to understand the social meanings of beef and milk. This is especially the case since cow protectionists elevated the archetypically whitened, European-origin female dairy cow as an icon of national alimentary purity even as they at times also targeted those who owned, transported, sold, or slaughtered the full range of bovines including bulls and buffalo.[7]

As colonial integration enabled cosmopolitan practices of social reform and emergent radicalisms in the British Empire, the stereotype of the Hindu "sacred cow" became a primary icon of colonial difference in international representation of India. Charu Gupta explains that the figure of *gau mata* or mother cow came to represent the emergent nation in part because it could flexibly access varied tropes of feminine power and victimization, ranging from imagery of the vengeful goddess to the nourishing provider of milk to the mute wife.[8] At the same time, the Hindu nationalist discourse of cow protection existed in complex relation to broader discourses of animal welfare disseminated by international vegetarian and anticruelty societies, which were encoded into Indian colonial law in the same time period. Although some animal welfare advocates in England and India during this period embraced anticolonial politics, the most established animal welfare organizations were elite groups advocating the policing of worker and peasant treatment of animals.[9] It is no surprise that they advocated the expansion of both the colonial state as defender of animals and of early industrial farm operations as a pathway to standardizing animal care. The Calcutta Society for the Protection of Animals (CSPCA)—the first animal protection society in Asia—was founded in 1861, five years before the ASPCA was founded in New York. Colonial Bengal passed its first animal welfare laws in the 1860s, and the British Raj passed the first all-India animal welfare law in 1890. The animal welfare societies were largely run by members of the British colonial class, who saw themselves as social reformers aligned with a larger global network of anticruelty activists.

### Phooka Regulation and the Rise of Indian Animal Welfare Law

Colonial officials sought to repress the cow protectionist current in Hindu revivalism, attempting to clamp down on communal riots, especially during Eid and other Muslim holidays. At the same time, missionaries and state functionaries ridiculed what they viewed as Hindu hypocrisy over the "sacred" cow, often noting the public spectacles of malnourished and diseased bovines, dogs, and other animals roaming Indian streets. Ensconced in sentimental reform discourses of colonial humanitarianism, such animal welfare discourse often took cow protectionists to task as maintaining dilapidated cowsheds. Nonetheless, there were some notable transfer points where the cow protectionist current of Hindu revival overlapped with animal welfare advocacy within the colonial state. Key transfer points between the rhetorics and social logics of cow protection and anticruelty

216

movements appear in debates over animal welfare laws passed in Calcutta in 1890 and 1938. Dairy is significant in these debates given the shift toward industrialization of milk that begins in select cities (such as Bombay and Calcutta) by the end of the nineteenth century, as well as the publicity by cow protectionists of the link between the end of a cow's lactation period and its vulnerability to slaughter. In its uneven representation of human–bovine intimacies, the colonial archive—especially legislative debates and administrative memoranda concerning animal welfare and dairying practice—offers a path for rethinking the disjunction of beef and dairy that guides most historiography of cow protection.

Despite the reams of records of state investigation of cow protection riots, national legislation did not criminalize slaughter of bovine species (cattle and buffalo) during this period; in fact, colonial officials were largely viewed by Hindus in northern India as endorsing slaughter through their attempts to anticipate and prevent cow protection agitation. Instead of focusing primarily on slaughter, the main concerns over the cruel treatment of bovines in early animal welfare legislation in India concerned cruel milking practices, particularly a practice called *phooka*, which colonial officials left untranslated from Hindi and Bangla. This practice often appears undefined in colonial law, though in other contexts it is translated into English as blowing or insufflation. Why was there so little description of this criminalized practice despite the intense focus on it in legislative debates on animal cruelty in colonial Bengal? Answering this question requires an approach to the archive that emphasizes its ideological nature and limited scope of representation; it requires suspicion of the project of direct information retrieval for reclaiming a history of human–animal relations. This is so even as we should insist on careful attention to the rhetorical forms instantiated in the archive that reveal how state power shapes categories of historiographic inquiry, including species categories.[10]

The concomitant attempts to regulate slaughter and dairy production created conflicting imperatives for late colonial governance, not only in terms of humans' relationships to animals but also concerning the social management of nation, gender, class, and caste, as varied factions of the nationalist movement asserted increasing control over the state in the decades preceding independence and partition in 1947. Legal prohibitions of phooka helped frame the bovine question in a way that preserved the ideological contours of the milk/beef distinction, in the process masking the manner in which cow protectionism and the figure of gau mata were subtly utilized to expand the state's authority to police public spectacles of animal cruelty. This in turn allowed for an ongoing conceptual division of cow protection and animal welfare that would continue to obscure the investment of the state and the dairy industry in the exploitation of bovine life in the lead-up to independence and partition.

Although slaughter for meat production has been the primary preoccupation of cow protectionists since Dayananda Saraswati, founder of the Hindu nationalist Arya Samaj, launched the cow protection movement in Panjab in the early 1880s, national animal welfare laws have generally not prohibited killing cows. After independence, Article 48 of the Indian constitution encouraged slaughter prohibitions but delegated this authority to the states. National animal laws dating to 1890 have, in contrast, placed significant focus on dairy practices. This emphasis reflects an attempt on the part of the colonial state to manage contradictions between the symbolic and economic logics of Hindu nationalism, particularly as the Indian National Congress and other nationalist groups began to exercise increasing power within the state apparatus. If the rise of print capitalism, mass transit networks, organized nationalism, and cow protection converged in the 1880s and 1890s, by the 1930s there was a will to incorporate aspects of domestic cow protectionism into the apparently secular policing activities of the state, including in Bengal, where Muslim political forces had rising political power. Whereas Muslim workers came into open conflict with the CSPCA in Bengal over regulations concerning the use of oxen in draft labor, preventing the municipal policing of ox carts, Muslim elites joined Hindus in the moderate wing of the Congress in support of anti-phooka activism. The ability to provisionally hold together a political coalition around this form of animal law had an impact on the public character of emergent Indian humanism. As a result, Indian animal welfare law began to shape a particular kind of moral vision and rhetoric of witnessing with regard to cows and buffalo as a pathway to a broader domestic politics of animal welfare and social reform.

Although later depictions of phooka eventually unveiled the practice as an intimate violation of the cow's body, focusing on tropes of bestiality and rape by the male dairy farmer of the female cow, initially the legal text of the ban attempted to completely withhold description of the practice. Take, as a starting point, the first mention of the cow in India's Prevention of Cruelty to Animals Act of 1890, the first animal welfare act to apply to all of India. Section 4, part 1 reads as follows: "If any person performs upon a cow or other milch animal the operation called phooka or dhoom dev, or permits such an operation to be performed on any such animal in his possession or under his control, he shall be punished with fine which may extend to 500 rupees, or with imprisonment for a term which may extend to two years, or with both, and the animal on which the operation was performed shall be forfeited to the Government." In its original form, the bill did not elaborate further; there was no definition of "the operation called phooka or dhoom dev."[11]

Such elliptical legal prohibitions were not uncommon, especially given that laws regulating sexuality conventionally refused to name the prohibited practice. Unlike prohibitions on other social practices like *sati* (widow immolation), which were highlighted by colonial reformers as representing the worst of regressive Indian social norms,[12] regulation of sexuality coexisted with Victorian rhetorical norms that worked to constrain public representation of the law. The infamous 1866 ban on sodomy in Section 377 of the Indian Penal Code euphemizes homosexuality and bestiality as "intercourse against the order of nature," and instead of defining specific acts, states only that "penetration is sufficient to constitute the carnal intercourse necessary to the offense described in this section."[13]

In the case of cruelty against dairy cows, a paternalistic approach to enforcing the moral vision of the human involved the hope that censoring knowledge of cruel practices would geographically constrain their spread. Consider a flurry of notes passed between colonial officials following the publication of the 1890 act. The government attempted to define phooka as a particularly Bengali problem; even as the prohibition of phooka would apply to all of India, the state attempted to rhetorically contain it to Bengal in order to prevent a wider airing of the practice. A lawyer from Maharastra, P. R. Desai, published the following query in the *Bombay Gazette*: "Sir, Section 4 of Act XI of 1890, an Act for the Prevention of Cruelty to Animals, prescribes a penalty for practicing upon a cow an operation called 'phúka.' I have tried my best ever since the passing of the Act to ascertain the meaning of this word . . . the exact meaning of it should be given in the Act, as in the absence thereof justice is, I consider, likely to fail in cases intended to be dealt with under the section mentioned above." In internal communications upon receipt of this note, the legislative secretary suggests that the government could deny the request based on the hypothesis that phooka only occurs in a limited geographic region. In turn, puzzled officials in the Home Department themselves sought out the meaning of the practice and debated its prevalence. After several failed attempts to find the definition in published agricultural sources, one official received the following description, passed on through multiple colleagues, which emphasizes the low class status of the phooka practitioner: "Phúka is the inflation of the womb with air (introduced by means of a bamboo pipe inserted in the vagina). It is supposed to increase the flow of milk (by pressure on the udder, perhaps?) and destroys the fertility of the cow. This horrid torture is as far as I know specialty of the low Bengali gowala." Finally, the Home Department advised that the government continue to withhold public description of the practice and suggested its limited geographic range; the final letter from the legislative secretary to the lawyer reads as follows: "I am desired to state that the practice of Phúka is believed to be confined to Bengal, where the word is well understood, and that it was not therefore necessary to give it a legislative explanation. Signed, S. Harvey James, Secretary to the Govt of India."[14]

Although many colonial officials outside of Bengal were not aware of phooka, the legislative debate in Bengal prior to the enactment of the law included testimony that invoked medical discourse intended to prove the ineffectiveness and irrationality of the milking method. The legislative review committee quotes veterinarian R. Spooner Hart's testimony from a court case in which a Calcutta *goala*, or dairy farmer, was prosecuted in 1887:

Phooka is practised in two ways; in one case the operator applies his mouth to the vulva . . . and blows into the vagina; in the other case a piece of hollow bamboo is thrust into the vagina to the extent of 6 or 9 inches, and the operator blows through the tube. During the process the animal is held by the nostrils, completely under restraint. The animals are subjected to this practice twice daily, and exhibit the utmost possible distress as milking time comes round. Sometimes salt and water is injected into the vagina, and sometimes as much of the animal's tail as is available is thrust into the vagina. . . . The effect, in my opinion, is painful to the animal operated upon. I consider it a barbarous piece of cruelty. The immediate effect of blowing into the vagina is, the cow evinces signs of abdominal pain: the hind legs are abducted, the back arched up, the animal shows discomfort and displeasure at the operation by shifting away from the operator, shows restlessness, the cow urinates. These outward signs I have described lead me to conclude that the operation causes pain to the cow; the blowing introduces foreign matter into the uterus and into the bladder, the latter becoming artificially distended. The effect on milk is nothing. It is a perfectly useless operation. . . . The blowing being an unnatural process, the forcing in of air into the parts not intended by nature to receive it must be attended with pain. Ill-effects would follow from the process if continued.[15]

Although I agree with the normative animal welfare claims advanced by Spooner and other anti-phooka advocates that phooka (or for that matter many other extractive agricultural practices) are likely to cause various forms of suffering for animals rendered as agricultural property, it is also important to carefully attend to the colonial discursive context and scopic regimes of such statements. Expert opinions universally denounced insufflation as ineffective, given that the practice was understood by veterinarians and colonial officials as a method of manually forcing out the remainder of milk from udders rather than a method of endocrine stimulation to induce lactation itself. This reflects something of the state's views not only of cruelty and humanity, but of history itself. The assumption that colonial animal law would modernize inhumane traditional practices guided expert discourse on phooka within veterinary and legal contexts.

Although colonial elites understood that phooka constituted a coercive method intended to extend the reproductive capacity of animal capital to meet the extractive desires of farmers operating on tight margins,[16] the veterinary discourses on the ineffectiveness of phooka were unable to conceive of the intimate knowledge that dairy pastoralists had developed for exploiting mammalian reproductive processes. Prior to identification of the hormone oxytocin in the 1950s, Indian veterinarians did not have at their disposal the endocrine discourses that medicalized the operation of hormones in lactation. Although the embrace of a kind of hormonal determinism produces its own problems—evident in recent transphobic responses to endocrine-disrupting toxins[17]—historicizing the veterinary discourses on the ineffectiveness of phooka helps to reveal the provincialism of the colonial progress narrative. The assumption that phooka constituted an irrational traditional practice of poor, low-caste goalas reveals the regressive caste and class politics of the governmental anti-phooka rhetoric. As such, the colonial archive repeatedly figures phooka as one of a range of irrational or criminal practices of an unruly peasantry that existed on the margins of large landholdings where *zamindars* (aristocratic hereditary landowners) were organizing more modern industrial agricultural operations.[18]

In this sense, the colonial experts' assumption of the localization of phooka as a Bengali agrarian practice sidelines a larger interspecies history of cattle domestication in which intimate knowledge of lactation was a significant contributor to the rendering of milk as commodity. Historians of milk today point to endocrine functions to make sense of a broader

221

anthropological literature on pastoral milking practices. Colonial ethnographies suggest that insufflation for lactation stimulation was not only practiced outside of Bengal, but was in fact widely noted across the whole range of cattle domestication, with reports ranging from the Caucasus to China and Siberia, Arabia to Southern Africa, and Hungary to France. Archaeological debates on cattle domestication in Africa between 8000 and 5000 BCE turn on whether Saharan cave paintings and etchings depict insufflation.[19] The most widely cited account in histories of milk is a xenophobic passage describing horse blowing by Scythians in Herodotus's *Histories*, and books on the global history of milk explain that insufflation is among a variety of practices used to stimulate lactation after a calf dies or stops feeding.[20] Modern depictions of insufflation predictably emphasize the indigeneity of the practice to colonized peoples. The anthropological literature and its photographic archive invoke romantic descriptions of cow blowing among seminomadic pastoralists in Africa, notably in Edward Evans-Pritchard's study of the relationship between cattle and kinship among the Nuer of southern Sudan.[21] Although these materials thus shed light on the Raj's historically dubious colonial effort to limit the geography of phooka to Bengal, they in turn engage in another dubious colonial tradition of idealizing the pastoral (including its normalization of patriarchal social forms) against the depredations of the modern.

Veterinarians did make compelling arguments about the potential for suffering and pain caused by phooka. Yet, given the variety of other criticisms of cruelty against cattle in dairies, cow houses, draft labor, and private homes—ranging from malnutrition and dehydration to whipping, crippling, and overwork—the greater and ongoing legislative effort aimed against phooka reflected a commingling of rhetorical opportunities for reformers, linking animal welfare to established colonial frames for narrating gendered victimhood and humanitarian rescue. Thus it is necessary to query whether anti-phooka discourse can even theoretically remedy violence given its normalization of mass animal agriculture, its reconciling of the figure of the human with property in animals. Proto-industrial and industrial dairying in India did not minimize potentially cruel gendered forms of bovine exploitation. It replaced coercive vaginal practices for inducing lactation with coercive vaginal practices of impregnation under the banner of a scientific "animal husbandry," and did so on a larger scale as India has developed the world's largest herd of domestic bovines. The colonial narrative of phooka as a rape committed by a lowly goala thus requires

222

postponing questions of deep history and privileges and classed and racialized visions of moral and economic development.

## Witnessing Phooka: The Scopic Regime of Bestiality

The Raj ultimately permitted phooka's legal definition to be entered into the national code. The 1890 law was amended to include the following definition: "Phooka or dhoom dev includes any process of introducing air or any substance into the female organ of a milch animal with the object of drawing off from the animal any secretion of milk."[22] An authoritarian form of colonial liberalism seems to be at work in the logics of concealment and witnessing evident in the development of this public definition of the prohibition of phooka. As historian of science Pratik Chakrabarti argues in an article on how the 1890 animal cruelty law shaped and was shaped by Indian scientific research, the law was not a transposition of metropolitan animal welfarism. Instead, it enacted a discourse on the aberrant indigenous forms of Indian cruelty that at once buttressed the power of the colonial state and masked its own exploitation of animals as resource.[23] In this sense, colonial authoritarianism dovetailed with the sentimental romanticism of colonial elites, whose own ability to witness on behalf of Indian animals and other figures of colonial abjection (such as the Hindu woman victimized by patriarchal practices like sati) became the basis for an incipient form of animal welfare policing. The moralism of this colonial construction of the human in law is evident in the distinct scopic regime of bestiality evident in the legislative discussions. Naisargi Dave's essay "Witnessing" examines the centrality of visual metaphors—specifically the exchange of gaze between a witnessing human and a violated animal—as a central trope in Indian animal welfare politics. Focusing on the contemporary activism of BJP politician and cow protectionist Maneka Gandhi, Dave argues that the narration of witnessing cruelty operates similarly to a coming-out narrative: "animal rights activists in India (and perhaps elsewhere) stake their commitment to a way of life based on one critical moment after which nothing can be the same.... Animal rights activists describe this critical moment as an intimate event in which the sight of a suffering animal, the locking of eyes between human and nonhuman, inaugurates a bond demanding from a person a life of responsibility. That event is uniquely intimate because it occurs between two singular beings . . . the human's knowledge is not of all animals in general, but of this animal, at this moment."[24]

223

The dynamic between secrecy and witnessing in the public representation of phooka comes to a head in later debates over the persistence of
phooka, particularly in 1937–38 in Bengal, when animal advocates sought
to strengthen penalties and widen policing. In the years leading up to Indian independence, a recommitment to prohibiting phooka among elite
reformers was largely uncontroversial, but it was also related to rising cow
protection and animal welfare activism, which at times took on a communal character. In this context, the cruelty of the practice was repeatedly
witnessed through the rhetorical form of a rape narrative. After reviewing
various arguments about the economics and health aspects of lactation and
milking, the violence of phooka was rendered in intimate scenarios emphasizing both the horror and the unspeakability of the practice as a form of
bestial penetrative violence.

Lalit Chandra Das, a lawyer and member of the Moderate wing of the
Congress Party, made a number of key points in his lengthy speech as lead
sponsor of the bill adding additional penalties for phooka: the practice was
economically counterproductive because it harmed the cow; it was immoral and cruel; it precipitated the end of milk production, leading farmers
to sell the cows for slaughter; it produced unhealthy milk. After Das's long
and rambling speech, an allied Congress member, Bankim Chandra Datta,
notes that the sponsor had failed to describe the actual practice. Datta's
comments then provide an account of phooka that demonstrates the rhetorical transition from concealment to visibility that echoes the 1890 legislative history: "The hon'ble mover of the bill has . . . omitted to tell the
House definitely as to what the practice is. Perhaps he felt some diffidence
in doing so and I also labor under the same disability, but I am afraid the
story has got to be told even at the risk of chocking [sic] you." Datta then
quotes the description of phooka given by Mrs. F. Stanley, secretary and
superintendent of the Calcutta Society for the Prevention of Cruelty to
Animals:

> The animal in question was in a secluded place at the back of the shed
> not visible from the road but immediately under the window at which
> I . . . was stationed. With wooden shutters closed there was a small space
> through which I could clearly see as to what was passing without being
> seen. . . . The she-buffalo was first tied firmly to posts by all four feet,
> one or two men holding her while this was being done. The milkman
> then seized the animal by the hairy end of the tail and with the greatest
> possible violence thrust this together with his hand and arms up to the

224

shoulder inside the vagina of the animal. By the movements of the man's arm one could see that he was inserting the hairy end of the tail right inside the uterus. Having held the tail in this position for a few minutes the man withdrew his arm leaving the tail fixed inside the animal for the whole length of time. All this time the animal was obviously in agony, coughing and groaning. After very casually dipping his hand in a tub of water he started milking the buffalo.[25]

In this remarkable speech, which was later excerpted in the nationalist journal *Modern Review*,[26] a number of narrative displacements are evident. The passage works to underline the necessity of animal welfare policing while distancing the speaker, Datta, along with his colleague, Das, from the role of witnessing. The "disability" that Datta and Das experienced in hesitating to describe the practice performs their social distance from the bestial act of penetration described therein as it reinforces white femininity as the privileged site for witnessing sexual violence. Mrs. Stanley, the chair of the CSPCA, performs the labor of sentimentally witnessing suffering, which confirms her own virtue as moral arbiter of the horror of cruelty. She voyeuristically peers into the cowshed to witness the act, only to recoil from the sight after the horror is revealed.

Shortly after Datta's long quote from Stanley, he offers the following reflection: "She could not remain there more for even a minute to witness what happened afterwards. This is the harrowing story. This is the barbarous, inhuman and revoltary thing that is being practiced. . . . If you feel in the way in which Mrs. Stanley felt and which every one of us, I think, ought to feel, I think you have got to condemn it in no unmistakable terms and legislate in a way by which this evil can be effaced out of Bengal if not of India."[27] When Datta here comments, "this is the harrowing story," it is unclear as to whether he refers to phooka itself or to Stanley's act of witnessing it; regardless, Datta claims that each legislator ought to share the witness's revulsion and to "condemn it in no unmistakable terms." Like other Victorian narratives centering sexual violence, the coercive penetration of the feminized cow is an act that must be witnessed at the same time that it is rendered unspeakable. In this rhetorical movement, the Congress politicians enact their distance from the bestiality of the dispossessed pastoralist, allowing the white female witness to bridge that distance in order to enable the expansion of nationalist reform. In a scopic regime that appropriates white anticruelty discourse for the cause of the cow, nationalist animal welfare reform was in sync with at least two currents of nineteenth-century

225

elite governmentality: a gendered distinction of the humane and the inhumane and a related authoritarian class politics that configured elites as the
cultivators of sentiment. These currents significantly influenced the elite
sectors of the nationalist movement in India even as they affected debates
over migration and animal welfare across the empire.[28]

The sentimental fashioning of Stanley as the white female defender of
the violated gau mata reflects a logic of racialized colonial reform championed by US missionary Katherine Mayo in two key texts, *The Isles of Fear:
The Truth about the Philippines* (1925) and *Mother India* (1927). Figuring
rape and cruelty to children, women, and animals as interlinked signs of
the barbarity and inhumanity of Asiatic racial types, Mayo fashions herself
as objective observer of cruelty in the name of humanistic colonial reforms.
In her racist polemics against decolonization of both the Philippines and
India, Mayo paints Asiatic populations as subject to the inhumanity of ancient custom and mired in filth, disease, and irrational social stigma. In
both works this is characteristically rendered through the diminished status of indigenous women, whose subjection is rhetorically and ideologically
linked to cruelty to animals. Describing the patriarchal social structure
of the Moros of Mindanao, Mayo notes casually that each chieftain entering battle instinctively "shuts his wife and cattle in his fort for protection . . . and each would rather die a thousand deaths rather than cede
a point of religion, of custom, or of pride."[29] Her description of the Indian *gaushala* or home for cows anticipates Stanley's account of phooka,
shifting from a pleasant scene outside the cow home to a detailed, fright-
ful rendering of the neglected bodies of young calves as innocent victims
of barbarity:

> The first gaushala I saw for myself was in the suburbs of a central In-
> dian city. Over the entrance gate was a charming painting of the blue
> god Krishna in the forest, piping to white cows. Inside the high walls at
> a distance lay a large pleasant garden of fruit trees and vegetable beds
> encircling a pleasant bungalow. On the hither side of the garden was
> the place of the cows. This was a treeless, shrubless, shelterless yard of
> hard-trodden, cracked, bare clay . . . inhabited by animals whose bones,
> in some cases, were literally cutting through their skins. Some had great
> open sores at which the birds, perched on their hipbones or their staring
> ribs, picked and tore. Some had broken legs that dangled and flopped
> as they stirred. Many were diseased. All were obviously starved. Bulls
> as wretched as the cows stood among them, and in a little pen at the

side were packed some 250 small calves. From these last arose a pitiful outcry, at the sound of approaching steps; and as I looked down over the pen-wall at their great brown eyes, their hollow sides and their shaking legs, it occurred to me to ask what they were fed. The answer, frankly given by the gaushala attendant, was that each calf gets the equivalent of one small tea-cupful of milk a day, until it dies—which, as a rule, and happily, it shortly does—the rest of the milk being sold in the bazaar by the keeper of the gaushala.

Mayo's polemic is deeply invested in the rhetorical production of a differential humanity demonstrated in the divergent conception of proper treatment of animals among the English and the Hindus. She describes the indigenous gaushala as "creating monsters" of cows, criticizing M. K. Gandhi's promotion of cow-protectionist *pinjparoles* (animal shelters) as a flawed attempt to remedy phooka and other horrors of indigenous custom without turning to the purportedly more modern animal care techniques of colonial agriculturalists and welfare societies. On the practice of phooka in particular, Mayo repeatedly quotes Gandhi's publications criticizing phooka, but goes on to note that even Gandhi relies on an Englishman's account of the practice and to state that "if any mass of Hindu feeling exists against it, the vitality of that feeling is insufficient to bring it forth into deeds. In a long passage reviewing Gandhi's reflections on the problem of street dogs, Mayo argues that Hindus fail to properly apprehend cruelty, and thus ritually oppose the killing of animals even in instances when this prolongs suffering due to starvation, illness, or injury. Expedient killing was then, as it is today, one of the primary means for colonial reformers to enforce the diminution of suffering as humane care. The lesson is that late colonial reform, in which crown authority over animal protection is transferred to the Indian political establishment, is a failure: "given a people still barbarian in the handling of their own women, it is scarcely to be expected that they should yet have taken on a mentality responsive to the appeal of dumb creatures."[30]

## Cow Protection and Colonial Humanism

Although the legislative debate in 1937 refutes Mayo's claim that there is no sentiment against phooka among indigenous elites, there remain archival traces of concerns about the scope of the proposed updates to the law. The silence with which phooka was met in the media, the colonial apparatus,

227

and even at times in the actual legislative debates worked not only to rein-force the taboo on bestiality, but also to conceal gendered communal and caste concerns with the expansion of animal welfare policing. These dynam-ics are evident in discussions of at least two topics. First, immediately after his description of phooka during the legislative debate, Datta expands on his protest by invoking a discourse of pollution that traded on caste Hindu fears of improper touch and tainted food. He claims, "the importance of cow's milk cannot be over estimated. Right from the very time of our birth you get the first sip of vitality from the cow's milk. . . . Phooka milk has been examined and it has been found to be highly contaminated. . . . I think it has also been pronounced by medical men that diseases such as typhoid and scarlet fevers have been transmitted through this milk. You ought, there-fore, to be very careful as to what milk you use. In other countries and in England in particular I know there are such statutes as the Contagious Dis-eases Animals Act, the Sale of Milk Registration Act, Food and Drugs Act, and similar other statutes. There they have tried to find out as to how best they can get pure and healthy milk. We, however, in India do not turn our attention in the same way." The quality of milk has been a persistent con-cern before and after the anti-phooka agitation, and was a significant influ-ence in the broader push for industrialization of milk production follow-ing independence. However, the potential of disease transmission through phooka was overblown, and it traded on broader discourses of purity and pollution that could be mobilized especially effectively given the unique spiritual investments that Hindu nationalist iconography placed in the cow and in cow-derived foods and healing products.

Second, a persistent criticism of the animal welfare laws was the inva-sion of privacy and the potential instigation of communal hatred, especially given the history of lynching and mob violence deployed against Muslims accused of cow slaughter. Some Bengali legislators criticized the 1890 law because it limited enforcement to publicly visible sites; the 1938 Bengal amendments proposed expanding enforcement to suburban and rural areas and requiring *khatals* or cowsheds to be publicly visible. Given that it was common for households with the economic means to keep milch animals within the domestic space, this provoked fears of intrusion. In the debates over the 1890 law, the legislative committee that strongly endorsed the pro-visions banning phooka also sought to protect the *zenana*, the segregated women's space within the household, from the intrusion of the colonial state: "the general provision of giving a right of entry into private houses, especially zenanas, does not seem to the Committee to be warranted by the requirements of the case, as the power is likely to be abused to the great annoyance and irreparable injury of the parties subjected to it, the real instances necessitating such harsh measures being very few and isolated." Consequently, the phooka debates presented fear of a set of gendered reversals; if the archetypal pastoral dairy farmer was a low-caste Hindu or Muslim male who raped the cow and thus endangered the spiritual and bodily nourishment of the nation, the deputization of the CSPCA and other animal welfare organizations with policing powers risked the colonial state's intrusion into the feminized bourgeois domestic space and violation of practices of *purdah* or veiling that were often integrated into a bourgeois vision of woman as reproducer of national and communal tradition.

From here, we can witness how an apparently secular animal welfare regulation of dairy production interfaced with communal efforts to prohibit slaughter. Cow protectionists—including M. K. Gandhi, who claimed to resist the movement's communal tendencies—lamented that the end of dairy production frequently led to the sale and slaughter of former milch cows. Publishing the secretary of the Calcutta Anti-Phooka Society's description of phooka, Gandhi writes, "It is difficult to imagine anything more torturing or revolting than the process described by the Secretary. . . . They are therefore transferred to butchers after they yield milk even in spite of phooka."[31] Iconography of the movement highlighted the connection between slaughter and milk. In a 1912 image of the cow as a provider to the nation (figure 9.1), eighty-four Hindu deities are located in the cow's body, which in turn feeds the four national communities of Parsis, Hindus, Muslims, and Europeans. Although the forces that passed dairy regulations were varied and divergent, concern over the expansion of animal welfare policing reflected the inevitably messy relations for regulating treatment of cows.

The dairy cow is always at risk of slaughter—generally by a stereotyped figure of Muslim monstrosity—and thus regulations on milk accomplished something that cow protectionists were unable to accomplish in their failure to nationalize slaughter criminalization: the transference of the communal concern for the cow into the abstract, secular moral vision of "animal welfare." To render cow veneration in such universalizing language worked to grant it access to a colonial humanism. In her book *Juridical Humanity*, Samera Esemir describes reform movements in colonial Egypt as shaped by a British conception of the law as a site of humanization, of the production of the human as an end of law. One sign of this development for Esemir is the attempt to provide humane care to animals in Egypt, as the minimization

229

9.1 *Cow with Eighty-Four Deities*, Ravi Varma Press, 1912.

of suffering in itself produces the figure of the human in law. Like Mayo, the colonial reformers that Esemir discusses in the Egyptian context are proponents of animal use and euthanasia as long as the state promotes a utilitarian logic emphasizing the reduction of pain and suffering. Given the utility of animal suffering in the resulting figure of the human produced by colonial law, Esemir suggests that animality is formative of the juridical, that "the colonial history of animal laws . . . relates to the fate of the human by making it difficult to fully capture colonial humanity without a consideration of animal reforms."[32]

As in Egypt, in India counternarratives existed that worked to contest the colonial vision of humane moral sentiment. Given the long-standing differences in nationalist accounts of the significance of cows—as economic and nutritive bases of social reproduction, as well as spiritual symbols of purity—it is not surprising that suffering and the gaze of the witness to cruelty were not the only tropes offered to describe the injury to the cow. In fact, cow protectionist discourse reveals a different kind of universalizing vision of the human, one that could by the late nineteenth century be rendered in a mode that combined secular narratives of colonial difference with an emergent construction of Vedic tradition as the deep history that precedes the rise of colonial law. The novel approach to Hindu nationalism

230

proffered by the Arya Samaj developed a sense of Hindu ethnonationalism by conjoining religious populism to a vision of lost Vedic origins that was deeply submerged in India but also in Europe and across the Islamic world.[33] In the missive he wrote as part of his work to found the cow protection movement, Arya Samaj founder Dayananda Saraswati's 1889 pamphlet *The Ocean of Mercy*, the economic decline of Muslim-majority societies from the Mughal Empire to Turkey and the Maghreb is attributed to the rise in meat-eating, which the author claims depletes the capacity of cows and other food-producing animals to provide economic and nutritional sustenance to meet mass needs. Denouncing the Mughals and the Mongols as temporary empires based on plunder reflected in the extraction of meat from animal bodies, Dayananda moves on to the broader western frontiers of the Muslim-majority and Mediterranean worlds to situate slaughter as the basis of decline: "Contrast the modern and ancient histories of the west. Were not Turkistan, Afghanistan, Persia, Asia Minor, Egypt, Greece, Turkey, and Italy the famous residences of the goddess of wealth? Where is that wealth now? . . . Alas, they have not understood the commonest maxim that industry with the preservation of what it brings in is the surest way to wealth. They chose the profession of destruction and reaped the fruits thereof." More directly, Dayananda writes, "the killer of the cow robs millions of people of their valuable article of food." Despite its claim to vegetarianism's relevance in the deep history of the subcontinent and beyond, Dayananda's framing of Hindus and Muslims as locked into distinct communities and empires reveals as much about the contemporaneous construction of communalism emerging in the late nineteenth century. Integral to the Islamophobia of his proclamations, Dayananda inaugurates a tradition among cow protectionists of claiming a Quranic invocation against beef-eating, portraying modern Islam as a corruption of its essential spiritual practice that, like all major religions, draws inspiration from the Vedas: "the killer of the bovine species, the feller of fruit trees, the seller of the human species, the drinker of wine, do not obtain salvation."[34]

If the Arya Samaj thus claimed that cow protection was a human rather than a narrowly "communal" concern, the prohibition of phooka risked subtly undermining one of the primary Islamophobic tenets that helped to abstract its vision of cow protection toward a claim upon the colonial figure of the human. Hindus were among the small agriculturalists accused of phooka, so advertising the violence of this practice risked breaching the communal borders evident in the binaries between milk and beef, veg and non-veg, milking and slaughter. In fact, historical accounts of cow protectionist riots

231

suggest that although the primary discourse of the cow protection societies was aimed at Muslim slaughter, including ritual sacrifice (*qurbani*) on Eid, these same societies also at times aimed their criticism at Hindu castes that were seen as accomplices to slaughter.[35] The Vedic narrative of cow veneration worked to defend against the breaching of these binaries by envisioning a unique form of humanism, situating the defense of animal bodies against meat extraction as essential to both the subcontinent's indigenous traditions and a religious purity that was the basis of human social reproduction across faiths and geographic borders. Cow protection thus has a complex relation to animal welfarism and to broader, contested visions of the human in late colonial India.

Based on this history, right-wing cow protectionists have since independence couched their arguments against slaughter in terms of universalizing Hindu claims to the human. Analyzing images produced by Hindu nationalists in 1992, the year of the mob destruction of the Babri Masjid in Ayodhya, Christiane Brosius notes that paramilitary cow protectionists claim they argue for the protection of Muslims' personal religious beliefs but require that they accede to a nationalism that prohibits offense to public sentiment for the cow.[36] The public spectacle of lynching and threats targeting Muslims who own, transport, or slaughter cows, of course, undermines the rhetorical force of such a claim.

Although the animal welfarists at the CSPCA were not themselves invested in such an ethnonationalist historical narrative or conception of Indian humanism, the anti-phooka coalitions they formed during the creation of India's foundational animal welfare laws allowed the nascent cow protection movement to lay a claim for the cow as a violated figure of the nation. This prevented the kind of nationalist resolution to the bovine question of the sort that Partha Chatterjee has argued came about regarding debates over women's education in Bengal in the early nineteenth century.[37] Instead of suppressing the rhetorical reproduction of the vulnerability of the cow, it proliferated it, ensuring that the state management of bovine species would play an outsize role in the politics of the postindependence period. Ironically, in the post-1990 era of economic liberalism in India, the rise of cow protectionism has coincided with the expansion in trade in live bovines, leather, and beef, especially in the export markets. Even as Hindu nationalist BJP governments promote an economic nationalism on the international stage through the "India Rising" and "Made in India" branding, they have presided over the neoliberal expansion of these industries, which they cynically associate with political opponents and minorities through

232

communalist cow protection agitation. The analysis of the historical conjunctures opened in colonial debates over phooka is thus relevant to a thorough assessment of the fascistic thrust of cow protection in India today, especially as the nationalist discourses of cow protection aim to rhetorically capture both anticolonial and humanist sentiment.[38] In retrospect, the history of cow protection offers important lessons for understanding the complexities of colonial regulations of social difference, the intensification of "religious" or "communal" violence, and the rendering of the human as a site of contestation in the politics of empire and decolonization in South Asia.

In retrospect, anti-phooka agitation struck at the heart of social struggles to form class, caste, and religious identities and to define the role of the state in late colonial and postindependence India. Whereas the overtly communalist character of cow protection and its focus on slaughter was repeatedly refused legal sanction under the British Raj, the development of an anticruelty discourse around phooka allowed for the formation of a universalizing language of cow protection that could serve the purposes of multiple groups. It helped the largely white elite animal welfarists to transmute energies of cow protection into a new kind of coalitional politics, even as it enshrined in law a form of recognition of the plight of gau mata as a violated species in need of uplift by anticolonial nationalists. For these reasons, the Victorian taboo on representing bestiality could be momentarily suspended in order that the law might intervene in the bovine question as a question of the very colonial production of the human. This suspension allowed for an elite discourse on cruelty, the ideological nature of which is evident in the manner in which it rhetorically divides animal species and food products in order to distinguish forms of extractive animal capitalism. Writing on the international representation of animals in Gaza, Sara Salih productively asks whether such humane rhetorics and strategies "resolutely overlook certain kinds of suffering in order to continue . . . current ways of consuming."[39] It appears that the proto-industrialization of dairy in the Indian colonial context witnessed such divided public exercise of sentiment regarding cow exploitation. This occurred through a displacement of the communal violence surrounding slaughter onto the figure of an irrational, dispossessed pastoral dairy farmer who required moral reform in order to secure the agricultural basis of social reproduction in late colonial Bengal.

233

# Notes

This essay was presented at the Animals in the Archives Symposium, University of Pennsylvania, on October 28, 2016. Thanks to Harriet Ritvo, Zeb Tortorici, Projit Mukharji, Iris Montero, and other participants for feedback. Thanks also to Sushmita Chatterjee, Banu Subramaniam, Elspeth Probyn, the other contributors to this volume, and one unnamed reviewer for additional comments.

1 Christopher Pinney, *Photos of the Gods: The Printed Image and Political Struggle in India* (Chicago: University of Chicago Press, 2004), 106.

2 Gyan Pandey, *Rallying Round the Cow: Sectarian Strife in the Bhojpur Region, 1888–1917*, Occasional Paper no. 39 (Calcutta: Centre for Studies in Social Sciences, 1981), 78.

3 See Pandey, *Rallying Round the Cow*; Sandria Freitag, *Collective Action and Community: Public Arenas and the Emergence of Communalism in North India* (Berkeley: University of California Press, 1989); Anand Yang, "Sacred Symbol and Sacred Space in Rural India: Community Mobilization in the 'Anti-Cow Killing Riot' of 1893," *Comparative Studies in Society and History* 2, no. 4 (1980): 579–96; S. Krishnaswamy, "A Riot in Bombay, August 11, 1893: A Study in Hindu-Muslim Relations in Western India during the Late 19th Century" (PhD dissertation, University of Chicago, 1966); John R. McLane, *Indian Nationalism and the Early Congress* (Princeton, NJ: Princeton University Press, 2015 [1977]).

4 Christophe Jaffrelot, *The Hindu Nationalist Movement in India* (New York: Columbia University Press, 1998): 205–8.

5 For example, see Michael Miller, "A Mob in India Just Dragged a Man from His Home and Beat Him to Death—For Eating Beef," *Washington Post*, September 30, 2015, https://www.washingtonpost.com/news/morning-mix/wp/2015/09/30/a-mob-in-india-just-dragged-a-man-from-his-home-and-beat-him-to-death-for-eating-beef/; "Dalits Assaulted for Skinning Cow," *Indian Express*, July 19, 2016, http://indianexpress.com/article/india/india-news-india/una-dalit-thrashed-cow-skinning-beef-ban-gujarat-cm-anandiben-patel-order-probe-2922451/; Vasudevan Sridharan, "India Hindu Beef Lynching: Muslim Victim Ate Goat Meat Not Beef Reveals Forensic Report," *International Business Times*, October 9, 2015, http://www.ibtimes.co.uk/india-hindu-beef-lynching-muslim-victim-ate-goat-meat-not-beef-forensic-report-reveals-1523254. For initial statistics on the violence, see also Delna Abraham and Ojaswi Rao, "86% Killed in Cow-Related Violence since 2010 Are Muslim, 97% Attacks after Modi Govt Came to Power," *Hindustan Times*, July 16, 2017, https://www.hindustantimes.com/india-news/86-killed-in-cow-related-violence-since-2010-are-muslims-97-attacks-after-modi-govt-came-to-power/story-w9CYOksvgk9joGSSaXgpLO.html.

6 To this end, the Rashtriya Swayamsevak Sangh and other cow protectionists have recently been effective in banning academic books that debunk the historical myth of Vedic beef renunciation. See, most notably, D. N. Jha, *The*

234

*Myth of the Holy Cow* (London: Verso, 2004); Wendy Doniger, *The Hindus: An Alternative History* (New York: Penguin, 2009).

7  Anti-slaughter laws in India vary by state on the inclusion of Asian water buffalo, a bovine species historically employed in draft work and dairying and distinguished from domesticated cattle. Some laws reserve the harshest penalties for slaughter or consumption of female cows as opposed to male oxen and bulls. On the racialization of the cow/buffalo distinction, see Kancha Ilaiah, *Buffalo Nationalism: A Critique of Spiritual Fascism* (Kolkata: Samya, 2004). On the gendered differentiation of cow and buffalo, see Doniger, *The Hindus*.

8  Charu Gupta, "The Icon of Mother in Late Colonial North India: 'Bharat Mata,' 'Matri Bhasha,' and 'Gau Mata,'" *Economic and Political Weekly*, November 10, 2001, 4296. See also Peter Robb, "The Challenge of Gau Mata: British Policy and Religious Change in India, 1880–1916," *Modern Asian Studies* 20, no. 2 (April 1986): 285–319.

9  Leela Gandhi, *Affective Communities: Anticolonial Thought, Fin-de-Siècle Radicalism, and the Politics of Friendship* (Durham, NC: Duke University Press, 2005), 101–2.

10  See critiques of archival knowledge related to South Asian diasporic queer history, most notably Anjali Arondekar, *For the Record: On Sexuality and the Colonial Archive in India* (Durham, NC: Duke University Press, 2009); Nayan Shah, "Sexuality, Identity, and the Uses of History," in *Q&A: Queer in Asian America*, edited by David L. Eng and Alice Y. Hom (Philadelphia: Temple University Press, 1998), 141–56. There is parallel scholarship on the limits of animal history, which largely emphasizes that archives offer represented rather than "real" animals for historical research. See, most notably, Erica Fudge, "'A Left-Handed Blow': Writing the History of Animals," in *Representing Animals*, edited by Nigel Rothfels (Bloomington: University of Indiana Press, 2002), 3–18. However, by dismissing the archive as an inherently anthropocentric site in favor of capturing "real" animals, a refusal of the "represented" animal risks foreclosing analysis of how animals are rhetorically and materially mobilized by the colonial state.

11  The Prevention of Cruelty to Animals Act of 1890, http://pawspakistan.org/wp-content/uploads/2007/04/the-prevention-of-cruelty-to-animals-act-1890-optimised.pdf.

12  See Lata Mani, *Contentious Traditions: The Debate on Sati in Colonial India* (Berkeley: University of California Press, 1998).

13  The Indian Penal Code, 1860, Act No. 45 of 1860, http://ncw.nic.in/acts/THEINDIANPENALCODE1860.pdf.

14  Home/Public/8-1890/No. 255–257, National Archives of India.

15  L/PJ/6/272/f473, India Office Records, British Library.

16  See Nicole Shukin, *Animal Capital: Rendering Life in Biopolitical Times* (Minneapolis: University of Minnesota Press, 2009).

17 Robyn Lee and Roxanne Mykitiuk, "Surviving Difference: Endocrine-Disrupting Chemicals, Intergenerational Justice, and the Future of Reproduction," *Feminist Theory* 19, no. 2 (2018): 205–21; Giovanna di Chiro, "Polluted Politics? Confronting Toxic Discourse, Sex Panic, and Eco-Normativity," in *Queer Ecologies: Sex, Nature, Politics, Desire*, edited by Catriona Mortimer-Sandilands and Bruce Erickson (Bloomington: Indiana University Press, 2010), 199–230.

18 See David Gilmartin, "Cattle, Crime, and Colonialism: Property as Negotiation in North India," *Indian Economic and Social History Review* 40, no. 1 (2003): 33–56.

19 Jean-Loïc Le Quellec, "Provoking Lactation by the Insufflation Technique as Documented by the Rock Images of the Sahara," *Anthropozoologica* 46, no. 1 (2011): 65–125.

20 Deborah Valenze, *Milk: A Local and Global History* (New Haven, CT: Yale University Press, 2011), 26; Hannah Velten, *Milk: A Global History* (London: Reaktion, 2010), 16–18.

21 Edward Evans-Pritchard, *The Nuer: A Description of the Modes of Livelihood and Political Institutions of a Nilotic People* (London: Oxford University Press, 1940), 34.

22 The Prevention of Cruelty to Animals Act of 1890.

23 Pratik Chakrabarti, "Beasts of Burden: Animals and Laboratory Research in Colonial India," *History of Science* 48, no. 2 (2010): 125–52, https://www.ncbi.nlm.nih.gov/pmc/articles/PMC2997667/.

24 Naisargi Dave, "Witness: Humans, Animals, and the Politics of Becoming," *Cultural Anthropology* 29, no. 3 (2014): 434.

25 L/PJ/7/1899, India Office Records, British Library.

26 "The Anti-'Phooka' Agitation," *Modern Review* 61 (May 1937): 599–600. See also "Opposition Leader on Status of House—Privilege Question—Bengal Legislative Council," *Star of India* (Calcutta), September 15, 1937, 5; "Bengal Council—Cruelty to Animals Bill—Referred to Select Committee," *Advance* (Calcutta), September 15, 1937, 3.

27 L/PJ/7/1899, India Office Records, British Library.

28 Tejaswini Niranjana, *Mobilizing India: Women, Music, and Migration between India and Trinidad* (Durham, NC: Duke University Press, 2006), esp. 55–84; Gandhi, *Affective Communities*, 92, 101–2.

29 Katharine Mayo, *The Isles of Fear: The Truth about the Philippines* (New York: Harcourt, Brace, 1925), 296.

30 Katharine Mayo, *Mother India* (New York: Blue Ribbon, 1927), 255, 260, 265–66.

31 M. K. Gandhi, "Man's Inhumanity," *Harijan*, June 19, 1937, in *The Collected Works of Mahatma Gandhi*, vol. 71 (New Delhi: Publications Division, Government of India, 1999), 363.

32 Samera Esemir, *Juridical Humanity: A Colonial History* (Stanford, CA: Stanford University Press, 2012), 136.

33 Christophe Jaffrelot, "Introduction: The Invention of an Ethnic Nationalism," in *Hindu Nationalism: A Reader*, edited by Christophe Jaffrelot (Princeton, NJ: Princeton University Press, 2007), 9–10.

34 Dayananda Saraswati, *The Ocean of Mercy*, translated by Durga Prasad (Lahore: Virajanand, 1889), 27, 21, 33.

35 In eastern Uttar Pradesh, the Chamars were the largest Hindu caste and were vilified by the local Gorakhpur Gaurakshini Sabha. See Pandey, *Rallying Round the Cow*, 55.

36 Christiane Brosius, "'I Am a National Artist': Popular Art in the Sphere of Hindutva," in *Picturing the Nation: Iconographies of Modern India*, edited by Richard Davis (Hyderabad: Orient BlackSwan, 2007), 171–205. See also Christiane Brosius, *Empowering Visions: The Politics of Representation in Hindu Nationalism* (London: Anthem, 2005), 71–74.

37 Partha Chatterjee, "The Nationalist Resolution of the Women's Question," in *Recasting Women: Essays in Indian Colonial History* (New Brunswick, NJ: Rutgers University Press, 1990), 233–53.

38 For example, despite her criticism of cow protectionist violence, Vandana Shiva offers an anticolonial rearticulation of cow veneration that obscures nationalist responsibility for the violence of cow protection, focusing on British divide-and-rule and reifying the Vedic myth of "the holy cow." See Pooja Bhula, "In the Name of the Holy Cow, We Must Now Rise: Activist Vandana Shiva," *DNA India*, November 28, 2016, http://www.dnaindia.com/india/interview-in-the -name-of-the-cow-we-must-now-rise-vandana-shiva-2277653.

39 Sara Salih, "The Animal You See: Why Look at Animals in Gaza?," *Interventions* 16, no. 3 (2014): 301.

## Bibliography

Abraham, Delna, and Ojaswi Rao. "86% Killed in Cow-Related Violence since 2010 Are Muslim, 97% Attacks after Modi Govt Came to Power." *Hindustan Times*, July 16, 2017. https://www.hindustantimes.com/india-news/86-killed-in-cow -related-violence-since-2010-are-muslims-97-attacks-after-modi-govt-came -to-power/story-w9CYOksvgk9joGSSaXgpLO.html.

"The Anti-'Phooka' Agitation." *Modern Review* 61 (May 1937): 599–600.

Arondekar, Anjali. *For the Record: On Sexuality and the Colonial Archive in India*. Durham, NC: Duke University Press, 2009.

"Bengal Council—Cruelty to Animals Bill—Referred to Select Committee." *Advance* (Calcutta), September 15, 1937, 3.

Bhula, Pooja. "In the Name of the Holy Cow, We Must Now Rise: Activist Vandana Shiva." *DNA India*, November 28, 2016. http://www.dnaindia.com /india/interview-in-the-name-of-the-cow-we-must-now-rise-vandana-shiva -2277653.

Brosius, Christiane. *Empowering Visions: The Politics of Representation in Hindu Nationalism*. London: Anthem, 2005.

Brosius, Christiane. "'I Am a National Artist': Popular Art in the Sphere of Hindutva." In *Picturing the Nation: Iconographies of Modern India*, edited by Richard Davis, 171–205. Hyderabad: Orient BlackSwan, 2007.

Chakrabarti, Pratik. "Beasts of Burden: Animals and Laboratory Research in Colonial India." *History of Science* 48, no. 2 (2010): 125–52. https://www.ncbi.nlm.nih.gov/pmc/articles/PMC2997667/.

Chatterjee, Partha. "The Nationalist Resolution of the Women's Question." In *Recasting Women: Essays in Indian Colonial History*, edited by Kumkum Sangari and Sudesh Vaid, 233–53. New Brunswick, NJ: Rutgers University Press, 1990.

"Dalits Assaulted for Skinning Cow." *Indian Express*, July 19, 2016. http://indianexpress.com/article/india/india-news-india/una-dalit-thrashed-cow-skinning-beef-ban-gujarat-cm-anandiben-patel-order-probe-2922451/.

Dave, Naisargi. "Witness: Humans, Animals, and the Politics of Becoming." *Cultural Anthropology* 29, no. 3 (2014): 433–56.

di Chiro, Giovanna. "Polluted Politics? Confronting Toxic Discourse, Sex Panic, and Eco-Normativity." In *Queer Ecologies: Sex, Nature, Politics, Desire*, edited by Catriona Mortimer-Sandilands and Bruce Erickson, 199–230. Bloomington: Indiana University Press, 2010.

Doniger, Wendy. *The Hindus: An Alternative History*. New York: Penguin, 2009.

Esemir, Samera. *Juridical Humanity: A Colonial History*. Stanford, CA: Stanford University Press, 2012.

Evans-Pritchard, Edward. *The Nuer: A Description of the Modes of Livelihood and Political Institutions of a Nilotic People*. Oxford: Oxford University Press, 1940.

Freitag, Sandria. *Collective Action and Community: Public Arenas and the Emergence of Communalism in North India*. Berkeley: University of California Press, 1989.

Fudge, Erica. "'A Left-Handed Blow': Writing the History of Animals." In *Representing Animals*, edited by Nigel Rothfels, 3–18. Bloomington: University of Indiana Press, 2002.

Gandhi, Leela. *Affective Communities: Anticolonial Thought, Fin-de-Siècle Radicalism, and the Politics of Friendship*. Durham, NC: Duke University Press, 2005.

Gandhi, M. K. "Man's Inhumanity." *Harijan*, June 19, 1937. In *The Collected Works of Mahatma Gandhi*, vol. 71. New Delhi: Publications Division, Government of India, 1999.

Gilmartin, David. "Cattle, Crime, and Colonialism: Property as Negotiation in North India." *Indian Economic and Social History Review* 40, no. 1 (2003): 33–56.

Gupta, Charu. "The Icon of Mother in Late Colonial North India: 'Bharat Mata,' 'Matri Bhasha,' and 'Gau Mata.'" *Economic and Political Weekly*, November 10, 2001, 4291–99.

Ilaiah, Kancha. *Buffalo Nationalism: A Critique of Spiritual Fascism*. Kolkata: Samya, 2004.

Indian Penal Code, 1860, Act No. 45 of 1860. http://ncw.nic.in/acts/THEINDIAN PENALCODE1860.pdf.

Jaffrelot, Christophe. *The Hindu Nationalist Movement in India*. New York: Columbia University Press, 1998.

Jaffrelot, Christophe. "Introduction: The Invention of an Ethnic Nationalism." In *Hindu Nationalism: A Reader*, edited by Christophe Jaffrelot. Princeton, NJ: Princeton University Press, 2007.

Jha, D. N. *The Myth of the Holy Cow*. London: Verso, 2004.

Krishnaswamy, S. "A Riot in Bombay, August 11, 1893: A Study in Hindu-Muslim Relations in Western India during the Late 19th Century." PhD dissertation, University of Chicago, 1966.

Lee, Robyn, and Roxanne Mykitiuk. "Surviving Difference: Endocrine-Disrupting Chemicals, Intergenerational Justice, and the Future of Reproduction." *Feminist Theory* 19, no. 2 (2018): 205–21.

Le Quellec, Jean-Loïc. "Provoking Lactation by the Insufflation Technique as Documented by the Rock Images of the Sahara." *Anthropozoologica* 46, no. 1 (2011): 65–125.

Mani, Lata. *Contentious Traditions: The Debate on Sati in Colonial India*. Berkeley: University of California Press, 1998.

Mayo, Katharine. *The Isles of Fear: The Truth about the Philippines*. New York: Harcourt, Brace, 1925.

Mayo, Katharine. *Mother India*. New York: Blue Ribbon, 1927.

McLane, John R. *Indian Nationalism and the Early Congress*. Princeton, NJ: Princeton University Press, 2015. (Originally published 1977.)

Miller, Michael. "A Mob in India Just Dragged a Man from His Home and Beat Him to Death—For Eating Beef." *Washington Post*, September 30, 2015. https://www.washingtonpost.com/news/morning-mix/wp/2015/09/30/a-mob-in-india-just-dragged-a-man-from-his-home-and-beat-him-to-death-for-eating-beef/.

Niranjana, Tejaswini. *Mobilizing India: Women, Music, and Migration between India and Trinidad*. Durham, NC: Duke University Press, 2006.

"Opposition Leader on Status of House—Privilege Question—Bengal Legislative Council." *Star of India* (Calcutta), September 15, 1937, 5.

Pandey, Gyan. *Rallying Round the Cow: Sectarian Strife in the Bhojpur Region, 1888–1917*. Occasional Paper no. 39. Calcutta: Centre for Studies in Social Sciences, 1981.

Pinney, Christopher. *Photos of the Gods: The Printed Image and Political Struggle in India*. Chicago: University of Chicago Press, 2004.

Prevention of Cruelty to Animals Act of 1890. http://pawspakistan.org/wp-content/uploads/2007/04/the-prevention-of-cruelty-to-animals-act-1890-optimised.pdf.

239

Robb, Peter. "The Challenge of Gau Mata: British Policy and Religious Change in India, 1880–1916." *Modern Asian Studies* 20, no. 2 (April 1986): 285–319.

Salih, Sara. "The Animal You See: Why Look at Animals in Gaza?" *Interventions* 16, no. 3 (2014): 299–324.

Saraswati, Dayananda. *The Ocean of Mercy*. Translated by Durga Prasad. Lahore: Virajanand, 1889.

Shah, Nayan. "Sexuality, Identity, and the Uses of History." In Q&A: *Queer in Asian America*, edited by David L. Eng and Alice Y. Hom, 141–56. Philadelphia: Temple University Press, 1998.

Shukin, Nicole. *Animal Capital: Rendering Life in Biopolitical Times*. Minneapolis: University of Minnesota Press, 2009.

Sridharan, Vasudevan. "India Hindu Beef Lynching: Muslim Victim Ate Goat Meat Not Beef Reveals Forensic Report." *International Business Times*, October 9, 2015. http://www.ibtimes.co.uk/india-hindu-beef-lynching-muslim-victim-ate -goat-meat-not-beef-forensic-report-reveals-1523254.

Valenze, Deborah. *Milk: A Local and Global History*. New Haven, CT: Yale University Press, 2011.

Velten, Hannah. *Milk: A Global History*. London: Reaktion, 2010.

Yang, Anand. "Sacred Symbol and Sacred Space in Rural India: Community Mobilization in the 'Anti-Cow Killing Riot' of 1893." *Comparative Studies in Society and History* 2, no. 4 (1980): 579–96.

ten | ANGELA WILLEY

# Fake Meat

A QUEER COMMENTARY

IT'S A QUEER FEELING, sitting down to write about meat. Meat has been an important object in the development of my political thinking over the years, but I've never written anything about it. I've also never experimented with autobiography in my writing, but every time I sit down to write about meat, stories come, memories, intimate flashes of insight about meat—meat as flesh, meat as sustenance, meat as metaphor. Anything I might say about meat seems simplistic, flat, misleading. Meat is sometimes tough (factory farming, global economies of food distribution, the deskilling of butchering), sometimes tender (a food ritual marking peace in an otherwise chaotic family life, a way of life that tempers precarity, a context for human/nonhuman animal intimacies). It's an anemic craving that subsumes all other desires and at the same time is impossible to chew. Meat is without doubt a powerful naturecultural node of meaning making and (re)materializations of our human/human, human/nonhuman, posthuman/entangled worlds.

This essay is a meditation on "fake meat": a popular casual moniker for meat analogues; facsimiles of popularly consumed meat products, for those looking to minimize or cease consumption of animal-derived meats for any reason. Meat substitutes have long histories in Seventh-Day Adventist and Buddhist traditions (and their restaurants). They are essential to and (in my humble opinion) perfected in vegan soul food (look it up). In the twenty-first century United States, fake meat is growing in popularity, with its variety and accessibility expanding considerably over the last decade. Veggie burgers are on menus and in freezers of general stores in some of the smallest of US towns, sometimes even in the famously carnivorous Midwest. Fake meat ranges from the simplest bean-patty substitute to the most innovative of food inventions. It exemplifies simultaneously the wondrous possibilities, violent complicities, and sometimes devastating disappointments of technology. If I err on the side of under-theorizing the industry's peddling of "health," its waste-making culpability, or its place within the global economy of processed foods more generally, it is because my aim here is to suggest that fake meat is good to think with. I'd like to reclaim it for these purposes from righteous dismissal by the faithfully carnivorous, sure, but also by the new wave of vegan foodies and strict advocates of whole foods diets, whether or not wholly plant-based. All turn up their noses at its inauthenticity—not real meat, not real food. If you're a vegetarian, the logic goes, why would you not just eat (healthier and arguably better-tasting) vegetables? In experimenting with answering that question over the years, it has become clear to me that fake meat is political. This commentary is a meditation on that question: Why fake meat?

As a dyke, the question always has a little ring of familiarity. If you're attracted to (queer) masculinity, why wouldn't you just date a real man?[1] I think fake meat through a queer feminist and critical trans lens—one attentive to the work the supposed inauthenticity of fake sex/fake meat/fake masculinity and femininity does to naturalize the supposedly authentic original. This lens is trained at the same time on what the othered version's difference/distance from that naturalized form can teach us about the epistemic and other systems that render it ahistorical and obvious. In addition to these Butlerian concerns over making strange what passes as prediscursive (or natural), as a science studies scholar, I'm intrigued by the contingency of any edible's food status and about the conditions of possibility for the health and other purity discourses that shape food as an onto-epistemological category. And from the perspective of food ethics, I'm curious about what it means to eat something, be sustained by something, that someone else derogates as "not food." In many contexts, this something is of course "real" (animal-derived) meat, or, in others, specific kinds of meat. Among foodies, it's often anything considered "processed." And in light of these questions, what does it mean to navigate the politics and ethics of intimate choices about consumption and ingestion where all available options are overdetermined by market-making and the differential valuation of lives?

Non-animal-derived meat is fodder for the queering of the very category—for meat's undoing as a stable and self-evident object. The undoing of meat means the possibility of dislodging some of the more sedimented logics of debates about vegetarianism. Specifically, it unsettles the idea that material-affective investments in meat-eating and more esoteric commitments to naming and resisting logics of killability[2] (for human workers and nonhuman food-to-be) are in fundamental tension and mark different sorts of callousness and denial about the nature of life on this planet.

I use autobiographical storytelling and humor (as both archive and method) to guide this meditation on fake meat. I explore themes of eating (fake) meat, queer and feminist meat politics, and questions of authenticity vis-à-vis material practices of worlding. In the way that EAT FAT challenged dominant cultural narratives about fat and attendant feelings, I have the modest hope that this commentary will engage the reader viscerally to think with the appeal of meat made from nonanimal sources.[3] Not that they may see the proverbial light and give up the also real pleasures of animal flesh or purist politics, but that they may more deeply appreciate an ethos of making real a queer practice of bringing into being "hope for livable worlds."[4] This ethos, I think, opens more space for thinking pleasure alongside (not opposed to) resistance to the politics of killability.

## Prelude: Newly Vegan

I was standing in line at the register at a small vegan café after lunch. The New England town was small, so I was delighted to find the place. Near the register there were some items for sale: a bag of herbed popcorn coated in nutritional yeast, a couple of jams to choose from, cookies—classic treats without the cheddar or animal pectin or butter. My heart soared as my eyes lit on a narrow yellow tube labeled "McDonald's Sausage Biscuit" right next to the register. I snatched it up to show my dining companion—"Wow!" I gushed to the cashier. "This is amazing! I miss sausage biscuits so much! Do you have more of these things?" Her horror-struck face turned green as she whispered "that's not food. It's a display to show you how much animal fat is in fast food."

I grew up eating those foods. I grew up working class in the US South and Midwest. Veganism for me was a strictly political decision having to do with the cruelties of a factory farming economy, for both workers and animals, and with the then-still-popular *Diet for a Small Planet* insight that feed for food animals was part of the distribution problem that led to hunger and starvation worldwide. It was one of the problems for which racist overpopulation discourse often functioned as a proxy. The moral economy of waistlines and heart health was (obviously, given my faux pas) not much on my mind. My repertoire of vegetable dishes was limited to side items in those early years of meatless eating. And my most persistent culinary longings, well over a decade after the sausage fat incident, and two decades since I committed to vegetarianism, are still of the artery-clogging variety: Carolina dogs, piled high with beef chili and wet slaw; corned beef hash under runny fried eggs; chewy baked ham cold the next day; fried chicken; fried bologna; and, of course, sausage biscuits, biscuits with sausage gravy, or any other iteration of that satisfying combo. Food is of course cultural. The gap between affective investment in meat-centric foodways and resistance to logics of killability is bridged for many by the performative potential of meat substitutes.

Fake meat exists now in dazzling variety, from an array of burger-shaped veggie/fungus/wheat/legume/nut mush to the most impressive replicas of American processed meat classics like fish sticks, chicken nuggets and patties, and hot dogs, to the recent explosion of lab-rendered realistic meats. Increasingly popular as well are those vegetables whose textures lend themselves to less-processed veg-based meat products, like jackfruit, which makes a beautiful BBQ.[5] Fake meat—in all its mostly high-sodium, low-nutrient glory—has, to me, represented a strange, sometimes fragile, but vital potential for the commensurability of seemingly irreconcilable worlds and worldviews.

In my early days of plant-based eating, I was ever tickled to find a new vegan treat (nacho cheese, gravy, marshmallows), something food science created especially to help sate a taste for the bloodlust of American cuisine. Back then, none of my comfort foods or favorite meals were vegetable-centric. Canned French-style green beans and carrot sticks were my favorite vegetables. I would say yes to blanched mushrooms and green pepper bits on my pizza, and that marked me as a vegetable lover in my family. Fake meat felt familiar to me, not only because I grew up eating a lot of meat, but also because processed meats of the veg and non-veg variety are often similar in color, texture, and taste. The controversy over whether or not fake meat tastes "real" or "good" is classed. So, too, the debate over its healthfulness depends on what you'd be eating instead.

Fake meat, I think, can operate as a site for thinking about the post-moral ethics of consumption. It can represent a dreaming into being borne

244

of refusing unfair choices. It is rightly critiqued as a high-waste techno-fix for a problem with an easy opt-out alternative: just eat vegetables. And yet, like most such techno-fixes, its meanings exceed the bounds of anti-tech critique. And I hope it goes without saying that plant foods are also the fruits (and vegetables as it were) of relations of violence and exploitation that affect our human and nonhuman kin. As such, fake meat is rich fodder for thinking about how we parse the potentialities of technology from the exploitative consumer capitalist forms its developments usually take. It has proven difficult to think about the global political economy of food and its unequal distribution of harms and benefits without allowing our analyses to be reduced to the petty distraction of moralist consumer politics.

## The Deconstructed UnFish Taco

By deconstructed I mean in bits, laid out before us, rather than rolled up into a mystery package—a fancy, potentially pretty way of serving up a mess. And I use "unfish taco" as a metaphor for "vegan" on the menu of foodways from which we can order. I've had my share of run-ins with the vegan police (I've done my time patrolling too, I confess!). The rules are finite and more or less clear: no animal-derived or tested-on products, not to eat, wear, clean with, and so on. While I was new to vegan politics at the turn of the twenty-first century, I was quite familiar with some of the contexts for human/nonhuman animal contact the educational materials conjured. Sometimes that intimate knowledge fueled my passion for the movement. Other times I felt the rub between abstract values and material practices in ways that left me deeply frustrated.

At fourteen I moved to rural Maine, to a town of around seven hundred year-round residents, and got very close with my dad's younger brother (one of ten siblings), who raised rabbits, chickens, turkeys, pigs, dogs, and parakeets. Sometimes there was a cat or two hanging around. And sometimes ducks. He hunted and fished. The house was filled with other animals, too—taxidermied—a black bear, a fox, several deer heads, a big trout from an auction. Once a year he held a men's dinner with a ten-meat chili including various hunted and scavenged creatures. I was not unfamiliar with checking animals by the side of the road for warmth (freshness), with prepping birds for killing (not the parakeets), and with the handling and cooking of a range of meats. My uncle used a power wheelchair and operated trigger, knife, spatula, and so on in the same way: with his powerful jaw and toothy grip. As his niece I sometimes objected, argued, but I worked by his side for pay off and on for eight years, and my hands helped with his work.

That work included feeding, grooming, protecting, finding, nursing, corralling, comforting, and learning other species. My uncle spent much of his time alone among these animals. His door was always open and turkeys and dogs wandered freely in and out, off into the woods and back again for meals and company. I remember the heat of the woodstove one night, lying on his couch with my boots still on, a teenage turkey perched on my teenage tummy, three crammed on his chair, on him, the sound of twenty or so parakeets in cages by the window, and the earthy smell of black labs drying by the stove, mixed with our own B.O. and the other half of yesterday's pizza warming in the oven. It seems beyond trite to say that he loved them and taught me to and that death didn't seem antithetical to that love. The intimacy of the "becoming in kind" that marked this farm work made me sensitive to suffering. It also made casual denial about where food comes from forever impossible. Every meat meal represents the culmination of some life. I think about those lives and those deaths.

When I decided to go vegan, I visited a nearby farm with sheep when I was home working in the summer and bought some homespun, home-dyed wool. I brought it to my mom and asked her to crochet me a new winter scarf, an ethical scarf. It was beautiful—long, brightly colored. It was an early act of initiative in my new vegan life. I wore it like a badge of honor. Once. My defense: Sheep are not killed for wool and small farms hand-shear sheep like I shave my dog every June before the heat comes. Small family farms help poor humans survive in rural areas and provide safety and often loving care to animals. No, not vegan. There is no ethical exploitation. This is the fantasy of noncomplicity that makes veganism per se hard to swallow. "Veganism," as it turns out, isn't precisely the practice of the theory that nonhuman animal suffering is an ethical problem for humans. Unfish tacos weren't exactly what I wanted, but they were the best thing on the menu.

## Queer Vegan/Feminist Food Politics

I met vegetarians and learned about compulsory heterosexuality at the same time. My queer and vegetarian becomings were intimately intertwined. *Female Masculinity* changed my life in exactly the same way fake meat did.[6] They both represented the heady possibility of making more desirable worlds out of the systems we were dealt. They both opened space to think about ethics and pleasure.

A synopsis: I had family in prison growing up and in college (in NYC) learned about prison abolition. I began to go to protests at One Police Plaza and in Albany, and I started attending meetings where I was introduced to hummus. Coterminously, I read Adrienne Rich's "Compulsory Heterosexuality and Lesbian Existence" and promptly rethought my ongoing engagement to my high school boyfriend (NYC, 1998). I was arrested at the RNC and spent eleven nights in jail. Protesters filled the women's county jail for a week. I was one of the few who ate the food. When I got out, I visited a vegetarian restaurant with about two dozen other protesters and had fake meat for the first time (Philadelphia, August 2000). Among these activists were some of the first radical queers I befriended. They had fake families and ate fake meat. It all made sense. I was romanced by visions of a world without prisons, rapey relatives (and other intimate violences endemic to family life), meat processing massacres (and other capitalist workplace atrocities), and beakless chicken slaughter. I endeavored to build a life less invested in systems that perpetuate suffering. I gave up meat and monogamy (White Plains, December 2000). I began an intense friendship with a brilliant scholar and activist who was a political nonvegetarian. We sat across from one another in restaurants, longing to switch plates. Hungry for the bones and cartilage she couldn't quite bring herself to touch, I learned that context is everything. Political veg, political non-veg. Caste politics, communal violence, the deskilling of butchering, the destruction of subsistence agriculture, factory farms, what gets subsidized where and why and how. We were reading together, drinking and smoking, and eating a lot of egg curry when I stopped identifying as vegetarian outside the US (London, 2001–2; Delhi, 2003). I moved to another new city on my own again and was the only human in my own apartment for the first time. Sam (my longtime canine companion) and I swore off animal by-products[7] once and for all, and I officially called it quits with my on-again-off-again long-distance fella. In retrospect, I guess this was the moment I became a vegan dyke—which means more or less that I acquired a new toothpaste and haircut (Atlanta, 2004).

A staple of lesbian comedy, jokes about vegetarianism garner big laughs because of its intimate familiarity as a site of relationship, identity, and community-making and unmaking for queer feminists (and those who date and organize with us). Back in the late 1990s, Latina lesbian comedian (now performance artist) Marga Gomez riffed on the pre-presidential Trump as spokesman for a mail-order steak company, impersonating his spiel with emphasis on the declaration "Believe me, I understand steak." The humor here lies in part on how perfectly the prepared steaks ad captures the

247

arrogance and willful ignorance that connect the production and conspicuous consumption of meat to Trump's American nationalist brand—of course he's the face of factory-farmed bulk-buy steaks. Once she finishes her impersonation, she turns back to the premise for a quick one-liner: "If Trump understood steak, he'd be a vegetarian." Her humor relies on the ubiquity of PETA-esque knowledge and identification among her San Francisco audience members, as well as self-awareness about that stereotype. In the opening to her show *Hung Like a Fly*, Gomez says that she's used to performing at lesbian fundraisers where she would follow forty-five to fifty minutes of announcements.[8] Her loving parody of said announcements is called "The Serious People's Collective," a fictive grassroots collective that, in the storyline, organizes both the comedy night and the boycott of it. Therein, she of course references food: "as you know, all of our baked goods contain no wheat, no dairy, no sugar, no tuna, no taste, and no ingredients." That "we" might sponsor and boycott the same event—or hold a bake sale peddling treats with comically little of what goes into baked goods—marks a tension between critical and creative practices as constitutive of "lesbian community." It is this tension I want to bring from (through) comedy into our theorizing. It's a self-reflexive (fumorist[9]) poking fun that allows us to hold complicity with violence without either (a) moralizing or (b) letting ourselves off the hook.

Rich debate around Carol Adams's[10] highly influential and rigorously critiqued take on feminist meat politics and Donna Haraway's[11] generative and controversial positioning of the logics of killability against the moralism of veganism shape the contours of feminist food politics. We continue to grapple with the implications of their core ethical insights: that similar logics undergird the exploitation of some humans (here women) and nonhuman animals (Adams), and that we all occupy positions of noninnocence vis-à-vis the suffering of human and nonhuman others (Haraway). Some important work has traced the political economic and embodied complexities of the sourcing of animal-derived foodstuffs.[12] Others have theorized the vegan as a killjoy figure.[13] While many have critiqued the analogies of exploitation (eatability as objectification, factory farming as slavery or genocide) that constitute the liberal humanist intelligibility of the amalgam "feminist vegetarianism" or "queer vegan," others have opened new questions about political kinship between those dehumanized by racism and nonhuman animals as an alternative to distancing from animals and animal statuses.[14] Some provocative texts have explored more deeply ways in which food and sex ethics are enmeshed.[15]

248

In "Thinking Sex," Gayle Rubin[16] famously lamented feminist and popular moralism around sex and wished we could treat our varied tastes and proclivities with as casual an approach as we do our food preferences and habits. Her call to rethink the grounds of sexual ethics played its part in inaugurating a quarter century of theorizing about how to reconcile "pleasure" and "danger." If the metaphor of "taste" opened space for post–sex wars queer feminist sexual ethics, that work in turn has some valuable insights to offer our too often either moralistic or laissez-faire approaches to meat-eating: for example, pleasure and harm matter simultaneously; desire is both historically and culturally specific and deeply embodied in meaningful affective and libidinal attachments; identitarian categories are good to think with, but bad proxies for analysis.

## "Is This One Made from Beans or Pigs?"

The title of this section is a question asked me by a seven-year-old helping to prepare bologna sandwiches. Its wisdom comes from being exposed to different kinds of meat. Its logic displaces the naturalization of animal-derived meat. I don't put "faux bologna" on my shopping list, but rather "bologna." It is bologna to me. When I make pot roast, that's how I think of it. I don't call it a one-pot seitan dinner. As Lenny Breedlove sang in the musical culmination of his *One Freak Show*[17] performance, "her gaze / makes pecs / out of cupcakes." He uses "cupcakes" to refer to breasts and he's talking about practices of intimate resignification he has engaged in as a trans man. Not a real man, according to some, or a real feminist, in the estimation of others, but "loved into realness," he says, "like the Velveteen Rabbit." Throughout this piece, he describes the power of common queer practices of resignification that exist alongside practices of bodily transformation from the lowest of low-tech to the surgical. If we can come to see the supposed imposter object—the "fake"—as the real deal (as real as the idealized/naturalized "original"), and experience it as such, queer and vegan practices of resignification have undertheorized and underappreciated material consequences.

Queer feminist debates and insights about the ethics of sex (both gendered enfleshment and doing it) can offer some nuance and levity to readings of the politics of meat. Meat-eating, like gender and sexuality, is highly performative. By playing on/with this performativity, I hope to open a bit of space for more and different thinking-together about vegan politics (capaciously construed) as something more than abstinence. Narrative matters.

249

Against a politics of purity, and beyond liberal discourses of "choice" and preference, we must have space for considerations of desire/hunger/craving, pleasure, production/sustainability/political economy, distribution of harms and benefits, and so on, while resisting the use of these discourses as evidence or as moral fodder.

Vegan politics and queer feminism are indeed enmeshed in cultural stereotypes, and I believe those associations can help us think critically about the tendency to romanticize lower-tech solutions and vilify higher-tech ones, to privilege a vegan politics of opting out over a messier politics of resignification, invention, and play. There are lots of jokes about lesbians and tofu. Lesbians don't like meat. Lesbians don't like dick. Lesbians are either too bitterly repressed or too highly evolved to enjoy the fleshy pleasures of steak or fucking. Lesbians/vegetarians appreciate the simple pleasures of salad greens and sharing a cup of herbal tea. Or maybe that's too extreme—a nice nutloaf and the touch of soft hands? A woodland-creature-shaped dildo and a Thanks-taking Tofurkey™? A more "realistic" cut of meat . . . wheat gluten, cyberskin. Beet blood, lube ejaculate. Or what can we do with synthetic biology?

This little thought experiment does the work of making visible, first, the performativity of foodways in general and vegetarianism in particular, and, second, the fragile logic that undergirds hierarchical or typological distinctions between similar kinds of practices and technologies. When it comes to technologies of "meat," tissue cultured flesh provokes two readings in tension: (1) hurray for another queer/vegan experiment in the remaking of our material/discursive realities, or (2) beware of a line crossed that could mean the unmaking of those very categories (and cultures of resistance). I would like to encourage us to take the attitude of the former (despite the uncomfortable bedfellows), highlighting the continuity in low- and high-tech logics. As Talia Bettcher says of gender transitioning, the variables separating surgical and nonsurgical transition choices are highly idiosyncratic and so not a worthwhile analytic distinction.[18] Following this logic, let us consider how we might reorient ourselves away from knee-jerk technophobic disbelief—about, for example, the specter of a headless cow (I know, Tofurkey was already enough to alarm many)—and instead toward critical consideration of more specific questions of political economy, like, where does this knowledge come from, who stands to benefit, really, and at whose expense?[19]

Thinking with fake meat has the potential to nurture a queer feminist ethic of curiosity about the science/art of making worlds in ways that

(1) resist easy recourse to a romanticized before, (2) draw attention to the conditions of intelligibility for our complex relations with techno-fixes, and in so doing (3) challenge us to contemplate our storytelling practices. Fake meat marks the possibility of meat without killing and plant-based eating that privileges discourses of pleasure over discourses of health. In so doing, fake meat can disrupt entrenched narratives of veganism versus carnivory, thus complicating a monolithic (moralistic) veganism. Our stories should reflect the diversity of approaches to bearing witness to and disrupting logics of killability at the table. They should proliferate possibility. Let us share more about the various foodways we are inspired by, committed to, and have invested in as sites for the materialization of relations and circumstances that foster livability for human and nonhuman kin. In so doing, we might yet queer "veganism" by cultivating a far richer lexicon for practices of undermining logics of killability.

## Postscript

At the moment of getting this off to press (two-plus years after writing it), Burger King is releasing the Impossible Whopper™ nationwide and Beyond Meat's™ burgers, sausages, and chicken are being piloted regionally at McDonald's, Dunkin' Donuts and Kentucky Fried Chicken. Silicon Valley answered our hunger for the taste of blood. In that time Amazon acquired Whole Foods, and the one nearest me opened a vegan deli counter. It might be right to extend the metaphor of sexual ethics to questions of vegan-washing (pink-washing) and vegan-nationalism (homonationalism). Maybe a purist vegan politics, where less meat = more justice and context matters little, was always headed toward Amazon and fast food spearheading the revolution. Maybe we are always a bit compromised by desire. I remain deeply perturbed by technophobic moralism and its manifestation in classist condemnation of the consumption of processed foods, yet reading about the projected $85 billion worth of the "plant-based meat industry" over the next decade—so sanitized from association with the necropolitics of factory farming or corporate greed—I have a desperate longing for lentil-walnut loaf.

## Notes

1  A startling variety of similar questions are asked of trans and gender nonconforming folks.

2   See this "Lab Meeting" for a range of reflections on Haraway's generative and enduring concept: Astrid Schrader et al., "Considering Killability: Experiments in Unsettling Life and Death," *Catalyst: Feminism, Theory, Technoscience* 3, no. 2 (2017).

3   Richard Klein, *Eat Fat* (New York: Pantheon, 1996).

4   Donna Haraway, *When Species Meet* (Minneapolis: University of Minnesota Press, 2008).

5   See, for example, these jackfruit recipes: https://www.peta.org/living/food /jackfruit-recipes-that-will-blow-your-mind-and-taste-buds/, and a newer fake meat brand built up largely around jackfruit: http://www.uptonsnaturals.com.

6   Judith Halberstam, *Female Masculinity* (Durham, NC: Duke University Press, 1998).

7   The science, sourcing, and ethics of which, if any, meats a dog should eat has long been hotly debated. From the popular rise of raw meat diets to an explosion of commercial vegan options, pet feeding is deeply politicized in often highly polarizing ways.

8   Marga Gomez, *Hung Like a Fly*, Uproar Entertainment, 1997.

9   Cynthia Willett, Julie Willett, and Yael D. Sherman, "Politics and Comedy," *Social Research* 79, no. 1 (2012): 217–46.

10  Carol J. Adams, "The Sexual Politics of Meat: A Feminist-Vegetarian Critical Theory" (New York: Bloomsbury, 2015).

11  Haraway, *When Species Meet.*

12  See, for example, Greta Gaard, "Toward a Feminist Postcolonial Milk Studies," *American Quarterly* 65, no. 3 (2013): 595–618.

13  See treatments of the vegan as a killjoy figure: Richard Twine, "Vegan Killjoys at the Table: Contesting Happiness and Negotiating Relationships with Food Practices," *Societies* 4, no. 4 (2014): 623–39: Rasmus R. Simonsen, "A Queer Vegan Manifesto," *Journal for Critical Animal Studies* 10, no. 3 (2012): 51–81.

14  See Holland's reframing of debates about the place of race and racism in theorizing the non/posthuman. Sharon P. Holland, "Hum/Animal: All Together," *PMLA* 131, no. 1 (2016): 167–69.

15  See, for example, Elspeth Probyn, *Carnal Appetites: FoodSexIdentities* (London: Routledge, 2000); Parama Roy, *Alimentary Tracts: Appetites, Aversions, and the Postcolonial* (Durham, NC: Duke University Press, 2010).

16  Gayle Rubin, "Thinking Sex: Notes for a Radical Theory of the Politics of Sexuality," in *Social Perspectives in Lesbian and Gay Studies: A Reader*, edited by Peter M. Nardi and Beth E. Schneider (London: Routledge, 1998), 100–133.

17  Lynnee Breedlove, *One Freak Show*, live performance recorded at Rude Mechs Theater, Austin, TX, February 17, 2007.

18  Talia Mae Bettcher, "The Phenomenology of Illusion: On Gender Transitions and Existential Identity," presented at the University of Massachusetts Amherst, March 1, 2017.

19  See Jennifer Terry's newest book for a model for researching technology's entanglements: Jennifer Terry, *Attachments to War: Biomedical Logics and Violence in Twenty-First-Century America* (Durham, NC: Duke University Press, 2017).

## Bibliography

Adams, Carol J. *The Sexual Politics of Meat: A Feminist-Vegetarian Critical Theory.* New York: Bloomsbury, 2015.

Bettcher, Talia Mae. "The Phenomenology of Illusion: On Gender Transitions and Existential Identity." Presented at the University of Massachusetts Amherst, March 1, 2017.

Breedlove, Lynnee. *One Freak Show.* Live performance recorded at Rude Mechs Theater, Austin, TX, February 17, 2007.

Gaard, Greta. "Toward a Feminist Postcolonial Milk Studies." *American Quarterly* 65, no. 3 (2013): 595–618.

Gomez, Marga. *Hung Like a Fly.* Uproar Entertainment, 1997.

Halberstam, Judith. *Female Masculinity.* Durham, NC: Duke University Press, 1998.

Haraway, Donna. *When Species Meet.* Minneapolis: University of Minnesota Press, 2008.

Holland, Sharon P. "Hum/Animal: All Together." PMLA 131, no. 1 (2016): 167–69.

Klein, Richard. *Eat Fat.* New York: Pantheon, 1996.

Probyn, Elspeth. *Carnal Appetites: FoodSexIdentities.* London: Routledge, 2000.

Roy, Parama. *Alimentary Tracts: Appetites, Aversions, and the Postcolonial.* Durham, NC: Duke University Press, 2010.

Rubin, Gayle. "Thinking Sex: Notes for a Radical Theory of the Politics of Sexuality." In *Social Perspectives in Lesbian and Gay Studies: A Reader,* edited by Peter M. Nardi and Beth E. Schneider, 100–133. London: Routledge, 1998.

Schrader, Astrid, Elizabeth R. Johnson, Henry Buller, Deborah Robinson, Simon Rundle, Dorion Sagan, Susanne Schmitt, and John Spicer. "Considering Killability: Experiments in Unsettling Life and Death." *Catalyst: Feminism, Theory, Technoscience* 3, no. 2 (2017).

Simonsen, Rasmus R. "A Queer Vegan Manifesto." *Journal for Critical Animal Studies* 10, no. 3 (2012): 51–81.

Terry, Jennifer. *Attachments to War: Biomedical Logics and Violence in Twenty-First-Century America.* Durham, NC: Duke University Press, 2017.

Twine, Richard. "Vegan Killjoys at the Table: Contesting Happiness and Negotiating Relationships with Food Practices." *Societies* 4, no. 4 (2014): 623–39.

Willett, Cynthia, Julie Willett, and Yael D. Sherman. "Politics and Comedy." *Social Research* 79, no. 1 (2012): 217–46.

# The Ethical Impurative

## ELEMENTAL FRONTIERS OF TECHNOLOGIZED MEAT

Only fools argue whether to eat meat or not. They don't understand truth nor do they meditate on it. Who can define what is meat and what is plant? Who knows where the sin lies, being a vegetarian or a nonvegetarian?
—Guru Nanak

MEAT HAS HAD AN EERIE RESONANCE IN MY LIFE. I was born into a vegetarian family in which some of my relatives were "strictly" and virulently vegetarian; I turned omnivore as an act of rebellion, an ethical imperative against what I saw as a potent politics of purity. Some of my relatives were so virulently vegetarian that my family came up with a term, "molecular vegetarianism"! Molecular vegetarians are "pure" vegetarians, and their vegetarianism was elemental—their food could never have been in proximity to (and for some to even the memory of) meat at any stage, including pans that might have once held meat in them. In the last three decades, despite the liberalization and globalization of India's economy, such purity politics has grown, not diminished in contemporary India. Today, as campaigns against beef-eating and beef bans proliferate across India, confronting the politics of purity seems ever more urgent.

When I moved to the United States, I was introduced to a different form of vegetarian politics, one where the same radical and rebellious tendencies of childhood had had the opposite effect, turning some of my omnivorous friends into vegetarians. Looking across the United States and India, most vegetarian politics that I have encountered have been animated by an ethical imperative against carnivory—be it about animal cruelty, human exceptionalism, the inhumanity of industrialized agriculture, ecological unsustainability, greenhouse gases, overpopulation, or the survival of the planet. In this essay, I want to examine "meat" as a central node for a politics of purity. I argue that binaries and rigid boundaries around categories—religious identity, caste affiliations, and biological categories on the one hand, and the boundaries around species such as vegetable, animal, cow, buffalo, pork, chicken—have together led to a passionate politics of purity, categories that are in fact far more porous than such a politics claims. I do this through examining two sites—the politics of beef-eating in India and ethical issues raised by the emerging technologies of meat production. The politics on both sites are biologically elemental. In the first case site, in India and about religion, we confront the rabid politics of a political Hinduism that protects the sanctity of the cow by advocating violence against people who are beef-eaters, even while they render the closely related buffalo and other mammals as "killable." The second case site is in the realm of science and of industrialized agriculture in the United States; we confront the vegetal frontiers of meat as scientific engineering of animals renders them less sentient, less animal, and more like vegetables. I explore the categorical elisions and the ethical conundrums that surround meat as an object of purity discourses. In short, in using these two cases, one highlighting religion and the other of science, I argue the categorical confusions around the categories vegetable and animal, and distinctions between different kinds of animals, reveal the difficulties of approaching "meat" through a politics of purity. In particular, in the first case, religious allegiances have been policed through meat politics, and in the second, ethical problems around industrialized agriculture have largely been approached by technological fixes.

In biological terrains of life, the categories of animals and plants dominate as the two major categories of living organisms, presenting us with binary categories of the animal and the vegetable. At the heart of the binaries of animal and vegetable lie other binaries—animals characterized as alive, active, mobile, and sentient, while vegetable is assumed to be passive, sessile, and insentient. In response to critiques, technologies of industrialized agriculture have worked to vegetize animals through technologies of desensitizing and desentience. Meanwhile, other environmental activists and plant biologists have worked to reanimate plants as sites of agency, pain, and sentience. In the case of a political Hinduism, the cow is exalted as a unique mammal to the exclusion of other closely related animals. In this essay, I argue that the framings of "ethics" and "rights" have underestimated the limits and plasticity of biological and political thinking, and have therefore been ineffective in challenging religious nationalism and industrialized agriculture. Facing this new terrain of blurring boundaries between animal and vegetable, I explore other landscapes for political activism and mobilization. In particular, I worry that ethics is not the best frame through which to examine the politics of food. Similarly, the religious divides between Hindu and Muslim and long-enduring caste politics in India elide a historical and regional politics that a politics of benign vegetarianism suggests. I begin with describing the ethical impurative. I follow with a discussion of the impact of technoscientific innovations in the simultaneous vegetizing of meat and the animalizing of plants. I end with some thoughts on how feminists might reframe their critiques and concerns about industrialized agriculture and meat.

## The Ethical Impurative: A Brief Personal History

I am an ethically driven meat-eater—an ethical stance born in reaction to a superior morality claimed by Brahminism. In the Brahmin worldview, humans reign high among earthly creatures, and Brahmins claim the apex among human castes. Born in India into the much and rightfully maligned Tamil Brahmins (nicknamed TamBrahms), I was introduced to a virulent vegetarian fundamentalism suffused with an ethos of purity and pollution. The professed superiority was insufferable, the purity exclusive and isolating, and the pollution just begging to be violated! This is the context that called for a strong, engaged, and impassioned ethical imperative, an ethical impurative. To me, omnivory was the answer. Omnivory held the promise of the miscegenation of multispecies flesh and blood, of the conjoining of plant, animal, and human flesh, spirit and souls, the intermixture of molecules of a diverse nature into the molecules of my carbon-based life form. Such a mobile creature, I figure, forever pollutes sacred and sanctified spaces in her impure wake.

256　　To my young mind, raised in the more secular spaces of urban India, the TamBrahm world was a culture of ever-reproducing power and privilege. In the orthodox spaces where TamBrahmdom was celebrated, purity reigned, sustained through elaborate rituals against pollution. Meat-eating was wrong, and minimal culinary commingling with non-Brahmins was advocated. The more orthodox practiced a concomitant refusal of garlic, onions, and alcohol (for their "flaming" of the flesh). For the most orthodox and sanctimonious, not even a drop of water would pass their lips outside of the home. If a cook was hired for the home, she was always Brahmin (often poor and widowed, and thus powerless). However, the maids in the house were rarely Brahmin, and they were the ones who cleaned the floors and toilets, washed the dishes, including *puja* paraphernalia used by the priest each day for the rituals of worship. Here the hypocrisy was apparent. How do you purify such pollution? A Brahmin would sprinkle water on the utensils, rendering them "pure" and fit for the deities and the household. Money also was always accepted from anyone, if necessary, with a few sprinkles of Brahmin water. Thus, merely touching or befriending the polluted would never have sufficed. One could be cleansed and purified. Omnivory, however, polluted the flesh so thoroughly, so molecularly, that there was no return, the ultimate ethical imperative.

I reveled in omnivory. The food of our neighbors always wafted in with exotic aromas. I fantasized about the smells and eating the forbidden foods. I would imagine that the long slices of eggplant, with their symmetric veins along the central stalk, were fillets of fish with elegant skeletons; I took pains to consume it with delicate precision. The raw jackfruit I heard tastes just like chicken, and my imagination ran wild as I consumed its fibrous flesh. With age, I ate at friends' houses and then in restaurants. I wore my omnivory with a badge of pride, especially among my more conservative relatives, who viewed me with disapproving and sometimes bemused eyes. Even to this day, one of my uncles greets me with the rhyme "Are you still eating the *nandus* and *vandus*?" (crabs and beetles). I always gleefully answer, "Yes, everything!"

The Brahmin notion of purity was born from a history of privilege, not denial, a privilege that afforded a life of vegetarianism. Brahmins were the keepers of the temples, the interpreters of the written word, controlling access to the gods. Despite anti-Brahmin and anti-caste movements, especially in Tamil Nadu, their rich history is one of power and privilege; from colonial to modern times they have reinforced the hierarchies of caste. Omnivory, which began as my small rebellion as a child, has thoroughly rendered my body into liminality forever. Impure and polluted, it taught me how to join the natural world as a member of a global humanity.

**THE ETHICAL IMPURATIVE**

Today this individual act of gleeful childhood rebellion seems sobering in the light of a growing national campaign against beef-eating. The hypocrisy of a growing political Hinduism is breathtaking. There is no campaign against buffalo meat or any other meat—only the cow—allegedly because the figure of the cow and its suffering alone remains sacred in Hinduism. This ignores the fact that as a new independent postcolonial nation, India was founded as a multireligious, secular republic with equal rights and representation for all religions. While other religions do not share a ban on cow-eating, and have other culinary prohibitions, the growing Hindu nationalism of India attempts to impose majoritarian rule, singling out beef-eating as a singular prohibition. A judge in the Rajasthan's High Court suggested in a ruling in 2017 that the cow be adopted as the national animal of India because, in addition to millions of gods and goddesses residing in the cow, the "cow is the only living being which intakes oxygen and emits oxygen."[1] Yet for Muslims and Christians who have other religious culinary prescriptions, and the poor for whom beef is relatively cheap meat, the weight and violence of majoritarian will is staggering. Over eighteen states have banned the slaughter of cattle. This is not a rhetorical campaign. Numerous individuals have been assaulted and murdered because they appear or are alleged to be meat-eaters. Of all the points of friction, beef is what "has drawn the most blood."[2] During his electoral campaign, Narendra Modi complained about India's "pink revolution" or rising meat exports, and backed the idea of a national ban on cow slaughter. With encouragement from the center, many states have tightened their laws on cow slaughter. At times, these laws effectively banned beef overnight, putting predominantly Muslim butchers suddenly out of a job, and any beef-eater under risk of an arrest.[3] Raising cattle for slaughter or suspicion of eating beef have resulted in "beef lynchings."[4] Dozens have been killed, and over 124 people have been injured in cow-related attacks. Some 86 percent of those killed in cow-related violence since 2010 have been Muslim, and 97 percent of the attacks have emerged after a Hindu nationalist government came to power in 2014.[5] Yet, with a growing affluent middle and upper class of Indians, meat-eating is widespread. Indians now eat more meat, including beef (cow and buffalo meat) than ever before. New terminologies like "dietary profiling" and "food fascism" have been introduced, attempting to capture the volatility of the situation. Consumption of beef is said to have grown 14 percent in cities and 35 percent in villages in recent years.[6]

What is striking in these cases of violence is the claim of beef-eating that engenders such violence. As a consequence, in several cases, the purported

258

meat has been sent to laboratories to test for its animal of origin. In one case, the purported beef was in fact mutton.[7] While officials acknowledge that it should not matter what the source of meat is, specimens are still taken and sent to the vet, and sometimes to a second laboratory for forensic tests.[8] It is clear that Hindu nationalist governments have used this as a weapon of intimidation. For example, ahead of the Eid celebration, the police in Haryana's Mewat district were tasked with checking morsels of meat in the biriyani sold by vendors to check for the presence of beef (Haryana has some of the strictest laws on production and consumption of cow meat). An added wrinkle from the science of meat testing is that while raw meat retains much of the cells' DNA, cooking meat (especially cooking for long periods of time as in a biriyani), denatures DNA, making it more difficult to identify.[9]

Despite its reputation as a land of vegetarianism, in reality only one in every five Indians is really vegetarian.[10] Most importantly, and at the heart of contemporary politics of Hindu nationalism and its strong and virulent anti-Islam stance and upper-caste politics, Muslims and Dalits (members of an oppressed caste group) have been particularly targeted.[11] India also has a thriving multibillion-dollar beef and leather industry, a majority run by Muslims. Muslims and Dalits are among the poorest in India, and many of them work in the leather sector, which employs about 2.5 million people.[12] Beef has thus emerged as a potent site for "meat politics" through the imposition of majoritarian Hindu will against the minority Muslim population. The current prime minister, Mr. Narendra Modi, has used the issue in the past to goad the majority Hindu population through emotional speeches (available on YouTube) such as "Brothers and sisters, I cannot say whether your heart is pained by this or not, but my heart screams out in agony again and again. And why you remain silent, why you tolerate this, I cannot understand." Local economies around beef and leather have collapsed, with slaughterhouses and meat-processing factories shuttering their businesses, leading to lack of work for hundreds of local and migrant workers; factory and farm workers are hard-pressed to pay back their loans, and some factory owners are defaulting on their loans.[13] Small and vocal acts of beef-eating as declarations of resistance by journalists, celebrities, and others on social media have proliferated. A prominent journalist, as an act of bold rebellion, tweeted, "I just ate beef. Come and murder me!" A police complaint was swiftly launched against her.[14] "Eat More Beef" public campaigns have been launched as rebellions.[15] "Not in My Name" campaigns have erupted across India in protest against mob lynchings of presumed meat-eaters.[16] The Supreme Court suspended the government ban on the sale of cattle for slaughter.[17] All this is not new—beef-eating has a long and turbulent history in Indian politics, grounded in religious and regional politics. The south of India, and the state of Tamil Nadu in particular, has a long history of protesting the caste oppression of Brahmins through "Eat More Beef" campaigns. These continue today even in prestigious locations like the Indian Institute of Technology (IIT).[18] Without a doubt the charged politics of region and religion will continue to place meat at a critical center and object of a politics of purity and pollution, marking the pure from the profane.[19] In contemporary India, the politics of meat has literally become a politics of pitting animal life against human politics, and for humans, a politics of life and death.

## Life in Binaries: On the Categories of Animal and Vegetable

From the religious purity politics in India that permits the eating of buffalo and other mammals, but not cows, I'd like to consider a different set of purity politics in environmentalist responses to meat. In the biological sciences, living organisms are categorized into two main categories, animal and plant—or in taxonomic terms the Phyla Animalia and Plantae—as binary opposites, shaping both our understanding of the two and also our ethical responses to vegetarianism, carnivory, and omnivory (we now have additional phyla including Phyla Monera [prokaryotic organisms], Protista [simple eukaryotic organisms], and Fungi [various fungal species]). While there are similarities between animal and plant cells, since they are both eukaryotes, biologists also characterize plant and animal cells differently, including cell structures, cell organelles, plant and animal stem cells, and modes of cell division.[20] These histories have shaped the binary frames of active, sentient animal life and passive, nonsentient plant life that animate many biological views of life, and more importantly the politics of meat. This framing has long and deep roots in the history of biology. One sees it in many sites in biology. The egg, for example, is characterized as having a polarity—an animal pole and a vegetal pole. These terms also extend to categorizing animal and vegetal hemispheres of the egg and embryo, and animal and vegetal plate cells in some organisms. In biology, the term vegetal is also often defined to include organisms that are capable of growth and reproduction, but not feeling or reason. Hence we see use of the term "vegetal" or vegetative to describe the state of humans who sink into a coma or various nonresponsive states. In colloquial language, "vegetative states" contrast with "animated states."

260

What is particularly striking in the languages that surround animal and vegetal is that they are distinctly gendered and raced. The two names, for example, arise from a long history of gender and race politics. "Higher" organisms were seen as evolving an animal polar region, while the vegetal pole represented "lower" forms and organs necessary for reproduction and providing nutrition. Predictably, the animal pole consists of cells that divide rapidly and that form the primary germ layers. In contrast, the yolky vegetal pole has less active cytoplasm, divides slowly, and protects and nourishes the developing embryo. The animal is characteristically considered biologically more complex, and "advanced" and "superior," as opposed to the evolutionarily typed "lower" plants. Such distinctions and characterizations come from early genealogies that organized all living creatures into hierarchies such as the "Great Chain of Being" or a "ladder of being." Superior organisms occupied higher rungs of the ladder, with less evolved and inferior organisms on the lower rungs. Men, especially white, Western, heterosexual, upper-class men, were always assumed to inhabit higher rungs of such an evolutionary ladder, while women and colonized peoples were closer to lesser organisms.[21] The two poles are also characterized as distinctly gendered. The dividing, generative pole of an egg is always the animal pole, endowed with traditionally masculine characteristics of being alive, active, growing, and productive, while the vegetal pole is endowed with the more feminine characteristics of being nourishing. Animals are active, being more masculine, and the nourishing vegetal more feminine.

In the great hierarchy of organisms, humans are on top, followed by animals, plants, and unicellular organisms. The biological categories of gender, race, class, and sexuality became potent biopolitical categories for nations. "Less developed" humans such as women, colonized peoples, peoples of color, nonheteronormative subjects, the disabled, and so on have historically been denied many rights and privileges because they were viewed as inferior. And indeed, these scientific categories shaped the social categories and subsequently various struggles of civil rights groups. We have seen the category of the rights-bearing human expanded from white men to men of color, white women, colonized men, and queer men and women. Animal rights have also emerged, especially the rights of primates, which are seen as closer to humans. Indeed, some animal rights activists have used precisely this logic in our expanding sense of sentience. As our conceptions of human exceptionalism have diminished, calls for animal rights have grown.[22] These have taken many forms. Some have called for an extension of human rights to create an "Animal Bill of Rights."[23] Animal rights activists

261

present a wide spectrum. On one end, activists argue that human/nonhuman binaries are arbitrary and that, like humans, animals are social beings, and feel pleasure and pain, joy and grief, share a strong emotional register, and should have the same rights. These activists suggest that we abolish the use of animals in experimentation and testing, and as meat. They usually endorse veganism—where no animal or animal parts are eaten or used in any way. Other animal rights activists eschew this extreme position (for varying reasons), and suggest great regulation of the use of animals, such as preventing cruelty, encouraging humane conditions of livestock, and minimal standards of housing and animal care.[24]

## Vegetizing Animals: Technologies of Desentience

Is it inhumane to house too many horned animals in tight enclosures so they routinely harm each other? Solution: Let us dehorn animals through gene editing.[25] Is the process of slaughter inhumane because of how animals are treated during the process? Solution: Let us produce more humane slaughter practices so animals don't know what awaits them. Is killing animals unethical? Solution: Let us deploy tissue culture to produce petri-dish meat. Do animals transfer diseases to each other because they are housed too close together in tiny quarters? Solution: Let us genetically engineer disease-resistant organisms.[26] Do pigs or other organisms produce too much agricultural pollution? Solution: Let us produce the Enviropig™ that limits the amount of phosphorus released in its manure.[27] Do we only require one sex of an animal for the needs of industrialized agriculture? Perhaps we can produce only "female" chickens that can be used to lay eggs and "male" cattle that will produce better meat—together creating more efficient farms.[28]

The politics extend to plants. Does the tomato freeze too easily? Solution: Let us transfer genes from Arctic fish to produce a more frost-resilient tomato. Does a vegetarian burger appear too much like grain and not enough like meat? Solution: Let us create a bloody veggie burger. As with animals, genes beneficial to humans that have been introduced into plants so their products will benefit the humans who consume them, such as vitamin A in golden rice (although still not commercially available), we have also seen vitamins A and C as well as folate in enriched corn.[29] The modern Cavendish banana also has enhanced levels of vitamin A.[30] We also have bred herbicide- and pesticide-resistant crops, plants with new genes that cause fruits to delay ripening, rot slowly, have greater shelf lives, and be less prone to damage in transport. Also, genes beneficial to humans have been introduced into plants and animals so their products will benefit the humans who consume them, such as omega-3 fatty acids in pigs that rival levels in fish, or vitamin A in golden rice.[31] Animals and plants have also long been used to produce human drugs. Animals, bacteria, plants, and more recently cells have long been used as factories for insulin production.[32] More recently, ATryn, the first therapeutic protein produced by genetically engineered animals as a prophylactic treatment for patients with a hereditary antithrombin deficiency, was approved by the FDA in 2006.[33] By now most animals and plants in agriculture have been commodified through patents and restricted trademarks, and are routinely licensed, bought, and sold. Genetic engineering has increased productivity, yield, and enhanced the nutritional quality of industrialized products. We now have fast-growing salmon, the first genetically altered animal cleared by the government for human consumption.[34] Through a genomic technological tool called TALENS, companies can create pigs that can be fattened with less food and cattle that yield more tender meat.[35]

The question I want to ruminate on is whether such technological responses to ethical quandaries really solve the ethical problems. In tracing the development of new varieties of organisms through breeding or genetic engineering, a consistent pattern to the resolution of ethical problems emerges. In each instance, the problem is resolved by a technological fix that bypasses the ethical problem rather than actually solving it. For example, in response to critiques of the size of animal enclosures that routinely crowd organisms to such an extent that they cannot even move and end up hurting each other, leading to easy transmission of diseases and the wide use of antibiotics, the solution devised is to engineer disease-resistant breeds. Technology, it would seem, is infinitely inventive and agile in solving our ethical problems as we currently frame them.

Technologies of agriculture and animal sciences have historically worked to maximize production and profit—following strategies to produce the most meat efficiently at the least cost. From using eggs and semen from high-performance milk and beef producers, humans have produced hybrids of animals with increasing yields. Products have been bred to maximize texture, taste, freshness, and transportability. As industrialized agriculture has taken a more and more central role in food production, various ethical quandaries have emerged. In the last few decades, the technosciences have emerged as the site for producing technological solutions for the ethical quandaries of industrialized agriculture.

263

## CELLULAR AGRICULTURE

We have seen the advent of "cultured meat" and other "cellular agriculture" (for example, cultured meat, cultured milk, and cultured egg whites). In the case of meat, muscle cells are grown on a substrate in laboratories (and future factories) using tissue engineering. Once the muscle cells differentiate and develop into mature tissue and to the required size, they are harvested and processed into various meat products. These technologized foods are often presented as "foods of the future" because they present better alternatives, including more sustainability, because they use considerably less energy, produce fewer emissions, and have lower land and water use compared to industrial animal agriculture.[36] In addition to producing more sustainable meats, experts claim that they reduce animal suffering significantly and ensure chemically safe, healthier, disease-free meat that is produced more efficiently and with enhanced nutritional profiles.[37]

## TECHNOLOGIES OF TRANSFER

A vast array of genetic technologies have been developed that allow the genetic modification of organisms,[38] including intragenic, famigenic, transgenic, and xenogenic. These technologies expand on conventional plant-breeding techniques that allowed the creation of particular cultivars by crossing species that could reproduce together. Such technologies, however, might result in the reshuffling of genetic sequences in the rest of the genome. Genetic technologies allow the transfer of particular sequences across species. A wealth of techniques have emerged. Intra- and cis-genic transfers allow the transfer of gene sequences across closely related organisms; famigenic technologies transfer genes across species in the same family. Transgenic transfers involve transferring genetic material across unrelated species, and xenogenic transfers involve moving laboratory-designed genes into organisms.

## PLANT "ANIMAL" ALTERNATIVES

Biotechnologies have also produced a host of plant and synthetic protein alternatives, including plant-derived meats and insects. This is a growing and profitable industry, and their products using biotechnological innovations, including tissue engineering and synthetic biology, are promoted by entrepreneurs, scientists, and industry as "moral" solutions to climate change. Indeed, cellular agriculture has been touted as our savior from a wide array of crises, ranging from climate change, to animal welfare, to

264

human malnutrition. In response, there is concern that excessive use of soy, gluten, and plant protein as substitutes have in turn created their own set of problems such as the rise of environmental estrogen,[39] as well as allergic and autoimmune problems.[40] These technologies have become so good that they have impressed even discerning food critics.[41]

## TECHNOLOGIES OF HARM REDUCTION

Industrialized agriculture, where large numbers of animals are housed in the smallest amount of space possible, has produced innumerable problems horrifyingly chronicled in many videos. Chickens pecking each other to death, cows and pigs that cannot move, excessive antibiotic use from feeding animals extra-rich (and gas-producing) food, untreated gaping wounds and infections—just to name a few. Gene-editing technologies have opened up new possibilities. Rather than sawing the horns off animals that wound each other, dehorned animals can now be produced genetically. We have seen a plethora of genetically produced "innovations" that in reality are mostly solving the problems of industrialized agriculture, and are specifically touted as technologies that produce more humane practices.

### Animalizing Plants: Thinking with Plants

The most obvious site of the animalizing of plants is through transgenic introduction of animal genes into plants—frost resistance from Arctic fish introduced into vegetables, growth hormones from carp introduced into safflower, fungal resistance genes from chickens introduced into wheat, genes from rodents introduced into soybeans, glowing tobacco plants that will help indicate when certain genes are active, to name a few. These technologies have been much publicized in vegetarian circles, leading some vegetarians to worry about the purity of their vegetables.[42] Are you eating a vegetable if there are animal genes in it? What are the contours of the vegetable?

If industrialized agriculture has been animalizing plants, some environmental activists and plant biologists have been challenging human exceptionalism by expanding the contours of the sentient organism beyond the human; that is, they have begun animalizing plants. One of the growing contributions of biology and animal studies more broadly has been to demystify the exceptionalism of the human. Primates and other animals now are credited with many characteristics once exclusively the province of the

265

human. We now talk about animals having intelligence, empathy, jealousy, practices of mourning, rituals of sociality, and so on. As a result of decades of work, activists in many countries have argued that "nonhuman hominids" should enjoy the right to life in freedom and not be tortured. Projects such as the Great Apes Project[43] have pushed for laws similar to those governing humans. Considerable work in animal studies and animal behavior has revolutionized what we know about animals, and as a result much of the vocabulary of the human is now routinely used to describe animals as well as human–animal interactions.[44]

Similarly, plants are no longer the passive, soulless, insentient beings they once represented. Instead, nonhuman actors have been imbued with intelligence, sociality, and ability to communicate, feel pain, and support each other; they have been recognized and been accorded new agency so far little recognized. Arguments for animal and plant sentience and intelligence have long histories. Indeed, over a hundred years ago physicist and biologist J. C. Bose conducted a series of experiments measuring electrical responses in plants, arguing that even ordinary plants are sensitive, exhibiting excitability and stimulus responses.[45] This line of research has had a very popular following at various times in the last century. Books and films such as *The Secret Life of Plants* (1973) and *What Plants Talk About* (2013) have seen huge popular success even as they have been pilloried in some scientific circles as paranormal science, pseudoscience, and mysticism.[46] While animal and plant behaviorists have made more inroads in recent years, the shadow of the label of "pseudoscience" continues to haunt this work. In recent years, there has been a raging debate on whether we could talk about a "plant neurobiology"—do plants have neural networks, synapses? Biologists have argued strongly for and against such frameworks. At the heart of these debates lie questions of what it means to do comparative biological work. Must plant and animal neurons look identical? Some have vociferously argued that while the origin of the word "neuron" in Greek is "vegetable fiber," there is no evidence for neurons, synapses, or brains in plants.[47] Or should we consider "plant neurobiology" not as a literal concept, but as a metaphor for comparative thinking?[48] Or perhaps we should embrace a term like "plant behavior" that allows us to talk about plant and animal behaviors alongside each other without collapsing one into the other?[49] Indeed, there is considerable evidence that there is a sensory basis to plants and that they integrate signaling, the transport of electric pulses and complex biomolecules that result in adaptive behaviors.[50] While still at the margins of plant biology, there is an active field of plant neurobiology today, including a scientific society and journals such as *Plant Signaling and Behavior*, and numerous international symposia.

Taken together, the vegetizing of animals and the animalizing of plants show us how technologies of food production have reshaped and blurred the boundaries around the animal and vegetable. Technological innovations have emerged as the site of solutions, and have increasingly produced new patented beings that solve particular ethical problems. However, the products of biotechnologies resemble "animals" less and less. In order to deal with questions of suffering and rights, the solution has been to de-animalize animals. Further, much of the political economy of industrialized agriculture is globalized, corporatized, machine-driven, and mass production has steadily been reinforced. Organic and local production is constantly co-opted by economies of scale and the consolidation of the big players of industry. Responses to and fear of technologized food have ushered in a strong environmental response around the naturalness and purity of food.

### Frankenfood: The Ethical Frontiers of Technologized Meat

Our digression into technologies of meat that vegetize meats (alongside the animalizing of plants) was to bring us back into a politics of purity, especially of reaffirming the contours of what is "natural." Like the xenophobia and the politics of purity that haunt our discourses on invasive species,[51] these fears pervade other realms of the political, including food activism. For example, activists against technologized meat and other genetically modified foods have dubbed them Frankenfood. At the heart of the politics of Frankenfood is that any tinkering with the natural using technology risks the unleashing of monsters such as Frankenstein. Much work in science and technology studies has critiqued the rejection of technology in favor of a valorization of the "natural," and a zeal for "local foods" as a politics of purity.[52] As I have argued in my previous work, a politics of purity and the natural pervades environmental discourses. Several lines of argument promote such politics of purity.[53] First, we see arguments around the "genetic integrity" of the natural, native, and the nation. Indeed, the fear that foreign species might interbreed with natives yields discourses that have the familiar ring of old anti-miscegenation anxieties and laws.[54] Yet, as Forrest and Fletcher argue, when pressed for a definition of genetic integrity, "there is generally some reluctance on the part of those employing such terminology to come to the point, although emotive issues connected with the archival 'preservation of our priceless heritage' and perhaps a variety of 'ethnic cleansing' are seldom far from the surface."[55] Looking closely at activists against technologized meat, several factors are striking. First, technologized meat is usually represented as the "other"—not natural, not "real," and not animal, indeed Frankenfood. The rhetoric warns us of "playing God," "tinkering with the natural," and cautions us about producing the "bizarre" and the creation of possibilities that are unlikely to occur in our peculiarly gendered and raced world. The language reinscribes particular notions of the "other," simultaneously reinforcing the normative as the native, the natural, the pure. Second, with technologized meat that produces reproducing animals, these animals are often attributed with a "hypersexual" fertility. There is fear of transgenes crossing to "natural" populations and creating mutant populations, ultimately rendering the native or original species extinct. For example, this rhetoric is most visible in fears of genetically engineered salmon.[56] Third, the fears of technologized meat are linked to a valorization of nature and the "natural." Fundamentally in this framework, "nature" is a realm that is seen as removed from human interference but also human-friendly, safe, and trustworthy; that is, products of nature are safe for humans. By tinkering with nature, humans are argued to assume an unparalleled arrogance and are accused of playing God. In this vision, if respected and left undisturbed, nature nurtures native species, nature produces "wholesome natural products" with pristine seeds that are good for you. If, however, we disturb this coevolved nature, with its own checks and balances, we are at risk of unleashing monsters. Genetically modified organisms enable unnatural gene mixing. Interestingly, companies that produce transgenic plants and GM food have moved to use the same rhetoric to celebrate genetically modified food because it will allow the "natural" to be more "natural." They suggest that producing varieties with higher yields will save biodiversity and ultimately conserve native forestland. Similarly, transgenes that bring pesticide and weed resistance to plants will reduce the use of pesticides and herbicides and ultimately create more "pure" nature and sustainable agricultural practices. Fourth, the rhetoric of purity is striking—"pure" nature, "pure species," species fidelity. Anxieties abound about natural and technologically enhanced species cross-breeding, thus "contaminating" the native gene pool and gene purity. The rhetoric emphasizes purity by highlighting "leaking genes," "genetic pollution," and "contamination." Activists and policy makers have created a purity index and have developed standards to measure "seed purity."

## The Ethical Impurative: Challenging Politics of Purity

In the two cases that animate this chapter—one from the realm of religion and the other from science—we explored the ban on beef-eating in India and the engineering of more killable animals. With a focus on purity politics, the two cases are premised on identifying the sacred yet deeply political sites of beef and the sentient animal, we see that each obscures deeply problematic claims of the sacred and the ethical. Industrialized agriculture has long embraced technology as a central mode of innovation. Early technologies of plant breeding through careful crossing of related species have now expanded to rampant transfer of genetic material across species that would not be able to reproduce otherwise. In this essay, I have focused on two main aspects of the technologies of food. These technologies of food production have ushered in ethical concerns about animal use and its sustainability. Rather than interrogating the technologies of concern, industrialized agriculture has used the critiques as a mandate to further technologize meat. There is little left that might be called "natural" or species untouched by human interventions. This has led to a potent form of purity politics among environmental and food activists.[57] In this essay, I have juxtaposed two forms of purity politics: one around beef-eating in India that is grounded in a politics of region and religion, and the second, the purity politics against industrialized agriculture.

Insights from biological and feminist science and technology studies are useful here. First, there is little purity in the world, at least biologically speaking. Plants and animals share a great deal of genetic material. Rather than pure lineages, animal and plant species are genetically teeming with entangled and mixed genomes. Humans share the majority of their DNA with other primates, and indeed harbor genes from other organisms, including plants, microorganisms, and fungi.[58] The shared biological material comes not only from historical entanglements of species, but through horizontal transfer of genetic material through microorganisms, processes that continue today.

Here I would suggest that challenging industrialized agriculture around the traditional framing of "ethics" is perhaps an unproductive line of political activism, because biotechnological innovation keeps circumventing the particular ethical problem raised. Technological determinism is forever "solving" ethical problems by genetically engineering "new" organisms that build a "web of life."[59] Second, cultural purity politics also elides historical intermingling of human societies and cultures. Demographic patterns of meat-eating reveal that the anti–beef-eating campaigns are in reality a virulent and violent campaign to intimidate religious and caste-based minority groups into a recognition of living amid majoritarian rule. In a country like India, claims of purity along religious lines elide an entangled and commingled history. What both politics of purity share is a politics of mobilizing the public through a politics around consumption. As Julie Guthman writes, "heightened anxiety about the constitution of food underlies much of the new politics of consumption."[60] Reading food politics through a politics of purity allows us to understand the virulence of food activists in India and the West, be it about beef or technologized food. In constituting a nostalgic past where food and food practices were pure and natural, both groups organize their politics around the pollutions—of religious minorities and technological interventions. Feminist science and technology studies also remind us that such politics of purity also obfuscate larger shifts in the political economy of technoscience. A focus around purity ethics is a distraction from the larger trends, where life is being increasingly commodified, patented, and trademarked. In fact, most varieties of plants and animals in industrialized agriculture are "owned" by someone. In most cases, such patents are shrouded in secrecy and obscure the technologies of production. This seems to be the central issue that should consume feminists. Instead, in both cases, a politics of purity ethics celebrates a nostalgia that is grounded in the mythic and mystical past rather than in studied histories of India or the West. Such a politics can only be faced through a strong politics against purity[61] to embrace the entangled, co-constituted, and deeply imbricated histories of life on earth. Long live the Ethical Impurative!

## Notes

1   Amitava Kumar, "What's behind India's Beef Lynchings?," *The Nation*, October 13, 2017.

2   Michael Miller, "A Mob in India Just Dragged a Man from His Home and Beat Him to Death—For Eating Beef," *Washington Post*, September 30, 2015.

3   Miller, "A Mob in India."

4   Harrison Akins, "How Hindu Nationalists Politicized the Taj Mahal," *The Atlantic*, November 27, 2017, accessed January 28, 2018, https://www.theatlantic.com/international/archive/2017/11/taj-mahal-india-hindu-nationalism/546374/.

5   Delna Abraham and Ojaswi Rao, "86% Killed in Cow-Related Violence since 2010 Are Muslim, 97% Attacks after Modi Govt Came to Power," *Hindustan Times*, July 16, 2017, accessed October 25, 2017, http://www.hindustantimes

.com/india-news/86-killed-in-cow-related-violence-since-2010-are-muslims-97 -attacks-after-modi-govt-came-to-power/story-w9CYOksvgk9joGSSaXgpLO .html; "India's Supreme Court Suspends Ban on Sale of Cows for Slaughter," *New York Times*, July 11, 2017.

6  Soutik Biswas, "Is India's Ban on Cattle Slaughter 'Food Fascism'?," *BBC News*, June 2, 2017, accessed October 18, 2017, http://www.bbc.com/news/world-asia -india-40116811.

7  Krishnadev Calamur, "India's Food Fight Turns Deadly," *The Atlantic*, October 8, 2015.

8  "India Lynching: Meat in Muslim Man's Fridge Mutton Not Beef, Forensic Test Reveals," *Dawn*, October 9, 2015, accessed January 28, 2018, https://www.dawn .com/news/1211921.

9  Vasudevan Mukunth, "Haryana, Please Note: Lab Test to Check for Beef Works Best if Meat Is Uncooked," *The Wire*, September 15, 2016.

10  Nimisha Jaiswal, "Only One in Five Indians Is Really Vegetarian," *PRI International*, September 14, 2016, accessed October 25, 2016, https://www.pri.org /stories/2016-09-14/only-one-five-indians-really-vegetarian.

11  Shubhomoy Sikdar, "Beef Ban Meant to Target Poor Muslims, Dalits," *The Hindu*, March 31, 2015, accessed October 25, 2017, http://www.thehindu.com /news/national/other-states/beef-ban-meant-to-target-poor-muslims-dalits /article7050399.ece.

12  Afroz Alam, "Cow Economics Are Killing India's Working Class," *The Conversation*, June 22, 2017, accessed October 23, 2017, http://theconversation.com/cow -economics-are-killing-indias-working-class-79274.

13  Suhasini Raj and Ellen Barry, "Modi's Push for a Hindu Revival Imperils India's Meat Industry," *New York Times*, June 5, 2017.

14  "Complaint against Shobha De over Tweet on Eating Beef," *Hindustan Times*, October 14, 2015, accessed October 25, 2017, http://www.hindustantimes .com/india/complaint-against-shobha-de-over-tweet-on-eating-beef/story -x85nBqqfIxDjxWs3qXcubI.html.

15  Vidhi Doshi, "To Protest Modi, These Indians Are Cooking Beef in Public," *Washington Post*, June 6, 2017.

16  "Indian Veterans Decry Targeting of Minorities," *Al Jazeera*, July 31, 2017, accessed October 25, 2017, http://www.aljazeera.com/news/2017/07/indian -veterans-decy-targeting-minorities-170731091701277.html.

17  "India's Supreme Court Suspends Ban on Sale of Cows for Slaughter."

18  R. Sujatha and R. Sivaraman, "IIT-Madras Campus Tense after Beef Fest," *The Hindu*, May 31, 2017.

19  Shraddha Chigateri, "'Glory to the Cow': Cultural Difference and Social Justice in the Food Hierarchy in India," *Journal of South Asian Studies* 31, no. 1 (2008): 10–35.

20  Renze Heidstra and Sabrini Sabatini, "Plant and Animal Stem Cells: Similar Yet Different," *Nature Reviews Molecular Biology* 15 (2014): 301–12.

271

21  Londa Schiebinger, *Nature's Body: Gender on the Making of Modern Science* (New Brunswick, NJ: Rutgers University Press, 1993).

22  Bernard E. Rollin, *Animal Rights and Human Morality* (Amherst, NY: Prometheus, 1981).

23  "Animal Bill of Rights," Animal Legal Defense Fund, http://animalbillofrights.aldf.org/.

24  For an introduction, see K. W. Stallwood, ed., *A Primer on Animal Rights: Leading Experts Write about Animal Cruelty and Exploitation* (New York: Lantern, 2002).

25  Amy Harmon, "Open Season Is Seen in Gene Editing of Animals," *New York Times*, November 26, 2015.

26  Harmon, "Open Season Is Seen in Gene Editing of Animals."

27  Elisabeth H. Ormandy, Julie Dale, and Gilly Griffin, "Genetic Engineering of Animals: Ethical Issues, Including Welfare Concerns," *Canadian Veterinary Journal* 52, no. 5 (2011): 544–50.

28  Harmon, "Open Season Is Seen in Gene Editing of Animals."

29  Shaista Naqvi et al., "Transgenic Multivitamin Corn through Biofortification of Endosperm with Three Vitamins Representing Three Distinct Metabolic Pathways," *Proceedings of the National Academy of Science* 106, no. 19 (2009): 7762–67.

30  Sydney Brownstone, "Humans Are about to Taste the First Genetically Engineered 'Super' Banana," *Fast Company*, June 30, 2014, https://www.fastcompany.com/3032136/humans-are-about-to-taste-the-first-genetically-engineered-super-bananas.

31  Amy Maxmen, "First Plant-Made Drug on Market," *Nature Newsblog*, May 2, 2012, accessed October 20, 2017, http://blogs.nature.com/news/2012/05/first-plant-made-drug-on-the-market.html.

32  Nabih A. Baeshen et al., "Cell Factories for Insulin Production," *Microbial Cell Factories* 13 (2014): 141.

33  Ormandy et al., "Genetic Engineering of Animals: Ethical Issues."

34  Harmon, "Open Season Is Seen in Gene Editing of Animals."

35  Keith J. Joung and Jeffrey D. Sander, "TALENS: A Widely Applicable Technology for Targeting Genome Editing," *Nature Reviews Molecular Cell Biology* 14 (2013): 49–55; Harmon, "Open Season Is Seen in Gene Editing of Animals."

36  Z. F. Bhat and H. Fayaz, "Prospectus of Cultured Meat—Advancing Meat Alternatives," *Journal of Food Science and Technology* 48, no. 2 (2011): 125–40; H. L. Tuomisto and M. J. Teixeira de Mattos, "Environmental Impacts of Cultured Meat Production," *Environmental Science & Technology* 45, no. 14 (2011): 6117–23; P. D. Edelman et al., "Commentary: In Vitro-Cultured Meat Production," *Tissue Engineering* 11, nos. 5–6 (2005): 659–62.

37  Bhat and Fayaz, "Prospectus of Cultured Meat," 125–40; Tuomisto and Teixeira de Mattos, "Environmental Impacts of Cultured Meat Production"; Edelman et al., "Commentary."

38  M. Sticklen, "Transgenic, Cisgenic, Intragenic and Subgenic Crops," *Advances in Crop Science and Technology* 3 (2015): e123.

39  Cecilia Chighizola and Pier Luigi Meroni, "The Role of Environmental Estrogens and Autoimmunity," *Autoimmunity Reviews* 11, nos. 6–7 (2012): A493–A501.

40  David Bell and Fernando Ovalle, "Use of Soy Protein Supplement and Resultant Need for Increased Dose of Loveothyroxine," *Endocrine Practice* 8, no. 3 (2001): 193–94.

41  Mark Bittman, "A Chicken without Guilt," *New York Times*, March 9, 2012.

42  Karen Iacobbo and Michael Iacobbo, *Vegetarians and Vegans in America Today* (Westport, CT: Praeger, 2006).

43  Great Ape Project, homepage, http://www.greatapeproject.org/index.php.

44  F. de Waal, *Are We Smart Enough to Know How Smart Animals Are?* (New York: W. W. Norton, 2017); Virginia Morrell, *How We Know Animals Think and Feel* (New York: Broadway, 2014); J. Narby, *Intelligence in Nature: An Inquiry into Knowledge* (New York: Penguin, 2006).

45  J. C. Bose, *Researches on Irritability of Plants* (London: Longmans, Green, 1913); J. C. Bose, "Transmission of Stimuli in Plants," *Nature* 115 (1925): 457.

46  P. H. Abelson, "Pseudoscience," *Science* 184, no. 4143 (June 1974): 1233.

47  A. Alpi et al., "Plant Neurobiology: No Brain, No Gain?," *Trends in Plant Science* 12, no. 4 (2007): 135–36.

48  Anthony Trewavas, "Response to Alpi et al.: Plant Neurobiology—All Metaphors Have Value," *Trends in Plant Science* 12, no. 6 (2007): 231–33; Anthony Trewavas, "What Is Plant Behaviour?," *Plant, Cell and Environment* 32, no. 6 (2009): 606–16.

49  František Baluška and Stefano Mancuso, "Plant Neurobiology," *Plant Signal Behavior* 4, no. 6 (2015): 475–76.

50  Baluška and Mancuso, "Plant Neurobiology"; Stefano Mancuso and Alessandro Volta, *Brilliant Green: The Surprising History of Science of Plant Intelligence* (Washington, DC: Island, 2015); J. Silvertown and D. M. Gordon, "A Framework for Plant Behavior," *Annual Review of Ecology and Systematics* 20, no. 1 (1989): 349–66.

51  Banu Subramaniam, "The Aliens Have Landed! Reflections on the Rhetoric of Biological Invasions," *Meridians: Feminism, Race, Transnationalism* 2, no. 1 (2001): 26–40; Banu Subramaniam, *Ghost Stories for Darwin: The Science of Variation and the Politics of Diversity* (Urbana: University of Illinois Press, 2014).

52  George Myerson, *Donna Haraway and Genetically Modified Foods* (Flint, MI: Totem, 1996); J. Guthman, "Doing Justice to Bodies? Reflections on Food Justice, Race, and Biology," *Antipode* 46, no. 5 (2014): 1153–71; A. Shotwell, *Against Purity: Living Ethically in Compromised Times* (Minneapolis: University of Minnesota Press, 2016).

53  Subramaniam, *Ghost Stories for Darwin*.

273

54  Chris T. Smout, "The Alien Species in 20th-Century Britain: Constructing a New Vermin," *Landscape Research* 29, no. 1 (2003): 11–20.

55  Forest and Fletcher 1995: 99.

56  J. H. Bohling, "Strategies to Address the Conservation Threats Posed by Hybridization and Genetic Introgression," *Biological Conservation* 203 (2016): 321–27.

57  P. Hunter, "'Genetically Modified Lite' Placates Public but Not Activists," *EMBO Reports* 15, no. 2 (2014): 138–41.

58  Sarah Williams, "Humans May Harbor More Than 100 Genes from Other Organisms," *Science*, May 12, 2015, https://www.sciencemag.org/news/2015/03/humans-may-harbor-more-100-genes-other-organisms.

59  S. M. Soucy, J. Huang, and J. P. Gogarten, "Horizontal Gene Transfer: Building the Web of Life," *Nature Reviews Genetics* 16, no. 8 (2015): 472–82.

60  J. Guthman, "Doing Justice to Bodies?," 1175.

61  Shotwell, *Against Purity.*

## Bibliography

Abelson, P. H. "Pseudoscience." *Science* 184, no. 4143 (June 1974): 1233.

Abraham, Delna, and Ojaswi Rao. "86% Killed in Cow-Related Violence since 2010 Are Muslim, 97% Attacks after Modi Govt Came to Power." *Hindustan Times*, July 16, 2017. http://www.hindustantimes.com/india-news/86-killed-in-cow-related-violence-since-2010-are-muslims-97-attacks-after-modi-govt-came-to-power/story-w9CYOksvgk9joGSSaXgpLO.html. Accessed October 25, 2017.

Adler, Tamar. "Are Vegetables the New Meat?" *Vogue*, October 11, 2015. http://www.vogue.com/13359379/are-vegetables-the-new-meat/. Accessed May 3, 2016.

Akins, Harrison. "How Hindu Nationalists Politicized the Taj Mahal." *The Atlantic*, November 27, 2017. https://www.theatlantic.com/international/archive/2017/11/taj-mahal-india-hindu-nationalism/546374/. Accessed January 28, 2018.

Alam, Afroz. "Cow Economics Are Killing India's Working Class." *The Conversation*, June 22, 2017. http://theconversation.com/cow-economics-are-killing-indias-working-class-79274. Accessed October 23, 2017.

Alpi, A., M. Amrhein, A. Bertl, M. R. Blatt, E. Blumwald, F. Cervone, J. Dainty, M. I. De Michelis, E. Epstein, A. W. Galston, and M. H. M. Goldsmith. "Plant Neurobiology: No Brain, No Gain?" *Trends in Plant Science* 12, no. 4 (2007): 135–36.

Anuj, A. "Bombay High Court Strikes Down Ss. 5D, 9B of Maharashtra Animal Preservation Act." *Bar & Bench*, May 6, 2016. http://barandbench.com/beefban-bombay-high-court-strikes-ss-5d-9b-maharashtra-animal-protection-act/. Accessed May 6, 2016.

Baeshen, Nabih. "Cell Factories for Insulin Production." *Microbial Cell Factories* 13 (2014): 141.

Baluška, František, and Stefano Mancuso. "Plant Neurobiology." *Plant Signal Behavior* 4, no. 6 (2015): 475–76.

Bell, David, and Fernando Ovalle. "Use of Soy Protein Supplement and Resultant Need for Increased Dose of Loveothyroxine." *Endocrine Practice* 8, no. 3 (2001): 193–94.

Bhat, Z. F., and H. Fayaz. "Prospectus of Cultured Meat—Advancing Meat Alternatives." *Journal of Food Science and Technology* 48, no. 2 (2011): 125–40.

Biswas, Soutik. "Is India's Ban on Cattle Slaughter 'Food Fascism'?" *BBC News*, June 2, 2017. http://www.bbc.com/news/world-asia-india-40116811. Accessed October 18, 2017.

Bittman, Mark, "A Chicken without Guilt." *New York Times*, March 9, 2012.

Bohling, J. H. "Strategies to Address the Conservation Threats Posed by Hybridization and Genetic Introgression." *Biological Conservation* 203 (2016): 321–27.

Bose, J. C. *Researches on Irritability of Plants*. London: Longmans, Green, 1913.

Bose, J. C. "Transmission of Stimuli in Plants." *Nature* 115 (1925): 457.

Brownstone, Sydney. "Humans Are about to Taste the First Genetically Engineered 'Super' Banana." *Fast Company*, June 30, 2014. https://www.fastcompany.com/3032136/humans-are-about-to-taste-the-first-genetically-engineered-super-bananas.

Calamur, Krishnadev. "India's Food Fight Turns Deadly." *The Atlantic*, October 8, 2015.

Chamovitz, Daniel. *What a Plant Knows: A Field Guide to the Senses*. New York: Farrar, Straus and Giroux, 2012.

Chigateri, Shraddha. "'Glory to the Cow': Cultural Difference and Social Justice in the Food Hierarchy in India." *Journal of South Asian Studies* 31, no. 1 (2008): 10–35.

Chighizola, Cecilia, and Pier Luigi Meroni. "The Role of Environmental Estrogens and Autoimmunity." *Autoimmunity Reviews* 11, nos. 6–7 (2012): A493–A501.

"Complaint against Shobha De over Tweet on Eating Beef." *Hindustan Times*, October 14, 2015. http://www.hindustantimes.com/india/complaint-against-shobha-de-over-tweet-on-eating-beef/story-x85nBqqfIxDjxWs3qXcubI.html. Accessed October 25, 2017.

De Waal, F. *Are We Smart Enough to Know How Smart Animals Are?* New York: W. W. Norton, 2016.

Doshi, Vidhi. "To Protest Modi, These Indians Are Cooking Beef in Public." *Washington Post*, June 6, 2017.

Edelman, P. D., D. C. McFarland, V. A. Mironov, and J. G. Matheny. "Commentary: In Vitro-Cultured Meat Production." *Tissue Engineering* 11, nos. 5–6 (2005): 659–62.

Forrest, Ian G., and Alan M. Fletcher. "Implications of Genetic Research for Native Pinewood Conservation." *Our Pinewood Heritage*, ed. J. R. Aldhous, 97–106. Farnham, UK: Forestry Commission, The Royal Society for the Protection of Birds, Scottish Natural Heritage, 1995.

Guthman, J. "Doing Justice to Bodies? Reflections on Food Justice, Race, and Biology." *Antipode* 46, no. 5 (2014): 1153–71.

Harmon, Amy. "Open Season Is Seen in Gene Editing of Animals." *New York Times*, November 26, 2015.

Heidstra, Renze, and Sabrini Sabatini. "Plant and Animal Stem Cells: Similar Yet Different." *Nature Reviews Molecular Biology* 15 (2014): 301–12.

Hunter, P. "'Genetically Modified Lite' Placates Public but Not Activists." *EMBO Reports* 15, no. 2 (2014): 138–41.

Iacobbo, Karen, and Michael Iacobbo. *Vegetarians and Vegans in America Today*. Westport, CT: Praeger, 2006.

"In the Name of Cow Protection, Goons Strip and Brutally Beat Muslim Traders." *Milli Gazette Online*, June 2, 2016. http://www.milligazette.com/news/14369 -in-the-name-of-cow-protection-goons-strip-and-brutally-beat-muslims -traders. Accessed May 4, 2016.

"India Lynching: Meat in Muslin Man's Fridge Mutton Not Beef, Forensic Test Reveals." *Dawn*, October 9, 2015. https://www.dawn.com/news/1211921. Accessed January 28, 2018.

"Indian Veterans Decry Targeting of Minorities." *Al Jazeera*, July 31, 2017. http:// www.aljazeera.com/news/2017/07/indian-veterans-decy-targeting-minorities -170731091701277.html. Accessed October 25, 2017.

"India's Supreme Court Suspends Ban on Sale of Cows for Slaughter." *New York Times*, July 11, 2017.

Jaiswal, Nimisha. "Only One in Five Indians Is Really Vegetarian." *PRI International*, September 14, 2016. https://www.pri.org/stories/2016-09-14/only-one-five -indians-really-vegetarian. Accessed October 25, 2016.

Joung, Keith. J., and Jeffry D. Sander. "TALENs: A Widely Applicable Technology for Targeting Genome Editing." *Nature Reviews Molecular Cell Biology* 14 (2013): 49–55.

Koller, Dov. *The Restless Plant*. Cambridge, MA: Harvard University Press, 2011.

Korosec, Kirsten. "Meat 2.0: Vinod Kosla's Latest Bet Is on a Stealth Hamburger Company." *ZDNet*, September 14, 2011. http://www.zdnet.com/article/meat -20-vinod-khoslas-latest-bet-is-on-a-stealth-hamburger-company/. Accessed May 3, 2016.

Krumins, Aaron. "Eating 2.0: How the First FDA-Approved, Genetically Modified Animal Will Revolutionize Food." *ExtremeTech*, November 25, 2015. http:// www.extremetech.com/extreme/218466-eating-2-0-why-the-first-fda- approved-genetically-modified-animal-will-revolutionize-the-food-industry. Accessed May 2, 2016.

Kumar, Amitava. "What's behind India's Beef Lynchings?" *The Nation*, October 13, 2017.

Mancuso, Stefano, and Alessandro Volta. *Brilliant Green: The Surprising History of Science of Plant Intelligence*. Washington, DC: Island, 2015.

Maxmen, Amy. "First Plant-Made Drug on Market." *Nature Newsblog*, May 2, 2012. http://blogs.nature.com/news/2012/05/first-plant-made-drug-on-the-market .html. Accessed October 20, 2017.

Meek, James. "Genetic Chickens Get DNA Copyright Tag." *The Guardian*, July 30, 2000.

Miller, Michael. "A Mob in India Just Dragged a Man from His Home and Beat Him to Death—For Eating Beef." *Washington Post*, September 30, 2015.

Morell, V. *Animal Wise: The Thoughts and Emotions of Our Fellow Creatures*. New York: Crown, 2013.

Mukunth, Vasudevan. "Haryana, Please Note: Lab Test to Check for Beef Works Best if Meat Is Uncooked." *The Wire*, September 15, 2016.

Myerson, George. *Donna Haraway and Genetically Modified Foods*. Flint, MI: Totem, 1996.

Naqvi, Shaista, et al. "Transgenic Multivitamin Corn through Biofortification of Endosperm with Three Vitamins Representing Three Distinct Metabolic Pathways." *Proceedings of the National Academy of Science* 106, no. 19 (2009): 7762–67.

Narby, J. *Intelligence in Nature: An Inquiry into Knowledge*. New York: Penguin, 2006.

Ormandy, Elisabeth H., Julie Dale, and Gilly Griffin. "Genetic Engineering of Animals: Ethical Issues, Including Welfare Concerns." *Canadian Veterinary Journal* 52, no. 5 (2011): 544–50.

Pachelli, Nick. "I Love Meat. But These New 'Bleeding' Veggie Burgers Convinced Me to Give It Up for Good." *Vox*, December 8, 2016. https://www.vox.com /first-person/2016/12/8/13799096/beyond-meat-impossible-foods. Accessed December 10, 2016.

Parra-Bracamonte, Gaspar Manuel, Juan C. Martinez Gonzalez, Ana Sifuentes Rincon, Victor Moreno-Medina, and Eligio Ortega-Rivas. "Meat Tenderness Genetic Polymorphisms Occurrence and Distribution in Five Zebu Breeds in Medico." *Electronic Journal of Biotechnology* 18 (2015): 365–67.

Raisfeld, Robin, and Rob Patronite. "Vegetables Are the New Meat." *New York Magazine*, November 7, 2010.

Raj, Suhasini. "Man Tied to Hindu Vigilante Group among Five Held in Deaths of Two Muslims." *New York Times*, March 19, 2016.

Raj, Suhasini, and Ellen Barry. "Modi's Push for a Hindu Revival Imperils India's Meat Industry." *New York Times*, June 5, 2017.

Rollin, B. E. *Animal Rights and Human Morality*. Amherst, NY: Prometheus, 1981.

Rowe, Bradley. "Understanding Animals-Becoming-Meat: Embracing a Disturbing Education." *Critical Education* 2, no. 7 (2011).

Schiebinger, Londa. *Nature's Body: Gender in the Making of Modern Science*. New Brunswick, NJ: Rutgers University Press, 1993.

Sebastian, Kritika Sharma. "JNU Students Ate Beef, Worshipped Mahishasur." *The Hindu*, February 18, 2016.

Shotwell, A. *Against Purity: Living Ethically in Compromised Times*. Minneapolis: University of Minnesota Press, 2016.

Sikdar, Shubhomoy. "Beef Ban Meant to Target Poor Muslims, Dalits." *The Hindu*, March 31, 2015. http://www.thehindu.com/news/national/other-states/beef -ban-meant-to-target-poor-muslims-dalits/article7050399.ece. Accessed October 25, 2017.

Silvertown, J., and D. M. Gordon. "A Framework for Plant Behavior." *Annual Review of Ecology and Systematics* 20, no. 1 (1989): 349–66.

Smout, Chris T. "The Alien Species in 20th-Century Britain: Constructing a New Vermin." *Landscape Research* 29, no. 1 (2003): 11–20.

Soucy, S. M., J. Huang, and J. P. Gogarten. "Horizontal Gene Transfer: Building the Web of Life." *Nature Reviews Genetics* 16, no. 8 (2015): 472–82.

Stallwood, K. W., ed. *A Primer on Animal Rights: Leading Experts Write about Animal Cruelty and Exploitation*. New York: Lantern, 2002.

Sticklen, M. "Transgenic, Cisgenic, Intragenic and Subgenic Crops." *Advances in Crop Science and Technology* 3 (2015): e123.

Subramaniam, Banu. "The Aliens Have Landed! Reflections on the Rhetoric of Biological Invasions." *Meridians: Feminism, Race, Transnationalism* 2, no. 1 (2001): 26–40.

Subramaniam, Banu. *Ghost Stories for Darwin: The Science of Variation and the Politics of Diversity*. Urbana: University of Illinois Press, 2014.

Sujatha, R., and R. Sivaraman. "IIT-Madras Campus Tense after Beef Fest." *The Hindu*, May 31, 2017.

Trewavas, Anthony. *Plant Behaviour and Intelligence*. Oxford: Oxford University Press, 2014.

Trewavas, Anthony. "Response to Alpi et al.: Plant Neurobiology—All Metaphors Have Value." *Trends in Plant Science* 12, no. 6 (2007): 231–33.

Trewavas, Anthony. "What Is Plant Behaviour?" *Plant, Cell & Environment* 32, no. 6 (2009): 606–16.

Tuomisto, H. L., and M. J. Teixeira de Mattos. "Environmental Impacts of Cultured Meat Production." *Environmental Science & Technology* 45, no. 14 (2011): 6117–23.

Williams, Sarah. "Humans May Harbor More Than 100 Genes from Other Organisms." *Science*, May 12, 2015. https://www.sciencemag.org/news/2015/03 /humans-may-harbor-more-100-genes-other-organisms.

twelve | MEL Y. CHEN

# Fire and Ash

A POWERFUL THING HAPPENED in my critical animal studies class while I
was a visiting professor at a small liberal arts school, at a time when racially
gendered injury and the perpetuation of ignorance in the administration
were creating pain and distrust, while the national and global tightening of
oppression continued apace. To talk about animality at this time—to think
about creatures, human and nonhuman, to meditate on lines of difference
and union that are not species lines, to ask why rats are used to spatialize
homelessness, why a people's worth in colonial calculus banishes them to
animality or humanity, to think too about the strength, vulnerability, and
resistance that might be felt to reside in animality—each of these moments
had tendril ties to things we felt happening around us. In all the turns, one
of us noted, we kept using the word "interconnectedness"—as an indication
of complicit ties within a broad system of seemingly disparate elements, or
a gesture of hope and affirmation, and also inevitability in forms of harm. In
my observation, "interconnectedness" kept representing a kind of secular
tracking of capitalism and its structural coconspirators—and this is something the students were very good at. We discussed race, disability, industrial agriculture, capitalism, class, and how they mapped to one another—
all the while being quite certain of the identities we discussed, what they
were and were not, convinced of their integrity as things or structures.

Then one student said, with hesitation because of her perception of the ill "fit" of her comment: "I'd just like to know what you all . . . believe. Because for me interconnectedness came first out of my belief—which is Buddhism. It's that interconnectedness—you know, the grain of rice . . . ," and her voice trailed off. Then she commented as if in apology, "Look, I've taken up so much space to just talk about that." But another student picked up where she had left off—and, in a kind of rhyme, told a similar story that had no end, rather an ellipsis. Just an experience, one laterally, associatively, metonymically linked, but linked nevertheless. In this doing, we started to realize a different form of interconnectedness, one lurking beneath. It wasn't all Buddhist, it wasn't all anticolonial, it wasn't moving along a single axis of critique. But what it was—perhaps unnameable even in retrospect—transformed. The room shifted. Other emotions: laughter, surprise. Words faded, silence came in. We had reimagined and reenacted, somehow, what interconnectedness could mean. Along the way, we could lose some of the resolute edges, of species, of programmed and overdetermined relations, of value—that "meaty" web of determination—we could begin to shed the blanket of capitalism's and colonialism's animal meaning.

There are two things I need to note about this story. One is that, in the middle of an elite liberal arts school filled with wonderful students and yet committed (and structurally restricted, to the point of bodily conduct, civility, proper to education and made into habitus) to secular theorizing, something that could be called spirit broke through. Two, we didn't end up anywhere. We didn't know quite what we were saying. The takeaway point was to note the nature of the shift, to know that it constituted a reach for a different kind of interconnectedness.

At a political moment such as this, there is a need for many things, all at the same time. There is a need for clear, nameable perception of what is happening and what has happened, and meaningful and direct means of remedy. I wish deeply for research and educational institutions to consider this a fundamental goal, and I have seen powerful examples of this work. There is equally, however, a need to recognize what has begun to break or dissolve, what no longer works as diagnostic as we run after desperate conviction. This is where "system" doesn't work. It's not metaphysics; it's instead a kind of shifting coagulation. I wish deeply for research and educational institutions to foster and fuel this as well, to be part of a true sense of redeeming, actionally hopeful creativity.

But however its means of interconnectedness, meat is a truly weird thing. For one thing, it represents coreness, substance. There is the meat of an argument, its necessary grounds for operationality. When there is no meat, there is nothing of substance. And yet meat is itself a nonintegrity. It is a substance whose member categories seem to vary (perhaps most wildly in the United States, home of maximally denatured and alienated foods) as to whether they include insects, chicken, pork, or fish. It can be a cut of an animal, and these days what one calls "meat" can also be a vegetarian product shaped into a burger patty or a turkey (there are also the "imitation meat" wheat products in canned form to satisfy largely Chinese Buddhist diets, but then I confuse).

If meat is the grounds for argument, then what is its inverse (and hence its quiet cosubstantiator)?

## Air

Here I am thinking of the brilliant work of Tim Choy, who has written precisely on the quality of air—and the apprehension of that air, the variable "substantiation" of Hong Kong air, as he puts it—by different parties and communities in Hong Kong. Air is not undifferentiated nothingness, but quite lively in its own way, and it contains substances. Choy writes of a journey of epistemological revision following his and his partner Zamira's illnesses by way of the polluted air—he had to reject his "initial attempts to disavow difficulties with the air," because, particularly in social theory, "air is left to drift . . . neither theorized nor examined, taken simply as solidity's lack . . . air can only be insubstantial."[1]

Meat and air meet, not only in, say, the conceptual or ontological traffic of cosubstantiation or the place of representative pollution like Hong Kong, but also in the closed spaces of the slaughterhouse. The hacking and grinding of animal killing yields "ground meat" and airborne particulates, a soup that bears the mark of processing consequence, an abstraction that must be assimilated by the worker. And meat and air meet in all the other ways that animal substances travel into the air, or in the ways that air re-circulates into settled substance to be absorbed, managed, and sometimes kept by the human and nonhuman animal bodies that breathe or otherwise receive, that are porous to the world around them, which is everyone and everything.

These are not fictions, nor are they limited to either science or religion or practical life, for that matter. In the last few years, California, another nonintegrity, has been burning regularly at the scale of international spectacle. If climate disasters become characteristic of a given place, California's is

281

fire and landslides. In the last couple of fall semesters teaching at Berkeley, I have had to buy bulk masks in the midst of thick sunless air for my non-plussed students who have been told that (1) school will be canceled only according to federal air quality guidelines (meaning that all other schools closed before Berkeley), and (2) only the "sensitive" should take care when outdoors, because they may experience difficulty breathing. Maybe this is a broken record, but what exactly does that mean, sensitivity (I write as a classic asthmatic), if what is burning, what incinerates into the air, is not only some fantasized exterior "nature" of trees, grasses, dirt, and other distant flora and their seemingly mundane chemical contents, but also built "environments" including houses, cars, barns, garages, and their chemical contents, such as paints, fuel, solvents, insecticides, as well as living beings—insects, salamanders, bears, deer, frogs, and also people? So that not only are the absorptions particularly frictive (asthma), but chemical (intoxication)? What kind of ruddy, capacious meat-eater is the normative student supposed to be-in-becoming? (Is this the literalization of whiteness's incorporation?) Should only "the sensitive" be kept from eating/becoming differently, even if the advisory might keep them hale for just a little longer? If people are burning and the winds know no bounds, what of the comment that this reaches the level of cannibalism? Or isn't it simply a continuation of how we are—contiguous, intersubstantiating, because of course cannibalism has been deployed as an exoticizing, racist popular anthropology?

I don't want to be overly sweeping, but it really feels as if California's air has become something like meat (though I suppose the commonest metaphor has been that of "soup," but it's getting real); and if the sky looks and if the air feels clear on a given day, we've had the exceptional luck of a meatless Monday. Scientists have concluded that there will not be a time in California's foreseeable future in which there is no fire happening any-where in the state. After years of drought, any generous helpings of rain only now seem to feed the tipped balance in which tender new kindling is grown to feed the next fire as it comes. That is on top of the "kindling" making up the housing built into fire zones, pushing back the front of nature in order to be near it. The painful irony is that this meat bears the marks of its own history of erasure. The periodic prescribed burns that were the

12.1–12.3 (*opposite*) Fiona Foley, *Witnessing to Silence*, Brisbane, Australia, 2004. Photo: Mel Y. Chen

regular practice of Native Californians made such extravagant meatification so much less likely, before the typically misbegotten settler system of scientific-ecological state fire prevention (this is not my time to take on a tentative Anthropocene argument, by which, teleologically, the whole earth has become a slaughterhouse that the geological record will reflect).

Ultimately, I take heed from Tim Choy's thoughtfulness around air: that it is many things at once, it is multiply and even ambivalently substantiated depending. There is a permanent art installation at the Magistrates Court in Brisbane, Australia, by Fiona Foley, a multidisciplinary artist-scholar who is Badtjala (an Aboriginal people of Fraser Island).[2] Called *Witnessing to Silence*, it is the story of a victorious deception. She had initially presented the project proposal by way of a "natural disaster," the Australian bush fires, represented by a display of ashes in suspension, shards of black inside a vertical glass cabinet mounted into the ground. What she didn't reveal until later was that the "bush fires" marked genocide. They in fact represented the ash, not of, say, the ecological management's canonical objects of trees and scrub, but of Aboriginal bodies that had been "removed" (to use the language of colonial operations) by way of government-instigated massacres around Queensland, after which the bodies were burned. (In the ambiguity of "bush" might be a wry comment on the colonial conflation of Aboriginal people with "nature," as if to capitalize on indigenous relations to land.) Arrayed on the ground are stone panels, each bearing the name of one site of massacre. There is so much more to say about this particular work; its brilliance to me is its subterfuge—this is not just "structural ambivalence," but a before-and-after pedagogy by which the relative (but only relative—what are the preferential hierarchies of urgency?) mundanity of and sympathy for burnt trees gives way, necessarily and pointedly, to charred bodies of genocide. Foley's "meat," then, once bitten, forces digesting, in spite or because of the contents. (There is another ash, opium ash, to which her work often refers, which I write about elsewhere.) There are folded and layered lessons then of the inseparability of settler colonialism and scientific-ecological management (for an exposition of this in the context of Hawai'i, see the article by Jonathan Goldberg and Noenoe Silva, listed in the Bibliography), a nonneutral mutual enfolding of peoples and things of the environment around them, and the segregated fiction that the lay definition of "environment" (as nonhuman) has come to inhabit.

286

To substantiate air in ways like this is not to ignore the predictive density of certain relations—of the way blood travels, of the selective porosities of human skin, of the differential scales by which rock becomes air.

But if we remember, say at bottom rather than exceptionally or provisionally, the nonintegrity of things, the work we do changes quite dramatically. There are exclusively scientific ways to describe this—porosities, particulates, dust, smoke, wind. But then we are still stuck in the conceptual words of scientific-ecological management, using them for perhaps compromised ends and ever again ignoring the consistent call to indigenous sovereignty in a world whose apparent dissolutions too often seem only to serve the urgent rebuildings premised on broken universals (informed by already-default ableisms, settler ideologies, capitalist formations, and white supremacist patriarchies). In the context of a discussion on genomic models of indigenous identity, Kim TallBear writes of indigenous notions of peoplehood "as emerging in relation with particular lands and waters and their nonhuman actors differ from the concept of a genetic population, defined as moving upon or through landscapes." In the light of such ecological devastation, the meatiness of air, however perverse in this present circumstance, requires so much rethinking, and I feel suspicious of the urgencies that may predominate. The adoption of Aboriginal land management techniques has already begun in Australia and California, yet it seems only the beginning of a deeply needed epistemological shift and recognition of the multiple layers of violence, settlement, and resubstantiation beyond present-day capitalist mappings—the simplest forms of complex "interconnectedness"—that need first to be accounted for and addressed, even mourned, especially mourned, differentially mourned, with all the emotions and ellipses that obtain. On this, as I am among those of us in the San Francisco Bay Area who have settled on Ohlone land and who participate in academic and institutional epistemologies that require radical undoing and redoing, I have many of my own accountings to address.

This incinerator has many bodies. As they burn, they seem to become one, yet they are not the same ash. What to make of this historicity? How to recognize it, record it, face its differences? How to enflesh this air-meat's nonintegrity?

## Notes

1 Tim Choy, *Ecologies of Comparison: An Ethnography of Endangerment in Hong Kong* (Durham, NC: Duke University Press, 2011), 142, 145.

2 Fiona Foley, *Witnessing to Silence*, art installation at Brisbane Magistrates Court, Brisbane, Australia, 2004.

NEEL AHUJA is Associate Professor of Feminist Studies at the University of California, Santa Cruz, where he is a core faculty member in the Critical Race and Ethnic Studies Program.

IRINA ARISTARKHOVA is Professor at the Penny W. Stamps School of Art and Design and Digital Studies Institute, University of Michigan, Ann Arbor. She is the author of *Arrested Welcome: Hospitality in Contemporary Art* (Minnesota University Press, 2020) and *Hospitality of the Matrix: Philosophy, Biomedicine, and Culture* (Columbia University Press, 2012, Russian translation 2017, Ivan Limbakh Press, Saint Petersburg). She is editor of *Woman Does Not Exist: Contemporary Studies of Sexual Difference* (Syktyvkar University Press, Russia, 1999) and editor of the Russian translation of Luce Irigaray's *Ethics of Sexual Difference*. Prior to her work in the United States, she taught at the National University of Singapore and Lasalle College of the Arts. Her writing has been translated into Romanian, German, Chinese, Dutch, Serbian, Slovenian, Portuguese, and Greek.

SUSHMITA CHATTERJEE is Associate Professor and Director of the Gender, Women's and Sexuality Studies program in the Department of Interdisciplinary Studies at Appalachian State University. She is trained in gender studies and political theory. Her published works focus on feminist and queer theory, postcolonial theory, animal studies, transnational politics, and visual politics. She is currently working on a book about postcolonial play and hauntings and their resonances in transnational feminist and queer theory.

MEL Y. CHEN is Associate Professor of Gender & Women's Studies and Director for the Center for the Study of Sexual Culture at the University of California, Berkeley. Their 2012 book, *Animacies: Biopolitics, Racial Mattering, and Queer Affect* (Duke University Press, MLA Alan Bray Award), explores questions of racialization, queering, disability, and affective economies in animate and inanimate "life" through the extended concept of animacy. Chen's second book project concerns the conceptual territories of toxicity and intoxication and their involvement in archival histories of the interanimation of race and disability. Writing on cognitive disability and method, the racialization of pollution, and more can be found in *Journal of Literary and Cultural Disability Studies, Transgender Studies Quarterly, Discourse, Women in Performance, Australian Feminist Studies, Medical Humanities*, and GLQ. Chen coedited a Duke University Press book series entitled "Anima," highlighting scholarship in critical race and disability post/in/humanisms. They are part of a small and sustaining queer/trans of color arts collective in the SF Bay Area.

PSYCHE WILLIAMS-FORSON is Associate Professor and chair of American Studies at the University of Maryland College Park. Her research interests include the American history of the 19th and 20th centuries, especially the topics of race, gender, materiality, and food.

KIM Q. HALL is Professor of Philosophy and a faculty member of the Gender, Women's, and Sexuality Studies Program at Appalachian State University. She is the co-editor with Ásta of *The Oxford Handbook of Feminist Philosophy* (forthcoming with Oxford University Press) and guest editor of *New Conversations in Feminist Disability Studies*, a special issue of *Hypatia: Journal of Feminist Philosophy*. She is currently working on a book titled *Queering Philosophy*.

JENNIFER A. HAMILTON is Visiting Professor of Sexuality, Women's & Gender Studies at Amherst College and Director of the Five College Women's Studies Research Center. Her research and teaching focuses on the anthropology of law, science, and medicine, postcolonial feminist science and technology studies, and the contemporary politics of indigeneity. She is the author of *Indigeneity in the Courtroom: Law, Culture, and the Production of Difference in North American Courts* (Routledge 2009) and is currently completing a second book manuscript, *The Indian in the Freezer: The Genomic Quest for Indigeneity* (under contract with the University of Washington Press).

ANITA MANNUR is associate professor of English at Miami University. She is the author of *Culinary Fictions: Food in South Asian Diasporic Culture* (2010) and coeditor of *Eating Asian America* (2014) She lives in Cincinnati with her two cats.

ELSPETH PROBYN is Professor of Gender & Cultural Studies at the University of Sydney. She has published several groundbreaking monographs including *Sexing the Self* (Routledge, 1993), *Outside Belongings* (Routledge, 1996), *Carnal Appetites* (Routledge, 2000), *Blush: Faces of Shame* (Minnesota, 2006), and *Eating the Ocean* (Duke, 2016). She is the co-editor *Sustaining Seas* (Rowman & Littlefield, 2020). Her latest

290

project, funded by the Australian Research Council, is entitled *Selling the Sea: A comparative study of the cultural, economic, and environmental roles of urban fish markets in the global north and south.*

PARAMA ROY is Professor of English at the University of California, Davis. She is the author of *Indian Traffic: Identities in Question in Colonial and Postcolonial India* (1998) and *Alimentary Tracts: Appetites, Aversions, and the Postcolonial* (Duke University Press, 2010), and co-editor of *States of Trauma: Gender and Violence in South Asia* (2009). Her current book project is titled "Species, Sacrifice, and the Question of Empire."

BANU SUBRAMANIAM is Professor of Women, Gender, Sexuality Studies at the University of Massachusetts, Amherst. Trained as a plant evolutionary biologist, Banu's work engages the feminist studies of science in the practices of experimental biology. Author of *Holy Science: The Biopolitics of Hindu Nationalism* (2019), *Ghost Stories for Darwin: The Science of Variation and the Politics of Diversity* (2014), and coeditor of *Feminist Science Studies: A New Generation* (2001) and *Making Threats: Biofears and Environmental Anxieties* (2005), Banu's current work focuses on decolonizing botany and the relationship of science and religious nationalism in India.

ANGELA WILLEY is Associate Professor of Women, Gender, Sexuality Studies at the University of Massachusetts, Amherst, working at the interstices of queer feminist theory, critical relationality, and science studies. Her work on non/monogamy, colonial sexual science, and critical materialisms has appeared in *Feminist Studies*; *Signs: Journal of Women in Culture and Society*; *Feminist Formations*; *Journal of Gender Studies*; *Science, Technology, and Human Values*; *Archives of Sexual Behavior*; and *Sexualities* and in edited collections on monogamy, on materialism, and on the science of difference. She is author of *Undoing Monogamy: The Politics of Science and the Possibilities of Biology* (Duke University Press, 2016) and co-editor of *Queer Feminist Science Studies: A Reader* (2017) and special issues of *Catalyst: Feminism, Theory, Technoscience*—on "Science out of Feminist Theory," the *Journal of Lesbian Studies*—on "Biology/Embodiment/Desire," and *Imaginations: A Journal of Cross Cultural Image Studies* on "Critical Relationality: Indigenous and Queer Belonging Beyond Settler Sex and Nature."

291

295

evolution, 65–67, 261; evolutionary biology, 45; polygenist, 78; and race, 71, 78, 81; transgenic, 150. *See also* biology; genetic science

Exclusive Economic Zones (EEZs), 27, 31

exotic foods: in cuisine, 129–30; milk, 53; colonial views of, 62

exotic meats, 10, 124–26, 129–30, 134. *See also* exotic foods; toothfish

exploration, 66–67, 80

The Explorers Club, 61–64, 68, 84–86, 87n7

extinction, 67, 268; risk of, 23. *See also* mammoths

fake meat, 12, 241–47, 249–51, 252n5, 281; environmental impact of, 265; ethics, 246, 262; production, 244

FAO (United Nations Food and Agriculture Organization), 23–24, 135n3

feminism, 45, 51–52, 58n30, 106, 154n10, 242–43, 246–50; history of, 27. *See also* Dobkin, Jess; gender politics; maternal politics; queer feminism

Fenton, Gwen, 23, 33n36

fetishization of food, 54, 190n66

fish, 17–19, 22–25, 71, 124, 168; as meat, 17–19, 30–31; agriculture and, 26, 262, 265; Antarctic, 26–28; conservation, 21, 28–29; deep-sea, 19–20. *See also* fish stocks; fisheries; ice fishing; illegal fishing

fisheries, 19, 25, 28–29, 33n37, 35n56; Marine Stewardship Council certification, 23–24

fish stocks, 21, 26, 28, 77. *See also* fisheries

Foley, Fiona, 286

food activism, 267–70. *See also* animal rights activism; environmental activism

food ethics, 12, 14, 48, 143–44, 162–64, 270; fake meat and, 242, 244; maternal politics and, 42, 47,

51–52; sacrifice and, 183; technology and, 263, 267, 269; vegan, 246, 248, 250, 252n7; violence and, 41. *See also* ethics of meat eating; Haraway, Donna; Heim, Maria; meat production ethics; Pollan, Michael; Probyn, Elspeth; Roy, Parama

food politics, 13, 122, 248, 256, 257, 270. *See also* meat; veganism

food studies, 7, 51, 123, 134. *See also* animal studies

food technology, 263–65, 267–70. *See also* frozen food; genetic science; technologized meat

foraged food, 129

frozen food, 10, 67–69; imperial transit of, 62–65; Inuit technology, 84–86

Gandhi, M. K., 227, 229

Gandhi, Maneka, 223

gastroaesthetics, 110

gender politics, 25, 27, 139–40, 229, 261; African American, 194, 196; Indian, 110, 223; meat-eating and, 126, 136n7, 194, 136n7. *See also* Bishnoi; body politics; feminism; queer crip theory

genetically modified foods. *See* genetic science

genetic science, 45, 262–65, 267–68; pigs, 149, 153

Ghassem-Fachandi, Parvis, 101–2, 110–11

Global North, 18–19, 21, 24, 31

Global South, 18–19, 25, 31

global supply chain, 10, 64, 67–68

GM foods. *See* genetic science

goat meat, 124, 234n5

Gomez, Marga, 247–48

Grant, Matt, 198

Greenpeace, 24. *See also* environmental activism

Guru Jambheshwar, 177, 182

Guru Nanak, 254

Guthman, Julie, 128, 270

maternal politics, 39–40, 55, 57n16, 181; separation and, 43; food and, 44–50, 190n66. *See also* breast milk; Dobkin, Jess

Mayo, Katherine, 226–27

meat as politics, 2–6, 97–99, 243. *See also* body politics; feminism; purity politics; queer crip theory

meat consumption rates, 26, 258

meat production ethics, 26, 255, 263, 267–69; Indian, 127–28, 153, 229

meat production law: in India, 101, 259; US lawsuits, 152. *See also* Indian beef bans

memory and food, 206

milk, 40; in India, 110, 177, 181, 215, 228–29; contamination, 133; white culture, 18. *See also* breast milk; dairy industry; phooka

missionaries. *See* Jackson, Sheldon; Mayo, Katherine

mock meat. *See* fake meat

Modi, Narendra, 215, 258–59; on yoga, 100–101, 109

MSC. *See* Marine Stewardship Council (MSC)

mutton, 68, 259

Nancy, Jean-Luc, 152–53

*National Geographic* magazine, 82

Native American people. *See* American Indian people

New Zealand, 19–20, 22–24, 27, 33n37; colonial history, 68; Maori Fisheries Settlement, 29

Nilsson, Magnus, 122

Noma restaurant, 122, 129

Nordic cuisine, 122–23

nuclear contamination. *See* Chernobyl nuclear disaster

Obama, Barack, 109, 200–201

*The Omnivore's Dilemma. See* Pollan, Michael

omnivory, 52, 254–57. *See also* Pollan, Michael

Ong, Aihwa, 114

orange roughy, 22–23, 30

organ transplants, 142, 148–49, 152. *See also* xeno science

Osborn, Henry Fairfield, 65–66

overfishing, 23, 26, 30, 77

packaging design, 100, 126

paleo diet, 45

Patagonian toothfish. *See* toothfish

Patton, Kimberley, 164, 168

Pauly, Daniel, 18, 24

pet food, 252n7

phooka: class politics, 221; cow protectionism and, 12, 17, 229, 232–33; regulation, 217–20, 222–28; non-Indian, 222. *See also* cow protectionism

pigs, 148, 151; organ use, 140–43, 148–49; disease, 150, 153; hog waste, 152. *See also* pork

piracy, 28, 35n69. *See also* illegal fishing

placenta, 44–46, 50

plant-based meat. *See* fake meat

plants, 260–61, 269–70; genetic modification, 262–64, 267–68; sentience, 255–56, 266

political philosophy. *See* Hobbes, Thomas; Hardt, Michael; Negri, Antonio

Pollan, Michael, 127–28, 130, 147, 151

pork, 14; consumption, 139, 145, 148; religion and, 154n15; 263; production, 151–53. *See also* pigs

postcolonialism, 47, 57n16, 63–64, 86, 102, India, 258, studies, 25–27. *See also* colonialism; imperialism

poultry farms, 125, 127; in *Breaking Bad*, 204. *See also* chicken; industrial farming

preserved food, 18, 68, 84

Probyn, Elspeth, 7, 9, 52–54

protein: animal, 31, 145; nonanimal, 263–65

300

www.ingramcontent.com/pod-product-compliance
Lightning Source LLC
Chambersburg PA
CBHW071732270326
41928CB00013B/2649